*Issues in Children's and Families' Lives*

# Early Childhood Programs for a New Century

EDITED BY

**Arthur J. Reynolds**
**Margaret C. Wang**
**Herbert J. Walberg**

GREAT *Cities*

UIC'S METROPOLITAN COMMITMENT

**The University of Illinois at Chicago Series on Children and Youth**

**CWLA Press • Washington, DC**

CWLA Press is an imprint of the Child Welfare League of America. The Child Welfare League of America is the nation's oldest and largest membership-based child welfare organization. We are committed to engaging people everywhere in promoting the well-being of children, youth, and their families, and protecting every child from harm.

CHILD WELFARE LEAGUE OF AMERICA, INC.
HEADQUARTERS
440 First Street, NW, Third Floor, Washington, DC 20001-2085
E-mail: books@cwla.org

CURRENT PRINTING (last digit)
10 9 8 7 6 5 4 3 2 1

Cover and text design by Amy Alick

Printed in Canada
ISBN # 0-87868-834-X

## Library of Congress Cataloging-in-Publication Data

Early childhood programs for a new century / edited by Arthur J. Reynolds, Margaret C. Wang, Herbert J. Walberg.
     p.cm. -- (University of Illinois at Chicago series on children and youth) (Issues in children's and families' lives)
    Includes bibliographical references and indices.
    ISBN 0-87868-834-X
     1. Early childhood education. I Reynolds, Arthur J. II. Wang, Margaret C. III. Walberg, Herbert J., 1937- IV. Series. V. Issues in children's and families' lives (Washington, D.C.)

LB1139.23 .E274 2001
372.21--dc21

2001047130

# In Memoriam

Margaret C. Wang
(1938-2000)

# The University of Illinois at Chicago Series on Children and Youth

The University of Illinois at Chicago (UIC) Series on Children and Youth is published as a part of the annual book series *Issues in Children's and Families' Lives,* edited by Thomas P. Gullotta. Drawing upon multiple academic disciplines and the full range of human service professions, its goal is to inform and stimulate policymakers and professionals who serve children and youth. From such academic disciplines as psychology and sociology, as well as such professions as education, medicine, nursing, and social work, the contributors draw upon basic and applied research aimed at uncovering both "the truth" and "the good." Thus, the goal of the series is to bring together pertinent knowledge about children and youth as well as to identify policies, programs, and practices that well serve them.

Herbert J. Walberg
Roger P. Weissberg
Editors, University of Illinois at Chicago
Series on Children and Youth

# Contents

**Preface** ................................................................ **xi**

Herbert J. Walberg and Roger P. Weissberg

University Advisory Committee for the University of Illinois at Chicago
Series on Children and Youth ........................................... xiii

National Advisory Committee for the University of Illinois at Chicago
Series on Children and Youth ............................................ xv

**Introduction and Overview:
Trends in Early Childhood Programs** ................................. **xvii**

Arthur J. Reynolds, Margaret C. Wang, and Herbert J. Walberg

**Part I. Preschool Education and Care** ............................... **1**

1. The Federal Commitment to Preschool Education: Lessons from
   and for Head Start ..................................................... 3
   Edward Zigler and Sally J. Styfco

2. Understanding Efficacy of Early Educational Programs: Critical
   Design, Practice, and Policy Issues ............................... 35
   Sharon Landesman Ramey and Craig T. Ramey

3. Universal Access to Prekindergarten: A Georgia Case Study ....... 71
   Anthony Raden

4. Child Care Quality and Children's Success at School ............. 115
   Deborah Lowe Vandell and Kim M. Pierce

**Part II. Early School-Age Programs and Practices** ............... **141**

5. Kindergarten in the 21st Century ............................... 143
   Elizabeth M. Graue

6. The Added Value of Continuing Early Intervention into the
   Primary Grades ..................................................... 163
   Arthur J. Reynolds

7. Grade Retention, Social Promotion, and "Third Way" Alternatives ................................................. 197
*Karl L. Alexander, Doris R. Entwisle, and Nader Kabbani*

## Part III. National Investments ................................................. 239

8. The Three Types of Early Childhood Programs in the United States .................................................................. 241
*Lawrence J. Schweinhart*

9. The Science and Policies of Early Childhood Education and Family Services ..................................................... 255
*Robert B. McCall, Lana Larsen, and Angela Ingram*

10. Lessons from Europe: European Preschools Revisited in a Global Age ............................................................. 299
*Sarane Spence Boocock*

11. Understanding the Promise of Universal Preschool .............. 329
*Darcy A. Olsen*

## Epilogue:
## Themes and Recommendations for a New Century ............ 353
*Arthur J. Reynolds, Margaret C. Wang, and Herbert J. Walberg*

About the Editors ....................................................... 361

About the Contributors ............................................... 363

## Index

Author Index .......................................................... 369

Subject Index .......................................................... 383

## *Tables*

Table 3.1   Georgia Prekindergarten Program for 4-Year-Olds ....... 72

Table 3.2   The Evolution of Georgia's Lottery-Funded
Prekindergarten Program ............................................. 77

Table 4.1   Effect Sizes Associated with Child Developmental
Outcomes at 3 Years and Cumulative Child Care
Quality, Child Care Hours, and Home Quality ........ 123

Table 5.1   State Kindergarten Entrance Dates ............................. 146

Table 5.2   Conceptions of Readiness ......................................... 151

Table 5.3   Odds-Ratios of Entry and Promotion Interventions in
Relation to Normal Entry and Promotion by Child
Characteristics ........................................................... 154

Table 5.4   Does the Evidence Support Redshirting? ................... 157

Table 6.1   Primary Features of Four Extended Early Childhood
Programs for Low-Income Families .......................... 170

Table 6.2   Selected Effect Sizes on School Competence for
Studies of Extended Early Childhood Programs ........ 173

Table 7.1   Differences Between Retainee and Never Retained
CAT-R and CAT-M Averages ................................... 210

Table 7.2   Odds Ratios Predicting High School Dropout From
Measures of Grade Retention ................................... 214

Table 7.3   Mark Averages from First Grade Through Nine Years
for Promoted and Retained Youngsters..................... 218

Table 10.1  Preschool Participation Rates of European OECD
Member Countries, 1995 ........................................ 302

## *Figures*

Figure A    Public Investments in Early Childhood Programs ....... xix

Figure B    Percentage of Children in Early Childhood Programs .. xx

Figure 2.1  Intellectual Performance of Children in the
            Abecedarian Project During the Preschool Years .......... 44

Figure 2.2  Intellectual Performance as a Function of Treatment
            Group and Site (Infant Health and Development
            Program) .................................................. 47

Figure 2.3  Reading and Math Achievement Scores from the
            Abecedarian Project ....................................... 55

Figure 2.4  Rates of Special Education Placement and Grade
            Retention in the Abecedarian Project ..................... 57

Figure 4.1  A Conceptual Model of Relations Between Child Care
            Quality and Children's EducationalSuccess ............... 117

Figure 6.1  Alternative Paths Leading to Social Competence ....... 168

Figure 6.2  Child-Parent Center Program ................................... 177

Figure 6.3  Age 15 Comparisons in the CPC Program ............... 181

# Preface

This book is in The University of Illinois at Chicago (UIC) Series on Children and Youth. The UIC series began in response to the "Great Cities" initiative taken by our former Chancellor and current President, James Stukel, other senior administrators, trustees, and civic leaders in Chicago. Its purpose is to disseminate scholarly resources to better understand and assist in solving problems of American cities. We are grateful to the university for providing the continuing funds to support the series of books and conferences on a variety of topics within this broad and vital subject. As exemplified by the disciplines represented on our university and national advisory boards (listed in the front of this volume), the series draws on the many fields and professions that have bearings on, and implications for, children and youth. We hope that the books provide insights for policymakers and professionals in welfare and health agencies, schools, and other community settings.

The series is intended to provide an interdisciplinary and "inter-professional" approach to problems facing urban children. The first volume in the series, *Children and Youth: Interdisciplinary Perspectives*, was published by Sage Publications in the annual series called Issues in Children's and Families' Lives. The second volume of the series, *Promoting Positive Outcomes*, was published by the Child Welfare League of America. It focused on solutions to the problems facing young people in the first two decades of life.

Since the early years of life are the foundation for healthy and constructive childhood, youth, and adult life, we are particularly happy to offer to readers the present volume: *Early Childhood Programs for a New Century*. Under the leadership of Margaret Wang, the Temple University Laboratory for Student Success at the Center for Research in Human Development and Education financially and logistically supported the preparation of the chapters and a national invitational conference in November 1999 to draw policy and practical implications. Marilyn Murphy coordinated the chapter preparation and conference. Lou Iovino and Stephen Page provided valuable editorial support.

As senior editor of the Issues in Children's and Families' Lives Series for the Child Welfare League of America, Thomas P. Gullotta arranged for the publication of the volumes. We are grateful for his leadership in this effort. The editors of this volume, Arthur Reynolds, Margaret Wang, and Herb Walberg, thank the authors and the conference participants who drew a number of policy and practical implications from the chapters. We greatly appreciate the many people who helped make both this volume and the UIC Series on Children and Youth a reality. We thank the distinguished members of our University of Illinois at Chicago Advisory Board and our National Advisory Board.

Herbert J. Walberg
Roger P. Weissberg
Series Editors

# University Advisory Committee for The University of Illinois at Chicago Series on Children and Youth

Lascelles Anderson
Director
Center for Urban Educational
    Research and Development
College of Education

Boris Astrachan
Professor
Department of Psychiatry

Carl C. Bell
Clinical Professor
Department of Psychiatry

David C. Braddock
Director
Institute on Disability and
    Human Development

Elizabeth Burns
Head
Department of Family Practice

Suzanne K. Campbell
Professor
Department of Physical
    Therapy

Barry R. Chiswick
Head
Department of Economics

Victoria Chou
Dean
College of Education

Judith A. Cooksey
Assistant Professor
Health Research and Policy
    Centers
School of Public Health

Suzanne Feetham
Professor and Harriet Werley
Research Chair
College of Nursing

Stanley Fish
Dean
College of Liberal Arts and
    Sciences

Brian R. Flay
Professor
Health Research and Policy
    Centers
School of Public Health

Rachel Gordon
Assistant Professor
Department of Sociology

Creasie Finney Hairston
Dean
Jane Addams College of Social
  Work

Darnell F. Hawkins
Professor
African-American Studies

Donald Hellison
Professor
College of Kinesiology

Elizabeth Hoffman
Provost and Vice Chancellor for
  Academic Affairs

Christopher Keys
Chair
Department of Psychology

Jack Knott
Director
Institute of Government and
  Public Affairs

David Perry
Director
Great Cities Institute

Olga Reyes
Associate Professor
Department of Psychology

Susan C. Schrimshaw
Dean
School of Public Health

Gerald S. Strom
Chair
Department of Political Science

James J. Stukel
President
University of Illinois

Patrick H. Tolan
Professor of Psychology in
  Psychiatry
Institute for Juvenile Research

Wim Wiewel
Dean
College of Urban Planning and
  Public Affairs

# National Advisory Committee for The University of Illinois at Chicago Series on Children and Youth

# Introduction and Overview:
# Trends in Early Childhood Programs

*Arthur J. Reynolds, Margaret C. Wang, and Herbert J. Walberg*

Investments in children during the early years of life are regarded as one of the most effective ways to promote children's learning (Council of Economic Advisors, 1997; National Science and Technology Council, 1997). The first decade has received special attention as a crucial "intervention point" for healthy development (Carnegie Task Force on Learning in the Primary Grades, 1996). Several White House conferences also have convened to highlight the importance of the early years, including those on early childhood development and on child care. Federal and state expenditures on early childhood programs exceed $15 billion and are likely to continue to rise given that only about one-half of all young children enroll in preschool (U.S. General Accounting Office, 1999). Among the highest priorities in the future are the effects of these investments on children, families, and society, and how the knowledge base can be translated into the most cost-effective programs on the widest possible scale.

Expanding on the two previous books in this series *Children and Youth: Interdisciplinary Perspectives* (Walberg, Reyes, & Weissberg, 1997) and *Promoting Positive Outcomes* (Reynolds, Walberg, & Weissberg, 1999), this book summarizes the state of our knowledge about the effects of early childhood programs from birth to age 8. Early childhood programs, in the context of the chapters, are defined as the provision of educational, family, or health services, during any of the first eight years of life to children, many of whom are at risk of poor outcomes because they face socioenvironmental disadvantages or have developmental disabilities. Most of these programs can be regarded as preventive (see also Barnett & Boocock, 1998; Shonkoff & Meisels, 2000).

## Emerging Trends in Early Childhood Programs

Three emerging trends in early childhood programs are salient in the current push for improving this nation's capacity for healthy development and learning, and success of children in the new millennium: (1) investments in early childhood programs, (2) increasing participation in early childhood programs, and (3) advances in understanding effectiveness.

### Investments in Early Childhood Programs

In recent years, federal and state governments have made greater investments in early childhood care and education programs. Although the rationale of these investments ranges from preventing learning difficulties to subsidizing child care for low-income working parents, the broad aim is to improve children's readiness for school. In addition to the pronouncement that all children will start school ready to learn as the first national education goal (National Educational Goals Panel, 1995), there has been a significant increase in funding at the federal and state levels.

As shown in Figure A, 70% (or $11.4 billion) of the $15 billion invested in care and education programs from birth to age 5 in 1998–1999 were federal expenditures (U.S. General Accounting Office, 1999). The major categories are Head Start preschool ($4.66 billion), Child Care and Development Funds ($3.17 billion), Title I education funding to school districts ($936 million), block grants to the states through Temporary Assistance for Needy Families (TANF; $895 million), and special education funding through Individuals with Disabilities Education Act (IDEA; $744 million). Notably, Head Start funding has risen by 33% since 1994. The remaining 30% (or $3.6 billion) was for early childhood education programs in 32 states ($1.7 billion) and for child care and Head Start supplements ($1.9 billion, mostly for the former). With these funds, the states serve approximately one million children (U.S. General Accounting Office, 1999). This number is likely to increase in the future.

### Increasing Participation in Early Childhood Programs

Although funding for early childhood programs has increased substantially in recent years, growth in the percentage of children served has been

**FIGURE A. Public Investments in Early Childhood Programs**

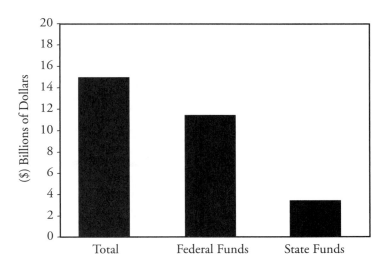

Source: U.S. General Accounting Office (1999).

incremental. Figure B shows the pattern of participation in early childhood programs from 1983 to 2000 for 3- to 5-year-olds as reported by the National Center for Educational Statistics (2002). Rates of participation in center-based care and education programs vary substantially by age. About one-third of 3-year-olds were enrolled in preschool programs (state and federal programs) in 1998, two-thirds of 4-year-olds, and one-half of 3- and 4-year-olds. As expected, about 90% of 5-year-olds are enrolled in early childhood programs, almost all of them as kindergartners. The largest increases in rates of participation were for 4-year-olds, reflecting the increased funding for Head Start and state-level early childhood education programs.

Nevertheless, trends in the demographics of work and evidence that participation in early childhood programs is associated with improved child development indicate that optimal levels of participation may not have been reached. Indeed, of the 7.9 million 3- and 4-year-olds eligible, 4.1 million were enrolled in preschool programs in 2000, leaving 3.8

Figure B. **Percentage of Children in Early Childhood Programs**

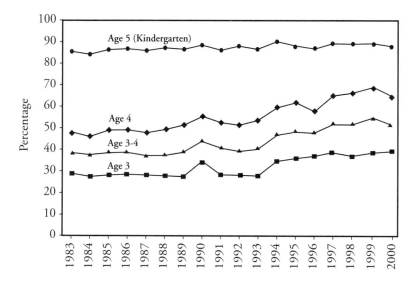

Source: National Center for Educational Statistics (2002).

million children unserved. Moreover, significant impediments to participation remain, including cost, availability of full-day programs, and the availability of well trained staff (Bowman, Donovan, & Burns, 2000).

As expected, preschool attendance differs substantially by family income and education. In 1997 for example, 40% of children living in poverty were enrolled in preschool programs compared to 51% of children above the poverty line (Forum on Child and Family Statistics, 1999). Differences by level of parent education were even larger as 71% of children of college graduates attended preschool programs, but only 47% of children of high school graduates and 37% of children of parents not completing high school. Since participation in preschool programs is associated with significantly greater levels of school readiness (Shonkoff & Meisels, 2000; Karoly et al. 1998), increasing access to early childhood programs of sufficient quality may improve child outcomes.

## *Advances in Understanding Effectiveness*

At the beginning of the 21st century, the field of early childhood education has amassed a large knowledge base about the effects on children's development. Relative to nonparticipation, participation in many early childhood programs has been consistently associated with higher levels of cognitive development, early school achievement, and motivation in the short term, and with lower rates of grade retention and special education during the elementary grades (Karoly et al., 1998; Reynolds et al., 1999). A few well-controlled studies (i.e., random assignment or matched groups) indicate that program participation is associated with higher rates of school completion and employment (Barnett & Boocock, 1998; Karoly et al., 1998).

A second major advance is the realization that both the timing and duration of intervention matter. In the past decade, empirical support for these program attributes has grown substantially. The most effective programs reported in the literature spanning home visitation to center-based preschool education have been those that begin during the early years of life, continue for multiple years, and provide support to children's school transitions. In ecological systems theory, for example, the impact of proximal processes as experienced in interventions is a function of their occurrence "on a regular basis over extended periods of time" (Bronfenbrenner & Morris, 1998, p. 996).

The third advance is support for the cognitive-scholastic advantage hypothesis as a mechanism of long-term effects of early education on child development outcomes. This advantage appears to culminate in better classroom adjustment and school commitment and in lower rates of grade retention and special education placement. In addition, there is emerging support for the significant role of the family and school support hypotheses in promoting effectiveness (Institute for Research on Poverty, 1997; Reynolds, 2000).

These emerging trends are the result of nearly four decades of progress and set the tone for future advancements in early childhood education. However, as much as knowledge has advanced about the effects of early childhood programs, many questions remain unanswered, and they need to be addressed from multiple perspectives: (a) What are the environmental conditions that promote the persistence of effects for a diversity of early childhood programs? (b) For whom are existing programs most effective and which program features are most associated with success? and (c) What are the effects of contemporary public programs over time? Can confidence in findings be strengthened, thus providing better guidance for policy and program decisions? (e.g., Karoly et al., 1998; U.S. General Accounting Office, 1997)

Despite the increased investments in early childhood programs and better understanding of effectiveness, several challenges remain. First, the nation's early childhood system is fragmented. The number of funding mechanisms and administrative systems makes coordination difficult and the continuity of services low. Relatively few children, for example, are enrolled in a single early childhood program or setting for more than a year. The most typical center-based arrangement for a 4-year-old is a part-day program for one year, with few opportunities for transition support in the early grades. Moreover, the quality of programs is uneven, many being mediocre or poor (Bowman, Donovan, & Burns, 2000). Calls for a better coordinated early childhood system that provides opportunities for increased length and quality of services have led to greater emphasis on collaboration among service providers, development of programs from birth to age 3, and efforts to support learning gains through successful transition programs.

Another area of concern is the large variation in services offered. Federally funded programs such as Head Start, IDEA, and Title I preschool are most likely to provide comprehensive services to children at risk. Block grants to subsidize day care provide far fewer services as they lack a broad educational mission. As reported by the U.S. General Accounting Office (1999), over 70% of center-based providers offer educational programs, but fewer than 10% provide medical services and referrals, parental support, and family social services. The number of services provided is far less in home settings; the percentage of providers offering educational programs is about 30%, and less than 5% of providers offer medical services and referrals, parent support, and family social services.

Because the effectiveness of early childhood programs is a function of length, quality, and breadth of services, the manner in which investments in early childhood programs are made is a crucial issue for cost-effectiveness (Guralnick, 1997; U.S. General Accounting Office, 2000). The changing demographics of the workforce, the work requirements of welfare reform, and increasing levels of disadvantage in inner cities mean that early childhood programs will need to be better tailored to the needs of families and children in the future. One of the continuing trade-offs is between providing more extensive services to a fixed number of children and providing less extensive services to larger numbers of children.

It is in this context of the need for taking stock of research on early child development and advances of research-based applications in early childhood programs that a series of papers were commissioned to serve as springboards for discussion at a national invitational conference on Early Childhood Learning: Programs for a New Age. The Conference, held in Washington, DC on November 29 to December 1, 1999, was sponsored by the Laboratory for Student Success, the Mid-Atlantic Regional Educational Laboratory established by the U.S. Department of Education at the Temple University Center for Research in Human Development and Education.

## Overview of the Volume

Nearly all the chapters included in this volume are the commission papers for the conference on Early Childhood Learning: Programs for a New Age. Leading scholars and leaders in early childhood education were asked to provide syntheses of the research base and the state-of-practice and to discuss emerging directions and next-steps. The authors were asked to address four major questions:

- What is the current state of knowledge about the impact of a variety of early childhood programs and services on children's well-being? For example, what programs are most effective and who benefits most from them? What are the limits of our current knowledge?

- What are the key components of effective programs and services? How should they be organized? What program components, levels of implementation fidelity, and environmental conditions increase effectiveness?
- What are the implications of the knowledge base on early learning for program development, modification, and expansion?
- How can the best or most promising practices be disseminated and used widely to promote early childhood development, especially for children at risk?

The chapters are organized under three topical sections. In Part I, the chapters consider programs during the first five years of life including Head Start, child care, and model programs. Part II covers kindergarten and the early school-age years. School readiness, grade retention practices, and extended interventions are discussed. Part III considers the broader implications of the knowledge base for program development and policy formulation. In the Epilogue, common themes and next-step recommendations are discussed.

## Part I. Preschool Education and Care

Four chapters are included in this section. Chapter 1, entitled "The Federal Commitment to Preschool Education: Lessons From and for Head Start," by Edward Zigler and Sally J. Styfco, traces the history of the nation's oldest federally funded preschool program, Head Start, and offers directions for research and practice in the coming years. Head Start was designed to provide comprehensive services to low-income and at-risk children in the areas of education, family support, social services, and health. While research on the effects of Head Start participation focused initially on children's cognitive skills, later studies revealed more persistent benefits in the reduced need for grade retention and special education. The influential Consortium for Longitudinal Studies reinforced these findings. An outgrowth of these studies is a consensus that the goal of Head Start is school readiness, meaning everyday effectiveness in meeting age-appropriate social and scholastic expectations. Several recent initiatives are discussed to improve the quality of research on the effects of Head

Start. Given that society at large is convinced of the payoff of investments in early education, Zigler and Styfco call for a unified federal approach for integrating early childhood programs. The guiding principles of this early childhood system are comprehensiveness of services, parent involvement, and the provision of high-quality services that are of sufficient length to impact children's development.

In Chapter 2, "Understanding Efficacy of Early Educational Programs: Critical Design, Practice, and Policy Issues," Sharon Landesman Ramey and Craig T. Ramey describe the philosophic and scientific history of the early intervention field. They note that the roots of the field came from studies documenting the tragic effects of environmental deprivation experienced by young orphan children in institutional care. This work and others provided the impetus for early preventive interventions in the first few years of life. The authors summarize the results of five of the most influential projects on model programs: the Consortium for Longitudinal Studies, Abecedarian Project and Project CARE, Perry Preschool, and the Milwaukee Project. All were university-based programs that included random assignment to intensive education and/or family services during at least one of the first five years of life. Together, these studies provide some of the best evidence that high-quality early childhood programs can impact not only the traditional outcomes of IQ and achievement test scores but also, and more importantly, the "real world" outcomes of educational attainment, employment, and reduced need for school remedial services. After discussing the evidence concerning the mediating mechanisms of effects and for whom services are most effective, the authors argue for targeted strategies of interventions for the highest risk children and families.

Chapter 3, entitled "Universal Access to Prekindergarten: A Georgia Case Study," by Anthony Raden, describes the history and development, implementation, and early evaluations of the State of Georgia program. As noted, the program was initially proposed by then-candidate Zell Miller in the 1989 gubernatorial campaign. It became a reality through a convergence of public support for using lottery proceeds for investments in education determined by competitive grants from outside the traditional education establishment. Coordinated by the State Department of

Education, the program opened in 1993 and served only low-income children. To increase political and public support, the program was expanded to all 4-year-olds regardless of income. Raden notes that the evaluations of the program have been limited, but they indicate that participants start kindergarten with higher levels of school readiness as rated by teachers, have fewer absences, and have lower rates of kindergarten retention, although fewer benefits were observed by first grade. The evaluations to date have not investigated longer-term effects, nor the extent to which the effects of participation vary by family income and later environmental conditions. Among the lessons learned from the Georgia experience, Raden describes the advantages of using the lottery as a funding mechanism for education investments, the importance of strong leadership in keeping programs alive, the importance of collaboration among service providers, and the critical role of space for facilities.

In Chapter 4, "Child Care Quality and Children's Success at School," Deborah Lowe Vandell and Kim M. Pierce highlight emerging evidence on the impact of child care experiences on children's social and academic development and offer recommendations for future research. The authors point out that child care quality can be defined by structural characteristics, such as child-to-staff ratios and caregiver education, and process characteristics, which are the specific learning experiences and activities of the care environment. In reviewing the recent literature on the effects of child care quality on children's development, the authors make clear that these characteristics can have significant influence on children's cognitive development, especially if the typical quality of the home environment is low. Data from the National Institute of Child Health and Development (NICHD) study, for example, show that child care quality contributes significantly to school readiness, expressive language, and receptive language. Other longitudinal studies of school-age children show a similar pattern of benefits for school achievement and work habits. As discussed, some of the most important work for the future will be to determine the mediators of child care effects on children's success, who benefits most from care settings, and how the quality of care carries over to later educational experiences.

## Part II. Early School-Age Programs and Practices

Three chapters are included in this section. Chapter 5, entitled "Kindergarten in the 21st Century," by Elizabeth M. Graue, describes the contribution of kindergarten programs and practices to children's school readiness. The near universal coverage of children in kindergarten (over 90% attended kindergarten) has made it an essential part of the early childhood system. As described, the definition of *readiness* varies considerably across parents and teachers and by socioeconomic status. Parents are most likely to define readiness by social skills while teachers see readiness as having good physical health and positive attitudes. Academic skills are emphasized more by parents and teachers in high-poverty schools, and by policymakers. According to Graue, these alternative definitions lead to different expectations for children that may or may not be well supported by schools. These become manifested in decisions about delayed kindergarten entry, often in the form of "redshirting." The author recommends that schools must continue to change to meet the educational needs of children.

In Chapter 6, "The Added Value of Continuing Early Intervention into the Primary Grades," Arthur J. Reynolds reviews the evidence concerning the effectiveness of extended early childhood programs. They can be defined as programs that begin during any of the first five years of life and provide continuation services through second or third grade. They are designed not only to support children's transition to school but also to help prevent the dissipating effects of preschool programs on academic achievement found in the literature. Reynolds reviews four of the most well-known extended intervention programs—Head Start/Follow Through, Chicago Child-Parent Center and Expansion Program, Carolina Abecedarian Project, and the recent Head Start/Public School Transition Demonstration Project. Findings from these studies show that continuation programs can promote children's school achievement and performance beyond levels achieved by preschool intervention alone. These extra benefits are especially the case for the Chicago Child-Parent Centers and the Abecedarian Project. Although extended programs are one element of larger school and social reforms, their main advantage over other reforms is that they can be more easily integrated with existing schools, and they do not require the creation of new service systems. Reynolds discusses several lessons for the future, lessons derived from 30 years of research on extended childhood programs.

Chapter 7, entitled "Grade Retention, Social Promotion, and 'Third Way' Alternatives," by Karl L. Alexander, Doris R. Entwisle, and Nader Kabbani, discusses the evidence concerning the controversial educational practice of grade retention with an eye toward more proactive ways to address children's learning needs. Findings from their Beginning School Study, one of the best for understanding the consequences of grade retention/promotion, indicate that retained students have an elevated risk of dropping out of school, especially in the case of children retained in first grade or retained twice. The authors argue that knowing the reasons for this increased risk is crucial for better understanding the conditions under which a child may benefit from retention and for determining which students are likely to benefit from retention and which are not. Continuing the theme of earlier chapters, Alexander and colleagues argue that any one-shot program or practice cannot be expected to solve children's academic or social difficulties when their always-present learning environments go unaltered. As noted by the authors, "Children at risk of academic failure require early and ongoing interventions, and to address their needs effectively calls for a more comprehensive reform agenda." Some of the promising enrichment strategies discussed include summer programs, reduced class size, one-on-one tutoring, and after-school programs.

## Part III. National Investments

Four chapters are included in this section. They address cross-cutting issues in early childhood programs. Chapter 8, entitled "The Three Types of Early Childhood Programs in the United States," by Lawrence J. Schweinhart, outlines the major similarities and differences among Head Start, public school prekindergarten, and preschool child care programs. These programs represent the major categories of early childhood programs today. The challenges and implications for evaluation research are also discussed. As Schweinhart describes, there are major differences among the programs in staffing, goals, and definitions of quality (and, by implication, effectiveness) that must be taken into account in evaluating and understanding effectiveness. Public school programs, for example, are primarily focused on educational services in the classroom provided by baccalaureate-educated and relatively well-paid teachers. Historically, these programs have a clearer focus on school readiness than do the other models. Schweinhart concludes that it is difficult to compare the effects of the three programs against each other because they serve different populations. He strongly concurs that their established and interactional components should be a major focus of research. Schweinhart argues that policymakers and funders need to rise above the politics of their positions to support thorough evaluations of the effects of alternative programs.

Chapter 9, entitled "The Science and Policies of Early Childhood Education and Family Services," by Robert B. McCall, Lana Larsen, and Angela Ingram, discusses evidence concerning the effects of alternative early childhood programs for different lengths of time on children's development and the implications of recent advances in knowledge for specific policy alternatives. The authors show that both model (e.g., pilot) and large-scale early education programs have accomplished many of their short- and long-term goals, including enhancing children's cognitive skills, increasing social maturity, and reducing rates of grade retention and special education placement. Although the overall pattern of findings is similar between model and large-scale programs, the effects of large-scale programs such as Head Start are smaller in size and less consistent from program to program. The characteristics of the successful programs discussed include the quality and quantity of treatment dosage (e.g., more is generally better), provision of developmentally appropriate services, use of smaller class sizes, implementation by well-trained staff, and quality of parent involvement. Based on the evidence reviewed, McCall and his coauthors indicate that in balancing cost and effectiveness, "lite" early childhood programs are unlikely to work, and that it is better to provide more extensive and longer lasting educational and family services to fewer children than less extensive services for shorter periods of time to greater numbers of children.

Chapter 10, entitled "Lessons from Europe: European Preschools Revisited in a Global Age," by Sarane Spence Boocock, reviews trends in preschool education policies and research throughout the European Union, trends with implications for preschool education in the United States. As Boocock explains, over half of the countries in Europe have publicly funded preschools that enroll 80% or more of children from ages 3 to 6. As in the United States, high quality preschool programs have been shown to lead to higher levels of cognitive and socioemotional development and to lower rates of grade retention and special education placement. These programs appear to especially benefit children in poverty. Boocock provides extensive evidence from studies conducted in France, United Kingdom, West Germany, and Sweden that show program success occurs across contexts, although long-term evidence is a continuing need. Among the programs and policies with implications for U.S. policy is Europe's more coherent system of education and care. As she explains, "Our nation continues to have one of the world's most fragmented, incoherent, and incomplete ECE systems." Boocock discusses the value of setting up a framework that provides more universal access to preschool education but with flexibility so that families could select from a variety of options, depending on their needs.

Like a year of grade school, one year of preschool is unlikely to result in marked and permanent behavioral change. Chapter 11, entitled "Understanding the Promise of Universal Preschool," by Darcy A. Olsen, critiques the knowledge base on the effects of preschool programs and discusses some implications of this evidence for universal preschool education. Although acknowledging that substantial amounts of research indicate that preschool positively affects children's school readiness and achievement, Olsen argues that the generalizability of this evidence to universal preschool is very limited. According to the author, this is because the best available evidence of the effects of preschool comes from studies of economically disadvantaged children. As noted by the author, it is clear that more and better research is needed on the effects of early education and care for children above the poverty line, and on the long-term effects of Head Start and other public programs. Olsen recommends that further research is needed to better justify universal preschool, with one major question being the environmental conditions and individual factors that contribute to the reduction of effects over time.

## Conclusion

This overview is no substitute for the chapters that follow. In highlighting the directions of the early childhood field, the authors provide many examples and recommendations. Major themes of the chapters and next-step recommendations are discussed in the Epilogue of the book. In many respects, the ideas and recommendations of the chapters are not entirely new. In February 1965, nearly four decades ago, the Head Start planning committee stated its vision for early childhood programs:

> It is clear that successful programs of this type must be comprehensive, involving activities generally associated with the fields of health, social services and education. Similarly, it is clear that the program must focus on the problems of child and parent and that these activities need to be carefully integrated with programs for the school years (Richmond, 1997, p. 122).

The major challenge for the future is how this vision can be tailored to the needs of children and families for the benefit of society.

## Acknowledgments

The National Invitational Conference on Early Childhood Learning: Programs for a New Age and publication of this volume were supported in part by funding from the Office of Educational Research and Improvement (OERI) of the U.S. Department of Education and by the Temple University Center for Research in Human Development and Education (CRHDE). However, the opinions expressed do not necessarily reflect the position of the funding agencies, and no official endorsement should be inferred. We thank Ruby Takanishi for a sterling keynote address at the conference and for advice in organizing the volume.

The volume editors would like to express their deep appreciation to the editorial staff at CRHDE for their editorial support in the preparation of this volume. The volume would not have come to fruition without the relentless efforts and superb administrative expertise of Lou Iovino, Marilyn Murphy, and Stephen Page. Finally, we are indebted to the series editors of the University of Illinois at Chicago Series on Children and Youth, professors Herbert J. Walberg and Roger P. Weissberg, and Tom Gullotta, Senior Editor of the Issues in Children's and Families' Lives Series for the Child Welfare League of America, for their encouragement and support throughout the preparation of this publication.

## References

Barnett, W. S., & Boocock, S. S. (Eds.). (1998). *Early care and education for children in poverty*. Albany: State University of New York Press.

Bowman, B., Donovan, M. S., & Burns, M. S. (Eds.). (2000). *Eager to learn: Educating our preschoolers: Executive summary*. Committee on Early Childhood Pedagogy, National Research Council. Washington, DC: National Academy Press.

Bronfenbrenner, U., & Morris, P. (1998). Ecological processes of development. In W. Damon (Ed.), *Handbook of child psychology: Vol 1. Theoretical issues* (pp. 993–1028). New York: Wiley.

Carnegie Task Force on Learning in the Primary Grades. (1996). *Years of promise: A comprehensive learning strategy for America's children*. New York: Carnegie Corporation of New York.

Council of Economic Advisors. (1997, April). *The first three years: Investments that pay*. Washington, DC: Office of the President.

Forum on Child and Family Statistics. (1999). *America's children: 1999* (Education indicator ED2.B). Washington, DC: U.S. Department of Education. (url:childstats.gov/ac1999/).

Guralnick, M. (Ed.). (1997). *The effectiveness of early intervention*. Baltimore: Paul H. Brookes.

Institute for Research on Poverty. (1997). Investments in young children [Special issue]. *Focus, 19*(1).

Karoly, L. A., Greenwood, P. W., Everingham, S. S., Hoube, J., Kilburn, M. R., Rydell, C. P., Sanders, M., & Chiesa, J. (1998). *Investing in our children: What we know and don't know about the costs and benefits of early childhood interventions*. Santa Monica, CA: RAND.

National Center for Educational Statistics. (2002). *Digest of educational statistics, 2001*(Chapter 2, Table 43, p. 59). Washington, DC: U.S. Department of Education.

National Educational Goals Panel. (1995). *National educational goals report: Building a nation of learners.* Washington, DC: U.S. Government Printing Office.

National Science and Technology Council. (1997, April). *Investing in our future: A national research initiative for America's children for the 21st century.* Washington, DC: Office of the President, Office of Science and Technology Policy, Committee on Fundamental Science, and the Committee on Health, Safety, and Food.

Reynolds, A. J. (2000). *Success in early intervention: The Chicago Child-Parent Centers.* Lincoln: University of Nebraska Press.

Reynolds, A. J., Walberg, H. J., & Weissberg, R. P. (Eds.). (1999). *Promoting positive outcomes.* Washington, DC: CWLA Press.

Richmond, J. B. (1997). Head Start, A retrospective view: The founders; Section 3: The early administrators. In E. Zigler & J. Valentine (Eds.), *Project Head Start: A legacy of the war on poverty* (2nd ed., pp. 120–128). Alexandria, VA: National Head Start Association.

Shonkoff, J. P., & Meisels, S. J. (Eds.). (2000). *Handbook of early childhood intervention* (2nd ed.). New York: Cambridge University Press.

U.S. General Accounting Office. (1997). *Head Start: Research provides little information on impact of current program* (Report no. GAO/HEHS-97-59). Washington, DC: Author.

U.S. General Accounting Office. (1999). *Education and care: Early childhood programs and services for low-income families* (Report no. GAO/HEHS-00-11). Washington, DC: Author.

U.S. General Accounting Office. (2000). *Preschool education: Federal investment for low-income children significant but effectiveness unclear.* (GAO/T-HEHS Publication No. 00-83). Washington, DC: Author.

Walberg, H. J., Reyes, O., & Weissberg, R. P. (Eds.). (1997). *Children and youth: Interdisciplinary perspectives.* Thousand Oaks, CA: Sage Publications.

# PART I

## Preschool Education and Care

# Chapter 1

# The Federal Commitment to Preschool Education: Lessons from and for Head Start

*Edward Zigler and Sally J. Styfco*

Forty years ago, federal preschool education programs did not exist. Nor did the federal government send preschool funds to the states, more than half of which did not even have kindergartens, not to mention classes for younger children. Today, the federal Head Start program enrolls over 900,000 children, ages 0 to 5, each year. All states have kindergartens, and partly in response to Head Start's success, more than half offer preschool to at least some groups of young children. The story of how we got from there to here and the lessons learned along the way are the subject of this chapter.

Head Start is not only the largest, but also the oldest federal preschool program. In fact, the federal commitment to early childhood education developed mainly in the form of what was christened Project Head Start (which, as we will explain, is a comprehensive intervention that includes but goes far beyond traditional preschool education). We begin by tracing the program's political origins, followed by brief descriptions of its structure, goals, and wandering history of evaluation. This background is used as a route toward understanding Head Start's current achievements and shortcomings. We glance at some other federal endeavors that involve young children, namely Part A of the massive Title I of the Elementary and Secondary Education Act, as well as the smaller Part B (Even Start). We conclude by taking a hard look at what we have learned from these collective efforts and how we can apply this knowledge to better prepare at-risk children for elementary school.

## The Development of Head Start

The history of education in America reveals few clues as to why the age for public schooling began at 6 or 7 years, moving down to 5 in more recent times. Suffice it to say that at these ages, local governments assumed responsibility for children's learning. Before children reached "school age," their care and education were the family's obligation. Therefore, with the exception of the war years, very few federal tax dollars were devoted to young children's development, and public policies were sparse because children's welfare was considered a private, family matter (Beatty, 1995; Michel, 1999; Takanishi, 1977). These conventions unwittingly changed in the early 1960s, when the nation began a huge campaign to eradicate poverty and promote social equality.

### *Birth of a Program for Poor Children*

Project Head Start was conceived during an optimistic period of American history, an era with ample amounts of prosperity and social activism, which joined to target domestic problems. The spirit of the times is captured in President Lyndon Johnson's dream to create a "great society" where all citizens share equally in the country's resources and democracy. Poverty was an anathema to this dream, so Johnson declared an all-out war against it. His attack, powerfully named the War on Poverty, was a major initiative to provide education and self-help opportunities to enable poor people to improve their lives. The 1964 Economic Opportunity Act (EOA) opened the "war" by creating several projects for poor adults, including the Community Action Programs (CAP).

CAPs were designed to help local communities establish and run their own antipoverty programs. However, some local governments opposed CAPs' requirement that poor people assume some control of program administration and funds and therefore refused to apply for the grants. Sargent Shriver, head of the Office of Economic Opportunity and Johnson's chief strategist in the war, needed a way to make CAPs more acceptable to local officials. He also wanted to do something about census data that truly dismayed him: The numbers showed that children comprised half of the population living below poverty. He thought it would make sense to target some CAP resources to the youngest of the poor.

Johnson's own life experiences had convinced him of the value of education as a way out of poverty. Shriver shared this belief and envisioned a program to prepare disadvantaged children to succeed when they got to school. A bonus was that local leaders might rally around such a program because no one could blame children for their financial straits or fear giving them too much power (Zigler & Anderson, 1997).

With the exception of a few small experimental projects, there was very little experience at the time to suggest how to meet the needs of economically disadvantaged preschoolers. Lacking a model for a national intervention project, but convinced that poor children could use help preparing for school, Shriver enlisted professional help. He appointed a planning committee of 14 experts from the fields of education, child development, social work, and physical and mental health. This diversity ensured that Head Start would become far more than an educational program. (For the history of the development of Head Start, see Zigler & Muenchow, 1992, and Zigler & Valentine, 1997.)

Dr. Robert Cooke, a noted pediatrician, chaired the group, which had only a few months to develop their plans. The committee's recommendations, presented to Shriver in February 1965, were based on a "whole child" philosophy that called for comprehensive programming: Head Start's goals were to improve physical health, enhance mental processes (particularly conceptual and verbal skills), and foster social and emotional development, self-confidence, relationships with family and others, social responsibility, and a sense of dignity and self-worth for both the child and family (*Recommendations for a Head Start Program by a Panel of Experts,* 1965). Note that only one of these seven goals specifically related to intellectual performance.

The committee's recommendations were unique not only because they outlined a multifaceted intervention, but because they included the family as well as the child. The planning document accorded parents a central role that was virtually unprecedented in education programs. Prior to Head Start, economically disadvantaged families had been treated as passive recipients of services dispensed by professionals. Head Start parents were to be involved in the planning, administration, and daily activities of their local centers.

One reason for this decision derived from Head Start's origins in CAPs, which were mandated to allow poor citizens "maximum feasible participation" in running antipoverty efforts. The EOA contained no clear definition of this slogan, and the Head Start planning committee interpreted it more literally than many local officials might have liked (Valentine & Stark, 1997). The planners were also influenced by the ideas of one member, Uri Bronfenbrenner, who was then conceptualizing his ecological approach to human development. Bronfenbrenner (1974, 1979) argued that families and communities have a potent influence on children's lives, so intervention must involve these agents to be effective. This insight was an astute one. Today, two-generation activities have become a hallmark of the Head Start model and a recommendation for programs that followed.

### Program Implementation

Expert advisors and the planning document itself recommended that a small, pilot program should be run and evaluated prior to mounting a large-scale effort. However, the Johnson Administration demanded that Shriver fire a major volley in the War on Poverty by beginning on a large scale. When Head Start opened in 1965, over half a million children were served in a summer program lasting six or eight weeks. Unfortunately, there was not enough time to screen the grant applications carefully, so variation in quality characterized Head Start from the very beginning.

Although Head Start has grown since that first summer, the basic format remains the same. The biggest change in structure occurred between 1966 and 1972, when Head Start centers converted from summer to school-year calendars. Today the program is generally a center-based preschool serving primarily poor children aged 3 to 5, with the majority (54%) being 4 years old (Administration on Children, Youth and Families, 2002). Most children attend a half-day session for one academic year, although some attend for two years. Full-day programs and home-based services are delivered in some locations. Federal guidelines require that at least 90% of the children enrolled be from families whose income falls below the poverty line; at least 10% of enrollment must consist of children with disabilities. Head Start programs by law receive 80% of their funding from the federal government ($6.5 billion in Fiscal Year 2002). The rest comes from other, usually local, sources, which may be in the form of donated services.

In 2001, there were over 1,500 Head Start grantees serving over 905,000 children and their families. (Statistics kept by the Administration on Children, Youth and Families, 2002, show that over 20 million children have attended Head Start since it began.) Each program is required to include early childhood education, health screening and referral, mental health services, nutrition education and hot meals, social services for the child and family, parent involvement, and family and community partnerships. Local programs are governed by Parent Committees, Policy Councils, and Policy Committees, collectively composed of parents, staff, and community representatives who are responsible for operating and staffing decisions. Although all Head Start programs must adhere to a body of national regulations, called the Program Performance Standards (U.S. Department of Health and Human Services, 1998), each is encouraged to adapt services to local needs and resources. Thus Head Start is not a formula intervention but a diversity of local programs that share a common structure and common practices.

This sketch of Head Start appears to depict a federal resolve to better the lives of poor children, which has only strengthened over time. Policymakers did become enamored with the program soon after it started because they believed it "worked," but they have questioned its effectiveness ever since. Several sources share the blame for the unfortunate fact that after all these years, Head Start's worth has not been satisfactorily documented: The planners designed a complicated program with complicated goals; the project's advocates promised too much; and policymakers expected too much and budgeted too little. We now turn to the empirical efforts that sometimes did more to cloud than to illuminate Head Start's accomplishments. Like the program, the science of evaluation has matured and improved over time. Thus, the research history is presented in two parts. The first covers the long period that generated a little knowledge but did a lot to illuminate the barriers to sound research. The second part describes recent activities that have evolved from these insights.

## Research: Then

Federal officials understandably wanted a national impact study to ascertain the effects of the costly new Head Start experiment. But exactly what effects were they looking for? The planning document referred to seven "objectives" such as boosting self-confidence and developing a responsible attitude. President Johnson had higher hopes that the few weeks children spent in Head Start would enable them to achieve more in all their years of schooling and to break the cycle of poverty when they grew up. None of these expectations were readily measurable, certainly not before the next election. Scientists were therefore free to be creative in choosing what effects Head Start might have and how to gauge them.

### *Cognition, Cognition, Cognition*

If policymakers in the early 1960s seemed too hopeful about the prospects of ending poverty, their enthusiasm was dwarfed by social scientists' dreams to raise intelligence. The decade was characterized by lofty promises that, given the "right" experiences at the "right" time, all children could develop into great intellects. Many psychologists devoted themselves to discovering just what those right experiences might be. Their efforts resulted in a growth industry for crib mobiles, talking typewriters, and books on teaching 2-year-olds to read. (The era's hype bears a strong—and frightening—resemblance to the 1990s craze over early brain development.) Although early childhood intervention programs also experienced growth at this time, few of them were designed explicitly to boost IQ scores. Yet considering the wild beliefs of the day concerning intelligence, it is easy to see how initial research on Head Start and other interventions came to dwell on cognition.

Beyond the fact that much of the social science community had embraced both naïve environmentalism and the notion of magical periods in development, there were practical reasons why Head Start research focused on intelligence test scores. For one, the project's broad scope, multiple objectives, and local diversity complicated evaluation because the standard design and measurement procedures available to researchers were not readily applicable; reliable commercial IQ tests were an easy alternative. Another complication was that there were no established measures of some program aims such as parent involvement and social relationships. Perhaps the most compelling reason that IQ and achievement tests were used nearly exclusively in research on Head Start and other interventions is that the results were so positive. Program designers of course wanted their efforts to succeed, and it was very tempting to employ measures—however inappropriate—that were sure to show success.

Early reports of IQ gains following almost any program ignited soaring hopes about the potential of intervention. For example, Eisenberg and Conners (1966) reported an amazing 10-point IQ increase for graduates of the first Head Start short summer program. Results like these grabbed public attention and made it easy to forget the program's other aims. Such findings also led people to expect too much and to feel duped when it was later revealed that the IQ gains were not sustained.

The catalyst for disillusionment was a study by the Westinghouse Learning Corporation (Cicirelli, 1969). The researchers evaluated children who attended Head Start summer sessions, sampling only a small group who had been in full-year programs (Datta, 1997); they did not administer IQ tests but their close proxy, achievement tests. These should have been cautionary flags to even cursory interpretations, but the Westinghouse findings, showing the achievement gains made in preschool purportedly faded away in the early grades of school, did much to cast doubt on the efficacy of early intervention.

Experts in statistics and evaluation eventually discredited the Westinghouse report after questioning the sampling procedures, data analyses, and appropriateness of the outcome measures. Yet, subsequent studies of Head Start and almost every other early intervention program led to the same conclusion: Preschool graduates generally do not continue to do better on cognitive or achievement tests. There are certainly many exceptions, but the more common findings of fade-out dashed hopes that brief preschool experiences could guarantee higher IQs or academic success for poor children. Disappointed federal officials began to entertain plans to phase out Project Head Start. Credit for its survival goes to Elliot Richardson, Secretary of the Department of Health, Education and Welfare, who fought with other members of the Nixon Administration against their phase-out ideas. Other heroes were the parents—a group newly empowered by their Head Start participation who lobbied Congress to save their program.

## Beyond IQ

In a welcome break from the narrow focus on IQ that characterized early research, the Consortium for Longitudinal Studies (1983) brought to light some of the noncognitive benefits of early intervention. The consortium consisted of researchers who had evaluated 11 preschool programs (two of them Head Start) during the 1960s and early 1970s. The researchers located original program participants and collected a uniform set of information about their current status. The findings confirmed that children who attend quality preschool programs do gain an initial boost in IQ and achievement scores that lasts for some years but appears to fade. However, lasting effects were found in other areas: Participants were less likely to be assigned to special education classes and were somewhat less likely to be held back a grade in school. The rigor of the consortium's methodology, and the findings of benefits that persisted until many children had reached 12 or more years of age, did much to restore public and scientific faith in the value of early intervention.

More recent studies and research reviews have also yielded encouraging results (Collins, 1989; McCall, 1993; Reynolds et al., 1997). Among the most comprehensive analyses of the literature are reviews by Barnett (1995), Haskins (1989), and Woodhead (1988). All were careful to separate experimental preschools (typically small and university-based; carefully designed, implemented, and evaluated; and of uniformly high quality) from Head Start. The reviewers noted that

Head Start and the smaller programs produced immediate gains in intelligence and achievement that generally dissipated within a few years. Haskins concluded that after that, there was very strong evidence that the experimental models improved school performance, including less grade retention and special education class placement. Although he described the evidence for Head Start in this domain as only modest, Barnett found it to be "significant" for large-scale programs, including Head Start. Life success indices (avoidance of delinquency, teen pregnancy, welfare, etc.) produced some evidence for the smaller projects but "virtually no evidence for Head Start" (Haskins, p. 278). This does not mean that Head Start has no such benefits, but that little or no data have been collected about them. In fact, because Head Start offers a wider variety of services than most of the comparisons, the program might have even greater benefits if the services are of high quality (Zigler & Styfco, 1994b).

There are several reasons why children leave the program testing well and then may lose this advantage. One is that performance on an IQ test reflects not only formal cognitive processes but experiential and personality variables as well. The IQ gains apparent after Head Start are not necessarily due to expanded intellectual capacity but may instead be explained by improved motivation, familiarity with test content, and comfort in the testing situation (Seitz et al., 1975; Zigler, Abelson et al., 1982; Zigler & Butterfield, 1968). Thus, participation in Head Start can enable children to develop the skills and attitudes needed to apply their abilities more fully. When they enter school, however, the environment may not continue to encourage full use of their potential; for example, there may be a poor curriculum or teaching practices that lower self-confidence and ignore individual learning styles (Lee, 1993; Lee & Loeb, 1995).

Another explanation for fade-out, at least for achievement gains, is that it is merely an artifact of measurement, statistical analysis, and sampling procedures (Barnett, 1992). A problem in many reviews, particularly the most inclusive, is that the results of good and poor programs (and sound and unsound studies) are combined so robust results from some investigations are statistically diluted by null effects from others (Gamble & Zigler, 1989). This dilution is what happened in the Synthesis Project (McKey et al., 1985), a meta-analysis of numerous Head Start studies. The results documented sustained benefits to children's health and adaptive behavior, but the authors reached the by-now common conclusion that positive effects on cognitive performance are impressive but short term. However, a close look at the individual study findings in the Synthesis Project report and in Barnett's review reveals a number that do not show fade-out. Other studies have found retention of benefits for some participant groups but not others (e.g., Currie & Thomas, 1995).

In sum, the sizable body of research on different intervention programs tentatively shows enduring effects on school adjustment and other aspects of social competence. The persistence of academic benefits is a possibility that warrants further review. Findings concerning immediate program effects are much more definite: When children leave preschool they have better IQ test scores and school readiness skills. In other words, they are better prepared for kindergarten. If this advantage later fades, the fault lies beyond the preschool.

## Research: Now

Our conclusion that Head Start has immediate effects on school readiness and possibly sustained effects on social adaptation reflects a general but by no means unanimous consensus. A significant dissenter is the U.S. General Accounting Office (GAO). The Office conducted a major review and concluded, "The body of research on current Head Start is insufficient to draw conclusions about the impact of the national program" (1997, p. 8) Screening out studies conducted prior to 1976 and those with inadequate methodologies, the GAO found only 22 studies to include in its analysis. These studies did not all measure the same type of impact, which is why the analysts felt there was simply not enough evidence to tell if Head Start makes a difference.

An appendix to the GAO report by the Department of Health and Human Services (DHHS) countered that "There is a large body of convincing research on the short and immediate effects of Head Start" (p. 48). The DHHS did not dismiss older studies because there are so many and because, collectively, their results are positive. The GAO chose 1976 as the cut-off date because the agency wanted to consider programs in operation after the initial implementation problems had been remedied and after the performance standards had begun to dictate services and quality. (The standards were not put into place until 1975, meaning Head Start operated for 10 years without quality controls.) This later work could conceivably have shown even stronger effects than the research on immature Head Start. We will never know because, as the GAO discovered, support for research was greatly reduced during the 1980s. In 1986, only $810,000 was spent on research, demonstration, and evaluation, representing only 0.08% of the program's $1 billion budget. It is therefore true that much of what is known about the effects of Head Start is based on older, sometimes problematic studies, and there is much that is not known. Happily, this is beginning to change.

## Goals and Measures

As we discussed earlier, a deterrent to informative research has been the lack of clearly defined goals so evaluators would know what type of progress to assess. In the early 1970s the goal of social competence was officially adopted, but, like most of the objectives in the original planning document, it too lacked reliable measurement (Zigler & Trickett, 1978). Over the following decade three major efforts were undertaken to define the construct and design an assessment battery of social competence for use in Head Start evaluations (see Raver & Zigler, 1991). But despite a staggering amount of work, difficulties in the laboratory and a political change of heart meant that a measure was never developed. This is sad because over all these many years of labor, a consensual definition of social competence emerged that involved four easily operationalized constructs: health, cognition, achievement, and motivational/emotional variables (Zigler & Trickett, 1978).

In 1993, the Administration on Children, Youth and Families (ACYF) began developing program performance measures for Head Start. Initiated to comply with the accountability mandate of the Government Performance and Results Act of 1993, the measures assess both quality and effectiveness of program services. The conceptual framework for the measures is built around the goal of social competence, encompassing various indices of health, cognitive and social development, and family functioning (Head Start Bureau, 1995). After the measures project began, Congress passed the Coats Human Services Reauthorization Act of 1998, which explicitly reworded Head Start's goal as school readiness. The importance of readiness is its strong bearing on school outcomes, such as being in the right grade for age and not being in special education.

Despite the differences in terminology, past teams of scientists, ACYF, and Congress are all on the same page: For young children, social competence and school readiness are indistinguishable (Zigler, 1998). To be competent, a child must be effective in dealing with his or her environment and be able to meet age-appropriate social expectancies. Children who cannot deal with their environments or demonstrate abilities that are reasonably expected of their age group are not ready for school. Discussions of competence and readiness in fact rely on the same themes. For example, the Head Start Bureau lists healthy growth and development, preschool education, and families who nurture their children's learning among objectives that support social competence. The three objectives for National Education Goal 1 (school readiness) are exactly the same (National Education Goals Panel, 1999). (The National Education Goals, adopted by the state governors in 1989 and signed into law in 1994, are used to guide school reform.) By changing the words of its goal statement to school readiness, the Bureau would bring some clarity to public thinking about why we invest in Head Start.

This explicit goal, and continued development of measures to assess it, will also make possible a sensible research agenda that fairly evaluates the program's effectiveness. Such an agenda will bring to fruition the efforts of scores of scientists who drafted wise research plans over the years. Implementation of these plans has been stifled in the past by a weak federal commitment to and support of Head Start research. These elements are now being strengthened, making it more likely than ever before that we will gain a coherent understanding of Head Start's benefits and ways to expedite them.

## Research Planning

The first wave of research on Head Start and other intervention programs had a myopic focus on cognitive benefits. Once these were documented and found to be temporary, investigators who were still interested used their imaginations in deciding what effects to assess. Many continued to search for results on IQ and achievement tests. A few examined the impact on health, parents, or communities. Researchers studying graduates of the Perry Preschool (an experimental project that ended in 1967) looked at novel data such as library patronage, juvenile delinquency, and teen pregnancy (Schweinhart et al., 1993). The use of such a variety of outcomes is valuable in that it conveys a broader sense of purpose to intervention. Collectively, however, this literature contributed little to our knowledge base because findings across studies were not easily compared and did not build upon one another.

This was the conclusion of the Advisory Panel for the Head Start Evaluation Design Project (1990), a group of experts who studied 25 years of Head Start research. They concluded that this expansive data set had not produced an organized knowledge set and drew up plans to attain one. The resulting "blueprint for Head Start research," as it came to be known, focused on studying which program services work best and for whom. The blueprint was not a detailed map for empiricists to follow but a general research strategy for studying the diversity of Head Start programs, participants, and outcomes.

More definitive plans were the responsibility of the Roundtable on Head Start Research (Phillips & Cabrera, 1996), a collaborative effort conducted by the National Research Council and the Institute of Medicine. Building on the blueprint, the Roundtable focused on the need to study the content and quality of Head Start services, the program's work with families in a changing world, mental health issues, and ways to invigorate the program's role as a national laboratory where effective service models are developed and disseminated to the early childhood fields. A practicum for the Roundtable's ideas was recently devised by the Advisory Committee on Head Start Research and Evaluation (1999).

This committee was charged with making recommendations for a national study of Head Start's impact on school readiness and on parental practices that promote readiness. The group's report, and the congressional charge that led to it, are notable for two reasons. First, the targeted outcomes focus on the immediate goal of preparing young children for school. Follow-up is planned until the end of first grade, a reasonable time frame to infer the value of readiness skills to early academic progress.

Also notable are the current plans for a longitudinal study to incorporate a random assignment design. Although random assignment characterized evaluations of many experimental projects, studies of Head Start have been limited to quasi-experimental designs. These are certainly informative but less rigorous than studies in which participants are randomly assigned to treatment and control groups. Applying this methodology to a national study should strengthen both the knowledge base and future evaluation science.

### Plans Realized

Research is also being conducted under the renewed federal interest in understanding and improving Head Start's effectiveness. In 1995, the Head Start Bureau created four Quality Research Centers that are each carrying out major independent studies. Together, they are also developing the program performance measures that will eventually be used to assess Head Start quality and results. Testing of the measures has become part of the Head Start Family and Child Experiences Survey (FACES), a national longitudinal study of ambitious breadth. Assessments include service quality and content; children's physical, cognitive, and social and emotional development; and parent involvement and family functioning. Results thus far indicate that quality in Head Start classrooms is good, children do become more ready for school, and that parent involvement and satisfaction are alive and well (Head Start Bureau, 1998).

Regardless of the final results of the massive planning and major empirical work now ongoing, this flurry of activity has already changed the tenor of thoughts about early intervention. First, research has regained importance as a vital function of program development that will no longer be considered "nonessential" when budgets are drawn. Second, the scope of this new empirical thrust should forever put to rest the simplistic notion that the only purpose of early intervention is to make children smarter. While cognitive gains are important to school success, so are children's physical and mental health and parents who take a proactive role in their child's learning. Finally, the sophistication of the current efforts lends credence to the worthiness of early intervention and its goals.

## Other Federal Interventions

Head Start was developed as an experiment because the planners had little information on which to base the project and had no assurance that it would work. The program was therefore conceptualized as a national laboratory for the design, evaluation, and dissemination of effective methods of early childhood education. After the initial summer trial, administrators launched different programs based on different approaches to meeting the needs of young children and families in poverty. Other federal agencies devised their own experiments to "win" the War on Poverty. Many of these projects failed or lost financial support. Several survived, at least thematically, and are briefly described here.

### The National Laboratory

The planners and early administrators did not believe that a summer of Head Start would inoculate children against the pervasive effects of poverty. Even as the program was extended to last for the school year, they began trials of ways to make it a more potent intervention (see Valentine, 1997). The Child Development Associate (CDA) program was launched to train a cadre of workers to provide quality care and education to children in Head Start and child care settings nationwide. The CDA credential is now recognized by many state child care agencies and has been mandated for Head Start staff. (A compliance rate of 100% has not yet been reached, even as recent legislation raised the bar to two- and four-year degrees by early in the 21st century.)

Recognizing that parents guide their children's development long before and after preschool, a number of family-focused interventions were also created. One was Education for Parenthood, a high school course to teach students the principles of child development and rearing before they have families. Another was the Child and Family Resource Program for parents and children ages 0 to 8 years. This program provided a variety of educational and support services, and families chose those they needed (Zigler & Seitz, 1982). Although the program was widely praised, the demonstration was ended in 1978.

A longer-lived model was the Parent and Child Centers (PCCs), which provided supportive services and parent education to families and children from birth to age 3. The PCCs operated for some 30 years, keeping the experiment alive but contributing little to our knowledge base. Without consistent performance standards and research attention, there was no way of knowing what services were generally delivered or how well they met the needs of participating families. Research was directed toward a more recent spin-off, the Comprehensive Child Development Program (CCDP), which connected families of children ages 0 to 5 with needed services in the community. Results of the pilot program showed few benefits, leading to the recommendation for more child-focused services (St. Pierre et al., 1997). The evaluation has been sharply criticized (Gilliam et al., 2000), leading us to conclude that it is premature to dismiss the CCDP as ineffective.

Over time, the premise of these early family support models earned strong scientific endorsement: Preventive services, beginning very early in a child's life, can be more effective—and more cost-effective—than remedial ones. On this basis, the Human Services Reauthorization Act of 1994 created Early Head Start, ending the PCC effort but subsuming some of the existing centers. Unlike the planners of the original Head

Start, the multidisciplinary committee convened by the Clinton Administration to design this younger version had an expansive knowledge base to guide them (Advisory Committee on Services for Families with Infants and Toddlers, 1994). Reauthorized in 1998, there are now 650 Early Head Start demonstrations across the country. Services for at-risk families begin prenatally and include comprehensive child development, parent education, and family support provided in the home, centers, and the community. The centers are covered by the new performance standards that, for the first time, govern the quality of services for the youngest Head Start participants. A research component was written into the project at its inception. The rationale of the project is clear: Waiting until a child is 3 or 4 years old is waiting too long. Children who are healthy, have sound relationships with their primary caregivers, and who have received adequate nurturing and stimulation will have the socioemotional foundations needed for learning in preschool and beyond (Zero to Three, 1992).

Administrators also experimented with continuing services to Head Start graduates. Just two years after Head Start opened, Follow Through was initiated to extend services through the early grades of elementary school. Plans were for this to be a national project of the same scope as Head Start, but the escalating costs of the Vietnam War depleted the expected funding before the demonstration phase was completed (Doernberger & Zigler, 1993). The concept survived as a tiny experiment in planned curriculum variation until the 1994 Reauthorization Act resurrected its original promise in the form of the Head Start-Public School Early Childhood Transition Project (described by Kennedy, 1993).

The Transition Project followed Head Start graduates from kindergarten through Grade 3. Local Head Start and public school personnel worked to introduce each child and family to the new school experience and to familiarize kindergarten teachers with the child's progress, program, and needs. Comprehensive services, parental involvement, and family support were continued for the next four years. The emphasis was on a smooth transition to school, drawing parents into the process.

Evaluation of the Transition Project demonstration has not yet been published. A small but convincing body of evidence supports the transition premise that longer, coordinated intervention produces longer lasting gains. Results of several projects—most notably the Chicago Child-Parent Centers, which closely resemble the Head Start model (Reynolds, 1994, 2000)—indicate that the advantages derived from preschool can be sustained by integrating preschool and school-age programming (see reviews by Barnett, 1995; Reynolds, this volume; Reynolds et al., 1997; Zigler & Styfco, 1993). This research offers hope that where well-implemented and of high quality, Transition Project sites will be shown to be effective in helping Head Start graduates become more competent students throughout school. While the demonstration has ended, the performance standards now require all Head Start grantees to engage in transitional activities with parents, children, and elementary school staff.

## *Title I*

The Department of Education has also implemented some programs for poor children before and after they reach school age. A large part of the Department's budget (over $10 billion annually) is spent on Title I of the Elementary and Secondary Education Act of 1965 (ESEA). Title I funds compensatory education for poor or at-risk children in preschool through Grade 12. Originally intended to enhance the educational services of impoverished school districts, the majority of the nation's schools now receive some Title I funds; in general, they are spent on remedial instruction for children who have fallen behind the academic expectations of their grade level.

Because of the scope of the program, evaluations of Title I are few, but those few show most students do not exhibit a meaningful gain in achievement (Abt Associates, 1997; Arroyo & Zigler, 1993). In a longitudinal study of Title I students in some 400 schools, Abt Associates found that academic standards were generally low and services too weak to close the achievement gap between children from poor and wealthier families.

Debate during reauthorization of the ESEA in 1994 focused on revamping the program by training classroom teachers, narrowing the target population, and encouraging schools in high-poverty districts to use their Title I funds for schoolwide programs instead of on individual students. These changes were incorporated in the Improving America's School Act of 1994, which also mandates that Title I do more to provide children with access to health and social services and to include their parents in the program. These components of the Head Start model have been legislated for Title I in the past but have been poorly implemented (Arroyo & Zigler, 1993).

Despite earnest efforts by educators, a major reason why Title I has proven recalcitrant to system-wide improvement is that it is more of a funding stream than a circumscribed program. Money is given to state educational agencies, which award it to local educational agencies, which direct it to school districts. When it eventually gets to individual schools, there is much flexibility in how it is spent. Without a discernible program, these funds have not made much of a difference in the achievement of low-income children, but several tangible projects supported by Title I resources have. Success for All, for example, began as a Title I grant for children in preschool until third grade (Slavin et al., 1996). With high-quality education in literacy and various degrees of parent involvement, students in this multiyear program exhibited significant gains in reading. Some Schools of the 21st Century (a model that adds a child care component to schools) are using Title I funds for expanding services beyond traditional academics. For example, they are supporting preschool teachers' salaries and quality before- and after-school care (Finn-Stevenson & Zigler, 1999).

A close reading of the reauthorizations of the ESEA over the years shows that policymakers have prodded Title I to adopt comprehensive services, parent involvement, and other elements of Head Start. Small but positive steps have been taken in this direction. In the final section of this paper, we explain our proposal for Title I to take the plunge and become the school-age version of Head Start.

## *Even Start*

In 1989, Part B of the ESEA's Title I authorized the Even Start Family Literacy Program. The general purpose is to improve adult literacy and education, parenting skills, and children's early literacy abilities. The target population is families in poverty who are eligible for adult education services and have a child 0 to 8 years old. In FY 1998, over 700 Even Start projects had combined appropriations of $124 million. Unlike Head Start, the program is now state administered.

Evaluation of Even Start shows that adult participants are more likely to attend adult basic education and parenting classes than controls not in the program; their children are also more likely to be enrolled in early childhood education programs (St. Pierre et al., 1998). Yet, this schooling did not catapult participants ahead of their comparisons. St. Pierre et al. reported that although parents in Even Start were more likely to obtain a GED, the reading and math gains they made were no larger than those made by control families. Even Start children acquired school readiness skills sooner than did peers who were not in the program, but this advantage disappeared when the peers gained experience in preschool or kindergarten. The investigators concluded that the apparent lack of benefits might have been due to differences in quality among Even Start programs, as well as to the difficulties inherent in conducting a national longitudinal study with various data collection and information tracking procedures.

# A Unified Federal Response

Americans and their elected officials are by now convinced that investments in programs for young children are monies well spent. To prove their commitment, policymakers have supported an array of programs directed toward the education of poor children. Head Start, Title I, and Even Start are three federal programs that concern preschool education. (A well-kept secret is that Title I also serves preschoolers, but even the GAO could not find the exact number. In a 2000 report, the agency cited the Department of Education's estimate of 2% of the Title I participants.) School-age children in low-income areas were, until recently, the target population of the four-year-long Head Start Transition Project; such children remain the target population of Title I. Family literacy services are common to Head Start and Even Start. All of these efforts have compatible goals and serve similar groups, yet they are authorized by different acts, subsections, and amendments, and compete with one another for shares of the federal budget.

Years of legislative tinkering with educational intervention programs have obviously created a frustrating maze. One analyst of all the entangled policies concluded that "supporters have exhausted any notion of whom they mean to help...or simply how" (Ralph, 1989, p. 396). The overlap in programs and policies suggests that time, effort, and money are being wasted at both the administrative and service delivery levels. We have now had decades of experience with early intervention and compensatory education. It is time to use this information to revamp our strategies for educating poor children.

## Elements of Effective Intervention

The literature on early intervention has generated some guiding principles that underlie the most salutary efforts (e.g., McCall, this volume; Price et al., 1988; Schorr, 1988; Zigler & Styfco, 1993). One is that programs must be comprehensive in scope, attending to the many factors that underlie the complex phenomenon of school performance. All children need certain learning experiences to be ready for school, but poor children often have myriad other needs as well. Children who are hungry, homeless, witnesses or victims of abuse, or live in neighborhoods governed by gangs and guns will not be able to give their full attention to school regardless of whether they attended preschool. The services poor children need may go beyond the traditional mission of the education establishment, but their absence makes that mission unattainable.

Another principle is that successful intervention programs target not only the child but also the family who rears the child. It makes sense that parents who have some of their basic needs met, feel a degree of social support, have some child-rearing skills, and have a sense of control over their own and their children's future can do a better job of parenting. The family systems approach provides an explanation of the long-term effects that have been found for early intervention. Several theorists (e.g., Lally et al., 1988; Seitz, 1990; Zigler & Seitz, 1982) have advanced the view that persistent benefits cannot be due to a half-day program experienced by the child during one year of preschool, but are rather due to the parents. As a result of their involvement with the intervention, parents become better socializers of the child throughout the rest of the day and, it may be hoped, throughout the child's development. On the other hand, the lack of commitment to parent involvement could account for the lackluster results of Title I.

The literature also makes clear that only quality services can deliver the intended benefits leading to school readiness. This point deserves emphasis because in recent years of Head Start expansion, efforts to serve more children proceeded more rapidly than efforts to serve them well. Years of inadequate funding, oversight, training, and technical assistance had left many Head Start centers struggling to provide adequate services and some unable to do so (Advisory Committee on Head Start Quality and Expansion, 1993; Chafel, 1992; National Head Start Association, 1990; Office of the Inspector General, 1993; U.S. Department of Health and Human Services, 1980; Zigler & Styfco, 1994a). These inadequacies, however, do not reflect pervasive quality problems at Head Start centers. Several studies have shown that Head Start is in fact better than many early care and education programs (Layzer et al., 1993; Ripple et al., 1999). Yet the existence of some poor centers taints the reputation of the many good ones and shortchanges their participants.

Quality improvement plans have now been drawn and are being implemented. Reauthorization of Head Start in 1998 continues the practice begun in 1990 of putting aside a portion of budget increases to upgrade quality. Research is showing that improvements are evident in key areas such as staff qualifications, caseloads, and turnover, especially among centers that had lower quality to begin with (Powell et al., 1998). Although there is still some way to go, these enhancements hold promise for boosting Head Start's overall effectiveness.

Finally, the many intervention attempts tried over the years have proven the difficulty of remediating the effects of poverty. No amount of early brain stimulation, no year of preschool, or no class periods of compensatory studies will ensure a bright future for a child raised in economic deprivation. Intervention must begin early and last long enough to have a meaningful impact on the child's development.

## A Unified Federal Policy

We have proposed a national system of extended intervention that builds on the scientific and theoretical bases created over the years (Zigler & Styfco, 1993). This system can be built upon and funded from existing programs that collectively, but not individually, capture the elements of successful intervention. In essence, our proposal calls for integrated services that begin with Early Head Start, followed by preschool Head Start and a Title I Transition in Grades K to three.

The Department of Education has made some inroads toward incorporating Head Start-like services into ESEA programs. Further, the Department's former Director of Compensatory Education Programs, Mary Jean LeTendre, has called for more collaboration with Head Start and other state and federal interventions. We should mention that the majority of states now offer prekindergarten to at least some children—typically the same at-risk groups served by Head Start and Title I. A very few states require or recommend that their public preschools adhere to the Head Start Program Performance Standards (Ripple et al., 1999). The others have the narrower, academic focus common to most Title I and elementary school programs. All states also serve children ages 0 to 3 who are eligible under Part H of the Individuals with Disabilities Education Act. The required comprehensive services and parental involvement are sometimes provided to these young children through Head Start or Title I. A significant benefit of a closer linking of Head Start and Title I is that they would form a visible model of service delivery for the state and other early childhood efforts.

The ultimate linking would be to fold Even Start into Early Head Start, have Head Start assume Title I preschool services, and have Title

I schools adopt the Transition Project model. This metamorphosis will give Title I an identity as an actual program based on knowledge and best practices. It will enable Head Start to serve more eligible children. Finally, these three programs will signify a coherent federal policy to meet the needs of at-risk children beginning prenatally—a policy states can emulate. Instead of funding a hodgepodge of programs with similar goals, tax dollars will be more efficiently spent on a system that can produce benefits greater than the sum of its parts.

## References

Abt Associates. (1997). *Prospects: Final report on student outcomes.* Washington, DC: U.S. Department of Education, Planning and Evaluation Service.

Administration on Children, Youth and Families (2002). *Head Start 2002 fact sheet.* Washington, DC: Author.

Advisory Committee on Head Start Quality and Expansion. (1993). *Creating a 21st century Head Start.* Washington, DC: U.S. Department of Health and Human Services.

Advisory Committee on Head Start Research and Evaluation. (1999). *Evaluating Head Start: A recommended framework for studying the impact of the Head Start program.* Washington, DC: U.S. Department of Health and Human Services.

Advisory Committee on Services for Families with Infants and Toddlers. (1994). *Statement of the Advisory Committee on Services for Families with Infants and Toddlers.* Washington, DC: U.S. Department of Health and Human Services.

Advisory Panel for the Head Start Evaluation Design Project. (1990). *Head Start research and evaluation: A blueprint for the future.* Washington, DC: U.S. Department of Health and Human Services.

Arroyo, C. G., & Zigler, E. (1993). America's Title I/Chapter 1 programs: Why the promise has not been met. In E. Zigler & S. J. Styfco (Eds.), *Head Start and beyond: A national plan for extended childhood intervention* (pp. 73–95). New Haven: Yale University Press.

Barnett, W. S. (1992). Benefits of compensatory preschool education. *Journal of Human Resources, 27,* 279–312.

Barnett, W. S. (1995). Long-term effects of early childhood programs on cognitive and school outcomes. *Future of Children, 5*(3), 25–50.

Beatty, B. (1995). *Preschool education in America: The culture of young children from the colonial era to the present.* New Haven: Yale University Press.

Bronfenbrenner, U. (1974). Is early intervention effective? *Day Care and Early Education, 44,* 14–18.

Bronfenbrenner, U. (1979). *The ecology of human development.* Cambridge, MA: Harvard University Press.

Chafel, J. A. (1992). Funding Head Start: What are the issues? *American Journal of Orthopsychiatry, 62,* 9–21.

Cicirelli, V. G. (1969). *The impact of Head Start: An evaluation of the effects of Head Start on children's cognitive and affective development* (Report No. PB 184 328, presented to the Office of Economic Opportunity). Washington, DC: Westinghouse Learning Corporation.

Collins, R. C. (1989). *Head Start research and evaluation: Background and overview.* Technical paper prepared for the Head Start Evaluation Design Project. Washington, DC: U.S. Department of Health and Human Services.

Consortium for Longitudinal Studies. (Ed.). (1983). *As the twig is bent: Lasting effects of preschool programs.* Hillsdale, NJ: Erlbaum.

Currie, J., & Thomas, D. (1995). Does Head Start make a difference? *American Economic Review, 85,* 341–364.

Datta, L. (1997). Another spring and other hopes: Some findings from national evaluations of Project Head Start. In E. Zigler & J. Valentine (Eds.), *Project Head Start: A legacy of the War on Poverty* (2nd ed., pp. 405–432). Alexandria, VA: National Head Start Association.

Doernberger, C., & Zigler, E. (1993). Project Follow Through: Intent and reality. In E. Zigler & S. J. Styfco (Eds.), *Head Start and beyond: A national plan for extended childhood intervention* (pp. 43–72). New Haven: Yale University Press.

Eisenberg, L., & Conners, C. K. (1966, April 11). The effect of Head Start on the developmental process. Paper presented at the Joseph P. Kennedy, Jr., Foundation Scientific Symposium on Mental Retardation, Boston.

Finn-Stevenson, M., & Zigler, E. (1999). *Schools of the 21st Century: Linking child care and education.* Boulder, CO: Westview Press.

Gamble, T., & Zigler, E. (1989). The Head Start Synthesis Project: A critique. *Journal of Applied Developmental Psychology, 10,* 267–274.

Gilliam, W. S., Ripple, C. H., Zigler, E., & Leiter, V. (2000). Evaluating child and family demonstration initiatives: Lessons from the Comprehensive Child Development Program. *Early Childhood Research Quarterly, 15,* 41–59.

Haskins, R. (1989). Beyond metaphor: The efficacy of early childhood education. *American Psychologist, 44,* 274–282.

Head Start Bureau. (1995). *Charting our progress: Development of the Head Start Program Performance Measures.* Washington, DC: U.S. Department of Health and Human Services.

Head Start Bureau. (1998). *Head Start Program Performance Measures: Second progress report.* Washington, DC: U.S. Department of Health and Human Services.

Kennedy, E. M. (1993). The Head Start Transition Project: Head Start goes to elementary school. In E. Zigler & S. J. Styfco (Eds.), *Head Start and Beyond: A national plan for extended childhood intervention* (pp. 97–109). New Haven: Yale University Press.

Lally, R. J., Mangione, P. L., & Honig, A. S. (1988). The Syracuse University Family Development Research Program: Long-range impact of an early intervention with low-income children and their families. In D. Powell (Ed.), *Parent education as early childhood intervention: Emerging directions in theory, research and practice* (pp. 79–104). Norwood, NJ: Ablex.

Layzer, J. I., Goodson, B. D., & Moss, M. (1993). *Life in preschool: An observational study of early childhood programs for disadvantaged four-year-olds.* (Vol. 1). Washington, DC: U.S. Department of Education.

Lee, V. E. (1993, April 8). Head Start: A band-aid on a serious wound. *The Detroit News,* Comment.

Lee, V. E., & Loeb, S. (1995). Where do Head Start attendees end up? One reason why preschool effects fade out. *Educational Evaluation and Policy Analysis, 17,* 62–82.

McCall, Robert. (1993). *Head Start: Its potential, its achievements, its future—A briefing paper for policymakers.* Pittsburgh, PA: University of Pittsburgh.

McKey, R. H., Condelli, L., Ganson, H., Barrett, B., McConkey, C., & Plantz, M. (1985). *The impact of Head Start on children, family, and communities: Final report of the Head Start Evaluation, Synthesis and Utilization Project* (DHHS Pub. No. OHDS 85-31193). Washington, DC: U.S. Government Printing Office.

Michel, S. (1999). *Children's interests/mother's rights: The shaping of America's child care policy.* New Haven: Yale University Press.

National Education Goals Panel. (1999). *The National Education Goals report: Building a nation of learners, 1999.* Washington, DC: U.S. Government Printing Office.

National Head Start Association. (1990). *Head Start: The nation's pride, a nation's challenge.* Report of the Silver Ribbon Panel. Alexandria, VA: Author.

Office of the Inspector General. (1993). *Evaluating Head Start expansion through performance indicators* (OEI-09-91-00762). Washington, DC: U.S. Department of Health and Human Services.

Phillips, D. A., & Cabrera, N. J. (Eds.) (1996). *Beyond the blueprint: Directions for research on Head Start's families.* Washington, DC: National Academy Press.

Powell, C. G., Brush, L. R., & Gaidurgis, A. (1998). The effects of Head Start's quality-improvement funding. *NHSA Dialog, 2,* 20–30.

Price, R. H., Cowen, E., Lorion, R. P., & Ramos-McKay, J. (Eds.) (1988). *Fourteen ounces of prevention: A casebook for practitioners.* Washington, DC: American Psychological Association.

Ralph, J. (1989, January). Improving education for the disadvantaged: Do we know whom to help? *Phi Delta Kappan*, 395–401.

Raver, C. C., & Zigler, E. (1991). Three steps forward, two steps back: Head Start and the measurement of social competence. *Young Children, 46*(4), 3–8.

*Recommendations for a Head Start Program by a Panel of Experts.* (1965, February). Washington, DC: U.S. Department of Health, Education and Welfare, Office of Child Development.

Reynolds, A. J. (1994). Effects of a preschool plus follow-on intervention for children at risk. *Developmental Psychology, 30,* 787–804.

Reynolds, A. J. (2000). *Success in early intervention. The Chicago Child-Parent Centers.* Lincoln: University of Nebraska Press.

Reynolds, A. J., Mann, E., Miedel, W., & Smokowski, P. (1997). The state of early childhood intervention: Effectiveness, myths and realities, new directions. *Focus: Newsletter of the Institute for Research on Poverty of the University of Wisconsin-Madison, 19,* 5–11.

Ripple, C. H., Gilliam, W. S., Chanana, N., & Zigler, E. (1999). Will fifty cooks spoil the broth? The debate over entrusting Head Start to the states. *American Psychologist, 54,* 327–343.

Schorr, L. B. (1988). *Within our reach: Breaking the cycle of disadvantage.* New York: Doubleday.

Schweinhart, L. J., Barnes, H. V., & Weikart, D. P. (1993). Significant benefits: The High/Scope Perry Preschool study through age 27. *Monographs of the High/Scope Educational Research Foundation, 10.* Ypsilanti, MI: High/Scope Press.

Seitz, V. (1990). Intervention programs for impoverished children: A comparison of educational and family support models. *Annals of Child Development, 7,* 73–103.

Seitz, V., Abelson, W. D., Levine, E., & Zigler, E. (1975). Effects of place of testing on the Peabody Picture Vocabulary Test scores of disadvantaged Head Start and non-Head Start children. *Child Development, 46,* 481–486.

Slavin, R. E., Madden, N. A., Dolan, L. J., & Wasik, B. A. (1996). *Every child, every school: Success for All.* Thousand Oaks, CA: Corwin Press.

St. Pierre, R., Gamse, B., Alamprese, J., Rimdzius, T., & Tao, F. (1998). *National evaluation of the Even Start Family Literacy Program: Evidence from the past and a look to the future.* Washington, DC: U.S. Department of Education.

St. Pierre, R., Layzer, J., Goodson, B., & Bernstein, L. (1997). *National impact evaluation of the Comprehensive Child Development Program: Final report.* Cambridge, MA: Abt Associates.

Takanishi, R. (1977). Federal involvement in early childhood education (1933–1973): The need for historical perspectives. In L. Katz (Ed.), *Current issues in early childhood education* (Vol. 1, pp. 139–163). Norwood, NJ: Ablex.

U.S. Department of Health and Human Services. (1980). *Head Start in the 1980's. Review and recommendations.* Washington, DC: Author.

U.S. Department of Health and Human Services (1998). *Head Start Program Performance Standards and other regulations.* Washington, DC: Author.

U.S. General Accounting Office. (1997). *Head Start: Research provides little information on impact of current program.* (GAO/HEHS Publication No. 97-59). Washington, DC: Author.

U.S. General Accounting Office. (2000). *Preschool education. Federal investment for low-income children significant but effectiveness unclear.* (GAO/T-HEHS Publication No. 00-83). Washington, DC: Author.

Valentine, J. (1997). Program development in Head Start: A multifaceted approach to meeting the needs of families and children. In E. Zigler & J. Valentine (Eds.), *Project Head Start: A legacy of the War on Poverty* (2nd ed., pp. 349–365). Alexandria, VA: National Head Start Association.

Valentine, J., & Stark, E. (1997). The social context of parent involvement in Head Start. In E. Zigler & J. Valentine (Eds.), *Project Head Start: A legacy of the War on Poverty* (2nd ed., pp. 291–313). Alexandria, VA: National Head Start Association.

Woodhead, M. (1988). When psychology informs public policy. The case of early childhood intervention. *American Psychologist, 43,* 443–454.

Zero to Three: National Center for Clinical Infant Programs. (1992). *Heart start: The emotional foundations of school readiness.* Arlington, VA: Author.

Zigler, E. (1998). By what goals should Head Start be assessed? *Children's Services: Social Policy, Research, and Practice, 1,* 5–17.

Zigler, E., Abelson, W. D., Trickett, P. K., & Seitz, V. (1982). Is an intervention program really necessary to raise disadvantaged children's IQ scores? *Child Development, 53,* 340-348.

Zigler, E., & Anderson, K. (1997). An idea whose time had come: The intellectual and political climate for Head Start. In E. Zigler & J. Valentine (Eds.), *Project Head Start: A legacy of the War on Poverty* (2nd ed., pp. 3–19). Alexandria, VA: National Head Start Association.

Zigler, E., & Butterfield, E. C. (1968). Motivational aspects of changes in IQ test performance of culturally deprived nursery school children. *Child Development, 39,* 1–14.

Zigler, E., & Muenchow, S. (1992). *Head Start: The inside story of America's most successful educational experiment.* New York: Basic Books.

Zigler, E., & Seitz, V. (1982). Social policy and intelligence. In R. Sternberg (Ed.), *Handbook of human intelligence* (pp. 586–641). New York: Cambridge University Press.

Zigler, E., & Styfco, S. J. (1993). Strength in unity: Consolidating federal education programs for young children. In E. Zigler & S. J. Styfco (Eds.), *Head Start and beyond: A national plan for extended childhood intervention* (pp. 111–145). New Haven: Yale University Press.

Zigler, E., & Styfco, S. J. (1994a). Head Start: Criticisms in a constructive context. *American Psychologist, 49,* 127–132.

Zigler, E., & Styfco, S. J. (1994b). Is the Perry Preschool better than Head Start? Yes and No. *Early Childhood Research Quarterly, 9,* 269–287.

Zigler, E., & Trickett, P. (1978). IQ, social competence, and evaluation of early childhood intervention programs. *American Psychologist, 33,* 789–798.

Zigler, E., & Valentine, J. (Eds.). (1997). *Project Head Start: A legacy of the War on Poverty* (2nd ed.). Alexandria, VA: National Head Start Association.

# Chapter 2

## Understanding Efficacy of Early Educational Programs: Critical Design, Practice, and Policy Issues

*Sharon Landesman Ramey and Craig T. Ramey*

### Origins of Early Intervention Research for At-Risk Infants and Children

One of the earliest documented accounts of efforts to enhance the development of young children was published in 1801 by a French surgeon, Jean Itard (1775–1838), who had enacted what is considered a classic educational intervention with an 11-year-old boy he had discovered running naked and wild in a forest (the "savage of Aveyron"; see Itard, 1932/1801). His work led to increased understanding about the role of early experience—and the degree to which subsequent education could compensate for earlier deficiencies. After five years of ambitious educational intervention, the child showed progress, yet many severe limitations in language and social behavior, as well as aberrant behavior, remained. These careful clinical observations supported the conclusion that certain types of early experience were essential for the emergence of higher order intellectual functioning. Later provision of comparable experiences or even highly individualized, intensive education could not adequately compensate for the developmental toll associated with extreme neglect and lack of early human stimulation and interaction.

Pioneering efforts to provide education for young children with normal development include the kindergarten movement and those efforts by other educational reformers who advocated the value of preschool experiences (cf. C. Ramey & Ramey, 1999). These include Johann Heinrich Pestalozzi (1746–1827), the Swiss educator who promoted early childhood education as a way to guide and enhance the individual child's true or natural self, rather than attempting to mold all children in a similar fashion. The ultimate goal of Pestalozzi's form of early education was to help each child think independently, essentially defining key elements of preschool and early elementary school education that continue to this day: group activities, vigorous physical exercise, field trips, collecting things, making models and maps, writing, and exploring nature. Later educational philosophers who were profoundly influenced by Pestalozzi include Fredrick Froebel (1782–1852), the father of modern-day kindergarten; Maria Montessori (1870–1952), a physician who abhorred conventional classrooms that emphasized regimentation and instead brought forth ideas of developmentally appropriate practices, now widely endorsed; John Dewey (1859–1952), who saw school as a microcosm of society and promoted children's independent thinking; and Jean Piaget (1896–1980), who devised innovative techniques to test children's reading abilities and helped to unravel the mysteries of very young children's reasoning and perceptions about the world and themselves.

Concerning the consequences of early deprivation, rather than planned educational experiences, a series of landmark studies of infants and young children in orphanages and institutions, begun in the 1930s and 1940s, raised grave concern about the serious and lasting harm caused by loss of a mother and subsequent care in a group setting. The work of Bowlby, Dennis, Goldfarb, Skeels, Skodak, and Spitz, among others, revealed that the conditions children faced in these institutions were horribly inadequate compared to the love, stimulation, and stability of a good family (see the review by S. Ramey & Sackett, 2000). This research set the stage for vigorous scientific inquiry that sought to identify precisely what children need early in life to ensure healthy growth and development.

The efforts included carefully controlled experiments using animal models, which systematically varied the type and timing of early experiences, as reviewed by Sackett et al. (1999). At first, these experiments concentrated on documenting the effects of social and sensory deprivation, although the paradigm subsequently was extended to study the consequences of early environmental enrichment. Collectively, the results provide compelling evidence that early experience matters—and matters a lot; and in the extreme, deprivation can produce functional mental retardation and aberrant social and emotional behavior in animals born healthy and with good genetic endowment.

A second line of research focused on understanding variation in young children's responses to nonoptimal settings and the extent to which environmental "habilitation" could reverse or minimize the negative effects of institutionalization or other forms of early deprivation (Landesman-Dwyer & Butterfield, 1983; Landesman & Butterfield, 1987). This work clearly confirmed a fundamental principle of social ecology, known as Person X Environment interaction: not all individuals respond similarly to the same environment (e.g., Bronfenbrenner, 1979; Landesman & Ramey, 1989). Based on this principle, the role of actual experience at the individual level, rather than mere exposure to environmental conditions, was directly implicated in mediating the effects of early deprivation. The factors hypothesized to contribute to the observed differences in children's responses to similar environments (e.g., orphanages and institutions) were biological and genetic differences (including gender), age when deprivation occurred, life history prior to deprivation, duration of exposure, and the child's own behavioral repertoire, which often serves to elicit different degrees of positive caregiving and social interactions from others.

A third and independent line of inquiry, also grounded in the landmark studies of orphanages and institutions, was a proactive effort begun in the 1960s to prevent the developmental toll observed all too frequently among children from extremely poor families. These efforts to provide early educational enrichment to infants and young children from low-resource families were also fueled by scientific findings from the fields of child development, mental retardation, and the new field of infant development, as well as a poignant national awareness of devastating conditions of poverty in the United States and tremendous inequality of educational opportunity (C. Ramey & Ramey, 1998a). Key findings included:

1. Evidence showed that rates of mental retardation—especially mild mental retardation with no documented biomedical cause—were markedly elevated among very poor families (for

an excellent review of the early epidemiological findings, see Garber, 1988). Further, this form of mental retardation displayed a time distributed onset reflecting a "curve of cumulative deficits" or "progressive mental retardation" (e.g., Deutsch, 1967; Klaus & Gray, 1968) and showed a strong familiar pattern (Zigler, 1967).

2. Numerous studies detected a strong association between the quality of a child's home environment—indexed by dimensions such as responsiveness and sensitivity of the mother to her child, the amount and level of language stimulation, direct teaching, and parenting styles—and children's intellectual and problem solving competencies (e.g., Bee, et al., 1969; Hess & Shipman, 1965; Hunt, 1961; Vygotsky, 1962). Over the next four decades, literally hundreds of additional studies have affirmed this strong association (e.g., see the reviews by Cowan et al., 1994; Huston et al., 1994; Maccoby & Martin, 1983).

3. Studies provided new demonstrations that very young infants, even newborns, could "learn," which challenged the then-dominant view that babies were essentially passive, unresponsive, and incapable (see Osofsky's 1979 first edition of *The Handbook of Infant Development* for a summary of these remarkable discoveries). Especially impressive were the experimental findings about the many different ways infants could learn, and how these learning experiences directly affected infants' responses to subsequent learning opportunities (cf. C. Ramey & Ramey, 1999).

Collectively, the scientific and social Zeitgeist favored the launching of enrichment programs "as antidote for cultural deprivation" (Hunt, 1964). Great optimism accompanied these efforts (e.g., Clarke, 1973), with a broad base of theoretical underpinnings and empirical findings to inform the experimental human research on early educational interventions (C. Ramey & Ramey, 1998a).

# The First Set of Experiments: Benefits and Limits

The first set of studies systematically designed to test the effects of providing enriched experiences to children from impoverished homes included many university-based preschool centers as the site of program delivery. These programs varied considerably in their intensity, as indexed by the amount of time children spent in the program, and their timing (age of onset, total duration). All were enacted with great care and concern for the well-being of the children and their families. Before reviewing the key findings, however, we want to acknowledge that much of the original writing about these early educational efforts would be subject to criticism today for endorsing a "deficit model" of extremely poor, often marginalized or oppressed families. Similarly, the approaches could be characterized as largely "compensatory" in that they sought to ensure that children had the seeming early "advantages" of middle-class families—interesting toys, books, music, and games; responsive, educated caregivers; a safe environment, nutritious meals, regular rest, and vigorous activity; and a cognitively rich environment where language and thinking skills were actively encouraged. Without doubt, there have been unfair and destructive negative stereotypes of those at the lowest socioeconomic levels, as well as bias in assuming that middle-class families are "optimal" in everything they do. Today, these programs of the 1960s and early 1970s would be described using different terms (less pejorative of families, less paternalistic of programs). Nonetheless, as best we can tell, the substantive content of what was offered to participating children and families was sound, conscientiously provided, well received by participants, and—as reviewed below—often successful.

## The Consortium for Longitudinal Studies

The Consortium for Longitudinal Studies represented a collaborative effort to conduct pooled analyses of findings reported from 11 studies that used experimental or quasi-experimental designs to test the efficacy of early intervention for children who were at risk based on sociodemographic characteristics (Darlington et al., 1980; Lazar et al.,

1982). Two major results emerged. The first was a reaffirmation that these programs did produce significant gains in the intellectual and cognitive performance of participating children. The second was that the magnitude of these gains, as indexed by IQ scores, was strongest at the end of the intervention, was maintained for 3 or 4 years thereafter, and then declined over time as children progressed with their formal schooling. Interestingly, the authors concluded that early education programs for children from low-income families resulted in long-lasting effects in four areas: school competence, developed abilities, children's attitudes and values, and impact on the family; however, these are rarely mentioned, in contrast to the findings about the IQ decline. In the early 1980s, the Consortium for Longitudinal Studies represented the authoritative word about early intervention effects, lending support for the value of early educational enrichment and what became widely known as the "fade-out effect" with respect to IQ.

## Subsequent Longitudinal Research Targeted to Prevent Mental Retardation

Continued longitudinal inquiry and new intervention studies have provided valuable data that allow for a better understanding of the course of development in children who receive different types and amounts of early intervention. Five studies—only one of which was included in the earlier Consortium for Longitudinal Studies—specifically focused on groups of children at high risk for mental retardation are particularly informative. These are the Perry Preschool Project (Schweinhart, et al., 1993; Schweinhart, et al., 1985; Weikart, et al., 1978), the Milwaukee Project (Garber, 1988), the Abecedarian Project (Campbell & Ramey, 1995; Ramey & Campbell, 1984), Project CARE (Burchinal et al., 1997; Ramey, et al., 1985; Wasik, et al., 1990), and the Infant Health and Development Program (Infant Health and Development Program, 1990; Ramey et al., 1992). All studies involved random assignment to intervention groups and were intensive, multipronged programs involving a minimum of one full year of intervention prior to 5 years of age.

When comparing effects across studies, there are several key issues to consider. The first concerns the comparability of the participants in terms of their risk factors. For example, the Milwaukee Project enrolled only children whose mothers were mentally retarded (IQs below 75), in contrast to the Perry Preschool Project, which enrolled children at age 3 or 4 who already showed developmental delay (IQs between 70 and 85). Both the Abecedarian Project and Project CARE enrolled all poverty families with additional social risk factors (e.g., low maternal education, unmarried parent, teen mother, mother with IQ below 90, absence of maternal relatives). In contrast, the Infant Health and Development Program enrolled infants based on being both low birth weight (below 2,500 grams) and premature (less than 37 weeks gestational age)—although this sample of 985 infants included a disproportionate number of low-income, socially at risk, and minority families, which is characteristic of premature, low-birth-weight infants in general. Theoretically, these differences in participants may be related to how much they need and how much they benefit from the intervention. Further, different types and amounts of intervention may be indicated for particularly vulnerable children, although this has not been rigorously tested.

Another important factor to consider is both the amount and nature of the intervention itself. In theory, interventions that provide the most intensive, direct, and individualized services to children are the most likely to alter the children's early experiences and, in turn, to result in the greatest benefits. The Perry Preschool Project provided one or two years of a two and a half hour day educational preschool experience, supplemented by home visits to promote more positive parenting skills. The Abecedarian Project afforded a minimum of five years of full-day early childhood education, health care, infant nutrition, and parenting and family supports; plus, half of the participants received three years of additional intervention in the form of a "home and school resource program" after they entered public school. The Milwaukee Project also provided a full-day educational program throughout the preschool years and continued through the kindergarten year. Special training for the low-IQ mothers for parenting and employment also were components of the Milwaukee Project. Project CARE systematically compared two forms of intervention, a center-based curriculum identical to that in the

Abecedarian Project and a home-based program of weekly home visits for the first three years, followed by biweekly visits for the next two years. The home-based intervention used the same educational curriculum as the center-based treatment, with special instruction and materials to assist parents in promoting their children's development. The Abecedarian Project, the Milwaukee Project, and Project CARE also included a very strong emphasis on language development. Finally, the Infant Health and Development Program concentrated intervention efforts on the first three years of life only, adapting key components of the Abecedarian Project and Project CARE, both of which had demonstrated efficacy at the time the project for premature, low-birthweight infants was initiated.

Another powerful factor that potentially influences the results of different studies, as well as the children's direct experiences, is the general ecological context. These projects were launched over a wide span of time and geography. The Perry Preschool Project was the first, launched in industrial Ypsilanti, Michigan, in the early 1960s, while the Infant Health and Development Program, an eight-city randomized controlled trial, was the last in the mid-1980s. The Milwaukee Project, begun in the late 1960s, was located in a concentrated inner city area, in contrast to the Abecedarian Project and Project CARE, which were carried out in the university town of Chapel Hill, North Carolina, enrolling families from the early to the late 1970s.

When comparing findings across studies, the performance of the control children—those who did not receive the intensive intervention—provides valuable information about the cumulative impact of the children's ecology on intellectual development. For instance, in the Infant Health and Development Program, children selected according to the same biological risk conditions at the same time in history showed markedly different courses of development across the eight sites. For example, in Boston, the average performance of the control children at age 3 was essentially at the national average and dramatically higher than that of children in Miami, whose average performance placed them in the mentally retarded range. It is noteworthy that in Boston there were early intervention supports readily available to the control children as part of a statewide program of early intervention, while these were not provided to control children in Miami. Further, there were many other ecological conditions that varied across the cities, such as differences in substance abuse, crime rates, parental literacy, and community supports of families with young children. We note further that ecological differences can influence development after intervention ends as well as before and during intervention.

## Major Findings at the End of the Intervention

For all five of these studies, significant main effects of the early intervention on children's intelligence were detected at the time the program ended. Figure 2.1 presents findings from the Abecedarian Project, one of the more intensive interventions, from infancy through school entry. In this study, group differences began to appear in the second year of life and continued thereafter, averaging about a 10 point IQ difference between the intervention and control group. The control group was not, however, untreated, since they received free nutritional supplements, medical care, and social supports to the family. These results were essentially replicated with the center-based educational treatment group in Project CARE. Quite disappointing, however, was the Project CARE finding that 5 years of home visiting, although well received and valued by the families, did not produce any detectable benefits for children.

The study that documented the largest group differences on IQ scores was on the Milwaukee Project, which served children who (a) were at the highest risk for mental retardation (i.e., their own mothers had very low IQs) and (b) had the greatest contrast between the treated and control groups in terms of the children's direct experiences and the supports provided to the families. At the end of the treatment period, the groups differed by 30 IQ points, with the treated children performing well above national average and the untreated controls somewhat below national average. Similar to the two North Carolina studies, the treated and control groups diverged in their development starting at 18 months of age. In addition, the children in the Milwaukee Project as well as the two North Carolina studies showed significant differences favoring the treated group in terms of many dimensions of language development

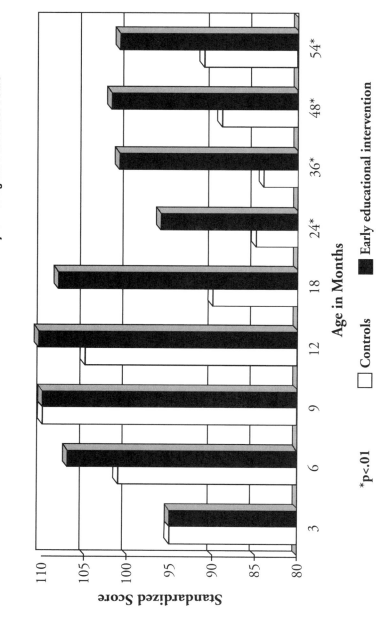

FIGURE 2.1 Intellectual Performance of Children in the Abecedarian Project During the Preschool Years

and the quality of mother–child interactions. Garber provided a thoughtful summary of the extensive mother–child dyadic interactions systematically coded from the Milwaukee Study where all the mothers had low IQs and low verbal skills:

> In summary, then, we found that the experimental dyads transmitted more information during structured mother-child interaction sessions than did the control dyads, and this was seen as a function of the quality of the experimental child's verbal behavior. The experimental children supplied more information verbally and initiated more verbal communication than did children in the control dyads. The children in the experimental dyads took responsibility for guiding the flow of information and providing most of the verbal information and direction. The mothers in both dyads indicated little differences in their teaching abilities during the testing session. However, in the experimental dyads the children structured the interaction session either by their questioning or by teaching the mother. As a result, a developmentally more sophisticated reciprocal feedback system seemed to have developed between the experimental children and their mothers, which contributed to faster and more successful problem completion. Thus, the intensive stimulation program undergone by the experimental children has benefited both the experimental child and the experimental mother by broadening their verbal and expressive behavioral repertoire. (Garber, 1988, p. 223)

The Infant Health and Development Program also reported significant group differences in each of the eight sites, although the magnitude of these differences varied considerably. Further, the children's birthweight category was a significant factor associated with the magnitude of group differences. For infants in the heavier low-birthweight group (2,001–2,500 gm), the IQ difference was 13 points at 36 months corrected age, while the group difference was half this much (6.5 points) for the lighter low-birthweight infants (less than 2,000 gm). This differential effect may reflect contributing, although not precisely specified, biological conditions that were more prevalent in the smaller premature children and in turn affected central nervous system integrity. Figure 2.2 presents these results for the two different birthweight groups. It is also noteworthy that the family characteristics of the heavier low-birthweight infants more closely resembled those of children in the other intervention studies—that is, low-income, minority status, low maternal education, and other demographic risk conditions. In terms of preventing mental retardation in this heavier low-birthweight group, 23% of the control children had IQ scores of 70 or below at 3 years of age, compared to 8% of the children who received early educational intervention. In this study, as in both the Milwaukee Project and the Abecedarian Project, direct benefits on the mother-child dyad were documented via quantitative observations of videotaped interactions (Spiker, Ferguson, & Brooks-Gunn, 1993).

## Long-Term Benefits

The most frequently asked question about early intervention is, how long do the benefits last? This question reflects an implicit assumption that high-quality, early experiences should be sufficient to ensure that a child will do well throughout later years. In early intervention circles, this is often referred to as "the inoculation hypothesis." What this question ignores is that the subsequent experiences a child has will also affect his or her rate of development and academic achievement. The quality of children's schooling, the nature of their peer groups, and the degree to which parents provide ongoing supports for learning (e.g., parent involvement with schools, quality after-school programs, opportunities for learning during the summer, and home literacy activities) all have been associated with differences in children's performance during the school years (S. Ramey & Ramey, 2000). Before presenting the results from the long-term follow-up of participants in

FIGURE **2.2 Intellectual Performance as a Function of Treatment Group and Site (Infant Health and Development Program)**

A. Heavier Low Birthweight Infants (2001-2500 grams)

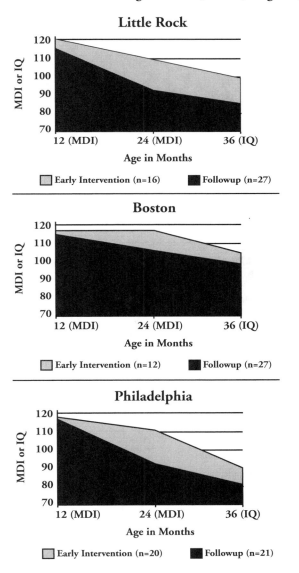

FIGURE **2.2** (CONTINUED) **Intellectual Performance as a Function of Treatment Group and Site (Infant Health and Development Program)**

A. Heavier Low Birthweight Infants (2001-2500 grams)

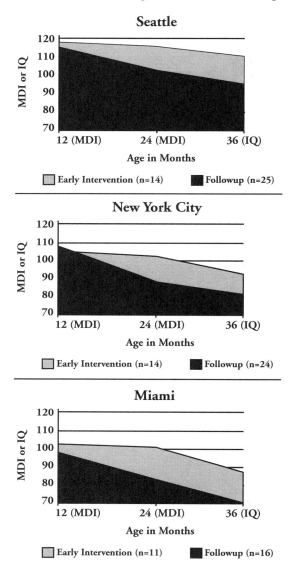

FIGURE 2.2 (CONTINUED) **Intellectual Performance as a Function of Treatment Group and Site (Infant Health and Development Program)**

A. Heavier Low Birthweight Infants (2001-2500 grams)

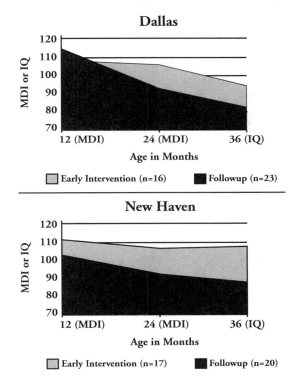

FIGURE 2.2 (CONTINUED) Intellectual Performance as a Function of Treatment Group and Site (Infant Health and Development Program)

B. Lighter Low Birthweight Infants (<2001 grams)

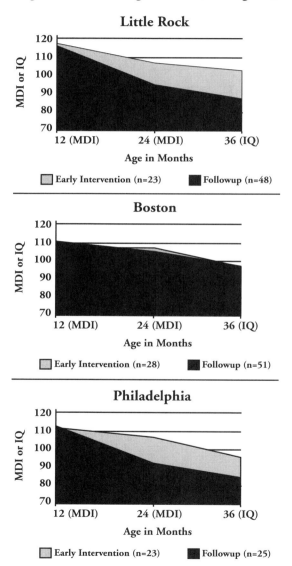

FIGURE 2.2 (CONTINUED) **Intellectual Performance as a Function of Treatment Group and Site (Infant Health and Development Program)**

B. Lighter Low Birthweight Infants (<2001 grams)

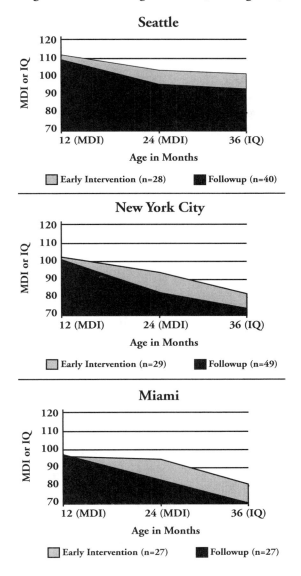

FIGURE 2.2 (CONTINUED) Intellectual Performance as a Function of Treatment
Group and Site (Infant Health and Development Program)

B. Lighter Low Birthweight Infants (<2001 grams)

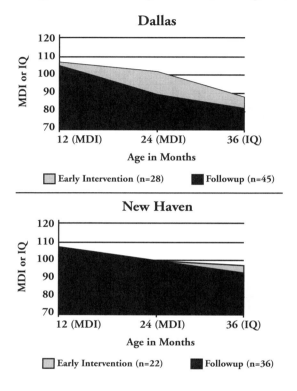

the above studies, we want to underscore that one of the greatest
scientific challenges is to understand the causal mechanisms that are
involved in the maintenance, or the loss, of the early gains associated
with participating in early intervention.

The study that has received the greatest amount of attention is the
one with results through the age of 27, the Perry Preschool Project. At
age 15, the treated children showed significantly greater academic

achievement in school, although their IQs were similar to that of controls, in the low 80s. These children were initially enrolled based on their low IQs in the preschool years. Thus, it appears that the IQ boost detected at age 5 was not sustained. Review of the longitudinal data indicates that the treated children showed a slight decline in tested IQ during the school years, while the control children showed a modest boost (Schweinhart et al., 1985). The latter is consistent with Ceci's (1991) conclusion about the general benefits of schooling on IQ.

What is so widely cited, however, are the "real world" benefits during the adolescent and adult years, including decreased school dropout and unemployment, increased college attendance, reduced teen pregnancy, and decreased criminal activity at 27 years (Schweinhart et al., 1993). For example, rates of special education placement and grade retention were 37% for the control children versus 17% for the treated children in the Perry Preschool Project. In fact, a cost–benefit analysis conducted by Barnett and Escobar (1987) estimates that the Perry Preschool Project resulted in a long-term savings of approximately $7 for every dollar invested in early intervention.

School-age results from the Abecedarian Project and Project CARE indicate long-term group differences in terms of a number of indicators, including reading and math achievement scores at ages 8, 12, and 15 (Campbell & Ramey, 1995; C. Ramey et al., 2000). Figure 2.3 summarizes the results comparing those who received the five years of preschool enrichment to those who received no systematic educational intervention during either the preschool or the school years. More detailed analyses indicate that children who received the additional three years of the home and school resource program tended to perform at the highest levels at most age periods, while the children who (S. Ramey & Sackett, 2000) received the home-and-school resource program showed only slight benefits. Thus, there is an orderly stepwise function for academic achievement for children who received eight, five, three, or no years of educational intervention. Other long-term benefits include large reductions in the rates of special education placement and grade retention, as Figure 2.4 shows. Unlike the Perry Preschool Program, significant IQ differences continued to be detected at 8, 12, 15, and 21 years, although the magnitude of the group differences was noticeably smaller during the school years (e.g., only a 5-point difference at ages 15 and 21 years of age, effect size of .31). The age 21-year follow-up results, recently released by the U.S. Department of Education, are especially encouraging and demonstrate that real-world indicators such as increased employment, greater likelihood of being enrolled in a 4-year college or university, and delayed age of childbearing are among the significant benefits of early intervention for a very high-risk group of African American children living in poverty. Indeed, reading and math skills also are significantly higher in young adulthood, as well as during the school years, in the Abecedarian Project cohort, which had 99% of the original sample of still-living children included in the adult assessment (Campbell et al., in press).

The Milwaukee Project published results of follow-up until the children were 10 years old. Significant IQ score differences persisted, although the treatment: 104 for the treated children as opposed to 86 for the control children. Somewhat surprising was the finding that the school achievement of the groups did not differ. Garber (1988) describes the poor quality of the inner-city schools these children attended and other complex educational policies and practices that may have affected children's school performance. Rates of placement in special education and referral for special services, however, did differ significantly for the two groups, as did the referral of children into "extended" primary grades (during the years when grade retention was a prohibited practice in the Milwaukee schools).

The Infant Health and Development Program was the only early intervention that ended several years before the children entered kindergarten. Many of these children's parents, regardless of original treatment group, were assisted in obtaining subsequent quality child care and other early intervention supports. By ages 5 and 8, the IQ differences had decreased considerably between the groups, such that an overall main effect of treatment was no longer present (Brooks-Gunn et al., 1994; McCarton et al., 1997). The heavier low-birthweight children,

FIGURE 2.3 Reading and Math Achievement Scores from the Abecedarian Project

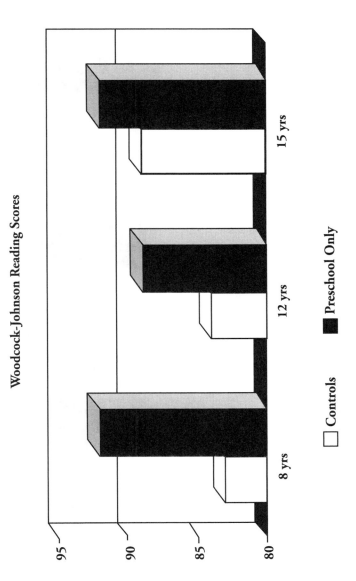

Woodcock-Johnson Reading Scores

**Figure 2.3** (CONTINUED) **Reading and Math Achievement Scores from the Abecedarian Project**

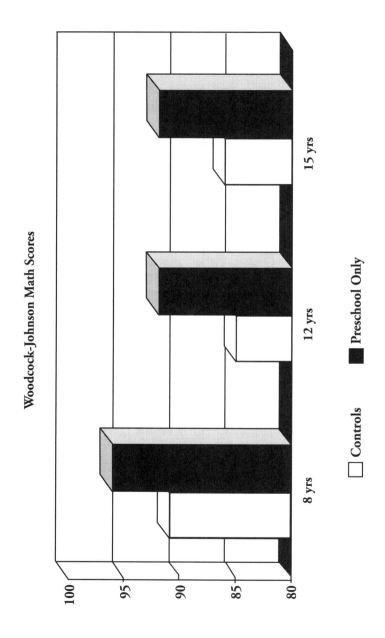

Woodcock-Johnson Math Scores

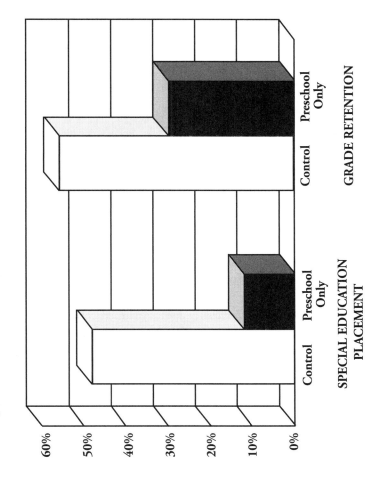

FIGURE 2.4 Rates of Special Education Placement and Grade Retention in the Abecedarian Project

however, continued to manifest significantly higher IQs as a function of early intervention. Specifically, by age 8, the early intervention group scored an average of 4.4 points higher than did the comparison children who received pediatric follow-up and social service referrals. In addition, other small magnitude but significant differences were detected in this group for mathematics achievement and receptive vocabulary scores. The consortium of investigators concluded that additional intervention strategies are needed for low-birthweight, premature infants to sustain the earlier benefits detected after the birth to age 3 educational enrichment.

## Summary of Results

The five major studies reviewed here all demonstrated benefits in terms of significant and clinically meaningful IQ increases and corresponding reduced rates of mental retardation during the preschool years. For four of the studies, multiple benefits persisted until middle childhood or later, although the IQ differences between groups declined and, in the case of the Perry Preschool Project, ceased to exist by adolescence. In contrast, more substantial benefits appeared in terms of everyday performance indicators, such as decreased rates of grade retention, special education, placement, and improved school achievement (except for the Milwaukee Project on the latter measure). For the one study that has followed children into adulthood, these benefits included more positive adult roles regarding economic self-sufficiency, greater educational attainment, and decreased criminal activity (Schweinhart et al., 1993).

The one study that did not show long-term benefits for the entire treated group was the Infant Health and Development Program. This program differed in two major ways: (a) children were selected solely on the presumed biologic risk factors of being low birthweight and premature, and (b) the educational intervention ended by 36 months corrected age, while all the other programs continued until children entered school or beyond (i.e., for some of the Abecedarian children and for all the Milwaukee Project children). The four studies with long-term benefits included three that identified children at high risk based on social demographic characteristics, especially maternal characteristics, while one (the Perry Preschool Project) selected children who already showed significant delays by 3 years of age. Virtually all of the children in these four studies were African American and came from families that predominately spoke Black Dialect English. What then did the early educational enrichment provide that either "boosted" the children's performance or, alternatively, prevented the developmental toll consistently observed in control children during the preschool years?

## Hypothesized Mediating Mechanisms: How Early Intervention Might Alter Children's Developmental Trajectories

Ramey and colleagues have been refining a complex, social ecological model of development over the past two decades. This incorporates principles of systems theory and social ecology, as well as findings from the literature about risk and protective factors (C. Ramey & Ramey, 1998a). In this conceptual framework, a child's individual competence is determined by a multitude of forces, including intergenerational factors, biological factors, parental competencies, and community social and cultural norms and practices. In this model, the important influences on intellectual competency are the direct transactions a child has with the immediate environment. Thus, early intervention programs that provide more intensive educational services, as well as start earlier and last longer, are hypothesized to be the most beneficial. Similarly, programs that directly target the child's everyday experiences, rather than indirectly seek to change this through increasing parental competency or the quality of the child's living conditions, are hypothesized to yield more immediate and greater effects. Although not reviewed here, there are many other early interventions reported for "at-risk" poverty children; many of these studies have serious design limitations (e.g., lack of random assignment, retrospective control groups), high rates of attrition (approaching 50% or higher), or relatively low rates of participation in the intervention program itself (for a review of the results of these studies, see Bryant & Maxwell, 1997). Typically, programs that have a very narrow focus, do not carefully control the content of the intervention, and do not last for one or more years have not produced changes in children's intellectual competency or academic achievement (Bryant & Maxwell, 1997; S. Ramey & Ramey, 1992). In essence, these ineffective early intervention programs are notably lacking in their provision of high-quality, developmentally supportive transactions for the children on a daily basis.

In a recent new analysis of the longitudinal findings from both the Abecedarian Project and Project CARE, Burchinal et al. (1997) calculated individual growth curves and related these to both family variables and children's direct experiences—that is, environmental transactions, including participation in early intervention day care experiences for those in the control condition. This analysis, more than any other to date, provides findings that support the hypothesis that efficacious early intervention provides developmentally normative learning opportunities for children who otherwise would not receive these to support normal intellectual development. The authors conclude that

> The results indicate that more optimal patterns of cognitive development were associated with intensive early educational child care, responsive stimulating care at home, and higher maternal IQ. In accordance with a general systems model, analyses also suggested that child care experiences were related to better cognitive performance in part through enhancing the infant's responsiveness to his or her environment. Maternal IQ had both a direct effect on cognitive performance during early childhood and, also, an indirect effect through its influence on the family environment. (Burchinal et al., 1997, p. 935)

This interpretation of likely causal mechanisms strongly agrees with the conclusions of Garber (1988) from the Milwaukee Study. The maintenance of school age benefits in the Carolina projects may be attributable to children attending a higher quality school system where children could apply their own competencies in learning and elicit positive social responses from adults, compared to the less resourceful school environments in Milwaukee and Ypsilanti.

A note of caution regarding the positive results from these studies is that the children performed, on average, below national norms—with the one exception of the average IQs of the treated children in the Milwaukee Study. Thus, even though early intervention was associated with significantly higher intellectual or academic performance compared to controls, the interventions did not completely eliminate the need for special education, grade repetition, or special services and educational supports. Children from high-risk families clearly benefited from compensatory experiences, although these did not entirely eliminate all risks. This is not surprising, since most of the children continued to live with their natural families, attended public schools in their locale, and also may have sustained intergenerational and biological risks that were not clinically detected (e.g., Moser, Ramey, & Leonard, 1990).

## Who Benefits the Most From Early Intervention?

A number of analyses on the North Carolina studies and the Infant Health and Development Program have confirmed a strong association between maternal education and/or maternal IQ and the magnitude of IQ benefits in children. In general, the lower the maternal educational level or maternal IQ level, the greater the degree of benefit associated with the early educational intervention (Brooks-Gunn, et al., 1992; Landesman & Ramey, 1989; Martin, et al., 1990). Garber (1988) also described in detail the microenvironment or the daily experiences of the highest risk children—those with very low IQ mothers who often experienced inadequate parenting and poor schooling themselves. He concluded that the home environment exerted a powerful influence on the development of children. Subgroup analyses, however, were not possible due to the small sample size and the relative homogeneity in the maternal and family characteristics of this sample.

The Infant Health and Development Program also indicated that the premature, low-birthweight children who sustained benefits from this form of early educational intervention were those who were biologically close to normal (i.e., heavier low birthweight) and also from families at greater social and economic risk.

## The Implications of Early Intervention Studies for Social Policy and the Prevention of Mental Retardation

The findings from carefully controlled, randomized trials of early intervention have been the basis for implementing many large-scale, Congressionally authorized programs to improve the outcomes for poverty children, such as Head Start (Zigler & Mueunchow, 1992; Zigler & Styfco, 1994), and many programs labeled "two-generation programs," including New Chance, the Comprehensive Child Development Program, the JOBS program (Smith, 1995), and the recently enacted Early Head Start. To date, none of these large-scale programs have demonstrated the same types or magnitude of benefits that have been documented in the smaller scale studies. The smaller scale, carefully controlled studies reviewed here were designed to adhere to high scientific standards, and further provided far more intensive educational supports to a greater proportion of enrolled children than have the large-scale, federally administered programs. For example, most children enrolled in Head Start receive only seven months of a half-day program for four days a week, starting when they are 4 years old—far less than any of the studies that produced significant intellectual benefits. A recently adopted set of higher standards for the Head Start program, which now serves approximately one million children, is intended to ensure that in the future these programs will be of more uniform high quality nationwide. Another notable difference is that most of these federal programs, including Head Start, have enrolled families solely based on poverty income. Accordingly, many of the participating children are not at comparably high levels of developmental risk for mental retardation or special education placement as the multi-risk children in the smaller scale studies were.

The research findings clearly support the conclusion that rates of mental retardation and special education placement among children at sociodemographic risk can be reduced by 50% or more. This means that the most prevalent form of mental retardation—namely, mild mental retardation associated with family conditions and not attributable to any known biological cause—could be drastically reduced if early intervention were successfully targeted to those at greatest risk.

The question for policy and decisionmakers then becomes twofold: What would be the estimated cost of such preventive interventions? Is it feasible to identify the highest risk families and provide the types of high-quality, intensive, multiyear, multipronged programs needed? Based on the costs of the early educational programs reviewed in this paper, the estimated annual cost of such preventive educational interventions would range from approximately $8,000 to $15,000 per year, with differences attributable primarily to variation in staff:child ratios, wages, and hours per day. In 1995, the nationwide average cost for special education was $6,335 above and beyond the cost of regular education, which averages between $6,000 to $7,000 in most local school districts. Similarly, the cost of grade retention is high—and is often preceded by school districts investing in several years of remedial summer programs, which historically have not been successful in significantly boosting children's school performance when provided after children "fail." Thus, the investment would appear to be a sound one in terms of cost savings, as well as the intangible benefits associated with a better educated citizenry. To place this in perspective, the cost of early intervention—especially if targeted to the highest risk groups rather than to all poverty families—is quite reasonable compared to the costs of many medical interventions, such as extended stays in neonatal intensive care units or to the cost of high-quality child care. There is, however, no third-party insurance to pay for such educational interventions, and these children have no strong parent advocacy or obvious professional group with national clout to lobby on their behalf. Worse yet, there are many home-visiting programs and local programs (Roberts et al., 1991) that would be jeopardized if a more intensive form of early intervention were adopted as the standard for high-risk children and their families. As with most prevention efforts, complex political, economic, and social factors are at play.

Given the increasing evidence that brain development is profoundly affected by early and cumulative life experiences (Shore, 1997), and the positive results of the research-based early interventions for truly high-risk children, there is ample theoretical and empirical support to justify launching systematic prevention efforts. Children from very low-income families whose parents have limited educational and intellectual resources need not be doomed to a life of incompetency. Yet without timely and highly intensive supports starting very early in life and probably extending into the school years, these children are likely to continue to fulfill their intergenerational prognosis of subaverage intellectual performance and marginal social and economic existence.

Perhaps the greatest challenge is sharing what the true options are with key decisionmaking groups, opinion leaders, the media, and the general public. The long list of large-scale government programs that do not yield the anticipated benefits is a chief factor in resistance to developing structured and targeted interventions that meet high standards and provide children with needed services. A comprehensive analysis of the reason such large-scale programs are disappointing must be conducted—by an objective group of scientists, practitioners, and policymakers—and reported in a fashion that will be constructive in redirecting the vast investments already being made in programs administered under the Departments of Health and Human Services and Education. Without an integration of scientific facts and political and practical realities, it is likely that we continue to "do good" that is undocumented and far less effective than would be possible with a concerted effort to provide the needed technical assistance, monitoring, and active community support needed for early childhood development. The opportunity is right, because of unprecedented high levels of money, to enhance the quality of child care nationwide (related to welfare-to-work initiatives largely) and the vigor and efforts of the programs, such as I Am Your Child and Zero to Three, that have increased awareness in the general citizenry.

# References

Barnett, W. S., & Escobar, C. M. (1987). The economics of early intervention: A review. *Review of Educational Research, 57*, 387–414.

Bee, H. L., Van Egeren, L. F., Streissguth, A. P., Nyman, B. A., & Leckie, M. S. (1969). Social class differences in maternal teaching strategies and speech patterns. *Developmental Psychology, 1,* 726–734.

Bronfenbrenner, U. (1979). *The ecology of human development.* Cambridge, MA: Harvard University Press.

Brooks-Gunn, J., & Furstenberg, Jr., F. F. (1987). Continuity and change in the context of poverty. In J. Gallagher & C. Ramey (Eds.), *The malleability of children* (pp. 171–187). Baltimore: Paul H. Brookes.

Brooks-Gunn, J., Gross, R. T., Kraemer, H. C., Spiker, D., & Shapiro, S. (1992). Enhancing the cognitive outcomes of low birth weight, premature infants: For whom is the intervention most effective? *Pediatrics, 89,* 1209–1215.

Brooks-Gunn, J., McCarton, C. M., Casey, P. H., McCormick, M. C., Bauer, C. R., Bernbaum, J. C., Tyson, J., Swanson, M., Bennett, F. C., Scott, D. T., Tonascia, J., & Meinert, C. L. (1994). Early intervention in low-birth-weight premature infants: Results through age 5 years from the Infant Health and Development Program. *Journal of the American Medical Association, 272,* 1257–1262.

Bryant, D., & Maxwell, K. (1997). The effectiveness of early intervention for disadvantaged children. In M. Guralnick (Ed.), *The effectiveness of early intervention* (pp. 23–46). Baltimore: Paul H. Brookes.

Burchinal, M. R., Campbell, F. A., Bryant, D. M., Wasik, B. H., Ramey, C. T. (1997). Early intervention and mediating processes in cognitive performance of children of low-income African American families. *Child Development, 68,* 935–954.

Campbell, F. A., & Ramey, C. T. (1994). Effects of early intervention on intellectual and academic achievement: A follow-up study of children from low-income families. *Child Development, 65,* 684–698.

Campbell, F. A., & Ramey, C. T. (1995). Cognitive and school outcomes for high risk students at middle adolescence: Positive effects of early intervention. *American Educational Research Journal, 32,* 743–772.

Campbell, F. A., Ramey, C. T., Pungello, E., Sparling, J., & Miller-Johnson, S. (in press). Early childhood education: Outcomes as a function of different treatments. *Applied Developmental Science.*

Ceci, S. J. (1991). How much does schooling influence general intelligence and its cognitive components? A reassessment of the evidence. *Developmental Psychology, 24,* 703–722.

Clarke, A. D. B. (1973). The prevention of subcultural subnormality: Problems and prospects. *British Journal of Mental Subnormality, 19* (Part 1, No. 36), 7–20.

Cowan, P. A., Cowan, C. P., Schulz, M. S., & Heming, G. (1994). Prebirth to preschool family factors in children's adaption to kindergarten. In R. D. Parke & S. G. Kellam (Eds.), *Exploring family relationships with other social contexts* (pp. 75–114). Hillsdale, NJ: Erlbaum.

Darlington, R. B., Royce, J. M., Snipper, A. S., Murray, H. W., & Lazar I. (1980). Preschool programs and later school competence of children from low-income families. *Science, 208,* 202–204.

Deutsch, M. (1967). *The disadvantaged child.* New York: Basic Books.

Garber, H. L. (1988). *The Milwaukee Project: Preventing mental retardation in children at risk.* Washington, DC: American Association on Mental Retardation.

Hess, R. D., & Shipman, V. (1965). Early experiences and socialization of cognitive modes in children. *Child Development, 36,* 869–886.

Hunt, J. McV. (1961). *Intelligence and experience.* New York: Ronald Press.

Hunt, J. McV. (1964). The psychological basis for using preschool enrichment as an antidote for cultural deprivation. *Merrill-Palmer Quarterly, 10,* 209–248.

Huston, A. C., McLoyd, V., & Garcia, C. (1994). Children and poverty: Issues in contemporary research. *Child Development, 65,* 275–282.

Infant Health and Development Program (1990). Enhancing the outcomes of low-birth-weight, premature infants. *Journal of the American Medical Association, 263,* 3035–3042.

Itard, J. M. G. (1932). *The wild boy of Aveyron.* Translated by G. & Muriel Humphrey. New York: Appleton-Century-Crofts. (Original work published 1801.)

Klaus, R. A., & Gray, S. W. (1968). The Early Training Project for disadvantaged children: A report after five years. *Monographs of the Society for Research in Child Development, 33* (4, Serial No. 120).

Landesman-Dwyer, S., & Butterfield, E. C. (1983). Mental retardation: Developmental issues in cognitive and social adaptation. In M. Lewis (Ed.), *Origins of intelligence: Infancy and early childhood* (2nd ed., pp. 479–519). New York: Plenum Press.

Landesman, S., & Butterfield, E. C. (1987). Normalization and deinstitutionalization of mentally retarded individuals: Controversy and facts. *American Psychologist, 42,* 809–816.

Landesman, S., & Ramey, C. T. (1989). Developmental psychology and mental retardation: Integrating scientific principles with treatment practices. *American Psychologist, 44,* 409–415.

Lazar, I., Darlington, R., Murray, H., Royce, J., & Snipper, A. (1982). Lasting effects of early education: A report from the Consortium of Longitudinal Studies. *Monographs of the Society for Research in Child Development, 47,* (2–3, Serial No. 195).

Maccoby, E., & Martin, J. (1983). Socialization in the context of the family: Parent-child interaction. In P. H. Mussen (Series Ed.) & E. M. Hetherington (Vol. Ed.), *Handbook of child psychology: Vol 4. Socialization, personality, and social development* (pp. 1–101). New York: Wiley.

Martin, S. L., Ramey, C. T., & Ramey, S. L. (1990). The prevention of intellectual impairment in children of impoverished families: Findings of a randomized trial of educational day care. *American Journal of Public Health, 80,* 844–847.

McCarton, C. M., Brooks-Gunn, J., Wallace, I. F., Bauer, C. R., Bennett, F. C., Bernbaum, J. C., Broyles, R. S., Casey, P. H., McCormick, M. C., Scott, D. T., Tyson, J., Tonascia, J., & Meinert, C. L. (1997). Results at age 8 years of early intervention for low-birth-weight premature infants: The Infant Health and Development Program. *JAMA, 277,* 126–132.

Moser, H. W., Ramey, C. T., & Leonard, C. O. (1990). Mental retardation. In A. E. H. Emery & D. L. Rimoin (Eds.), *The principles and practices of medical genetics* (Vol. 2, pp. 495–511). New York: Churchill Livingstone Inc.

Osofsky, J. D. (1979). *Handbook of infant development.* New York: Wiley.

Ramey, C. T., Bryant, D. M., Sparling, J. J., & Wasik, B. H. (1985). Project CARE: A comparison of two early intervention strategies to prevent retarded development. *Topics in Early Childhood Special Education, 5,* 12–25.

Ramey, C. T., Bryant, D. M., Wasik, B. H., Sparling, J. J., Fendt, K. H., & LaVange, L. M. (1992). Infant Health and Development Program for low birth weight, premature infants: Program elements, family participation, and child intelligence. *Pediatrics, 89,* 454–465.

Ramey, C. T., & Campbell, F. A. (1984). Preventive education for high risk children: Cognitive consequences of the Carolina Abecedarian Project. *American Journal of Mental Deficiency, 88,* 515–523.

Ramey, C. T., Campbell, F. A., Burchinal, M., Skinner, M. L., Gardner, D. M., & Ramey, S. L. (2000). Persistent effects of early childhood education on high-risk children and their mothers. *Applied Developmental Science, 4,* 2–14.

Ramey, C. T., & Ramey, S. L. (1998a). Early intervention and early experience. *American Psychologist, 53,* 109–120.

Ramey, C. T., & Ramey, S. L. (1998b). Prevention of intellectual disabilities: Early interventions to improve cognitive development. *Preventive Medicine, 27,* 224–232.

Ramey, C. T., & Ramey, S. L. (1999). *Right from birth: Building your child's foundation for life (birth to 18 months).* New York: Goddard Press.

Ramey, S. L., & Ramey, C. T. (1992). Early educational intervention with disadvantaged children—To what effect? *Applied and Preventive Psychology, 1,* 131–140.

Ramey, S. L., & Ramey, C. T. (2000). Early childhood experiences and developmental competence. In J. Waldfogel & S. Danziger (Eds.), *Securing the future: Investing in children from birth to college* (pp. 122–150). New York: Russell Sage.

Ramey, S. L., & Sackett, G. P. (2000). The early care-giving environment: Expanding views on non-parental care and cumulative life experiences. In M. Lewis & A. Sameroff (Eds.). *Handbook of developmental psychopathology* (2nd ed., pp. 365–380). New York: Plenum Publishing Company.

Roberts, R., Wasik, B., Casto, G., & Ramey, C. T. (1991). Family support in the home: Programs, policy, and social change. *American Psychologist, 46,* 131–137.

Sackett, G. P., Novak, M. F. S. X., & Kroeker, R. (1999). Early experience effects on adaptive behavior: Theory revisited. *Mental Retardation and Developmental Disabilities Research Reviews.* New York: Wiley.

Schweinhart, L. J., Barnes, H. V., Weikart, D. P., Barnett, W. S., & Epstein, A. S. (1993). *Significant benefits: The High/Scope Perry Preschool Study through age 27.* Ypsilanti, MI: High/Scope Press.

Schweinhart, L. J., Berrueta-Clement, J. R., Barnett, W. S., Epstein, A. S., & Weikart, D. P. (1985). Effects of the Perry Preschool Program on youths through age 19: A summary. *Topics in Early Childhood Special Education, 5,* 26–35.

Shore, R. (1997). *Rethinking the brain: New insights into early development.* New York: Families and Work Institute.

Smith, S. (Ed.). (1995). Two generation programs for families in poverty: A new intervention strategy. *Advances in Applied Developmental Psychology, 9.*

Spiker, D., Ferguson, J., & Brooks-Gunn, J. (1993). Enhancing maternal interactive behavior and child social competence in low birth weight, premature infants. *Child Development, 64,* 754–768.

Vygotsky, L. S. (1962). *Thought and language.* (E. Hanfmann & G. Vakar, Trans.). Cambridge: MIT Press.

Wasik, B. H., Ramey, C. T., Bryant, D. M., & Sparling, J. J. (1990). A longitudinal study of two early intervention strategies: Project CARE. *Child Development, 61,* 1682–1696.

Weikart, D. P., Bond, J. T., & McNeil, J. T. (1978). The Ypsilanti Perry Preschool Project: Preschool years and longitudinal results through fourth grade. *Monographs of the High/Scope Educational Research Foundation.*

Zigler, E. F. (1967). Familial mental retardation: A continuing dilemma. *Science, 155,* 292–298.

Zigler, E., & Muenchow, S. (1992). *Head Start: The inside story of America's most successful educational experiment.* New York: Basic Books.

Zigler, E., & Styfco, S. J. (1994). Head Start: Criticisms in a constructive context. *American Psychologist, 49,* 127–132.

# Chapter 3

## Universal Access to Prekindergarten: A Georgia Case Study

*Anthony Raden*

Despite mounting evidence that high-quality early education programs enhance children's development and chances of succeeding in school (Barnett, 1998), the nation's early care and education systems remain fragmented, underfunded, and insufficient to meet the needs of American families (Kagan & Cohen, 1997). Over the last several years, as research affirming the importance of early development has begun to affect public policy debates, decisionmakers at all levels of government have been paying more attention to the availability and quality of early education. Forty-two states now invest in at least one form of Pre-K initiative (Schulman et al., 1999). To date, 18 states have chosen to allocate supplemental state funds to expand and/or improve federal Head Start services for low-income children. Many more states have established independent state-run Pre-K programs located in public schools and/or community-based sites (Schulman et al., 1999).

While most states continue to target early education resources to children believed to be at the highest risk of school failure (Blank & Poersch, 2000), in recent years advocates, educators, and policymakers have increasingly begun to call for more states to progress toward the provision of universal early education (Wilgoren, 2000). This is an account of one such effort—Georgia's Prekindergarten initiative. While other states are establishing large-scale programs—notably New York, Massachusetts, and Oklahoma—Georgia's initiative is the most far-reaching and mature. In 1993, Georgia became the first state to establish a Pre-K program for 4-year-olds funded entirely with lottery revenues. At the outset, the means-tested program served only low-income children. But in 1995, Georgia expanded the initiative, becoming the first state to offer universal, voluntary preschool for all 4-year-olds. In

TABLE 3.1
**Georgia Prekindergarten Program for 4-Year-Olds***

| Population Served | Children who are Georgia residents and 4 years old on September 1. No income requirements. |
|---|---|
| Hours of Operation | Minimum is 6.5 hours/day; 5 days/week; 180 days/year. |
| No. of Children Served | 63,500 (2001-02 school year) |
| % of Children Reached | State Pre-K and Georgia Head Start together serve approximately 75%–80% of eligible 4-year-olds in the state. |
| Eligible Pre-K Providers | Public school districts, which may subcontract to private schools, community agencies, Head Start centers, and child care centers. During the 2001–02 school year, 43% of Georgia Pre-K students were located in school-based programs and 57% were in nonpublic school (i.e., private) sites. |
| Administrative Auspices | Office of School Readiness (OSR) (1996–present) Originally administered from the State Department of Education (1992–1996) |
| Program Standards | **Ratios:** 1:10, with class size maximum of 20<br><br>**Staff Qualifications:** Teachers must have a CDA Credential, or teacher certification in early childhood education, or a college degree with specialization in early childhood education, or teacher certification in elementary education or a Montessori or vocational early childhood education degree.** Aides must be at least 20 years old, and high school graduates.<br><br>**Educational Program:** Must use an OSR approved curriculum and adhere to state child care licensing requirements. Curriculum choices include: Bank Street, Creative Curriculum, High/Scope, High Reach, Montessori, and Scholastic Workshop. |

TABLE 3.1 (CONTINUED)

| Program Standards (continued) | **Parental Involvement:** Parent volunteering, participation in meetings, group activities, teacher conferences, voluntary workshops. |
|---|---|
| **Funds** | Funding on a formula basis related to enrollment and teacher credentials. Average cost per child: $3,748. State appropriations: $238 million (2001-02) |
| **Assessment of Performance** | Consultants conduct 2–3 site visits annually to each program to assess program performance and offer technical assistance as needed. |

\* Adopted from Mitchell, 1998, Office of School Readiness
\*\* "For the 2002-03 school year, CDA/CCP will no longer be an option as a
   lead teacher credential"

1996, Georgia demonstrated an unprecedented commitment to early education by establishing an independent agency, the Office of School Readiness, to administer Prekindergarten. Now serving approximately 60% of the 4-year-olds in the state (more than 60,000 children), Georgia's Pre-K program has been lauded as the most comprehensive state early education initiative in the nation.

The development of universal prekindergarten in Georgia illustrates the complex and often unpredictable processes through which ideas are translated into policy. An analysis of the program's history also underscores that the establishment and growth of Georgia Pre-K were not inevitable; policymakers and administrators encountered conflicting interests, confronted crucial decision points, and made distinct choices that shaped the evolution of a prominent education policy. Clearly in the vanguard of state-funded early education, Georgia provides an illuminating example of the dilemmas and pressures with which other states will have to grapple as legislators and other policymakers seek to improve opportunities for children to experience early care and educational systems.

## Zell Miller and the Georgia Lottery for Education

The story of Georgia's Prekindergarten initiative begins with a political campaign. In 1989, Lieutenant Governor Zell Miller faced three opponents in a crowded race to become the Democratic nominee in Georgia's 1990 gubernatorial election. Early in the primary campaign, Miller announced his support for a state lottery that would earmark all proceeds for education programs. To establish a "Lottery for Education," as Miller called it, the Georgia legislature would have to vote by a two-thirds majority to amend the state constitution. Voters would then have to ratify the decision through a statewide referendum. Although Miller initially did not provide specifics on how the lottery-generated education revenues would be distributed, during the campaign (and in later years) he filled in the details of his education program. Thirty-five percent of lottery sales would be transferred by the Georgia Lottery Commission to an education account and distributed to three education priority areas: (a) scholarships for accomplished Georgia high school graduates to attend Georgia colleges (later called the HOPE scholarship program), (b) the purchase and distribution of equipment and technology for public schools, and (c) a voluntary preschool program for at-risk children.[1]

The battle Miller waged to establish the lottery proved to be grueling. Staking his political future on the lottery—and clearly using the issue to define himself in opposition to his political rivals—Miller faced daunting opposition from all sides of the political and ideological spectrum, including the incumbent governor of his own party, a hostile legislature that would eventually reject his lottery bills during the 1989 and 1990 legislative sessions, an anti-lottery coalition supported by church leaders and the politically powerful Religious Right, Georgia's major newspapers, and much of Georgia's educational establishment. Contending that the lottery would actually decrease overall education spending, the Georgia State PTA and the Georgia School Board Association both opposed plans that would tie lottery funds to education. The *Atlanta Journal and Constitution* argued in several editorials that Miller's lottery proposal was a cheap political ploy that was being oversold and offered false education promises ("The Lottery and Other

Trivia," 1990). One columnist, Jim Wooten, claimed that the connection between education and the lottery was a ruse. "Lottery proceeds, inevitably, will displace general fund dollars, so that education is unlikely to enjoy any lasting gain," Wooten wrote. "Are we willing to create a new bureaucracy to devise games to rip off the poor and entertain the middle-class? I don't know yet. But funding education is not even remotely a factor in determining whether we put the state in the lottery business (Wooten, 1989)." Political writers accused Miller of cynically embracing the idea of a lottery at the urging of his political advisor, James Carville (see Beinart, 1998).[2]

Zell Miller, who would later support his own prolottery coalition (Georgians for Better Education) to counter antilottery claims, had a ready response to the criticism that funds would not enhance education. He promised to earmark lottery revenues directly into distinct, innovative educational programs, thereby ensuring that funds would not be blended and lost within the State Education Department's $3 billion general budget. The earmarked funds could be redirected for other purposes only by means of another constitutional amendment.

After vowing to make the 1990 election a referendum on the lottery amendment, Miller won both the Democratic primary and the general election by comfortable margins. Political analysts attributed his victory to his championship of the lottery—a stand that took on a populist flavor. The *Atlanta Journal and Constitution* wrote, "[I]n the public mind it will be Mr. Miller's lottery. Few politicians have ever been so totally identified with a single issue" (McAllister, 1991).

Once in office, Miller stood firm on the need for an independent commission, controlled by the governor, to spend the lottery revenues on specific education programs. "I'm not going to let the General Assembly appropriate that money," Miller said. "The point is to make sure that the lottery money is not lost in the education bureaucracy or is not lost on the local level" (May & Watson, 1990). With popular support for the lottery abundantly clear, and the power of the Governor's Office committed to the issue, Miller's bill establishing the Georgia Lottery for Education was passed during the 1991 legislative session. The following year, after a costly and often bitter lobbying campaign, voters of Georgia approved a constitutional amendment establishing a state lottery.

## Why Prekindergarten?

According to numerous political aides and education observers, Zell Miller's commitment to educational improvement was genuine and profound. In later years, the *Atlanta Journal and Constitution* ("Lottery Numbers Add to Education," 1997) would refer to Miller's "missionary zeal for education." Miller's vigorous defense of the lottery reflects the urgency of education reform in Georgia, whose education system perpetually ranks near the bottom in the nation on measures of academic expenditures and achievement.[3] Moreover, Miller's proposal did not take shape in a vacuum. During the 1980s and early 1990s, the number of states supporting some form of Pre-K initiative tripled (Adams & Sandfort, 1994; Mitchell, et al., 1989). In 1990, approximately 56% of American 4-year-olds were enrolled in a preprimary education program—a 100% increase from 1970 (U.S. Department of Education, 1997b).

Political considerations may have been as compelling as educational factors. Gary Henry, a professor from Georgia State University who closely monitored the movement to create Georgia's lottery, speculates that Miller may have been convinced that the relatively small amount of projected lottery funds would never produce meaningful change in the K-12 system. Henry suggests that in the final analysis, education experts may have been less influential than strategic advisers who stressed the potential political benefits. Henry said:

> In the campaign in '90, when trying to think about the lottery, [Miller] knew that he had to have a funding source, he knew that he had to have some campaign issues. And it was clear that the pairing of the lottery with education was a clear winner. Our polls at the time were showing that the support went up for the lottery if it was paired with education. And so he had to create programs that would be

**TABLE 3.2**
**The Evolution of Georgia's Lottery-Funded Prekindergarten Program**

| January 1989 | Georgia Lieutenant Governor and candidate in the 1990 gubernatorial campaign, Zell Miller, proposes the establishment of a state lottery with proceeds earmarked for education. |
|---|---|
| December 1989 | Miller's campaign announces that lottery proceeds will create a voluntary preschool program for 4-year-olds. |
| November 1990 | Zell Miller elected Governor of Georgia. |
| November 1991 | Governor Miller specifies that lottery proceeds will be earmarked to three priority areas: (a) a voluntary preschool program for low-income 4-year-olds; (b) college scholarships for Georgia high school students; (c) technology and equipment for public schools. |
| September 1992 | At Governor Miller's direction, Georgia's Department of Education establishes a pilot Pre-K program. 750 low-income 4-year-olds attend pilot program during 1992–93 school year. |
| November 1992 | Voters of Georgia approve constitutional amendment establishing a state lottery. |
| June 1993 | Georgia's Lottery for Education officially opens. |
| September 1993 | First year of program implementation. 8,700 low-income students attend lottery-funded Georgia Pre-K during 1993–94 school year. |
| September 1994 | Pre-K program serves 15,500 low-income students during 1994–95 school year. |
| November 1994 | Governor Miller reelected to a second term. |
| January 1995 | Miller announces that Pre-K eligibility requirements will be dropped. All Georgia 4-year-olds now eligible to attend a universal and voluntary program. |

**TABLE 3.2** (CONTINUED)

| September 1995 | First year as a universal program. 44,000 students attend Pre-K during 1995–96 school year. |
|---|---|
| April 1996 | Pre-K program moved from Georgia Department of Education to a newly created Office of School Readiness. |
| September 1996 | Pre-K program serves 57,500 students during 1996–97 school year. |
| September 1997 | Pre-K program serves 60,000 students during 1997–98 school year. |
| October 1997 | Georgia's Voluntary Universal Pre-K program awarded the prestigious Innovation in American Government award from Harvard's Kennedy School of Government. |
| September 1998 | Pre-K program serves 61,000 students during 1998–99 school year. |
| January 1999 | Zell Miller leaves the Governor's Office. |
| September 1999 | Pre-K program serves 62,000 students during 1999–2000 school year. |
| September 2000 | Pre-K program serves 62,500 students during 2000–2001 school year. |

distinctive, yet educational in focus. He knew that putting the money just right back into the funding stream for K-12 was not going to capture the public or do much for public education. So he came up with these programmatic ideas.[4]

## Designing and Implementing the Pre-K Initiative

Governor Miller assigned the task of developing and implementing the Pre-K program to the Georgia State Department of Education (DOE).

The Early Childhood Division of the Department, working with an advisory committee composed of educators and leaders from Georgia's early education and child care fields, sought to integrate the program into a comprehensive system of services for children and families. A DOE official involved in the early stages of the planning process, who chose to remain anonymous, recalls that two policy initiatives shaped the Pre-K program's guiding vision: (a) Goals 2000, a set of national education goals that prioritized school readiness; and (b) Family Connections, a statewide policy initiative launched in the early 1990s that sought to restructure and integrate state and federal programs to deliver services more efficiently and effectively to families in need.

### Early Program Guidelines

The DOE developed guidelines that stressed the program's comprehensive, family-centered goals. Although many programmatic features would be altered in later years (e.g., eligibility rules, program length, administrative structure, funding mechanisms), these initial guidelines would serve as the blueprint for the program:

**Eligible children.** As initially envisioned, the means-tested program would serve at-risk 4-year-olds. The program categorized "at-risk" children eligible for Medicaid; Aid to Families with Dependent Children (AFDC); the Women, Infants, and Children nutrition program (WIC); other child nutrition programs; subsidized federal housing; or those referred by an agency serving children and families.[5]

**Coordinating councils.** DOE required each Pre-K site to form a local council responsible for (a) developing the program application, (b) establishing collaborations to provide available services to the children and families, and (c) developing and evaluating the program on an ongoing basis.

**Competitive open funding.** Through a competitive process, all grants or contracts would be awarded to sites located in communities with an identified population of at-risk children. Entities eligible for funding included school systems, public and private nonprofit agencies, and private for-profit child care providers.

**Staff-child ratios.** The total number of children served could not exceed 12 in home settings. Classrooms and centers were required to have at least one adult for every 10 children and could not exceed 20 children.

**Curriculum.** All curricula were to be submitted to and approved by the Department of Education. During the first years of implementation (1992–1995), the Pre-K program approved four curriculum choices: Montessori, Bank Street, Creative Curriculum, and High/Scope.

**Staffing.** The original guidelines did not require providers to staff sites with certified teachers. Programs had the option to hire (a) a child and family development specialist, (b) a parent educator, (c) a paraprofessional with a Child Development Associate (CDA) credential, (d) a certified teacher with training in instruction of children younger than 5; (e) or an individual from other related fields with appropriate training or experience.

**Support services.** Providers were required to offer basic health and developmental screenings (EPSDT) for all participating children; parent-focused services, such as literacy, job training, and parent education; and coordinated access to mental health, drug treatment, or crisis intervention programs if needed. Beginning in the 1993–1994 year, programs were required to employ Family Service Coordinators to provide targeted case management for the participating families and to facilitate the integration of needed services.

**Program length.** Early guidelines and funding formulas granted programs the flexibility to provide services of varying length and intensity. The guidelines called for "consideration [to be] given to the coordination of services which address the child care needs of working parents" (Georgia Department of Education, 1994, p. 4). While some sites offered half-day and traditional school-day services, many sites were funded to provide extended-day and full-year programming.

## Meeting Two Key Challenges: Partnering With Head Start and Private Child Care Providers

After piloting the program in 1992, program implementation began the following school year (1993–1994) when 8,700 children attended Pre-K at a cost of $4,258 per child. During the second year of implementation, the program served 15,500 children at an average cost of $5,018 per child.

Creating a new system of early care and education out of whole cloth would prove to be a difficult and complex task. Some of the toughest challenges involved trying to stitch new policies and services together with existing programs, including Head Start, diverse private child care programs (both nonprofit and for-profit), and a wide range of family and child services. Two challenges proved to be crucial during the first three years.

## Resolving Tensions with Head Start

Governor Miller's decision to create an independent state-run Pre-K program—not to supplement Head Start as some states opted—had immediate consequences for Head Start in Georgia. According to Celeste Osborn, the Director of Georgia's Office of School Readiness, relations between the state and Head Start were somewhat strained even before the Pre-K program was introduced. Georgia's establishment of universal kindergarten in the 1980s engendered lingering resentment among Head Start providers who believed that their 5-year-old participants were being unfairly taken away by the state. Robert Lawrence, the DOE administrator in charge of Georgia's Head Start/Pre-K Collaborative, agrees that fear of competition for Pre-K children and mistrust of the state "caused tremendous problems with the Head Start community. They thought the state was coming in to take over the program." Lawrence believes that Head Start's unique historical legacy in the South, where the program is viewed as a triumph of the Civil Rights movement and largely a program for African American children, contributed to the tense political climate.

In an effort to build bridges to Head Start, to the school systems, and to private providers, the state held collaborative conferences. DOE's Early Childhood Division also attempted to address community tension through the program's local coordinating councils. During the 1993–94 academic year, administrators amended the program guidelines to recommend that representatives from Head Start serve on the councils. The guidelines stated specifically, "It is not the intent of this program to be in competition with Head Start or any other preschool or child care provider" (Georgia Department of Education, Office of Instructional Services, 1994, p. 1).

## Integrating For-Profit Providers into the System

In Georgia, as in many states across the nation, a shortage of appropriate classroom space and facilities was a steep obstacle to developing a large-scale initiative. With Georgia's over-crowded public school population already "bursting out of the buildings" in the early 1990s, making room for preschoolers would have required considerable investments for facilities expansion. Complicating the significant facilities problem, Miller was pushing to have the program serve substantial numbers of children as soon as possible. This was a powerful argument for opening up the program to proprietary child care providers, using their buildings instead of allocating funds towards public school expansion. "In Georgia (Universal Pre-K) simply couldn't have happened (without private for-profit child care providers)," said an education reporter from Atlanta. "We didn't have space in schools. It's a whole lot cheaper to take somebody who's already got a building and give them a trained teacher, or give them money to hire a trained teacher, (and) stock the room with toys and games and everything than it is to build a building from scratch." Providing a similar rationale, Celeste Osborn says:

> On the facilities issue, we decided to bypass it.
> Instead of spending money on bricks and mortar, we
> decided to put the funding with the children. That's
> a major reason we started a major public-private
> partnership here in the state of Georgia with the
> private child care associations. Because they had the
> available classroom space, that also allowed us a very
> quick implementation schedule because we didn't
> have to go through a long building process.

Thus, from the start, Georgia invited for-profit child care centers to participate. However, according to a DOE employee, while the program focused on at-risk children, for-profit providers showed little interest in participating. In 1995–1996, when the program expanded to provide free

Pre-K to all 4-year-olds in the state, for-profit providers could no longer stand on the sidelines. According to Rachael Kronchite, president of an organization representing the interests of the state's child care industry, for-profit providers began to fear that the state would jeopardize their businesses by not giving them equal access to Pre-K grants. Susan Maxwell, President of the Georgia Child Care Council, recalls the child care industry's anxiety, "Private providers knew they had to get in the game, but [were] not sure how the game would be played." Maxwell remembers that DOE enraged private providers when, in some crowded school districts, it awarded Pre-K grants to place 4-year-olds in mobile trailers, while private day care centers with empty classrooms were turned down. Maxwell believes that the private child care industry, a powerful lobby in Georgia, "would have tried to kill the [state's Pre-K] program if they had not been allowed to participate."[6] Another child advocate similarly recalls the intense political pressure applied by the industry, "The private child care providers started saying, 'You are stealing our business!' They told the governor that his policies were hurting small business development.... It was a brilliant argument on their part."

In 1995, Miller mandated that private child care centers would have equal access to Pre-K grants. Integrating into a public program hundreds of private child care centers, which have historically operated outside the influence of public school policy, proved to be a daunting challenge. DOE staff members recall tense, complex interactions with private child care associations over requirements for developmentally appropriate practices, curriculum, staff training, and auditing. Particularly intense disagreements ensued concerning credential-based funding formulas and the program's first-come, first-serve open enrollment procedure. Commenting on the Department's frustration with the child care industry, a DOE Pre-K staff member said:

> The private for-profit providers really... just wanted
> the money to be sent to them and [had a] 'leave me
> alone and let me do my job' kind of attitude....
> They didn't want oversight, no curriculums. They
> wanted to be able to use what they considered to be
> their curriculum, which in many cases was a
> worksheet kind of mentality. They wanted to be able
> to make a profit.

As the program operated from 1993–1995, much of the tension involving the for-profit providers revolved around the state's efforts to monitor sites and enforce standards, which private providers tended to perceive as overly bureaucratic, rigid, burdensome, and punitive. "There is the perception that (private child care providers) are in the business, for the money and only for the money," Kronchite says of DOE. "There is a perception that if we give you money, you're not going to use it the way we said to use it, and so we have to look at this so carefully."

DOE's Early Childhood Division instituted training sessions and conferences to try to overcome barriers to effective collaboration. Despite an initial mistrust between program administrators and private child care providers, Georgia's Prekindergarten program has become one of the nation's most extensive public–private education ventures. By the 1997–1998 school year, more than half (57%) of the children in Pre-K were located in nonpublic-school programs.

## Expansion, Controversy, and Change

The Georgia Lottery proved to be more profitable than even Zell Miller had predicted. For Fiscal Year 1994, the state appropriated $242 million in lottery funds for the specified education programs. By 1995, the figure increased to $475 million, surpassing the projected budget appropriation by $250 million (Council for School Performance, 1998).

As the lottery proceeds grew and lottery-funded education programs received more attention, an increasing number of Georgians began to seek access to the services. Middle-class families began demanding to know from their state representatives why they should have to pay for preschool or child care when the Governor had promised a lottery-funded program for Georgia's 4-year-olds.[7] Pressures mounted to expand Pre-K beyond low-income families.

A Democrat in an increasingly Republican state, Governor Miller had been reelected in 1994 by a narrow margin.[8] Convinced that his education programs would remain tenuous if they focused exclusively on low-income children, Miller stepped back to consider how larger-than-expected lottery revenues might be used to address the problem that had inspired the lottery in the first place: improving Georgia's education system. Some advisors in DOE recommended using the funds to expand Pre-K downward to serve at-risk 3-year-olds. But Miller made a different choice: offering free Pre-K to all 4-year-olds whose parents wanted to enroll them, regardless of income. Miller clearly saw the political advantages of extending benefits to middle-class parents and thereby strengthening his political base; he also saw educational advantages, believing that his education programs would be strengthened through middle-class involvement and support. According to Gary Henry, Miller calculated, "If he could get a strong commitment from the middle-class and a perception of a real benefit for having their kids in this program, he might be able to keep the program during politically bad times or the program might outlive his administration if he had strong public support for it." Mike Volmer, an advisor to Miller who would later administer the Pre-K program, recalls the logic behind the decision to open the program's enrollment:

> I guess I always come from the practical school. And
> the practical school said to me that with the political
> conservative environment that we are living in, if we
> come out and try to push a program for poor kids,
> we're not going to get a whole lot of support. And so,
> what we made the decision to do is push a program
> that would touch all Georgians. So I don't know
> whether middle-class or upper-class people really need
> the program. But we needed their support.

Consequently, in January 1995, Governor Miller officially announced that the state's Prekindergarten program for 4-year-olds would drop income eligibility requirements; all 4-year-olds in Georgia would now be eligible to attend a universal and voluntary program.[9]

For the 1995–1996 academic year, Pre-K enrollment nearly tripled, from 15,500 to 44,000 children. By most accounts, the DOE Pre-K administration was understaffed and unprepared to adequately handle the pace and scope of Miller's promised Pre-K expansion. During the first year of expansion to universal access, the program had a difficult time securing sufficient classroom space; some school districts were forced to locate their Pre-K classes in mobile trailers, while more than 12,000 Pre-K applicants remained on waiting lists. Rapid expansion led to logistical nightmares setting up adequate systems to deal with enrollment, regulations, and reimbursement; at public hearings many providers complained bitterly about program administration. A current DOE staff member who faults policymakers for their "inability to thoughtfully plan ahead" contends that Pre-K administrators did a good job with limited staff. "From the outside, it was clear there was a lot of chaos," he added.

In November 1994, political winds further shifted the course of Georgia's Pre-K program. In the 1994 campaign for State Superintendent of Schools, Linda Schrenko, a conservative Republican closely aligned with the Religious Right, upset the incumbent Democrat, Werner Rogers. Schrenko found herself nominally in charge of a Prekindergarten program that was under the control of the Democratic Governor and that would bring her no credit, even if it succeeded. Moreover, the idea of a state-run Pre-K program stood in stark contrast to her own conservative principles. According to one early childhood advocate, Schrenko and the department she headed "really didn't want the Prekindergarten program, because it does go in opposition to what a lot of the extreme conservative population believe about where children belong, and that's at home with their mommies." Another DOE staff member said, "[Shrenko] has no real understanding of early education. She knew that the governor was going to run it. It was his legacy; she didn't want that interference and confusion."

Governor Miller, in turn, mistrusted Schrenko's motives. "If you're a governor and this is your baby, you're not quite confident that somebody who's calling (Pre-K) 'glorified baby sitting' is going to be somebody who's going to really try to make the program work," an education professor from Atlanta observed. Consequently, "the program was held hostage," a DOE staff member recalled, as Miller and Schrenko "were playing politics and trying to figure out how to maneuver around each other and to get what each party wanted." As a result of the political infighting, the Superintendent's

Office prevented Pre-K administrators from filling basic staffing requests, adding to the program's administrative problems.

The behind-the-scenes feud eventually reached the public stage, as education reporters began writing about tension between Miller and Schrenko over control of the program. Schrenko derided the program publicly, complaining to the press about her limited input into the Pre-K standards and the expectation that she would merely "implement" the Governor's program ("Governor, Schrenko Pass Buck on Pre-K," 1995). The *Atlanta Journal and Constitution*, now an enthusiastic supporter of Pre-K, pointed out that key decisions were looming, such as requirements for teacher training and support services, and argued that Schrenko and Miller were "passing the buck" on these issues. "Who's in charge," the paper wondered, "the Governor or the Superintendent? Indeed this is the most troubling issue of all" ("Governor, Schrenko Pass Buck on Pre-K," 1995).

In 1995, the political atmosphere surrounding Pre-K became even more charged. Aware of the program's endorsement of standards promulgated by the National Association for the Education of Young Children (NAEYC), conservative organizations accused Pre-K of using and promoting an anti-bias curriculum distributed by NAEYC (Derman-Sparks & the A.B.C. Task Force, 1989). Although the curriculum was never, in fact, part of Georgia's Pre-K curriculum, conservative politicians and activists, including the state's Christian Coalition, claimed that the program was implementing a curriculum that undermined families and traditional values and promoted a prohomosexual agenda. Schrenko inflamed an increasingly public controversy by erroneously informing Miller that the antibias curriculum had in fact been implemented in Pre-K.

Eventually, reporters established that the NAEYC antibias curriculum had never been adopted by the Pre-K program (White, 1996). Nevertheless, by late 1995, Zell Miller had had enough. Concerns over program administration and the hostile political environment—both within and outside the Department of Education—convinced the Governor that he would have to act boldly to save Pre-K.

## Creating an Office of School Readiness and Changing Public Perceptions

With one of his pet programs—an important part of his legacy—under siege, Governor Miller devised a strategy to save the Georgia Prekindergarten Program. To administer universal Pre-K he would establish a separate office outside of the State Department of Education, staffed with appointees directly responsible to the Governor. According to Mike Volmer, Miller took the controversial step of establishing another bureaucratic department to prevent the program's demise:

> It was a very weak program without any real propo-
> nents. And when I say real proponents, yes, you had
> educators, but the general public, the media,
> members of the general assembly, they were really
> against it…. But there was [enough] conflict in the
> state that the Governor felt he had to pull out of
> [the Department of Education], and there was just
> enough support that he went ahead and created that
> new department.

Despite objections from Republican legislators and conservative organizations about increasing bureaucracy, the Georgia legislature authorized creation of the new Office of School Readiness (OSR). To set up and run OSR, Miller turned to Mike Volmer, the Director of the HOPE Scholarship Program. Volmer had Miller's confidence and a well-earned reputation as a loyal and politically astute fix-it man with extensive experience overseeing governmental initiatives. What he lacked was training in education in general or early education in particular. Governor Miller granted Volmer the freedom to staff OSR with employees who would be loyal to him. Rather than hiring education experts, for the most part Volmer sought individuals with administrative, budgetary, legislative, and technological skills.

In March 1996, Miller and his Democratic allies successfully defeated Republican proposals to cut Pre-K funds and scale back enrollment by reinstating income-eligibility requirements. Volmer's political instincts convinced him that altering negative perceptions of

Pre-K was the new agency's top priority. He calculated that he had 60 days to accomplish this goal, or the legislature would not authorize funding. In retrospect, he believes that his background proved helpful because in the final analysis, the program's survival would hinge on political factors, not educational ones. "What needed to happen was not so much bringing in educational expertise," Volmer said, "but bringing in some political expertise." Volmer contends that the key was to stress academics: "Now, educators will argue that we don't need to stress academics for 4-year-olds. But what I was trying to say in a general way is: 'We ain't no babysitting service.' We are going to focus on math concepts, science concepts, English concepts, and all that. Because that's what the general public wants."

To improve public perception of the program, Volmer brought a marketing perspective to OSR that had been lacking at DOE. Volmer and his staff quickly developed six "learning goals" that focused entirely on children's learning and development and de-emphasized social services and family-centered objectives. OSR staff also distributed a brochure describing the program's academic orientation, and spoke to groups and journalists around the state about the program's academic benefits.[10] Volmer believes that these public relations steps helped to turn the political tide within three to four months. "I do not want to diminish the role of qualified, good educators, and what needed to be done in the substance area," Volmer says. "But to me, the… most important thing, initially, was to change the perception in people's minds." Volmer adds, "I will market the hell out of anything. They say I could market soap real well. But my feeling is that if you have a successful program and no one knows about it, you're not going to last."

## Midcourse Corrections

By the time the Office of School Readiness was up and running, the Prekindergarten program had been in existence for approximately four years. OSR staff scrutinized its operation and found substantive changes were needed in many aspects of program implementation. They embarked on an ambitious set of midcourse corrections.

### Streamlining Program Administration

The most pressing need was to bring efficiency to program administration. Volmer and his staff inherited a large and complex program without basic management tools, such as adequate databases or descriptive materials for public distribution. During its first year in operation, OSR staff revamped the application review process that it had inherited from DOE and significantly upgraded the program's technological and administrative capacity. As they streamlined program administration, OSR also eliminated the requirement for community coordinating councils, which had been a hallmark of the DOE-run program. OSR staff members state that the councils generally served their purposes well in the early years of the program, but later became bogged down in conflict in many communities, resulting in an inefficient and unnecessary level of bureaucracy.

### Introducing a Customer Service Orientation

Volmer and his staff made a concerted effort to bring a business perspective to the administration of Pre-K. Osborn speaks of instituting a customer service orientation in relations with parents, providers, and school system representatives. OSR has established a website and database to give parents information on available Pre-K openings. The business orientation was most evident in a new attitude toward the private Pre-K providers that constitute the majority of Pre-K sites.[11] Pamela Shapiro, OSR's Deputy Director, points out that the DOE Pre-K administrators had no experience working in the private sector. "They really had a difficult time seeing outside the box and understanding that child care is a business and preschool is a business," she said. Volmer also stresses that DOE administrators failed to appreciate the legitimate business concerns of the private child care providers. Without loosening regulations, Volmer tried to change the program's perception of the child care industry from one of mistrust to "treating them as business partners that we needed." OSR's 18 field consultants—who are trained to monitor Pre-K grantees from a more consultative, less regulatory orientation—visit each Pre-K site in the state three to four times per year. OSR has also established public/private partnerships in which public schools provide resource coordinators for private sites. According to OSR, the more consultative approach has (for the most part) defused conflict with for-profit providers.

### Strengthening Teacher Qualification Requirements

Task forces in California and New York have identified the recruitment and retention of qualified teachers as one of the major impediments to implementation of universal preschool (Superintendent's Universal Preschool Task Force, 1998). Carrying out a key recommendation of the Quality 2000 Initiative, Georgia's Pre-K guidelines provide for flexibility in the range of degrees or achievement that can satisfy teacher preparation requirements. For certification, lead teachers must have one of the following credentials: (a) full certification in early childhood education; (b) a four-year college degree, with a major in education, child development, early education, psychology, or social work; (c) a two-year/vocational/Montessori degree, with a focus in child development; or (d) a Child Development Associate (CDA) or Child Care Professional (CCP) credential. In addition, while not requiring Pre-K teachers to have full certification in Early Childhood Education, the program's funding formulas create incentives for all Pre-K grantees to hire well-qualified teachers and for teachers to obtain advance certification. For example, during the 2001-02 school year, OSR provided each Pre-K site funding based on the qualifications of the lead teacher, which ranged from $2,219 per child/per year for a public school teacher with a CDA, to $3,162 per child/per year for a certified teacher in early education at a private site.[12]

### Revising and Standardizing the Educational Program

OSR has made instructional changes in Pre-K, standardizing, and in some cases, abbreviating educational programming. Children now receive 6.5 hours of instructional services five days per week for 36 weeks—the length of a typical academic year. Pre-K centers have the option of providing extended-day services at the parent's expense. Moreover, OSR revised staff/child ratios and has offered Pre-K providers greater flexibility in selecting curriculum models (see Table 3.1 for details).

### Program Expansion or Comprehensive Services?

When the Pre-K initiative served primarily at-risk children, it placed great emphasis on the provision of comprehensive, family-focused social services. As the program moved toward universal coverage, this aspect of the program was criticized as expensive and overly intrusive. Volmer decided that for political and budgetary reasons, Pre-K would have to deemphasize and scale back some of these comprehensive services. Arguing that it would be necessary to "have the program focused only on education," Volmer concluded, "As important as social services are, as important as other human services may be, this program (was) in deep trouble.... I just felt like we couldn't be all things to everyone." Governor Miller supported reorienting Pre-K away from family-focused support services. "I was unhappy with the Pre-K program in its infancy," Miller said. "It was too much of a social program, too much of a babysitting program." Miller stated publicly that "the whole purpose of setting up a separate office [OSR] was to shift emphasis toward school readiness skills."

The most significant change involved replacing mandatory social services for low-income families with a voluntary "brokerage of services." OSR recast the Family Service Coordinator position, creating Resource Coordinators (RCs). Pre-K providers who serve more than six at-risk students may apply for funds to offer voluntary RC services for at-risk children and families. OSR redefined the objectives of resource coordination as identifying child health problems; offering parents seminars, volunteer opportunities, and conferences to enhance knowledge of child development; information that will increase knowledge of community resources; and providing help in obtaining necessary documentation required for kindergarten (Office of School Readiness, 1998).

OSR also changed the program's health requirements. In the initial years of the program (1992–1995), all children received full EPSDT screenings through the Pre-K providers, which are no longer required. OSR amended the guidelines to state that Pre-K providers should work with health departments and health professionals to ensure that the children receive the screenings within 90 days (Office of School Readiness, 1998).

As a result of the cuts in comprehensive services, per-pupil expenditures decreased considerably over time. During the second year of implementation (1994–95), the approximate cost was $5,018 per child. During the 1997–98 school year, the program spent about $3,516 per child.[13]

While many advocates and educators believe that Georgia Pre-K has been strengthened by its narrower focus on educational goals, scaling back the family support component has sparked criticism among some providers and child advocates in the state who believe that the program no longer meets the substantial needs of at-risk children and their families. For example, a professor of early education who chose not to be identified argues that the move to OSR compromised the provision of comprehensive services and developmentally appropriate practices. "When the program was initially developed," she says, "it included a family support program… As the family support position was eliminated, [there was a decline] in the quality of services for the individual. They cut out the piece that tied the services of the program to the child and family. It was detrimental." An education reporter from Atlanta expresses similar concerns about the state providing funds for middle-class children whose parents would have paid for child care, while not serving adequately all eligible low-income children. "[I]f you're going to have the scarce resources in a public program, you ought to spend them on who's going to benefit the most," she says. A local education administrator, critical of the revised services, contends that Miller and OSR have oversold the benefits of the program. "The whole story is not numbers served," he says. It is the quality of the services. As the program expanded to serve every child, the icing on the cake started to fall off. Family support was watered down to almost nothing…. The health component was watered down as well…. In some way it has been watered down over the desire to serve more children." He contends that Miller could have used the program's popularity to retain and enhance quality comprehensive services.

### *Partnering with Head Start*

The Office of School Readiness sought to reduce any lingering tension with Georgia's Head Start administration and providers. Robert Lawrence, the coordinator of Georgia's Head Start/Pre-K Collaborative now located within OSR, credits OSR with reaching out to him and local Head Start providers to build a trustful working relationship. This collaboration and blended funding allows some Georgia Pre-K children to receive Head Start health and social services. In turn, Head Start receives state funding to provide some participants with full-day programming. Steven Golightly, Regional Hub Director for the Administration for Children and Families within the U.S. Department of Health and Human Services and the federal officer overseeing Head Start in the region, credits OSR's collaborative efforts and respectful attitude toward Head Start with reducing fear of competition to "a nonissue." Golightly expresses confidence in the quality of the state-run Pre-K programs. "The standards are high, the quality is high," he says. "We don't think it's as high as Head Start, but that probably is a moot point. We have… our Head Start children in wraparound services that are funded by Pre-K after the Head Start class ends. If we felt they were doing a shoddy job, we wouldn't condone the collaboration of the wraparound."

By most accounts, the programs now complement each other well. Together Head Start and Georgia Pre-K provide early education to approximately 80% of the 4-year-olds in the state. The saturation rate varies from 30%–45% in a few (typically rural) counties to 90%–100% in other counties.

## Gauging the Impact of Georgia's Pre-K Program

### *Measuring Early Results*

During the first year of statewide implementation (1993–1994), researchers recruited a random sample of 317 Pre-K participants from 18 program sites geographically distributed throughout the state. A year later, when these children were finishing kindergarten, 267 of them (84%) were located and compared to a randomly selected matched group of 267 Pre-K–eligible students who had not participated in the Pre-K program (Pilcher & Kaufman-McMurrain, 1995). The results indicated that near the end of kindergarten, Pre-K participants scored significantly higher than the comparison children on measures of academic development ($F(1,532) = 23.72, p < .001$, Ms = 4.87 and 3.98, respectively), communication ($F(1,532) = 21.77, p < .001$, Ms = 4.96 and 4.14), physical development ($F(1,532) = 25.48, p < .001$, Ms = 5.20 and 4.30), self-help ($F(1,532) = 23.13, p < .001$, Ms = 5.18 and 4.31), and social development ($F(1,532) = 11.44, p < .01$, Ms = 5.11 and 4.52). The Pre-K participants also had significantly fewer absences ($F(1,532) = 4.90, p < .05$, Ms = 9.3 and 11.1) and were retained less frequently ($F(1,532) = 5.55, p < .02$, 4.5% and 9.4%, respectively) than were the comparison children (Pilcher & Kaufman-McMurrain, 1995).

The same cohort of students was evaluated the next year near the end of first grade (Pilcher & Kaufman-McMurrain, 1996). Researchers located and assessed 97% of the previous sample: 262 Pre-K participants and 255 comparison children. The evaluation revealed that nearly two years after completion of the Pre-K program, fewer programmatic effects were evident. First graders who had participated in the Pre-K program did have significantly fewer absences during the school year ($F(1,501) = 5.17, p < .05$, Ms = 7.42 and 9.38, respectively), but did not differ on referrals for special services or rates of grade promotion. Pre-K children continued to score significantly higher than the comparison children on academic development ($F(1, 514) = 7.55, p < .01$, Ms. = 85.22 and 81.99), but not on social development, physical development, or communication.[14] Researchers obtained achievement scores from the Iowa Test of Basic Skills for a subsample of students (98 Pre-K and 91 comparison). The Pre-K students tended to score higher than the comparison children on math problem solving ($z = 1.75, p < .10$, Ms = 56.39 and 49.84, respectively), total math ($z = 1.65, p < .10$, Ms = 54.89 and 48.55) and total reading ($z = 1.66, p < .10$, Ms = 53.21 and 46.16), but not on reading comprehension. The findings also showed that parents of participants and comparison children did not differ on school participation, employment status, or reliance on public assistance programs (Pilcher & Kaufman-McMurrain, 1996).

Overall, these findings suggest that Pre-K significantly enhanced the children's development and improved their chances for benefiting from kindergarten. The fading of some program effects, however, raised questions (particularly among policymakers) about the program efficacy during these early years of implementation. Consistent with evaluations of many early intervention programs, these early evaluations showed that in the absence of consistent follow-through in the primary grades, many significant developmental gains tend to diminish over time.

## Evaluating Universal Pre-K

Because the program changed so significantly when it expanded to universal provision, policymakers and administrators do not view the early evaluations as indicative of the effectiveness of the current universal program.

During the 1996–97 school year, OSR initiated a 12-year longitudinal evaluation of the Georgia Pre-K program (Basile et al., 1998). A process evaluation focusing on Pre-K service delivery during the first year of the study demonstrated that most Pre-K teachers are well trained and satisfied with their jobs. Of the sample studied, 83% of Pre-K teachers were fully trained in their respective curricula, 85% had a four-year degree or better, and 79% were certified in early childhood education. Furthermore, based on teacher responses to a series of questions examining teaching practices and attitudes, researchers concluded that most teachers use developmentally appropriate practices in their Pre-K classes (Basile et al., 1998). Overall, 93% of Pre-K teachers responded that they were working in a supportive environment.

The evaluation, however, revealed discrepancies in the training and treatment of teachers at public school and private (including both nonprofit and for-profit) Pre-K sites. Lead teachers in public schools were significantly more likely than their counterparts at private sites to hold state certification in an early childhood field of study (97% to 65%), to believe that salaries are fair (Ms = 2.67 and 1.86, respectively), and to report a favorable work environment (Basile et al., 1998).[15] Moreover, although parents as a whole demonstrated an extremely high level (90%) of satisfaction with the program, satisfaction and program experience varied by organization type. Parents of children enrolled in public schools reported higher levels of satisfaction with Pre-K, and were more likely to attend special programming, to say that they learned from Pre-K staff, and to believe that their interactions with their child changed as a result of the program (Basile et al., 1998). Overall, the results suggest that while the program meets parental expectations and has succeeded in attracting qualified staff, important questions remain about the consistency of program quality and implementation.

For the second year of the longitudinal evaluation, 3,201 randomly selected Pre-K children were followed through their kindergarten year (Henderson et al., 1999). Findings indicated that a majority of kindergarten teachers believed that as a result of Pre-K, students were better prepared for kindergarten in specific skill areas such as prereading (60%), premath (58%), gross motor skills development (64%), and social interactions with adults (68%) and children (70%). Kindergarten teachers rated approximately two-thirds (64%) of the students as well prepared (i.e., ready for schooling) at the start of kindergarten. These findings are promising and suggest that the program may be accomplishing its school readiness goals. However, because the researchers could not recruit a comparable comparison group of children who did not attend the Pre-K program, it is not possible to make reliable causal interpretations of these data.[16]

The evaluation also assessed the impact of differences in Pre-K programs' educational orientation on student outcomes in kindergarten.[17] Based on classroom observations and teacher interviews, findings indicate that Pre-K teachers (49%) report more "child-centered" beliefs and practices than do kindergarten teachers (42%). Consistent with research demonstrating that developmentally appropriate early childhood education and care (ECEC) programs have positive effects on children's academic performance and motivation (Marcon, 1992, 1999; Stipek et al., 1995), children benefited more when their Pre-K teachers used a "child-centered" teaching approach (Henderson et al., 1999). Teachers rated children from child-centered classes as better prepared for kindergarten, and they progressed more during the kindergarten year, especially when the kindergarten teacher also used a consistent child-centered teaching style (Henderson et al., 1999).

## Looking Ahead

### *The Viability of Lottery-Funded Pre-K*

In part, the program's future hinges on the ability of the lottery to continue to raise revenues that can be earmarked for educational programs. From a financial perspective, Georgia's lottery has exceeded all expectations and projections. Independent reports released by the Georgia State Auditor and Georgia State University's Council for School Performance confirm that lottery proceeds have supplemented traditional educational expenditures, resulting in substantial increases in appropriations for education (Council for School Performance, 1998). Despite predictions that lottery revenues would taper off after a few years, ticket sales have increased each year the lottery has been in operation (Council for School Performance, 1998). By 1998, the lottery had generated over $2.7 billion in lottery revenues, with over $713 million appropriated for Georgia's Pre-K program. Lottery funds covered virtually the entire $212 million operating budget for Pre-K in 1998, including all grants to providers and administrative costs. [18]

### *The Necessity of Popular Support*

A consensus seems to have formed among most policymakers, child advocates, and program administrators that OSR and Zell Miller were so skillful in building political support that leaders from both parties will remain committed to Pre-K in the foreseeable future. Zell Miller's successor, Governor Roy Barnes, pledged full support for Pre-K.

Mike Volmer believes that expanding Pre-K to include middle-class parents ensured the program's sustainability. He recalls:

> Legislators were shooting holes in this program [in 1996]. Now if you talk to them, I don't think they'd say anything negative in a public manner anyway. Because they've got too many [middle-class] families… that are utilizing the program. And that's what we were aiming to do—make sure this was perceived as a middle-class program. It just so happened [to be] helping 30,000 at-risk children.

Volmer also believes that emphasizing educational benefits to middle-class parents was critical in building political support. He says:

> It's remarkable the level of support we did get from the middle-class folks. And their level of support really came from—not that it was a babysitting program, but their children were actually learning something. And so, I think in the end it will show that the program benefited children from all economic [groups].

Advocates and educators inside and outside OSR also stress the importance of Pre-K's broad constituency. OSR's Kathleen Gooding credits Miller with the foresight to understand that programs that exclude middle-class populations are vulnerable to shifting political forces. "Whenever there is a change in government, there is a chance that programs that work with at-risk populations will be cut," Gooding says. "They're the easiest to cut. The population base that it comes from, they do not fight. They don't know how to fight the system. They're pretty much a silent majority." Robert Lawrence agrees and suggests that other states should take note: Even though research demonstrates that low-income children are the primary beneficiaries of early education programs, "you can't mount a sustainable program without support from the middle-class that votes." Gary Henry contends that states must ultimately determine mechanisms to ensure that middle-class families, who may be more skilled at obtaining services, do not benefit at the expense of lower income families. Nonetheless, Henry concludes, "I think the big lesson is that making services available to a broad array of children and not just economically disadvantaged children probably will increase geometrically the support for the program over time."

## Lessons for Other States

### *Universal Access May Be a Key to Winning Support*

Georgia opted to shift the goals of its Pre-K program away from targeting services to the state's neediest children to the provision of services for all children. While establishing equal access to state services, an important rationale for the expansion was the calculation that incorporating the middleclass into the program would build a powerful base of support that would secure the program's future. Georgia's state-run Pre-K program, now the most far-reaching in the nation, has developed overwhelming popular approval (over 85%) and survived political opposition that might have terminated a weaker program (Council for School Performance, 1998). Most informed observers believe that the decision to move toward universal coverage saved Pre-K in Georgia. Although some educators and advocates oppose a policy of a state providing resources to families capable of paying for their own child care or preschool, the irrefutable fact remains: Programs geared toward economically disadvantaged, politically weak populations tend to remain inherently vulnerable and limited.[19]

States must determine if the goals of expansion and broad public acceptance require trade-offs that compromise the scope of program services. Early childhood programs have generally shown more effectiveness for low-income children than for children from other populations (Barnett, 1998). From the start, policymakers need to address the issue of support services. How will Pre-K fit into the spectrum of existing services available for children and families? Can voluntary services be of sufficient intensity to accomplish the comprehensive, two-generational goals of traditional early intervention programs targeted to low-income families (Yoshikawa, 1994; Zigler & Styfco, 1993)? Universal Pre-K, stripped of these services, may fail to meet the significant, multidimensional needs of many low-income families.

Universalizing access to programs, however, may erase the stigma attached to targeted services for at-risk children. The nation's largest early care and education program, Head Start, has never shaken the stigma of being a program for children in poverty. Some advocates in Georgia suggest that one of the lasting contributions of Georgia's Pre-K program may be in launching an early education program in which children, and the program itself, are not stigmatized by class.[20] Within universal initiatives, equity becomes a pervasive concern. Some analyses suggest that when human services are offered on a universal basis, middle- and upper-class families may benefit disproportionately (Magenheim, 1995).

## State Lotteries and Financing

A state lottery is a viable mechanism for financing universal Pre-K classes. It is highly unlikely that a state as conservative as Georgia would have appropriated large sums of tax revenues to fund a comprehensive early education program—Georgia's Pre-K initiative would probably not exist without the lottery. With its substantial and consistent lottery-generated revenue base, Georgia's Pre-K program has avoided the gaps in funding and blending of funding streams that routinely plague early education initiatives (Kagan & Cohen, 1997). Across the nation, as states seek solutions to inequities in school funding (Crampton & Whitney, 1996; Jones, 1994) and revenue sources to establish comprehensive early education programs (Mitchell et al.,1997), lotteries will remain attractive funding options. However, in most other states, which have significantly higher cost-per-pupil funding rates, even Georgia's substantial lottery resources would not cover the entire costs of a universal preschool program.

Increasingly embraced by political consultants, lotteries allow politicians to provide constituents with the gambling games they seek while generating seemingly tax-neutral revenue sources to shape popular policies (Beinart, 1998; Sack, 1999). Nevertheless, important questions remain about the capacity of lotteries to generate sufficient revenues to sustain educational policies; in most states, lottery revenues simply supplant previous funding sources, resulting in no net increase in actual education spending (Jones, 1994; Perlman, 1998). Georgia set an important precedent by stipulating in an amendment to the state constitution that lottery funds be spent on specific and distinct educational programs.

Despite the potential benefits to education, the social consequences of state-sponsored gambling are still not well understood (Shepherd et al.,1998; Wood & Griffiths, 1998). An analysis by the *Atlanta Journal and Constitution* documented that Georgians living in lower income neighborhoods spend more than twice as much on lottery tickets than do residents in higher income areas (Watson, 1994). This discrepancy raises a question posed by lottery opponents: Are lotteries a form of regressive, albeit voluntary, taxation geared toward the poor? Educators and policymakers must determine whether the benefits outweigh the possible negative consequences of state lotteries.

## *Leadership*

Creating a large-scale Pre-K program requires powerful, consistent leadership. Georgia's Pre-K program would not have taken root or survived without a skilled and powerful governor willing to risk political capital on the program. Unfortunately, few states have governors with Zell Miller's strong interest in education and formidable political skills necessary to implement meaningful education change.[21] Georgia's establishment of Pre-K thus provides a potent example of the prioritizing of education policy at the highest levels of state government. More often, education reform is a "bottom-up" process of policy formation, with advocates, educators, and sympathetic legislators crafting proposals and seeking support from leaders.

The evolution of Georgia's Pre-K initiative illustrates that successful program development requires input from policymakers and administrators with a range of backgrounds and skills. While most state-run Pre-K programs across the nation are administered within state Departments of Education (Mitchell, 1998), it may be naive to expect education policy analysts to possess the expertise and experience needed to administer and grow a complex initiative. Initially administered within the State Department of Education, Georgia's prekindergarten program benefited from the early contributions of informed education experts familiar with essential components and principles of quality early education. But these experts were not always well equipped to address the political and administrative problems that threatened to destroy the program. Thus, the success of Georgia's Pre-K has been due, in no small part, to the contributions of individuals with knowledge of legislative dynamics, budgetary policy, technology, public relations, and political strategy.

To protect Pre-K from intense political opposition, Governor Miller removed the program from the auspices of DOE. He established a separate Office of School Readiness staffed with administrators who reported directly to him. Intentionally seeking politically savvy appointees skilled at building a broad base of support, Miller grasped a reality that leaders in other states must also confront: Early education policy cannot be created in a political vacuum. Ultimately, states must analyze carefully under what auspices programs will be placed, and what skills key personnel will bring to initiatives.

## Understanding the Ecology of Early Childhood Programs

Success hinges on understanding the fragile ecology of early childhood education and care programs. States must consider carefully how Pre-K initiatives may affect the fragmented systems of care that already exist for young children. An infusion of resources—including money and technical support—can improve the overall quality of the state's programs for preschoolers. But implementing a statewide early education program affects existing programs in predictable and unpredictable ways. States, therefore, must monitor whether universal Pre-K positively and/or negatively affects the quality and availability of early care and education services.

Child care analysts fear that some proprietary centers may eliminate slots and resources for younger children as Pre-K classes become more profitable to operate. While there has been no systematic data collection addressing the systemic ramifications of universal Pre-K, a particular concern is that infants and toddlers—especially those from low-income families—may end up concentrated in unmonitored settings or low-quality centers that are unable to qualify for state Pre-K funds.

## The Challenge of Integrating Private Providers

Program planners and administrators faced the dual reality that (a) including both nonprofit and for-profit child care providers into a state-based program significantly enhances program capacity support and (b) an increasingly powerful and competitive proprietary child care industry is prepared to fight to protect its customer base (Magenheim, 1999). They also had to respond to the distinct needs of for-profit child care providers and recognize the expertise that for-profit providers brought to the enterprise. Georgia's efforts to create a public–private education partnership suggest that states must understand the legitimate business concerns of for-profit industry and learn to work with organizations and institutions with diverse cultures, priorities, and goals.

By including the proprietary child care industry in its state-run education initiative, Georgia Pre-K challenged many basic tenets about what constitutes—and who is qualified to provide—early education. Although program administrators have clashed with representatives of the child care industry over such issues as reimbursement rates, curriculum, enrollment requirements, and community collaboration, the number of well run for-profit Pre-K centers demonstrates that a profit motive and a commitment to developmentally appropriate education are not mutually exclusive. However, states should not assume that providing materials, curriculum training, and technical support necessarily results in quality programs that meet high standards. To date, only for-profit programs have had Pre-K sponsorship revoked based on failure to meet standards. Moreover, program evaluations point to significant discrepancies between public and private sites in terms of staff credentials and possibly the quality of instruction (Basile et al., 1998). More information is needed about variations in services among the wide variety of nonpublic-school Pre-K sites, including large corporate child care chains, small "mom and pop" businesses, religious institutions, and nonprofit community-based organizations.

### Intergovernmental Dynamics

Complex dynamics may ensue among the different levels of government in the provision of early education services. An enhanced state role in providing early education has considerable implications for the future of Head Start. From the outset, Georgia Pre-K caused strain between state education authorities and Georgia's Head Start programs over control of resources and competition for participants. Because Head Start tends to be viewed in Southern states as an outgrowth of the Civil Rights movement and largely a program for African American children, the conflict had implicit racial overtones. Pre-K administrators have deliberately worked to reduce conflict and establish a collaborative partnership with Head Start.

Some policy analysts assert that the role of the federal government in the provision of early education ought to be reduced and fundamentally reconstituted (Ripple et al.,1999). Instead of Head Start being funded and administered from Washington, some critics contend that federal early education funds should be devolved to the states in block grants (Besharov & Samari, 1998). Advocates of devolution suggest that states can more efficiently meet the unique needs of their residents. In contrast, Head Start supporters may fear that the elimination of a singular federal early education program will result in state programs of inferior quality, possibly less equipped to meet the needs of low-income children and their families (Ripple et al., 1999). Georgia's model of state and federal partnership suggests that complementary state and federal initiatives can coexist to help create a more coherent and responsive ECEC system. But states must enforce standards to ensure that universal initiatives do not result in a two-tiered—possibly segregated—early education system, in which low-income families are concentrated in Head Start or lower quality Pre-K settings.

## Teacher Preparation

Program success hinges on the quality of teacher preparation, and a shortage of teachers with early childhood training threatens the successful implementation of universal Pre-K in many states (Kagan & Cohen, 1997; Whitebook et al.,1989). Georgia Pre-K has upgraded teaching at hundreds of childcare centers through incentive-based funding mechanisms. In the 1997–98 school year, 85% of Georgia Pre-K teachers held certification in Early Education (Basile et al., 1998). As an indication of the strength of Georgia's systems of training and incentives, evaluations have found that the vast majority of Pre-K teachers consistently use developmentally appropriate teaching practices in their Pre-K classrooms (Basile et al., 1998). Nonetheless, inadequate compensation threatens program quality. Surveys reveal significant discrepancies in the education, credentials, and compensation of teachers at public and private Pre-K sites (Basile et al., 1998). Public schools, which provide higher wages and full benefits, are better equipped than private child care centers to recruit and retain certified teachers. States, therefore, must determine additional strategies to professionalize all Pre-K staff and establish parity between counterparts in the public and private education and care systems. Responding to this problem, in the 2000–2001 school year, OSR required all Pre-K teachers to receive a minimum salary based on teacher credentials.

### Infrastructure

The challenge of creating a Pre-K infrastructure cannot be underestimated. States seeking to provide early education to a significant proportion of eligible children will face similar options as those in Georgia: (a) large-scale investment in building or expanding public school facilities, or (b) using existing space beyond school settings, typically in private nonprofit or for-profit child care centers. Georgia's solution was to engage for-profit and nonprofit child care providers into a public-private education partnership.

Although the program encountered some difficulty finding room for all new enrollees during the first year of expansion, adequate facilities have been identified in most communities. However, evidence suggests that suitable facilities may be scarce in low-income neighborhoods, especially those in urban areas (Handy, 1996; Superintendent's Universal Preschool Task Force, 1998). States must develop creative strategies to ensure that families in these neighborhoods are not shortchanged in program funding, access, and quality.

## Acknowledgments

This chapter is based on a longer and more detailed working paper published by the Foundation for Child Development, which provided support for the project.

# Endnotes

[1] Although Georgia would later earn acclaim for developing the nation's first universal prekindergarten program, Miller initially envisioned a Pre-K program for at-risk (i.e., low-income) children.

[2] James Carville, who would two years later become one of the architects of Bill Clinton's campaign for the presidency, is viewed by some political analysts as the "father" of "Lotteries for Education" (Beinart, 1998).

[3] In 1990, over 30% of Georgia's adults did not graduate from high school—the 10th highest percentage among the 50 states (U.S. Department of Education, 1997a). With an average per pupil expenditure of $4,416 during the 1990–1991 academic year, Georgia ranked 37th on state spending on elementary and secondary school (U.S. Department of Education, 1997c).

[4] This case study is based on interviews (phone and in-person) conducted between June 1998 and May 1999 with numerous Pre-K providers, program administrators, educators, reporters, and child advocates. Many of the individuals interviewed opted for their comments to remain anonymous; thus, several unattributed but influential voices are interwoven throughout the chapter.

[5] Most of the children eligible for the program were also eligible for other means-tested education programs, such as Head Start or Title I.

[6] According to Roger Neugabauer of the Child Care Information Exchange, in several southern states—where many of the large corporate child care chains had their early growth—the proprietary child care industry tends to be better organized and exert more political influence (personal communication).

[7] The Governor had never, in fact, promised prekindergarten for all 4-year-olds. But constituents' expectations seemingly changed how they viewed previous pronouncements.

[8] By 1998, the Republican transformation of the South had rendered Georgia the only state in the region not to have elected a Republican governor in recent years.

[9] The prekindergarten program now classifies at-risk children as "Category 1." All other children are labeled "Category 2."

[10] According to the Office of School Readiness in 1998, "The school readiness goals of the Georgia Prekindergarten Program are to provide appropriate preschool experiences emphasizing growth in language and literacy, math concepts, science, arts, physical development, and personal and social competence." The OSR has recently altered these learning goals slightly by substituting the phrase "to provide a developmentally

appropriate preschool program" for the earlier "to provide appropriate preschool experiences."

[11] During the 1996–1997 school year, the program provided grants to 825 nonpublic-school sites and 663 public sites.

[12] Reimbursement rates differ slightly for public school and nonpublic-school Pre-K sites. Because of differences in salary, benefits, and operating expenses for the core program, OSR reimburses private providers at a slightly higher rate per child. However, local school systems receive additional funds for the training and experience of teachers based on the state salary scale, which are not reflected in the published weekly rates. Furthermore, to upgrade teacher preparation, OSR is phasing in more rigorous credential requirements. By the 2002–2003 school year, all lead Pre-K teachers will be required to have a minimum of an associate degree in early childhood education or a two-year vocational-technical diploma in Early Childhood Care and Education.

[13] Increased administrative efficiency may also contribute to the decline in per-pupil expenditures.

[14] These scores were based on a different measure of development (the Developmental Profile-II (DP-II)) than the one that was used during the first year of the evaluation, which raises questions about the validity of the findings. For both years, the research protocol included the Developmental Rating Scale (DRS), a teacher-rating instrument that assesses the same domains as the DP-II. While Pre-K children scored significantly higher than the comparison children on the five DRS domains (academic, social, communication, physical, and self-help) during kindergarten, by first grade no significant differences were found. See Pilcher & Kaufman-McMurrain, 1996 for details.

[15] These evaluation reports, written for a general audience, do not include all relevant statistical information, such as $F$ scores and alpha values.

[16] Incorporating random assignment to treatment and control group, the most rigorous evaluation design, is virtually impossible when evaluating a universal program, thus limiting the interpretation of the results.

[17] To date, evaluations have not included subgroup analyses that examine (a) whether the program has differential effects for children from different income levels, or (b) the outcomes of children who receive different levels of services (i.e., comprehensive or less comprehensive).

[18] There are two exceptions to lottery-funded Pre-K expenditures: Many Category One (i.e. low-income) children in Pre-K receive Department of Family and Children

Services funds for the provision of extended-day services and Child and Adult Care Food Program funds for free and reduced-price meals.

[19] Around the country, there are numerous examples of popular initiatives for low-income children championed by leaders who successfully communicated the need and/or strong research base for the program. However, many policy analysts contend that in a conservative region such as the South, significantly increasing the number of families and communities reached by an initiative is a key to institutionalizing a program.

[20] Although the program may be integrated by race, ethnicity, and socioeconomic background, OSR has not released statistics indicating that children are attending integrated classrooms.

[21] As a "strong governor state" with concentrated gubernatorial power (Rosenthal, 1990), Georgia provides opportunities to exert leadership that are somewhat diminished in other regions.

# References

Adams, G., & Sandfort, J. (1994). *First steps, promising futures: State prekindergarten initiatives in the early 1990s.* Washington: Children's Defense Fund.

Barnett, W. S. (1998). Long-term effects on cognitive development and school success. In W. S. Barnett & S. S. Boocock (Eds.), *Early care and education for children in poverty.* Albany: State University of New York Press.

Basile, K., Henderson, L., & Henry, G. (1998). *Prekindergarten longitudinal study 1996–1997 school year report 1: Program implementation characteristics.* Atlanta: Georgia State University Applied Research Center

Beinart, P. (1998, November 16). The Carville trick: The Clinton consultant found a way to win the South for the Democrats—the lottery. But is it fair? *Time*, p. 58.

Besharov, D., & Samari, N. (1998, October). Child care vouchers (and cash payments). Paper prepared for Vouchers and Related Delivery Mechanisms: Consumer Choice in the Provision of Public Services, conference sponsored by the Urban Institute, The Brookings Institute, and the Committee for Economic Development, Washington, DC.

Blank, H., & Poersch, N. O. (2000). *State developments in child care and early education: 1999.* Washington, DC: Children's Defense Fund.

Council for School Performance. (1998). *Report on the expenditure of lottery funds fiscal year 1997.* Georgia State University Council for School Performance. Atlanta: Georgia State University.

Crampton, F., & Whitney, T. (1996). *The search for equity in school funding. Education Partners Working Papers.* Denver, CO: National Conference of State Legislatures. (ERIC Document Reproduction Service No. ED 412 601)

Derman-Sparks, L., & the A.B.C. Task Force. (1989). *Anti-bias curriculum: Tools for empowering young children.* Washington, DC: National Association for the Education of Young Children.

Georgia Department of Education, Office of Instructional Services (1994). *Georgia's pre-kindergarten program: FY '94 phase II program guidelines.* Atlanta: Author.

Governor, Schrenko pass buck on Pre-K. [Editorial]. (1995, July 27). *Atlanta Journal and Constitution,* p. 16.

Handy, J. (1996). *The allocation of Georgia lottery education funds.* Atlanta, GA: Research Atlanta, Inc.

Henderson, L., Basile, K., & Henry, G. (1999). *Prekindergarten longitudinal study: 1997–1998 school year annual report.* Atlanta: Georgia State University Applied Research Center.

Jones, T. (1994, November). *America's gamble: Lotteries and the finance of education.* Paper presented at the Annual Meeting of the American Education Studies Association, Chapel Hill, NC. (ERIC Document Reproduction Service No. ED 380 903)

Kagan, S., & Cohen, N. (1997). *Not by chance: Creating an early care and education system for America's children.* New Haven: Bush Center for Child Development and Social Policy, Yale University.

The lottery and other trivia. [Editorial]. (1990, February 1). *Atlanta Journal and Constitution,* p. 14.

Lottery numbers add to education. [Editorial]. (1997, January 7). *Atlanta Journal and Constitution,* p. 6.

Magenheim, E. (1995). Information, prices, and competition in the child care market: What role should government play? In M. Pogodzinski (Ed.), *Readings in Public Policy* (pp. 269–307). Cambridge, MA: Blackwell.

Magenheim, E. (1999, April). *Preschools and privatization.* Paper presented at Teachers College, Columbia University, NY.

Marcon, R. (1992). Differential effects of three preschool models on inner-city 4-year-olds. *Early Childhood Research Quarterly, 7,* 517–530.

Marcon, R. (1999). Differential impact of preschool models on development and early learning of inner-city children: A three-cohort study. *Developmental Psychology, 35*(2), 358–375.

May, A., & Watson, C. (1990, November 23). "The governor's race 1990: Candidates at odds on lottery funds: Views differ on who gets control," *Atlanta Journal and Constitution,* p. B1.

McAllister, D. (1991, January 29). Lottery is Governor Miller's baby; he needs to watch it," *Atlanta Journal and Constitution,* p. A10.

Mitchell, A. (1998). *Prekindergarten programs funded by the states: Essential elements for policymakers.* New York: Families and Work Institute.

Mitchell, A., Seligson, M., & Marx, F. (1989). *Early childhood programs and the public schools.* Dover, MA: Auburn House Publishing Company.

Mitchell, A., Stoney, L., & Dichter, H. (1997). *Financing child care in the United States: An illustrative catalog of current strategies.* Ewing Marion Kauffman Foundation, Kansas City, MO; Pew Charitable Trusts, Philadelphia, PA. (ERIC Document Reproduction Service No. ED 413 988.)

Office of School Readiness. (1998). *Georgia Prekindergarten Program: 1997–1998 school year Pre-K providers' operating guidelines.* Atlanta, GA: Author. See also: http://www.osr.state.ga.us/whatisprek.html

Perlman, E. (1998, January). The game of mystery bucks. *Governing,* 28–29.

Pilcher, L. C., & Kaufman-McMurrain, M. (1995). The longitudinal study of Georgia's prekindergarten children and families: 1994–1995. Atlanta: Georgia State University, Department of Early Childhood Education.

Pilcher, L. C., & Kaufman-McMurrain, M. (1996). *The longitudinal study of Georgia's prekindergarten children and families: 1995–1996*. Atlanta: Georgia State University, Department of Early Childhood Education.

Ripple, C., Gilliam, W., Chanana, N., & Zigler, E. (1999). Will fifty cooks spoil the broth? The debate over entrusting Head Start to the states. *American Psychologist, 54*, 327–343.

Rosenthal, A. (1990). *Governors and legislators: Contending powers*, Washington, DC: Congressional Quarterly Press.

Sack, K. (1999, January 14). Dixie sees a jackpot in the lottery: More southern states, among last holdouts, are set to join in. *The New York Times,* p. A9.

Schulman, K., Blank, H., & Ewen, D. (1999). *Seeds of success: State prekindergarten initiatives 1998–99*. Washington, DC: Children's Defense Fund.

Shepherd, R., Ghodse, H., & London, M. (1998). A pilot study examining gambling behavior before and after the launch of the national lottery and scratchcard in the UK. *Addiction Research, 6*(1), 5–12.

Stipek, D., Feiler, R., Daniels, D., & Milburn, S. (1995). Effects of different instructional approaches on young children's achievement and motivation. *Child Development, 66,* 209–223.

Superintendent's Universal Preschool Task Force. (1998). *Ready to learn: Quality preschools for California in the 21st century*. Sacramento, CA: California Department of Education.

U.S. Department of Education. (1997a). *Digest of education statistics: 1997*. Table 12—Educational Attainments of Persons 25 Years Old and Over: April 1990. Washington, DC: Author.

U.S. Department of Education. (1997b). *Digest of education statistics: 1997.* Table 46—Enrollment of 3-, 4-, and 5-year-old children in preprimary programs, by level and control of program and by attendance status: October 1965 to October 1996 (in thousands). Washington, DC: Author.

U.S. Department of Education. (1997c). *Digest of education statistics: 1997.* Table 168—Current Expenditure Per Pupil in Average Daily Attendance in Public Elementary and Secondary Schools by State: 1959–1960 to 1994–1995. Washington, DC: Author.

Watson, C. (1994, June 26). Has the gamble paid off? *Atlanta Journal and Constitution,* p. D1.

White, B. (1996, February 8). Schrenko backs up on Pre-K controversy; school chief admits anti-bias material never part of the Pre-K program," *Atlanta Journal and Constitution,* p. B1.

Whitebook, M., Howes, C., & Phillips, D. (1989). *Who cares? Child care teachers and the quality of care in America: Final report of the National Child Care Staffing Study.* Oakland, CA: Child Care Employee Project.

Wilgoren, J. (2000, February 23). Secretary of Education proposes that teachers work all the year. *The New York Times,* p. A19.

Wood, R., & Griffiths, M. (1998). The acquisition, development and maintenance of lottery and scratchcard gambling in adolescence. *Journal of Adolescence, 21*(3), 265–273.

Wooten, J. (1989, January 18). Funding education and state lottery are unrelated. *Atlanta Journal and Constitution,* p. A14.

Yoshikawa, H. (1994). Prevention as cumulative protection: Effects of early family support and education on chronic delinquency and its risks. *Psychological Bulletin, 115,* 28–54.

Zigler, E., & Styfco, S. (1993). Using research and theory to justify and inform Head Start expansion. *Society for Research in Child Development Social Policy Report, 7,* 2.

# Chapter 4

# Child Care Quality and Children's Success at School

*Deborah Lowe Vandell and Kim M. Pierce*

Major changes in the care of young children have clearly occurred in the United States during the past half century. The present norm, in contrast to the norm 50 years ago, is for children to accumulate substantial nonparental child care experience prior to the start of elementary school. Almost 60% of preschool children (5 years or younger) are now in nonparental care on a regular basis (Hofferth et al.,1998). Child care is especially common by the late preschool years, when 77% of 4-year-olds and 84% of 5-year-olds are reported to be in nonparental care on a regular basis. This care occurs in a variety of settings, including community-based child care centers, Head Start programs, and family day care homes.

Several recent studies have found the quality of these care settings to be highly variable. For example, the National Institutes of Child Health and Human Development (NICHD) Early Child Care Research Network (2000a) assessed child care quality across the gamut of arrangements for children who were 3 years and younger. They observed that 8% of the settings were of poor quality, 53% were fair quality, 30% were good quality, and only 9% were excellent. Similarly, the Cost, Quality, and Outcomes of Child Care Study reported that 11% of center-based care for older preschoolers was poor in quality, 65% was medium quality, and 24% was high quality (Peisner-Feinberg et al., 1999). It is within this ecological context of widespread reliance on child care of variable quality that questions about contemporary child care have been framed. Researchers and policy makers have asked whether children's success at school is related to their earlier participation in child care of varying quality. As is apparent in the review that follows, a number of recent research studies can inform this question.

## Conceptual Framework

In considering the research evidence regarding child care quality, we are guided by the conceptual framework presented in Figure 4.1. Quality is conceptualized in terms of structural-regulable characteristics and child care processes. Structural-regulable characteristics are aspects of child care settings such as group size, child-adult ratio, caregiver education, and caregiver training that potentially are subject to regulation by communities or states. Child care processes are the experiences that children have in their care settings, including their interactions with caregivers and peers and their opportunities to participate in different activities. In the sections that follow, available research is used to evaluate the three propositions delineated in Figure 4.1: (a) that process quality predicts children's educational success, (b) that structural-regulable characteristics predict children's educational success, and (c) that structural-regulable characteristics predict process quality. Diverse indicators of children's subsequent educational success are considered: cognitive and preacademic skills, language skills, and social competence as positive indicators, and behavior problems as a negative indicator. Surveys of teachers and school administrators concur with empirical research that these areas are building blocks for success at school (Alexander & Entwisle, 1988; Johnson et al.,1995; Kagan et al., 1995; Knudsen-Lindauer & Harris, 1989; Lewit & Baker, 1995).

As indicated in Figure 4.1, questions about the effects of child care quality are considered after controlling for the characteristics of the families who use particular arrangements. Controlling for family characteristics is necessary because child care choices are not random. Parents who have higher incomes and more education are more likely than parents who have less income and education to place their children in care arrangements that have lower child–adult ratios and better trained teachers (NICHD Early Child Care Research Network, 1999a). Children whose mothers are more sensitive to their needs tend to be placed in child care arrangements that offer more sensitive and positive caregiving (NICHD Early Child Care Research Network, 1999b). Children whose home environments are cognitively stimulating are more likely to attend cognitively stimulating child care (NICHD Early

FIGURE 4.1. A Conceptual Model of Relations Between Child Care
Quality and Children's Educational Success

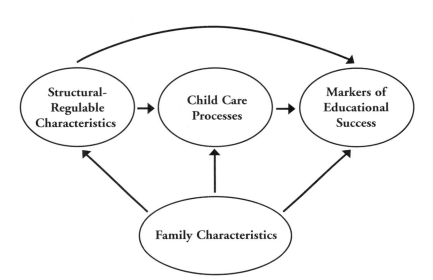

Child Care Research Network, in press-b). Because these family characteristics—income, parental education, maternal sensitivity, stimulating and supportive home environments—are predictors of many child outcomes, they represent significant confounding factors in studies of the effects of child care quality on children's adjustment. The concern is that putative effects of child care quality are actually family effects. In order to address this concern, it has become standard practice for researchers to identify and then to control family characteristics statistically. In the review that follows, studies are reported in which family selection effects are controlled.

## Are There Meaningful Relations Between Process Quality and Markers of Educational Success?

Several reliable measures of process quality have been developed. Some process measures evaluate experiences across several areas and then combine ratings of these experiences into global scores. The Early Childhood Environment Rating Scale (ECERS; Harms & Clifford, 1980), for example, combines ratings from seven areas—personal care routines, furnishings, language reasoning experiences, motor activities, creative activities, social development, and staff needs—into an overall evaluation of program quality. Other process quality measures such as the Observational Record of the Caregiving Environment (ORCE; NICHD Early Child Care Research Network, 1996, 2000a) focus on specific aspects of the child care environment, such as caregivers' behaviors with individual children. A high positive caregiving score on the ORCE indicates a caregiver that is sensitive and responsive to the child's needs, warm and positive, cognitively stimulating, and not detached or hostile.

In his comprehensive review published in the *Handbook of Child Psychology*, Lamb (1998) examined studies of relations between process quality measures and children's developmental outcomes. With respect to infant care, he concluded, "High-quality day care from infancy clearly has positive effects on children's intellectual, verbal, and cognitive development, especially when children would otherwise experience impoverished and relatively unstimulating home environments. Care of unknown quality may have deleterious effects" (p. 104). In terms of care for older preschool children, Lamb offered that "Center-based day care, presumably of high quality, can have positive effects on children's intellectual development, regardless of family background, and does not seem to have negative effects on any groups of children" (p. 110).

Lamb's view is not shared by all child care researchers, however. In the same year that Lamb's chapter was published, Scarr (1998) published a paper in the *American Psychologist* that presented a decidedly different conclusion: "Widely varying qualities of child care have been shown to have only small effects on children's concurrent development and no demonstrated long term impact, except for disadvantaged children" (p. 95). Scarr based her conclusion on what she perceived to be serious shortcomings of child care research: failures to control adequately for family selection factors and failures to document long-term relations between early child care quality and subsequent child functioning.

Not surprisingly, Scarr's views were heavily influenced by her own research conducted in Bermuda and in the United States. In her initial work conducted in Bermuda in collaboration with Kathleen McCartney and Deborah Phillips, concurrent associations were reported between process quality as measured by the ECERS and child developmental outcomes. In particular, overall quality in nine child care centers correlated with children's scores on standardized cognitive and language tests (McCartney, 1984). Children who attended higher quality centers, as measured by the ECERS, also were rated as more sociable, considerate, and task oriented than children in poorer quality centers (Phillips, McCartney, & Scarr, 1987). In addition, correlations were found between specific experiences and child performance: Children's language scores were higher when they attended centers in which verbal interactions between children and caregivers were more frequent (McCartney, 1984).

In 1994, Chin-Quee and Scarr published the results of the longitudinal follow-up for 97 of the 166 children in the original Bermuda sample. Teachers rated children's social competence (peer relations and cooperative behavior) and academic achievement when children were in Grades 1 and 2 (Time 2) and Grades 3 and 4 (Time 3). Associations between the quality indicators during the preschool years and social competence at school were tested with hierarchical regressions in which parental values, age of entry into care, and total amount of child care prior to school entry were controlled. In the regressions that predicted academic achievement, maternal education and maternal IQ also were controlled. Neither the ECERS global score nor the specific measures of caregiver language were associated with children's social competence and academic achievement at Time 2 or Time 3.

Although Scarr argues that the Bermuda Study demonstrates that child care quality has minimal (or no) long-term impact on children's development, the results must be interpreted with caution because they are based on child care assessments that were collected at a single point in time. We have no way of knowing how representative the single quality assessment was of the children's cumulative experiences in child care. Such an assessment might be sufficient if care arrangements and quality are stable; a single observation is not adequate if care is unstable or changing. In the Bermuda sample, Chin-Quee and Scarr (1994) reported that half the children experienced one, two, or three arrangements during the intervening period, and half experienced more than three arrangement changes. The absence of significant long-term associations between process quality and children's later adjustment may be the result of the failure of the one-time quality score to reflect the cumulative quality of children's early child care experiences.

Scarr's conclusion of minimal long-term effects of child care quality also is based on a second longitudinal study that was conducted in the United States. Time 1 assessments of child care quality were obtained in 363 classrooms located in 120 child care centers in three states (Georgia, Virginia, Massachusetts). Quality scores were based on teacher-child interaction scores created from items on the ECERS and the ITERS (a version of the ECERS designed for infant/toddler classrooms) and the Assessment Profile (a process measure similar to the ITERS/ECERS). Unlike the Bermuda study in which significant concurrent relations between process quality and child developmental outcomes were found, few concurrent relations were found in the three-state study (McCartney et al., 1997).

For the follow-up component of the three-state study (Deater-Deckard et al., 1996), parents and caregivers/teachers reported children's adjustment four years later for 141 of the original 718 children, when the children were 6 to 8 years old (Time 2). Hierarchical regressions were conducted that controlled for child characteristics (Time 1, child adjustment; Time 2, age and child gender) and family characteristics (socioeconomic status, a composite of parenting stress and low emotional support, maternal harsh discipline practices). In these analyses, the child care quality composite score at Time 1 did not predict changes in children's behavior problems or social withdrawal from Time 1 to Time 2. Given the absence of concurrent relations between process quality and concurrent child adjustment, the lack of significant longitudinal findings is not surprising.

The results from the three-state study also must be interpreted cautiously. The lack of correlation between process quality and child adjustment may reflect measurement limitations. The global measures of process quality had only moderate cross-site reliability: Interobserver agreement was reported to be .58 for the ECERS and .55 for the ITERS (McCartney et al., 1997). Lower relations between process quality and child outcomes would be expected when the measure of process quality is less reliable. A second concern with the three-state longitudinal analyses is the adequacy of the process quality score. Because no information is provided about child care quality after its single assessment, the assessment's reliability as an indicator of the quality of children's experiences in child care is impossible to determine.

Scarr's arguments are important in that they have underscored the value of moving from the identification of concurrent associations between quality and child outcomes to longer term effects of child care quality. It is fortunate that additional longitudinal results have become available since Lamb and Scarr published their reviews. These studies begin to address Scarr's call to move beyond concurrent designs to longitudinal designs. They represent a further advancement in that they consider patterns of child care quality over time by including quality assessments from more than a single year and by focusing on children whose care arrangements were stable.

## NICHD Study of Early Child Care

One comprehensive study that has considered child care quality over time is the NICHD Study of Early Child Care (SECC), an ongoing project being conducted at 10 research sites in the United States. Two or three sites are located in each of the four major geographic areas; the sites are placed in a variety of settings: in large and mid-size cities, suburbs, small towns, and rural areas. Almost 9,000 families were approached in hospitals shortly after their child's birth. One month later, 1,364 families were enrolled in the study, based on a stratified random sampling plan. This sample included children of color (24%), mothers with less than a high school degree (10%), and single mothers (14%). Families were recruited regardless of their child care plans.

Extensive information about the children, the families, and child care was collected during home visits, child care visits, and laboratory assessments. Phone interviews were conducted with mothers every three months in order to track hours and types of child care. Because families were recruited at their child's birth, the sample was not biased by containing only participants who were pleased with their child care.

A major focus of the study was consideration of possible effects of child care quality on children's development. To this end, children in nonmaternal care for 10 or more hours a week were observed during two half-day visits at 6, 15, 24, and 36 months. Caregiver behaviors (sensitivity, detachment, cognitive stimulation, and positive regard) were rated and a composite positive caregiving score was created. The SECC investigators asked if cumulative positive caregiving (the average of positive caregiving scores across all ages at which care was observed) was related to seven child developmental outcomes that were assessed at 36 months (NICHD Early Child Care Research Network, 1999b). School readiness was measured in the laboratory using the Bracken School Readiness Scale (Bracken, 1984), which assesses knowledge of color, letter identification, number/counting, shapes, and comparisons. Expressive and receptive language skills were measured in the laboratory using the Reynell Developmental Language Scales (Reynell, 1991). Mother and caregiver reports of child behavior problems were composite scores created from the Child Behavior Checklist (Achenbach, 1991) and reflected scores from the Adaptive Social Behavior Inventory (Scott, Hogan, & Bauer, 1992). Peer skills were assessed during a videotaped semistructured play session with a friend.

In order to evaluate relations between cumulative positive caregiving and child development, regression analyses were conducted. For these analyses, family factors (maternal education, family income, maternal psychological adjustment, home quality in terms of cognitive stimulation and emotional support as assessed by the Caldwell and Bradley (1984) HOME scale, and observed maternal sensitivity during videotaped mother-child interactions), other child care factors (proportion of time in center care and total hours in care from 3 to 36 months), research site, and child gender were entered as control variables. Cumulative quality during the first three years was related to children's school readiness, expressive language, and receptive language at age 3. These effects were

## TABLE 4.1
### Effect Sizes Associated with Child Developmental Outcomes at 3 Years and Cumulative Child Care Quality, Child Care Hours, and Home Quality

| Developmental domain at 3 yrs | Cumulative child care quality | | Cumulative child care hours | | Cumulative home quality | |
|---|---|---|---|---|---|---|
| | $r$ | $d$ | $r$ | $d$ | $r$ | $d$ |
| School readiness | .14*** | .39*** | .00 | .04 | .25*** | .83*** |
| Expressive language | .14*** | .44*** | .00 | .04 | .28*** | 1.01*** |
| Receptive language | .09*** | .28* | .06 | .01 | .19*** | .71*** |
| Behavior problems (mother) | −.03 | −.14 | .05 | .08 | −.06 | −.10 |
| Behavior problems (caregiver) | −.06 | −.25 | .04 | .12 | −.15*** | −.56*** |
| Peer skills | −.04 | −.05 | .06 | .06 | .17*** | .57*** |

*Note:* From *Effect Sizes from the NICHD Study of Early Child Care,* by NICHD Early Child Care Research Network, 1999b. Partial *r*s associated with child care quality were obtained from regression analyses that controlled for family factors (maternal education, family income, maternal psychological adjustment, observed home quality, observed maternal sensitivity), other child care factors (cumulative time periods in center care, cumulative child care hours), research site, and child gender. Partial *r*s associated with child care hours were determined in comparable regressions that controlled for child care quality in addition to the other covariates. Partial rs for home quality were determined after controlling for child care hours and quality in addition to the other covariates. *d* statistics were obtained from MANCOVA analyses that contrasted children who experienced the highest and lowest quartiles of child care quality, child care hours, and home quality, controlling for the same covariates.

$^*p < .05.$ $^{***}p < .001.$

evident for analyses conducted for all children who were observed in care and for children in the top and bottom quartiles of quality (see Table 4.1). Not surprisingly, effect sizes in those two quartiles were larger than the partial correlation coefficients obtained in the analyses that included all children.

One way of evaluating the magnitude of these findings is to compare them to other obtained effects (McCartney & Rosenthal, 2000). To this end, the SECC investigators conducted parallel analyses that tested relations between quality of the home environment during the first 3 years and the child developmental outcomes, and between child care hours during the first 3 years and the child outcomes. Table 4.1 shows the effect sizes computed for these parallel analyses. Effects associated with quality of the home environment (the cumulative composite scores created from the HOME scale and the mother-child interaction rating) were roughly twice the size of the child care quality effects. Effects associated with child care hours were substantially smaller than effects associated with child care quality. Thus it appears that effects of child care quality assessed longitudinally to age 3 years were neither huge nor trivial, but were large enough to be meaningful.

### A Second Longitudinal Study: The Otitis Media Study

A second standard by which to judge effects is replicability (McCartney & Rosenthal, 2000). Replicated findings, even if they are not large, can signal effects of some importance. It is notable, then, that results from a second recent longitudinal study are consistent with those reported in the SECC. Burchinal et al. (2000) tested effects of process quality on children's cognitive and language development at ages 12, 24, and 36 months. Eighty-nine infants (aged 4 to 9 months) initially were enrolled in a study of the effects of middle-ear infections (otitis media) on children's development. The children attended 27 child care centers that were rated annually with the ITERS or ECERS.

Hierarchical linear models were tested in which the annual observations of classroom quality were used to predict children's adjustment outcomes. Higher quality child care over time was associated with better cognitive development, better receptive and expressive language skills, and better functional communication skills over time, after controlling for child gender, family poverty status, and the quality of the home environment.

A significant limitation of the analyses reported by both the SECC and Burchinal et al. (2000) was that children were studied only to age 3 years. Thus, it is not clear if early differences in children's adjustment associated with child care quality are harbingers of later differences or if these differences dissipate by the time children enter grade school. As additional findings from these ongoing investigations become available, they should help to identify conditions under which early child care quality differences continue to be associated with children's development over time.

### Cost, Quality, and Outcomes of Child Care Study

A third project—the Cost, Quality, and Outcomes of Child Care Study (CQO; Peisner-Feinberg et al., 1999)—asked whether effects of child care quality on child adjustment continue to be in evidence in the early grade school years. Initiated in 1993, the CQO was conducted in four states (California, Colorado, Connecticut, and North Carolina). The initial sample consisted of 579 children (30% ethnic minority) who were enrolled in 183 preschool classrooms. At the start of the study, the children were in their next-to-last year of child care before entering school. Classrooms were observed and rated for quality of the classroom environment, teacher sensitivity, and teaching style (didactic vs. child centered). These quality indicators were combined into a single process quality composite. Children were followed through two years of child care and the first three years of school (kindergarten through second grade) and completed tests of receptive language ability, reading ability, and math skills. Child care staff and schoolteachers rated the children's cognitive and attention skills, sociability, and problem behaviors yearly.

Longitudinal hierarchical linear model analyses tested relations between the child care quality composite collected during the first year (Time 1) and children's developmental outcomes through second grade. In all analyses, selection factors (maternal education, child's gender and ethnicity) were controlled statistically. Children who were enrolled in high-quality child care classrooms demonstrated better receptive language skills. Effect sizes for receptive language were moderate for the preschool period (.60 and .51 for the two years preceding school entry), more modest in kindergarten (.30), and not significant in second grade. Child care quality also was related to children's math skills: Children who were enrolled in higher quality child care classrooms demonstrated better math skills prior to school entry, in kindergarten, and in second grade, with modest effect sizes across the years (.20 to .29). This relationship was stronger for children whose mothers had less education. Relations between child care quality and children's math skills were maintained even when quality of the elementary school classroom in kindergarten and second grade was controlled.

### Conclusions

The results of three recent longitudinal studies are consistent with the point of view articulated by Lamb (1998), that high-quality child care can have positive effects on children's development in several domains. A strength of all three of these recent investigations is that the quality of children's experiences in child care and/or school classrooms was assessed at several ages, rather than a single point in time.

## Are There Meaningful Associations Between Structural-Regulable Factors and Children's Developmental Outcomes?

As indicated on Figure 4.1, child care researchers also have considered relations between structural-regulable characteristics and child outcomes. The seminal National Day Care Study (Ruopp et al., 1979) addressed this question by studying children attending child care centers in Atlanta, Detroit, and Seattle. As part of the study, a clinical trial was conducted in which 3- and 4-year-olds were randomly assigned to 29 preschool classrooms that varied by group size, child-staff ratio, and teacher education and training. Child behaviors were assessed at baseline and 9 months later. Children assigned to classrooms with fewer children obtained greater gains on measures of receptive language, general knowledge, cooperative behavior, and verbal initiations, and exhibited less hostility and conflict in their interactions with others than did children assigned to classrooms with larger numbers of children. Children whose assigned teachers had more education and training achieved greater gains in cooperative behavior, task persistence, and school readiness than did children whose teachers had less education and training.

Other studies considered relations between structural-regulable features of child care and child development over longer time periods. Howes (1988), for example, examined structural-regulable factors at three years in relation to children's first-grade adjustment. Quality in 81 child care settings was defined in terms of meeting five specified standards: teacher training in child development, child–adult ratio of 8:1 or less, group size of fewer than 25 children, a planned curriculum, and adequate physical space. During the intervening period, the 87 children attended the same university lab school, meaning that they experienced classes with the same or similar structural-regulable characteristics. In analyses that controlled for family selection (maternal work status, family structure, and maternal education), Howes determined that children whose early care (prior to enrollment in the university school) had met more of the structural-regulable standards had fewer behavior problems and better work habits according to their first-grade teachers, in comparison to children whose prior child care had met fewer standards. Additionally, boys (but not girls) had better academic performance in first grade when their early child care programs had met more of the standards.

## Criticism of Structural-Regulable Factors as Predictors of Outcomes

Blau (1999) has been critical of much of the prior research that has examined associations between structural-regulable factors and child developmental outcomes. Blau argues that these studies were flawed because they were based on small nonrepresentative samples, failed to control adequately for family factors, failed to take into sufficient account relations between different child care features, and were based on "uninterpretable" composites. In an effort to address these perceived limitations, Blau used data from the National Longitudinal Survey of Youth (NLSY) to consider three structural-regulable characteristics (group size, child-adult ratio, and caregiver training) in relation to child developmental outcomes.

The NLSY is an ongoing survey of a nationally representative sample of 12,652 youth who were 14–21 years old at the beginning of the study in 1979. Beginning in 1986, information about children of the female respondents was collected. Mothers also reported information about primary child care arrangements—the number of children cared for in the group, the number of adult care providers in the arrangement, and whether the main caregiver had specialized training in early childhood education or child development. Blau averaged these maternal reports to create structural-regulable scores for child care from birth to 2 years and from 3 to 5 years. These scores were examined in relation to children's developmental outcomes. Children completed the Peabody Picture Vocabulary Test (PPVT), a measure of receptive language skills, beginning at 3 years old. Mothers reported on children's behavior problems beginning at 4 years. At 5 years or older, children completed math and reading subscales of the Peabody Individual Achievement Test (PIAT).

Simple correlations revealed statistically significant but small correlations between mothers' reports of caregiver training when the children were in infant/toddler care and the children's later performance. Children whose mothers reported that their caregivers had more specialized training obtained higher math and receptive language scores. When type of care was controlled, these associations continued to be significant. Blau then asked if caregiving training, group size, and child–adult ratio were uniquely associated with child performance. Regression models were tested that included 64 child care factors (e.g., number of arrangements, hours per week in care, months per year in care, paid cash for care, cost of care, center care, family day care home, relative care) and family factors (e.g., child gender, cognitive stimulation, emotional support, Latino ethnicity, African American ethnicity, grandmother worked when mother was 14, mother's education, grandmother's education, fraction of mother's preschool years her mother was present, fraction of mother's high school years her father was present, month of pregnancy in which mother first received prenatal care, child's birth order, Catholic, child received well-care visit in first quarter, mother's age, mother's age at birth of child, siblings in various age groups, fraction of pregnancy during which mother worked). In ordinary least squares regression analyses, relations between maternal reports of caregiver training and children's math and receptive language scores were no longer evident when these other variables were controlled. Blau (1999) concluded, "There seems to be little association on average between child care inputs experienced during the first three years of life and subsequent child development, controlling for family background and the home environment" (p. 805).

## A Response to the Criticism of Structural-Regulable Factors as Predictors of Outcomes

We believe that Blau's conclusion is not warranted for several reasons. First, the lack of findings may be the result of measurement problems associated with maternal reports, especially retrospective reports, of group size, ratio, and caregiver training. If the maternal reports of structural-caregiver characteristics are unreliable, then obtained associations are likely to be reduced and "real" effects may go undetected. Evidence from other data sets indicates that concurrent maternal reports of group size and child-adult ratio are, at best, only moderately reliable. In the NICHD Study of Early Child Care, for example, the correlation between concurrent caregiver and mother reports of group size was .55 on average (range = .51 to .63 for interviews conducted at 6, 15, 24, and 36 months). The correlation between concurrent maternal and caregiver reports of child-adult ratio in the NICHD Study was lower, .33 on average (range = .27 to .42). Maternal retrospective reports of group size and ratio appear to be considerably less reliable. Near-zero correlations were obtained between observational assessments of group size and child-adult ratio when children were age 4 years (Vandell & Powers, 1983) and maternal retrospective reports of these same structural variables four years later (Vandell, Henderson, & Wilson, 1988). There are no available data, to our knowledge, from which the accuracy of maternal reports of caregiver training can be evaluated. We suspect, based on our own personal experiences, that most mothers do not know about their caregivers' training. Taken together, serious questions about the quality of the mother-report data can be raised. Such measurement problems would result in an underestimation of effects of structural-caregiver characteristics.

In addition to problems in measurement, Blau considered some very long time lags between child care quality and child outcomes. Child outcomes were assessed a minimum of two years after mothers reported structural-regulable features, with an average of a five-year lag. There are indications in Blau's report that associations were evident for shorter, but not longer, lags. For example, significant relations were found between child–adult ratios and caregiver training during the first 3 years and children's behavioral adjustment and math performance for those children who were less than 9 years of age. Significant relations were not found for children who were older than 9 years. It also is the case that Blau detected relations between structural-regulable scores during the preschool period (3–5 years) and children's later adjustment. Within this somewhat briefer time lag, smaller group sizes were associated with better math, reading, and language performance, and better child-staff ratios were associated with fewer behavior problems.

A third factor that may have minimized effects was Blau's strategy of isolating structural-regulable factors and examining them as unique and independent predictors. Although such an approach makes sense as a rigorous academic exercise, it does not take into account that structural-regulable factors occur in combination in the real world. Because of collinearity between factors, individual coefficients may be reduced and unstable.

Other approaches to examining structural-regulable factors include looking at the factors in combinations that are common in child care settings, an approach used in the Howes (1988) study described above. Still other studies have focused on an individual factor approach, in which each factor is examined in separate analytic models. Both approaches avoid the artificiality of identifying unique variance when individual factors are, in fact, intercorrelated in child care settings.

The NICHD Study of Early Child Care examined concurrent relations between structural-regulable factors and child outcomes using both the combination and individual factor approaches (NICHD Early Child Care Research Network, 1999a). These analyses focused on 163 children at 24 months and 250 children at 36 months who were enrolled in child care centers. Four structural-regulable factors were assessed in relation to guidelines recommended by the American Public Health Association: child–staff ratio (3:1 in infant/toddler rooms and 7:1 in preschool rooms), group size (6–8 in infant toddler rooms, 14 in toddler rooms), caregiver specialized training with certification or a college degree in child development or early childhood education, and caregiver formal education (some college courses). At 24 months, 10% of child care classrooms met all four standards, whereas 34% of the classrooms at 36 months did so. Children who attended centers that met more of the recommended guidelines had fewer behavior problems at 24 and 36 months, and higher school readiness and language comprehension scores at 36 months, even after controlling for family income-to-needs and observed maternal sensitivity. There were significant linear trends in the associations between the number of recommended standards that were met and children's concurrent adjustment. Threshold effects were not evident: When children attended classrooms that met more standards, their cognitive, language, and social development was better than when they attended classrooms meeting fewer standards.

Child adjustment also was related to enrollment in classrooms that met specific individual standards. At 24 months, children displayed fewer behavior problems and more positive social behaviors when centers met the recommended child-adult ratio. At 36 months, children exhibited fewer behavior problems and obtained higher school readiness and language comprehension scores when caregivers had specialized training or more formal education.

Burchinal et al. (2000) have reported longitudinal findings using the individual factor approach. Children exhibited better receptive language and functional communication skills over time when enrolled in classrooms that met recommended guidelines for child-staff ratios, even after controlling for gender, family poverty, and home quality. Caregiver education also predicted children's adjustment, but only for girls: Girls whose caregivers had at least 14 years of education evinced better cognitive and receptive language skills over time than girls whose caregivers had fewer than 14 years of education.

### Conclusions

Structural-regulable characteristics, although more distal than process quality indicators to children's experiences in child care, have been shown to be associated with children's academic, cognitive, and social development. Smaller group sizes and child–caregiver ratios, and more caregiver training and education, appear to have positive effects on these important developmental outcomes. Future work might consider threshold levels for these child care characteristics to ascertain the point at which further improvements in structural-regulable quality do not yield additional developmental benefits for children.

## Are There Relations Between Structural-Regulable Factors and Process Quality?

As indicated in Figure 4.1, the third set of relations is between structural-regulable factors and process quality. If such relations are identified, they may illuminate ways by which process quality can be improved. In his chapter in the *Handbook of Child Psychology*, Lamb (1998) considered findings from 20 studies and concluded that "there is substantial evidence that scores on diverse structural and process indices of quality are intercorrelated" (p. 89). These studies included the National Day Care Study, in which lower child–staff ratios were associated with children engaging in more creative, verbal, and cooperative activities (Ruopp et al., 1979), and the Child Care Staffing Study, in which lower ratios were associated with more sensitive, less harsh, and less detached caregiver behavior (Howes et al., 1992).

The NICHD Study of Early Child Care (NICHD Early Child Care Research Network, 1996, 2000a) also has considered this issue using a broader range of child care settings, including centers, child care homes, nannies, and grandparents. Consistent associations between structural-regulable features and process quality were obtained for observations conducted when children were 6, 15, 24, and 36 months of age. Smaller group sizes and lower child–adult ratios were associated with more positive caregiving behaviors. Caregivers with more education and/or more training were observed to offer more positive caregiving than caregivers with less education and less training. These relations were evident in both simple correlations and regression analyses that took into account multiple factors simultaneously.

## *Unobserved Determinants?*

Blau (2000) has cautioned that much of the research evidence pertaining to structural-regulable factors and process quality is problematic because investigators have failed to account for additional observed and unobserved determinants of child care quality that might be confounded with group size, child–adult ratio, caregiver education, and caregiver training. These additional factors, he argues, might include center policies, caregiver pay and benefits, curriculum, leadership skills of the director, and the energy and motivation of the caregivers. To address this perceived shortcoming, Blau reanalyzed data collected by the Cost, Quality, and Outcomes Study. In his first set of analyses, Blau conducted regressions to determine if individual structural-regulable features were associated with process quality when other factors (teacher, parent, and center characteristics) were controlled. His findings were consistent with those of other reports: When child-adult ratios were larger, process quality as measured by the ITERS or ECERS tended to be lower. When caregivers had attended college or training workshops, or when caregivers had college degrees in fields related to child care, ECERS scores tended to be higher.

### The Fixed-Effects Model

Blau then tested relations between structural-regulable characteristics and process quality using a much more stringent fixed-effects model that included center as a control variable. This fixed-effects approach was possible because, typically, two classrooms were observed in each center. In centers in which there were both infants and preschoolers, one classroom of each age was observed. In centers serving only preschoolers, two preschool classrooms were selected randomly. With both specific center and type of classroom (infant vs. preschool) controlled statistically, relations between structural-regulable characteristics and process quality were reduced. Blau interprets this reduction to mean that unobserved center characteristics play a larger role than structural-regulable factors do in process quality variations. Our concern, however, is that the center fixed-effects control used by Blau is inappropriate. As Blau himself noted, this approach requires variability in structural-regulable factors within a given center. It is unlikely that classrooms in the same center are highly variable in terms of caregiver training, ratio, or group size, especially given that the regression model also controlled for type of classroom (infant/toddler or not). Thus, the inclusion of center as a control variable will result in an underestimate of associations.

### Conclusions

Significant associations have been found between structural-regulable characteristics of child care settings and the quality of care that children receive. Process quality is likely to be higher when group sizes and child-adult ratios are smaller and when caregivers are more highly educated and more highly trained. These associations suggest one approach that might be taken to improve process quality.

## Summary and Recommendations

Some scholars recently have challenged the view that child care quality is associated with meaningful differences in children's developmental outcomes. A number of specific criticisms of prior research have been raised, including that investigators have failed to document long-term effects within community-based samples and have failed to include appropriate statistical controls in their analyses. This chapter summarizes findings from several recent research reports that sought to address these problems. These reports considered child care quality in relation to children's longer term performance as well as concurrent performance. These studies indicate that both structural-regulable and process quality are related to children's readiness for school. Children whose child care meets higher structural-regulable standards are more likely to demonstrate better cognitive and language skills and better behavioral adjustment than do children whose child care does not meet these standards. Stronger, more robust associations are evident between process quality and child developmental outcomes. All of these adjustment indicators play a role in children's readiness to learn and ability to profit from instruction. Furthermore, recent longitudinal research demonstrates that child care quality during the infant and preschool years has positive effects on children's school performance and academic progress into the early elementary years.

Many challenges remain in the study of the effects of child care quality variations on children's educational success. One area that has just started to receive attention is the quality of the school classroom and how variations in this environment moderate the long-term influence of child care quality on children's development. Future research is needed to consider the effects of child care quality over time in conjunction with the quality of school classroom environments that children experience subsequent to child care.

A second challenge is determining when and how to control appropriately for prior child adjustment in examinations of long-term effects of child care quality on children's development. Some researchers have argued that stronger tests of child care quality can be made if controls for children's prior adjustment are included in the tests. These controls are difficult to achieve because children typically begin child care during their first year of life, prior to the time that robust and reliable measures of child cognitive, language, and social adjustment can be administered. Using measures of child adjustment collected at some later period after substantial child care experience has accrued is problematic because these measures may well be a reflection of the effects of quality to that point. By using child adjustment measures that may well be affected by quality as controls, we may eliminate (or at least minimize) the very quality effects that are of interest.

Another research challenge is the explicit test of the mediational model delineated in Figure 4.1. To date, individual studies have considered three sets of relations: those between structural-regulable features and process quality, those between structural-regulable features and child outcomes, and those between process quality and child outcomes. We lack, however, explicit tests of the proposition that structural-regulable factors exert their influence by altering the quality of the care provided to children. Tests of a full mediation model should be conducted, the results of which may allow us to draw firmer conclusions about how best to improve child care quality so that all children can benefit developmentally from their experiences in these settings.

## Acknowledgments

This chapter was completed while the authors received support from the National Institutes of Child Health and Human Development, Grant HD27040.

## References

Achenbach, T. M. (1991). *Manual for the Child Behavior Checklist/4-18 and 1991 Profile.* Burlington: University of Vermont Department of Psychiatry.

Alexander, K. L., & Entwisle, D. R. (1988). Achievement in the first 2 years of school: Patterns and processes. *Monographs of the Society for Research in Child Development, 53*(2, Serial No. 218).

Blau, D. M. (1999). The effects of child care characteristics on child development. *Journal of Human Resources, 34,* 786–822.

Blau, D. M. (2000). The production of quality in child care centers: Another look. *Applied Developmental Sciences, 4,* 136–148.

Bracken, B. A. (1984). *Bracken Basic Concept Scales.* San Antonio, TX: Psychological Corporation.

Burchinal, M. R., Roberts, J. E., Riggins, R., Jr., Zeisel, S. A., Neebe, E., & Bryant, D. (2000). Relating quality of center-based child care to early cognitive and language development longitudinally. *Child Development, 71,* 339–357.

Caldwell, B. M., & Bradley, R. H. (1984). *Home observation for measurement of the environment.* Little Rock: University of Arkansas.

Chin-Quee, D. S., & Scarr, S. (1994). Lack of early child care effects on school-age children's social competence and academic achievement. *Early Development and Parenting, 3,* 103–112.

Deater-Deckard, K., Pinkerton, R., & Scarr, S. (1996). Child care quality and children's behavioral adjustment: A four-year longitudinal study. *Journal of Child Psychology and Psychiatry, 37,* 937–948.

Harms, T., & Clifford, R. M. (1980). *Early Childhood Environment Rating Scale.* New York: Teachers College Press.

Hofferth, S. L., Shauman, K. A., Henke, R. R., & West, J. (1998). *Characteristics of children's early care and education programs: Data from the 1995 National Household Education Survey* (Report No. 98-128). Washington, DC: U.S. Department of Education, National Center for Education Statistics.

Howes, C. (1988). Relations between early child care and schooling. *Developmental Psychology, 24,* 53–57.

Howes, C., Phillips, D. A., & Whitebook, M. (1992). Thresholds of quality: Implications for the social development of children in center-based child care. *Child Development, 63,* 449–460.

Johnson, L. J., Gallagher, R. J., Cook, M., & Wong, P. (1995). Critical skills for kindergarten: Perceptions from kindergarten teachers. *Journal of Early Intervention, 19,* 315–349.

Kagan, S. L., Moore, E., & Bredekamp, S. (Eds.). (1995). *Reconsidering children's early development and learning: Toward common views and vocabulary.* Washington, DC: National Education Goals Panel.

Knudsen-Lindauer, S. L., & Harris, K. (1989). Priorities for kindergarten curricula: Views of parents and teachers. *Journal of Research in Childhood Education, 4,* 51–61.

Lamb, M. E. (1998). Nonparental child care: Context, quality, correlates, and consequences. In W. Damon, I. E. Sigel, & K. A. Renninger (Eds.), *Handbook of child psychology: Vol. 4. Child psychology in practice* (pp. 73–133). New York: Wiley.

Lewit, E. M., & Baker, L. S. (1995). School readiness. *The Future of Children, 5,* 128–139.

McCartney, K. (1984). Effects of quality of day care environment on children's language development. *Developmental Psychology, 20,* 244–260.

McCartney, K., & Rosenthal, R. (2000). Effect size, practical importance, and social policy for children. *Child Development, 71,* 173–180.

McCartney, K., Scarr, S., Rocheleau, A., Phillips, D., Abbott-Shim, M., Eisenberg, M., Keefe, N., Rosenthal, S., & Ruh, J. (1997). Teacher-child interaction and child-care auspices as predictors of social outcomes in infants, toddlers, and preschoolers. *Merrill-Palmer Quarterly, 43,* 426–450.

NICHD Early Child Care Research Network (1996). Characteristics of infant child care: Factors contributing to positive caregiving. *Early Childhood Research Quarterly, 11,* 269–306.

NICHD Early Child Care Research Network (1999a). Child outcomes when child care center classes meet recommended standards for quality. *American Journal of Public Health, 89,* 1072–1077.

NICHD Early Child Care Research Network (1999b, April). *Effect sizes from the NICHD Study of Early Child Care.* Paper presented at the biennial meeting of the Society for Research in Child Development, Albuquerque, NM.

NICHD Early Child Care Research Network (2000a). Characteristics and quality of child care for toddlers and preschoolers. *Applied Developmental Sciences, 4,* 116–135.

NICHD Early Child Care Research Network (2000b). The relation of child care to cognitive and language development. *Child Development, 71,* 960–980.

Peisner-Feinberg, E. S., Burchinal, M. R., Clifford, R. M., Culkin, M. L., Howes, C., Kagan, S. L., Yazejian, N., Byler, P., Rustici, J., & Zelazo, J. (1999). *The children of the Cost, Quality, and Outcomes Study go to school: Technical report.* Chapel Hill: Frank Porter Graham Child Development Center, University of North Carolina.

Phillips, D., McCartney, K., & Scarr, S. (1987). Child-care quality and children's social development. *Developmental Psychology, 23,* 537–543.

Reynell, J. (1991). *Reynell Developmental Language Scales.* Los Angeles, CA: Western Psychological Service.

Ruopp, R., Travers, J., Glantz, F., & Coelen, C. (1979). *Children at the center: Final report of the National Day Care Study.* Cambridge, MA: Abt Associates.

Scarr, S. (1998). American child care today. *American Psychologist, 53,* 95–108.

Scott, K. G., Hogan, A., & Bauer, C. (1992). The Adaptive Social Behavior Inventory (ASBI): A new assessment of social competence in high risk 3-year-olds. *Journal of Psychoeducational Assessment, 10,* 230–239.

Vandell, D. L., Henderson, V. K., & Wilson, K. S. (1988). A longitudinal study of children with day-care experiences of varying quality. *Child Development, 59,* 1286–1292.

Vandell, D. L., & Powers, C. P. (1983). Day care quality and children's free play activities. *American Journal of Orthopsychiatry, 53,* 493–500.

# PART II

## Early School-Age Programs and Practices

# Chapter 5

# Kindergarten in the 21st Century

*Elizabeth M. Graue*

Kindergarten is both a beginning and an ending. It is the end of a particular type of parental control and the beginning of what many would call "real school." Kindergarten is a bridge from early to elementary school, from home to school, from the role of child to the role of student. This bridge is complex, framed emotionally, politically, socially, and psychologically. Its practices are filled with ritual, folk wisdom, and solid logic based on development theory. These beliefs and rules for practice shape the interactions among teachers and their students and play a vital role in policymaking related to kindergarten.

## Kindergarten Today

Many of us use our memories of our own or our children's kindergarten and to frame our decisionmaking on what exists and what is appropriate. But kindergartens have changed in substantive ways in the last 25 years, resulting in a curious gap between memory and practice. This gap was captured recently in an article in *Time* magazine entitled "The Kindergarten Grind." It contrasted the warm memories of snack, naptime, and rhythm band, with a competitive, academically oriented boot camp that looks much more like the elementary grades than an early childhood setting. In this section, I provide a brief overview of today's kindergarten, with a focus on the policy-practice connections that impact the activities presented to young children.

### State Policies Related to Kindergarten

Kindergarten is in the unique position of being simultaneously almost universal and merely an option. Ninety-eight percent of all first graders have had prior experience of school by attending kindergarten (Zill et al.,

1995), with attendance virtually expected of all children entering first grade. At the same time, if policies for program provision are an indicator of the instantiation of an institution, then kindergarten is still seen as merely an option. Only 39 states require districts to offer some form of kindergarten program (29 require half-day program offerings, 10 require full-day program availability). Some states require districts to offer both. Seventeen states impose no programming requirements related to kindergarten. A total of 15 states require kindergarten attendance (10 require half-day, 5 require full-day) and a stunning 44 states have no kindergarten attendance requirement at all (National Center for Education Statistics, 1997).

This curious combination of expectation and option sets up some of kindergarten's most thorny dilemmas. Most people assume that kindergarten is a standard part of our educational system. At the same time, we leave open the possibility that parents might choose another year at home for their child. Although kindergarten is a part of our educational consciousness, it also represents our ambivalence about inducting children into formal educational settings. A key concern linked to kindergarten programming is the age at which children are deemed old enough to enter school.

### Kindergarten Entrance Age

Traditionally age 5 is the year of enrollment in kindergarten. But the point in the calendar year at which a child turns 5 determines when he or she will enter kindergarten. In the East and West, children have been younger at school entry than they have been in the Midwest and the South because of winter cutoffs as opposed to fall cutoffs. Thirty years ago children were required to be five by December 1, making the youngest of them 4 years 9 months at the start of the school year. Over time, however, the entrance date used to mark kindergarten entry has shifted subtly. We are now more likely to require a child to be 5 by September 1 (Graue & Shepard, 1992). Indiana distinguishes itself as being the state with the oldest kindergartners, requiring them to be five by June 1 in the year they enter. Only eight of the fifty states include children of age 5 within the range of compulsory attendance for school (National Center for Education Statistics, 1997). Table 5.1 illustrates the variability in current kindergarten entry dates for those states with state legislated entry cutoffs.

This shift to older kindergartners has occurred when growing numbers of preschool children are having out-of-home educational experiences. In 1975, 31.5% of 3- and 4-year-olds attended some kind of preschool program; that number grew to almost 50% in 1996 (National Center for Education Statistics, 1997). In addition, more mothers have been employed outside the home, requiring increases in the availability of day care. At the same time, because of curriculum escalation, the pedagogical approaches used in kindergarten have changed (Shepard & Smith, 1988). The first grade curriculum has slowly migrated into kindergartens, changing its activities and expectations. This bundle of trends has been linked to increased accountability pressures in schools, with a pounding press for performance, even among our youngest students. (Cunningham, 1988; Meisels et al., 1993). In such a social and educational context, forestalling the start of formal education in the form of kindergarten is curious and sensible at the same time.

## Program Configuration

Kindergarten programs are moving from half-day to full-day offerings.[1] Full-day programs are more likely to be offered in low-income than in affluent schools, 55% versus 28% (Love et al., 1992). In 1996, 52% of 5-year-olds were in full-day programs, a fourfold increase from 1965 (National Center for Education Statistics, 1997). In 1993, approximately 54% of kindergarten teachers taught full-day classes, with two-thirds of those teachers working in high-poverty areas (Heaviside, Farris, & Carpenter, 1993).

Kindergarten programming is clearly in transition. More children attend kindergarten, but that experience is changing from a voluntary half-day program to an all but mandated full-day program. Half of all children come to kindergarten with some type of formal schooling as a

TABLE 5.1
State Kindergarten Entrance Dates

| December–January | September10–October 16 | August 31–September 2 | June 1–August 15 |
|---|---|---|---|
| California | Iowa | Alabama | Alaska |
| Connecticut | Kentucky | Arizona | Arkansas |
| District of | Louisiana | Delaware | Indiana |
| Columbia | Maine | Florida | Missouri |
| Hawaii | Montana | Georgia | Puerto Rico |
| Maryland | Nebraska | Idaho | |
| Michigan | Nevada | Illinois | |
| New York | North Carolina | Kansas | |
| Rhode Island | Ohio | Minnesota | |
| Vermont | Tennessee | North Dakota | |
| | Virginia | Oklahoma | |
| | Wyoming | Oregon | |
| | | South Carolina | |
| | | South Dakota | |
| | | Texas | |
| | | Utah | |
| | | Washington | |
| | | West Virginia | |
| | | Wisconsin | |

*Note:* From Education Commission on the States (1997). Clearinghouse Notes. Denver, CO.

foundation, and children entering kindergarten are more likely to be 5 years old or even 6 rather than 4 turning 5. One way of understanding these changes is to examine an idea that is uniquely linked to kindergarten—the notion of readiness. This construct, much argued about, shapes many of our programming and policy decisions.

## Readiness

Readiness for school is a notion widely used in discussions about education in the United States. It is the first of our national education goals, the source of anxiety for many parents, and the target of an array of activities designed by policymakers and educators. And it is the catalyst for a very lucrative industry of test makers, parent literature, and developers of early education materials, experiences, and settings. Given all the concern about readiness, what exactly do we know about it? Common ideas about readiness involve age and skill levels; more recently, educators have begun to extend the idea to include the child's whole learning environment.

Readiness typically connotes an age range when most children are deemed old enough to benefit from formal school experiences. Readiness also connotes a constellation of skills considered precursors to school success. These skills combine a complex of physical/biological maturation, prior experience, and dispositional qualities. For those who focus on skills, the notion of readiness is a threshold needed to guarantee success. Current knowledge about readiness reminds us that it is not a static entity, a single target that all children achieve at one time. Instead, readiness is a process that spans a critical period of early learning and development (Meisels, 1999).

Readiness must also include an environment that promotes education. For those who focus on achieving this environment, that is, a "ready school" (Shore, 1998), discussions focus on policies and practices that help children thrive in the educational environment. The Goal 1 Ready Schools Resource Group, for example, suggests ten Readiness Goals for schools to create the environment most conducive to learning:

1. Smoothing the transition between home and school.
2. Striving for continuity between early care and education programs and elementary schools.
3. Helping children learn and make sense of their complex and exciting world.
4. Committing to the success of every child.

5. Committing to the success of every teacher and every adult who interacts with children during the school day.

6. Introducing or expanding approaches that have been shown to raise achievement.

7. Altering practices and programs if they do not benefit children.

8. Serving children in communities.

9. Taking responsibility for results.

10. Having strong leadership.

From the ready for school perspective, responsibility for readiness rests in inclusive programming that welcomes children and their families into the activities of the school. Exclusionary policies, in which children are deemed either ready or not ready and, therefore, inside or outside the boundaries of pedagogy, are discouraged.

Ideas about readiness are linked to conceptions of children and the options available to children, families, and educators (Graue, 1993a; Shepard & Smith, 1986). It is therefore important to understand how the notions of readiness set contexts for opportunity.

### Parents' Views

Parents, more than teachers, appear to have a checklist approach to readiness. When asked to rate a set of skills as essential/very important to success in school, parents had highly developed images of prerequisite skills. At least 80% of parents focused on social skills such as communication, sharing, enthusiasm, and a sufficient attention span as essential to kindergarten success. At least half felt that more basic academic skills like using pencils, counting, and knowing the ABCs were necessary. These ideas of what a child needs to know in order to succeed are related to parent characteristics, such as educational attainment (National Center for Education Statistics, 1995) and socioeconomic status (Graue, 1993b; Lareau, 1989, 1994). An inverse relationship exists between level of formal education and the degree to which parents feel that particular skills are necessary for readiness: College graduates are less likely than parents with less formal education to expect success to be linked to particular skills.

Does this imply that higher education breeds lower expectation for children? Just the opposite. Middle income professionals are likely to expect schools to adapt to the needs of their children and further assume that they can advocate for services that will promote success (Lareau, 1989). This attitude is less likely for parents with lower levels of income and education, who assume that their children need to be fully prepared for school upon entry. Lower income parents are highly aware of requisite skills for kindergarten success, but are also likely to present their children in kindergarten on the basis of the legislated entry date (Graue, 1993b).

## Teachers' Views

Examinations of public school kindergarten teachers' conceptions about readiness range from large-scale surveys to ethnographic explorations of the interplay of beliefs and practices. These teachers see physical health, good communication skills, and enthusiasm as most essential to school readiness (Heaviside et al., 1993). Least important for school readiness were "skills" that are often seen as academic—problem-solving skills, ability to identify primary colors and shapes, ability to use pencils/paintbrushes, knowledge of the alphabet, or ability to count to 20. Fewer than one in four kindergarten teachers cited these as necessary for school success.

Following the patterns of parents, teachers in low-income schools are more likely than those in more affluent contexts to expect specific academic skills for readiness. In addition, teachers in high-poverty schools and those who teach primarily students of color are more likely to think that children with readiness problems should come to school as soon as they are legally eligible. Mechanisms for enhancing readiness are a curious mixture of maturationist and interventionist views. Virtually all teachers (94%) see readiness as amenable to enhancement by good teaching, and a slightly smaller number (88%) see it as invariably tied to maturation. This apparent contradiction reveals the complexity of readiness: It is nature and nurture at the same time.

Kindergarten teachers' philosophies of readiness shape their practices with young children (Graue, 1993b; Smith & Shepard, 1988). Curriculum, retention practices, and advice about when to enter a child into school are all linked to readiness beliefs. One typology of readiness beliefs has been suggested by Meisels (1999). Table 5.2 provides an overview of how these various conceptualizations position individuals in early education.

Descriptively these categorizations are interesting, but thinking about implementing them raises concerns. Different assumptions about students depend on ideas held about their home life, their ability to learn, and the interventions that might enhance their success. We have different readinesses for different children. Nativist approaches to readiness tend to be applied to children from privileged backgrounds on the assumption that appropriate nurturing of emerging abilities are part of ongoing home activities. In contrast, environmental approaches tend to be used for children living in poverty and for those whose first language is not English. For these children, early intervention is applied on the grounds that the parenting practices supporting the child are inadequate to provide them with the necessary skills for school readiness (Graue, 1992).

What are the implications of different expectations for groups of children beginning kindergarten? Given the patterned nature of the beliefs and practices, one way to examine the differences is in terms of equity. Is it equitable to have different readinesses for different children? Or is it simply a matter of embracing the incredible developmental diversity present in our young children? Concerns about equity would never dictate equal treatment for all children, which would not make sense given the developmental differences that children present to us. What must be equitable are the outcomes that come out of the educational choices we make. It requires an inclusive, or interactionist approach that is process oriented (Meisels, 1999), an approach that locates explanations and possibilities in the intersection of the child and context. It requires the type of thinking that Meisels calls for in his definition of readiness:

> Readiness is not something we wait for and it is not
> something we impose. It is not a within-the-child

**TABLE 5.2**
**Conceptions of Readiness**

| Type | Readiness | Mechanism | Teacher Role |
|---|---|---|---|
| Ideal/Nativist | A level of maturity that allows productive interactions with peers and appropriate attention in the classroom. Development occurs before learning. | Internal maturation supported secondarily by parental support and developmentally targeted opportunities. | Nurture the naturally unfolding maturity but do not attempt to accelerate learning beyond the internally bounded limits. |
| Empiricist/ Environmental | Skills-oriented view in which experiences provide for accumulation of skills absolutely necessary for school success. | Externally driven, with the environment providing the catalyst for readiness. | Identifying needs and generating experiences that will develop readiness skills. |
| Social Constructivist | Shared set of meanings constructed by local participants in the kindergarten experience. | Social and cultural meanings and demands shape readiness. | Social actor holding a particular framework for students. |
| Interactionist | A bidirectional concept focusing on the children's characteristics and material conditions in communities to enhance readiness. | Children's readiness reflects joint contributions of the internal and external forces on development. | Teachers apply well- stated standards for learning through appropriate assessment of performance, formulating plans for instruction from the results of assessment. |

*Note.* Adapted from Meisels, 1999.

phenomenon, nor something specifically outside the
child. Rather, it is the product of a set of educational
decisions that are differentially shaped by the skills,
experiences, and learning opportunities the child has
had and the perspectives and goals of the community, classroom, and teacher. (1999, p. 19)

This conception of readiness is certainly more complex and more
dynamic than those concerning just age, skills levels, or environment, yet
includes all those as well. And it will require more reflexive practices on
the part of teachers, parents, policymakers, and researchers as they search
for ways to enhance child success.

## Delayed Kindergarten Entry

In the 1980s, early childhood educators noticed that increasing numbers
of parents delayed their child's kindergarten entry. Boys born close to the
kindergarten entrance cutoff were seen as good candidates for waiting a
year because they were believed to mature more slowly and would be the
youngest in their kindergarten class. It even developed its own labels—
"holding out" or, more colorfully, "academic redshirting," from the term
used in athletics. Kindergartners are redshirted when parents delay entry
because of concerns about readiness for school.

Some researchers suggest that kindergarten is no longer perceived as
a place to develop readiness; instead, children are expected to be ready at
school entry (Graue, 1993b; Kagan, 1990; Powell, 1995; Shepard,
1990). In addition, changes in kindergarten programming have shifted
what kindergartners are expected to cope with—engaging in abstract
workbook tasks rather than developmentally appropriate activities
(Bredekamp, 1987). This escalated curriculum has made parents and
teachers fearful that young 5-year-olds would fail (Hatch & Freeman,
1988; Smith & Shepard, 1988).

The practice of redshirting has been studied through analysis of
student records (Bellisimo et al., 1995; Brent et al., 1996; Cosden et al.,
1993; Graue & DiPerna, in press; Kundert et al., 1995; May et al., 1995;

McCaig, 1990; Shepard et al., 1989; Spitzer et al., 1995), through long-term interpretive studies (Graue, 1993a, 1993b; Lareau, 1994), and through large scale survey work (Byrd et al., 1997; Graue & DiPerna, in press; Zill et al., 1997). Each of these studies found that substantial numbers of children were coming to school later than legally eligible. Redshirting is more frequent for relatively younger boys (Bellisimo et al., 1995; Brent et al., 1996; Byrd et al., 1997; Graue & DiPerna, in press; May et al., 1995; McCaig, 1990; Shepard et al., 1989; Zill et al., 1995) and affluent families (Bellisimo et al., 1995; Lareau, 1994; Shepard et al., 1989; Zill, 1992).

The profile of the typical redshirt can be gleaned from the depiction of data from a Wisconsin study of redshirting presented in Table 5.3, which illustrates the odds of different entry and promotion patterns given certain child characteristics. Boys are nearly twice as likely as girls to be redshirted and retained.

## Individual Outcomes

There are differences in academic achievement between the oldest and youngest children in primary grades; the youngest typically do slightly less well than the oldest, and in many studies the differences disappear by third grade (Cameron & Wilson,1990; Graue & DiPerna, in press; Morrison et al., 1997; Shepard & Smith, 1986). Younger first graders outperform their age-mates who are a year behind them in school, indicating that entrance age alone is not a risk factor. Schooling effects are larger than age effects (Morrison et al., 1997). Redshirts appear to have an IQ or ability advantage, which when used as a covariate, narrows the differences in achievement between the youngest and oldest children (Cameron & Wilson, 1990; Kundert et al., 1995). In contrast, placement in special education programs occurs at higher rates for redshirts than for their normally entered and promoted peers (Byrd et al., 1997; Graue & DiPerna, in press; May et al., 1995).

Concerns for redshirts are primarily social, with parents hoping to help their child be a good worker and a leader in the class (Graue, 1993a, 1993b; Lareau, 1994). Social outcomes do not appear to favor redshirts,

TABLE 5.3
**Odds-Ratios of Entry and Promotion Interventions in Relation to Normal
Entry and Promotion by Child Characteristics**

|  | Early entry | Redshirt | Retention K-3 |
|---|---|---|---|
| **Race-ethnicity** (vs. Caucasian) |  |  |  |
| **African American** | 1.02** | 1.00 | 1.03 |
| **American Indian** | 0.01 | 1.09 | 0.58 |
| **Asian American** | 1.76 | 0.87 | 1.35 |
| **Hispanic** | 1.5 | 1.40 | 1.78** |
| **Sex** (vs. female) |  |  |  |
| **Male** | 0.43*** | 1.91*** | 1.78*** |
| **Economic status** (vs. not eligible) |  |  |  |
| **Eligible for free/ reduced lunch** | 1.17 | 1.6*** | 3.25*** |
| **Birth quartile** (vs. Fall) |  |  |  |
| **Winter** | 0.20*** | 2.19*** | 2.06** |
| **Spring** | 0.05*** | 3.43*** | 2.65*** |
| **Summer** | 0.04*** | 13.32*** | 4.86*** |

*Note.* From Graue & DiPerna, in press.
*p < .05. **p < .01. ***p < .001.

with self-concept, peer acceptance, and teacher ratings of behavior for oldest and youngest children being about the same (Spitzer et al., 1995). In retrospective and cross-sectional analyses, redshirts fare less well than their peers on measures of behavioral problems (Byrd et al., 1997; Zill et al., 1997). Redshirting has not caused the increased rates of social and emotional difficulty; it has not solved these problems, either.

## Social Influences

When communities embrace redshirting, parents feel pressure to redshirt even the most ready younger boys (Graue, 1993a, 1993b). Parental decision making is quite varied. Some parents make the decision to redshirt even before their child is born, even going so far as to time conception, seeing great advantage to the child being the oldest in the group (Graue, 1993a; Noel & Newman, 1998). Others choose redshirting after being advised by significant others in their lives (Graue, 1993b; Lareau, 1994; Noel & Newman, 1998). There are large differences in the rates of redshirting from neighborhood to neighborhood, with levels ranging from 3%–94% (Graue & DiPerna, in press). It is unlikely that child readiness varies to such a great degree. Instead, social meanings of readiness, which vary from community to community, support entry in one community and delay in another, with limited attention to child characteristics.

Parents often request a more advanced curriculum for their now 6-year-olds when they enter kindergarten (Graue, 1993a). Teachers report dropping many basic kindergarten concepts because their students, as a group, come in knowing more (Graue, 1993b). Shepard (1990) suggests that redshirting may have consequences not only for redshirts themselves but for the students who enter on time:

> To the extent that 6-year-olds help to define kindergarten norms, meeting their needs moves the kindergarten curriculum further away from instruction attuned to the needs of children who have just turned 5. Redshirting obviously increases the age heterogeneity of kindergarten classrooms. And to the extent that the middle class hypothesis is true, it increases the "disadvantage" of normal 5-year-olds from poor families who come to school at 5 years 0 months and are asked to compete with children who are 6 years 3 months old, come from affluent homes, and have three years of Montessori preschool experience. (p. 163)

## *Evaluating the Investment of the "Gift of Time"*

Although public schools cannot deny entrance to legally eligible students, some school personnel advise parents that another year might provide the kind of maturation that will ensure a child's success. They claim that redshirting will help the child avoid troubles adjusting to formal education settings, become a leader who is able to meet the challenges of early schooling academically and socially, and avoid later problems that lead to retention or placement in special education (Uphoff, Gilmore, & Huber, 1986).

But is redshirting a good investment, and have these claims been verified? Redshirting certainly does not come without costs. It requires an additional year of care that is paid for on a cash basis or with lost wages by parents. For this reason, it is an intervention that is only available to families that can afford it. Furthermore, the claims made in favor of redshirting are based on research that does not allow unambiguous comparisons. Studies have not provided initial measures prior to redshirting, so it is difficult to assess the impact of the extra year. Table 5.4 provides a comparison of the assertions made by those who advocate redshirting and empirical support for the assertion.

There is no denying that there are vast differences in the maturity and readiness of children who are eligible for kindergarten. That variability in the developmental dimensions of interest to early educators is staggering. Is redshirting the answer? Developmental variability is an essential consideration in working with children. We should expect it, incorporate it into our programming, and in our most flexible and optimistic moments, celebrate it. Comparing the claims to the evidence, I suggest that redshirting is overapplied as parents and teachers try to reduce developmental variability for the sake of educational similarity. While it would be imprudent to say that no child should delay school entry, it is an egregious error to support the old saying, "When in doubt, hold them out." It makes more sense to say, "When in doubt, support them in every way you can. Provide a developmental curriculum that is appropriate for their needs and strengths. And attend to that very

**TABLE 5.4**
**Does the Evidence Support Redshirting?**

| Claim | Evidence |
|---|---|
| Promotes higher academic achievement provided by an additional year of maturation and learning. | Equal achievement with grade peers (including those children who enter on time but are relatively young), particularly by Grade 3. |
| Creates leaders with social maturity. | Equal teacher ratings of social interaction. Higher than expected incidence of later social-emotional difficulties. |
| Helps avoid later retention in grade. | The extra year provided by redshirting is, for many, a form of retention. In fact, many retention checklists argue against retaining a child who is already overage. The rationale is that the extra year hasn't helped. Therefore, retention is not likely to be chosen for this group. |
| Helps avoid later placements in special education. | Redshirts have a higher than expected referral rate for special education, despite the intervention. |

important social aspect of their development by making it part of the curriculum." Not nearly as catchy, it is nonetheless more inclusive, more equitable, and more responsible in the long run. This approach is one that applies equally to those we might consider eligible for redshirting and the broader kindergarten population. Joining concerns of child and context will provide us much more leverage in our actions on behalf of young children and will help us avoid easy responses to complex questions.

## Conclusion

Kindergartens are changing in subtle and not-so-subtle ways, causing turbulence, resistance, and worry. We are in a transformational period in which we must revisit our goals for kindergarten, articulating what we want children to experience. As early childhood educators, we must reflect on the social and cultural changes that are shaping the kindergarten agenda. Kindergartens must change because the children and families they serve are evolving. We must also link practice in more coherent ways with our developing empirical knowledge base on the effects of educational policies and activities.

As program changes are contemplated, the benefits and costs to individual children, families, teachers, and programs should be contemplated in terms of current conditions rather than memories of days gone by. For example, shifts to full-day programming must be considered in the context of kindergarten's voluntary status. Programs focusing on enhancing readiness must be constructed, recognizing the considerable variability in readiness beliefs and practices, and premised on equity. Finally, we must reconsider the tacit support provided for delay of kindergarten entry, acknowledging that it is an intervention not without costs. Given our murky diagnostic skills, we are not able to know who will benefit from academic redshirting.

Approaches to early education are variably inclusive of diverse children, who present us with an immense range of ability, skill, readiness, maturity, and resources. Our decisions about who is ready, who is mature, and who is competent hold assumptions about the nature of development and our responsibility to educate the children in our care. We need to be more aware and open about those decisions, recognizing our obligations for developing positive outcomes that are fair. If we can manage our way through these challenges, kindergartens will again be an experience in which children can thrive.

## Endnotes

[1] Full day might be construed as a misnomer if you compare a parental work day with a typical elementary school day. A full-day kindergarten typically follows the same schedule as an elementary school program.

## References

Bellisimo, Y., Sacks, C. H., & Mergendoller, J. R. (1995). Changes over time in kindergarten holding out: Parent and school contexts. *Early Childhood Research Quarterly, 10*(2), 205–222.

Bredekamp, S. (1987). *Developmentally appropriate practice in early childhood programs serving children from birth through age 8.* Washington, DC: National Association for the Education of Young Children.

Brent, D., May, D. C., & Kundert, D. K. (1996). The incidence of delayed school entry: A twelve-year review. *Early Education and Development, 7*(2), 121–135.

Byrd, R. S., Weitzman, M., & Auinger, P. (1997). Increased behavior problems associated with delayed school entry and delayed school progress. *Pediatrics, 100,* 654–661.

Cameron, M. B., & Wilson, B. J. (1990). The effects of chronological age gender, and delay of entry on academic achievement and retention: Implications for academic redshirting. *Psychology in the Schools, 27*(3), 260–263.

Cosden, M., Zimmer, J., & Tuss, P. (1993). The impact of age, sex and ethnicity on kindergarten entry and retention decisions. *Educational Evaluation and Policy Analysis, 15*(2), 209–222.

Cunningham, A. (1988). *Eeny, meeny, miny, moe: Testing policy and practice in early childhood.* Berkeley, CA: National Commission on Testing and Public Policy.

Education Commission on the States. (1997). *Clearinghouse Notes.* Denver, CO: Author.

Graue, M. E. (1992). Meanings of readiness and the kindergarten experience. In S. Kessler & B. Swadener (Eds.), *Reconceptualizing early childhood education* (pp. 62–90). New York: Teachers College Press.

Graue, M. E. (1993a). Expectations and ideas coming to school. *Early Childhood Research Quarterly, 8*(1), 53–75.

Graue, M. E. (1993b). *Ready for what? Constructing meanings of readiness for kindergarten.* Albany, NY: State University of New York Press.

Graue, M. E., & DiPerna, J. C. (in press). The gift of time: Who gets redshirted and retained and what are the outcomes? *American Educational Research Journal.*

Graue, M. E., & Shepard, L. A. (1992). School entrance age. In L. Williams and D. Fromberg (Eds.), *The encyclopedia of early childhood education* (p. 311). New York: Garland Publishing.

Hatch, J. A., & Freeman, E. B. (1988). Who's pushing whom: Stress and kindergarten. *Phi Delta Kappan, 70,* 145–147.

Heaviside, S., Farris, E., & Carpenter, J. (1993). *Public school kindergarten teachers' views on children's readiness for school* (NCES 93-410). Washington DC: National Center for Education Statistics.

Kagan, S. L. (1990). Readiness 2000: Rethinking rhetoric and responsibility. *Phi Delta Kappan, 72,* 272–279.

Kundert, D. K., May, D. C., & Brent, D. (1995). A comparison of students who delay kindergarten entry and those who are retained in grades K-5. *Psychology in the Schools, 32,* 202–209.

Lareau, A. (1989). *Home advantage.* London: Falmer.

Lareau, A. (1994). *Delayed kindergarten entrance: Social class, parent involvement, and redshirting.* Unpublished paper, Temple University, Department of Sociology, Philadelphia.

Love, J. M., Logue, M. E., Trudeau, J. V., & Thayer, K. (1992). *Transitions to kindergarten in American schools.* Washington, DC: Office of Policy and Planning, U.S. Department of Education.

May, D. C., Kundert, D. K., & Brent, D. (1995). Does delayed school entry reduce later grade retentions and use of special education services? *Remedial and Special Education, 16*(5), 288–294.

McCaig, R. (1990). *The practice of holding back children from entry to kindergarten: How widespread is it?* Research Report No. 10. Grosse Point, MI: Grosse Pointe School System.

Meisels, S., Steele, D. M., & Quinn-Leering, K. (1993). Testing, tracking, and retaining young children: An analysis of research and social policy. In B. Spodek (Ed.), *Handbook of research on the education of young children* (pp. 279–292). New York: Macmillan.

Meisels, S. J. (1999). Assessing readiness. In R. Pianta & M. J. Cox (Eds.), *The transition to kindergarten* (pp. 39–66). Baltimore: Paul H. Brookes.

Morrison, F. J., Griffith, E. M., & Alberts, D. M. (1997). Nature-nurture in the classroom: Entrance age, school readiness, and learning in children. *Developmental Psychology, 33*(2), 254–262.

National Center for Education Statistics. (1995). *Readiness for kindergarten: Parent and teacher beliefs* (Statistics in Brief NCES 93-257). Washington, DC: National Center for Education Statistics.

National Center for Education Statistics. (1997). *Digest of Education Statistics 1997* (98–105). Washington, DC: National Center for Education Statistics.

Noel, A. M., & Newman, J. (1998, April). *The decision to delay school entry: Profiles of two groups of mothers and implications for school psychological practice.* Paper presented at the National Association of School Psychologists, Orlando, FL.

Powell, D. R. (1995). *Enabling young children to succeed in school.* Washington, DC: American Educational Research Association.

Shepard, L. A. (1990). Readiness testing in local school districts: An analysis of backdoor policies. In S. F. B. Malen (Ed.), *The politics of curriculum and testing: 1990 Yearbook of the Politics of Education Association* (pp. 159–179). New York: Falmer Press.

Shepard, L. A., Graue, M. E., & Catto, S. F. (1989, March). *Delayed entry into kindergarten and escalation of academic demands.* Paper presented at the American Education Research Association, San Francisco.

Shepard, L. A., & Smith, M. L. (1986). Synthesis of research of school readiness and kindergarten retention. *Educational Leadership, 44*, 78–86.

Shepard, L., & Smith, M. L. (1988). Escalating academic demand in kindergarten: Counterproductive policies. *Elementary School Journal, 69*, 135–145.

Shore, R. (1998). *Ready Schools*. Washington, DC: National Education Goals Panel.

Smith, M. L., & Shepard, L. (1988). Kindergarten readiness and retention: A qualitative study of teachers' beliefs and practices. *American Educational Research Journal, 25*(3), 307–333.

Spitzer, S., Cupp , R., & Parke, R. D. (1995). School entrance age, social acceptance, and self-perceptions in kindergarten and 1st grade. *Early Childhood Research Quarterly, 10*(4), 433–450.

Uphoff, J., Gilmore, J. E., & Huber, R. (1986). *Summer children: Ready or not for school*. Middletown, OH: J & J Publishing.

Zill, N. (1992). *What we know about the school readiness of young children in the United States*. Washington, DC: National Education Goals Panel.

Zill, N., Collins, M., West, J., & Hausken, E. G. (1995). *Approaching kindergarten: A look at preschoolers*. Washington, DC: National Center for Education Statistics.

Zill, N., Loomis, L. S., & West, J. (1997). *The elementary school performance and adjustment of children who enter kindergarten late or repeat kindergarten: Findings from national surveys* (Statistical analysis report NCES 98-097). Washington, DC: U.S. Department of Education, Office of Educational Research and Improvement.

# Chapter 6

# The Added Value of Continuing Early Intervention into the Primary Grades

*Arthur J. Reynolds*

> The question is to what extent does this deterioration [of effects] occur.... This may be due to the discrepancy realized by the child between his Head Start experience and the conditions actually existing in public schools. As Dr. William Glasser has written, sending a child to Head Start and then putting him into a public school is like preparing a soldier for combat by sending him on a vacation to the French Riviera. (Mendelsohn, 1970, p. 448)

> Relatively brief periods of intervention, or even more extended ones, cannot assume the whole burden of care for society's ills; they cannot reverse the downward spiral of progressively greater inadequacy, the fate of too many children whose homes have not been able to provide them with the many advantages... taken for granted in middle-income families. (Gray, 1983, p. 81)

> Do we really want to believe that a year of preschool can ultimately shape the course of human life? To do so is to ignore the many, many factors ranging from the quality of schooling to socialization influences from the family and community.... Development is a continuous process and, while it is important to give the child a sound beginning, that does not mean the future is secured. (Zigler et al., 1993, pp. 21–22)

Three decades of research and practice in early childhood have led to greater attention to children's transitions to school and how parents and educators can better promote positive outcomes. The purpose of this chapter is to review the evidence about the added value of early childhood programs that continue into early grades. I find substantial evidence that the effects of early childhood programs that begin in preschool and continue to second or third grade are greater than the effects of programs that begin and end in preschool. Consequently, extending preschool programs upward into the primary grades has significant empirical support.

Few issues have greater significance for the early childhood field than the optimal timing and duration of service participation. While it has long been posited that the earlier intervention begins, the greater and more lasting the impact on children, the duration of program participation is also believed to be an important principle of effectiveness. The supposition about early entry perspective has been most recently highlighted by the implementation of family support programs for young children such as Early Head Start and Parents as Teachers. The urgency to intervene during the first 3 years of life has been accentuated by research on early brain development and by the public attention such findings often generate. To many observers, the implication of this research is that neurological growth in infants' brain circuitry is so rapid and dynamic that intervention after ages 2 or 3 may be too late to prevent serious learning difficulties and their negative long-term consequences.

Alternatively, the supposition about duration of service posits that the continuity of children's development from infancy to preschool and beyond is more important than experiences or developmental changes that occur just in infancy. Thus, there is an equal balance of influences in the learning environments between infancy and early childhood. This perspective is best represented by the ecological model of development in which children's outcomes are conceptualized as a function of a nested structure of influences emanating from the individual child to the larger systems of family, school, and community. Bronfenbrenner and Morris (1998) discuss this through the concept of proximal processes, whereby learning activities and experiences will have optimal impact if they "occur on a regular basis over extended periods of time" (p. 996). Their conclusion supports the role of relatively intense and multiyear programs. Recent examples of this approach to intervention include the National Head Start/Public School Early Childhood Transition Demonstration Project and the FAST Track Program for the prevention of conduct disorders.

Extended early childhood programs are defined as planned interventions that begin during any of the 5 years of a child's life before kindergarten and continue through at least second grade. These programs typically include both center-based child education, family services, and community outreach to children from low-income families or who have special needs. Because other chapters in this book address the effects of early childhood programs in infancy and preschool, I do not discuss this research in any detail. For reviews of this evidence, see Barnett (1995), Ramey and Ramey (1998), and Weissberg and Greenberg (1998). I also do not discuss evidence on the relative effects of school-age programs alone versus preschool programs alone (e.g., see Reynolds, 2000). For complementary perspectives, see Slavin, Karweit, and Madden (1994).

## Rationale for Extended Early Childhood Programs

Many studies of preschool programs have indicated that, for at least some outcomes, effects fade with the passage of time (Barnett, 1995; Weissberg & Greenberg, 1998). Although there are many reasons for the dissipation of effects, the key rationale for extended interventions is that the continuation of programs into the primary grades will not only promote more successful transitions but also help prevent the fading effects of preschool intervention. Most developmental theories indicate that environmental support during the transition to formal schooling is important for children's continued success (Entwisle, 1995). This process of change is called an ecological transition. An ecological transition is any change in the role, function, setting, or expectations of a developing person. The transition from preschool to kindergarten and the primary grades necessitates changes in the roles, settings, and expectations of an individual child.

Participation in extended early childhood interventions (continuation programs) may lead to greater and longer lasting effects than interventions that end in preschool for several reasons. First, longer periods of implementation may be necessary to promote greater and longer lasting changes in scholastic and psychosocial outcomes. Early interventions are often comprehensive, and they provide many services to children and parents that require significant coordination. They may be more effective if they have more time to work. Two recent reviews of social programs for children and youth (Durlak & Wells, 1997; Weissberg & Greenberg, 1998) indicate that a common element of successful programs is that they provide comprehensive services for at least two years. Another factor that reinforces the need for longer lasting interventions is that children in many urban settings are more at risk today than in the past (Wilson, 1996); hence early interventions must be more extensive than before to be equally effective.

Second, extended early childhood programs are designed to encourage more stable and predictable learning environments, both of which are key elements in optimal scholastic and social functioning (Garmezy & Rutter, 1988; Masten & Garmezy, 1985). Participation in extended interventions, for example, may encourage higher rates of school and home stability than would otherwise be expected. Certainly, environmental forces continue to operate after preschool and kindergarten. One assumption of early interventions that continues into the primary grades is that the postprogram learning environment at home and in school can reinforce, limit, or neutralize earlier gains in learning, and thus should not be left to chance.

A third rationale for extended childhood interventions is that they occur at a time increasingly viewed as a sensitive if not "critical" period in children's scholastic development (Entwisle, 1995; Entwisle & Alexander, 1993). It is expected that the provision of additional educational and social support services to children and families during this key transition would promote greater success and would help prevent major learning problems by third grade, a primary marker that presages later academic and social development. In the past decade, many studies provide empirical validation for the strong link between early school adjustment and educational success during the entire schooling process (Alexander & Entwisle, 1988; Entwisle & Alexander, 1993; Reynolds, 1991; Reynolds et al., 1996).

As a result of these features, continuation programs may not only promote children's learning but help prevent the dissipation of the effects of earlier intervention, which is a pattern that occurs for many kinds of social programs. Figure 6.1 shows several paths through which early childhood interventions are hypothesized to affect later social competence, the consensus goal of these programs. The literature indicates that five hypotheses of effects can promote effectiveness, and they are a major focus of extended childhood programs: (a) motivational advantage hypothesis (children's motivation or perceived competence), (b) cognitive advantage hypothesis (as measured by developed cognitive and scholastic abilities), (c) social adjustment hypothesis (prosocial behavior), (d) family support hypothesis (changes in the family behavior), and (e) school support hypothesis (classroom and school learning environments). To the extent that continuation programs strengthen the factors associated with these intervening mechanisms, long-term success is more likely (Reynolds, 2000).

## Four Extended Early Childhood Interventions

Several continuation programs described below have provided preschool and school-age services to children and families at risk due to economic disadvantage and other socioenvironmental conditions. These include Head Start/Follow Through, the Chicago Child-Parent Center and Expansion Program, the Carolina Abecedarian Project, and the National Head Start/Public School Early Childhood Transition Demonstration Project. Although there are other programs with similar features, these four programs are the best known. Because each is based on a different ordering of the paths of influence (see Figure 6.1), they provide

**FIGURE 6.1  Alternative Paths Leading to Social Competence**

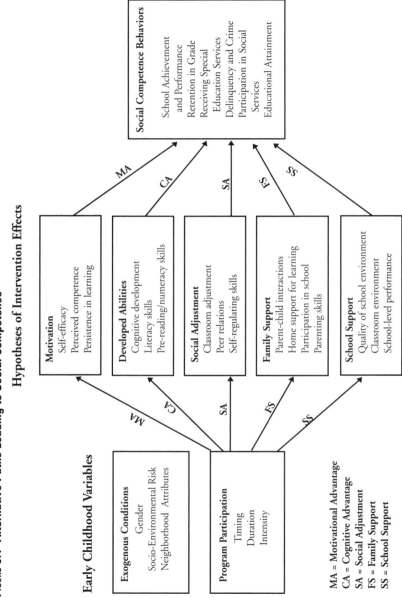

contemporary perspectives on program effectiveness and particularly evidence about the effectiveness of continuation interventions.[1]

Table 6.1 provides key attributes of these programs. Table 6.2 summarizes findings from selected evaluations. In reporting the findings of these programs, I consider the benefits of both (1) participation in the school-age components of the program and (2) the added value of this participation above and beyond participation in earlier preschool intervention. Of course, the latter benefits are emphasized.

## Head Start/Follow Through

As conceived by the planners of Head Start, the purpose of Follow Through (FT) was to enhance children's transition between preschool and the early elementary grades by providing Head Start–like services in public schools. It was believed that a continuous early childhood experience for low-income children from preschool to third grade would have the best chance to strengthen children's long-term school success. In 1967, President Johnson noted that this approach would "preserve the hope and opportunity of Head Start by a 'follow through' program in the early grades" and further advocated that in order "to fulfill the rights of America's children to equal educational opportunity, the benefits of Head Start must be carried through to the early grades" (cf. Rhine, et al., 1981, p. 27). Indeed, the original plan was to serve 200,000 children in the fall of 1968 at an expenditure of $120 million. However, only $15 million was allotted to FT in the first year by the U.S. Office of Education, and funding declined thereafter. As a result of the deep cutbacks in funding plus the observed incompatibilities between the social-service orientation of Head Start centers and the more regimented educational establishment of public schools, FT never achieved its original goal as a coordinated continuum of early childhood intervention (see also Doernberger & Zigler, 1993; Rhine, 1981).

Instead, FT became a social experiment on the effects of alternative instructional methods on children's educational development in kindergarten to third-grade classrooms. It was implemented as a series of "planned variations" of five instructional models and some mixtures

**TABLE 6.1  Primary Features of Four Extended Early Childhood Programs for Low-Income Families**

| Program | Organization | Classroom learning environment | Parent involvement | Social & health services |
|---|---|---|---|---|
| Chicago Child-Parent Centers (1967–present) | One administrative system for PK–Grade 3<br>Head teacher at each site<br>Teacher aides<br>Reduced class sizes | Indiv. instruction in lang. and math<br>Curricular resources<br>Staff inservices | Parent room at each site<br>Coordinator<br>School and home support activities<br>Advisory council | Services of school community rep<br>Outreach & referrals |
| Head Start/Follow Through (1968–1996) | Elementary school<br>K–Grade 3<br>Program coordinator<br>Most had teacher aides | Distinct curriculum model (e.g., DI, BS)<br>Curricular resources<br>Staff inservices | Class volunteers<br>Home visitors<br>Advisory council | Examinations<br>Referrals |
| Carolina Abecedarian Project (1972–1985) | Elementary school<br>K–Grade 2<br>Home-school resource teacher | Limited to activities of home-school teacher | Home visits, school support, outreach | Outreach & referrals |
| Head Start/Public School Early Childhood Transition Demonstration Project (1991–1998) | Elementary school<br>K–Grade 3<br>Family service coordinator | Developmental curricula<br>Inservice training and workshops | Parent resources at each site<br>Home visits<br>School involvement<br>Trans. gov. board | Nutrition services<br>Family outreach<br>Dental care |

*Note:* DI=Direct Instruction, BS=Bank Street

including (a) Parent Education Model, (b) Direct Instruction Model, (c) Behavioral Analysis Model, (d) High/Scope Cognitively Oriented Curriculum Model, and (e) the Bank Street Model of Developmental-Interaction. Each model had its own philosophy of education and emphasized somewhat different mechanisms of effects described in Figure 6.1. As described by Abelson, Ziger, and DeBlasi (1974), the distinguishing features of the Bank Street FT program in New Haven highlighted the motivational and cognitive advantage hypotheses:

> (a) an individual rather than a group-oriented approach, (b) an explicit interest in socio-emotional development of the child or what is often called the "whole child" approach, and (c) an emphasis on learning how to learn through the mastery of underlying principles and concepts. These features led to more frequent contacts between teachers and individual children in FT classrooms than in NFT classrooms. They also resulted in the use of a broad array of teaching methods. (pp. 758–759)

The High Scope model also followed a "whole child" approach but focuses on broader cognitive development. Alternatively, the Direct Instruction and Behavioral Analysis models emphasized the development of academic skills within more structured, group-oriented approaches. The Parent Education model adhered most to the family support hypothesis through extensive home visitation and activities between parents, children, and teachers.

Like Head Start, FT also provided a variety of health and social services, and encouraged family participation in children's education. Home visits by paraprofessionals and participation on school advisory councils were major elements of the parent component. Moreover, most classrooms had teacher aides (see Table 6.1). Because the program was sponsored by entire schools and was implemented at the classroom level, FT participants were not required to be graduates of Head Start. However, 50% or more of the students in FT classrooms were required to be graduates of Head Start. Comparison groups for determining the effects of FT were comprised of classrooms in non-FT schools in which most children did not enroll in Head Start.

**Research findings.** The results from previous studies of FT defy easy description, and a full accounting is well beyond the scope of this chapter. One overall finding reported in the national evaluation (Stebbins et al., 1977) and in critical reviews (e.g., House et al., 1978) was that substantial modifications in the classroom learning environment in kindergarten and the early primary grades can enhance children's early educational success and social and emotional development, thus improving the transition to school. As emphasized in the national evaluation (Stebbins et al., 1977), the instructional models were not equally associated with student academic achievement. The Direct Instruction and Behavioral Analysis models were most consistently associated with higher achievement test scores across location and time. As shown in Table 6.2, studies based on the High Scope, Bank Street, and Direct Instruction models found that participation in FT after Head Start was associated with higher school achievement in the short-term (Abelson et al., 1974; Schweinhart & Wallgren, 1993), but these effects were reduced over time (Becker & Gersten, 1982; Seitz et al., 1983).

Nevertheless, the variation in program effectiveness between schools was often larger than variation among the methods of instruction (House et al., 1978). Greenwood, Ware, Gordon, and Rhine (1981) found that in the Parent Education model, the number of completed home visits was significantly associated with growth in achievement in Grades 1 to 3 in two communities but not in other communities. Such findings are repeated often and indicate differences in implementation across sites and in the capacity of schools to coordinate transition activities.

The most important conclusion about the effectiveness of continuation programs from this research is that FT does not provide an optimal test of the added value of extended early childhood programs. As noted previously, FT was not implemented for this purpose. Because the vast majority of children who participated in FT classrooms graduated from Head Start, adequate samples of Head Start children who did not participate in FT—the key comparison for determining the added value

**TABLE 6.2 Selected Effect Sizes on School Competence for Studies of Extended Early Childhood Programs**

| Program and studies | Program sample and experiences/ Control sample and experiences | Effects at ages 8–9 | | | | Effects at ages 12–15 | | | |
|---|---|---|---|---|---|---|---|---|---|
| | | Read | Math | Retn | Sped | Read | Math | Retn | Sped |
| **Head Start/Follow Through** | | | | | | | | | |
| Abelson, Zigler, & DeBlasi, 1974/ Seitz et al., 1983 (up to age 14) | 35 in Bank Street FT in K–3; 91% had HS<br>26 other-school controls; 28% had HS | .00 | .51 | -- | -- | .00 | .13<br>(> boys) | -- | -- |
| Becker & Gersten, 1982 (up to age 12) | 1,097 in Direct Inst. FT in 1–3<br>907 in non-FT classrooms in same schools | >.50 | >.50 | -- | -- | .19 | .26 | -- | -- |
| Schweinhart & Wallgren, 1993 (up to age 9) | 281 in High/Scope FT in K–3<br>528 same-school controls; 1% had HS | .39 | .29 | -- | -- | -- | -- | -- | -- |
| **Chicago Child-Parent Centers** | | | | | | | | | |
| Fuerst & Fuerst, 1993 (up to age 14) | 419 with 4 or more years CPC<br>503 in feeder-school controls; no CPC | -- | -- | -- | -- | .33 | .20 | -- | -- |

TABLE 6.2 (CONTINUED)

| Program and studies | Program sample and experiences/ Control sample and experiences | Effects at ages 8–9 | | | | Effects at ages 12–15 | | | |
|---|---|---|---|---|---|---|---|---|---|
| | | Read | Math | Retn | Sped | Read | Math | Retn | Sped |
| Reynolds, 1994 (up to age 11) | 462 in CPC Pre-K and K plus grades 1–3 / 207 in CPC Pre-K and K only | .55 | .48 | -13.0 | -.03 | -- | -- | -- | -- |
| Reynolds & Temple, 1998 (up to age 13) | 426 in CPC Pre-K and K plus grades 1–3 / 133 in CPC Pre-K and K only | .48 | .35 | -- | -- | .43 | .28 | -.15 | -.06 |
| Carolina Abecedarian Project | | | | | | | | | |
| Campbell & Ramey, 1995 (up to age 15) | 25 in daycare(0 to age 5)+ Kind–Grade 2 / 24 in daycare from birth to age 5 only | .27 | .33 | -- | -- | .20 | .00 | +.02 | +.24 |
| Head Start/Public School Early Childhood Transition Demonstration | 31 sites across the country | Only evaluation results from local sites are available | | | | | | | |

*Notes:* Values for reading and math achievement are proportions of standard deviations. Values for grade retention (Retn) and special education (Sped) are percentage-point differences (negative numbers favor the intervention group). In Abelson et al. study, the effect sizes for the cross-sectional sample were .34 and .51, respectively for third-grade reading and math achievement. In Schweinhart & Wallgren, average effect across grades 1 to 3 was .63.

of continuation programs—were not readily available and hardly ever investigated (one exception is Abelson et al., 1974). The effects of timing and duration of participation in Head Start and Follow Through were confounded. Although it is difficult to know precisely the added value of FT, this research does generally indicate that enhancements in the quality of schools in the early grades promote children's educational success with or without earlier intervention.

Another major limitation of the FT experience was that Head Start and Follow Through were administered in systems—community action agencies and public schools—that differ in significant ways. These differences reduced the continuity, integration, and coordination between preschool and school-age services, which are crucial features of continuation programs. Another program begun at the same time as FT did implement a coordinated early childhood program within a single administrative system that was much closer to the original vision of Head Start planners. This was the Child-Parent Education Centers in the Chicago Public Schools.

## Chicago Child-Parent Center and Expansion Program

Like Head Start/Follow Through, the Child-Parent Center and Expansion Program (CPC; originally Child-Parent Education Centers) is a school-based early intervention that provides comprehensive educational and family-support services to economically disadvantaged children from preschool (ages 3 or 4) to early elementary school (second or third grade). The CPC program was established in 1967 through funding from Title I of the landmark Elementary and Secondary Education Act of 1965. It is the second oldest (after Head Start) federally funded preschool program in the United States, and it is the oldest extended early childhood intervention. Initially implemented in 4 sites and later expanded to 25, the program intends to promote children's academic success in early childhood and beyond and to facilitate parent involvement in children's education. Today, 24 centers operate in the Chicago schools, and since 1977, the primary grade component has been integrated with regular elementary school programs.

The development of the CPCs can be traced to the middle of 1966 when the General Superintendent of the Chicago Public Schools asked Dr. Lorraine M. Sullivan, District 8 Superintendent and program founder, to report on ways to improve student attendance and achievement. The district was located in the Garfield Park and Lawndale community areas, which had the highest concentrations of poverty in the city. After the preschool and kindergarten programs began in four sites, the principals agreed to continue to provide services to the kindergarten graduates up to third grade beginning in 1968.

The CPC program has three features that contrast sharply with Head Start/Follow Through. Figure 6.2 shows the organization and major elements of the program. First, the total program is implemented within one administrative system, the Chicago Public Schools. This strengthens continuity of service delivery in several ways, including providing centralized oversight by the school principal and having geographic proximity between preschool/kindergarten and school-age components. Moreover, the program operates in early childhood centers that are physically separate from the elementary schools (either in wings or in separate school sites), and are called small-school homes ("schomes"). A third difference with FT is that there is substantial variation in the number of years that children participate (from 1 to 6 years). Children can enroll for 1 or 2 years of preschool. Because they live in neighborhoods outside the CPCs, some children do not enter the primary-grade component of the program and instead enroll in other elementary schools. By administrative design, six centers provide services up to third grade for a total of six years; the remaining centers provide services up to second grade for a total of five years. The four major features of the program are:

- A structured and diverse set of language-based instructional activities designed to promote academic and social success. Curriculum materials vary by site but many combine elements of the Bank Street, High/Scope, and Behavioral models.
- A multifaceted parent program that includes participating in parent room activities, volunteering in the classroom, attending

**FIGURE 6.2 Child-Parent Center Program**

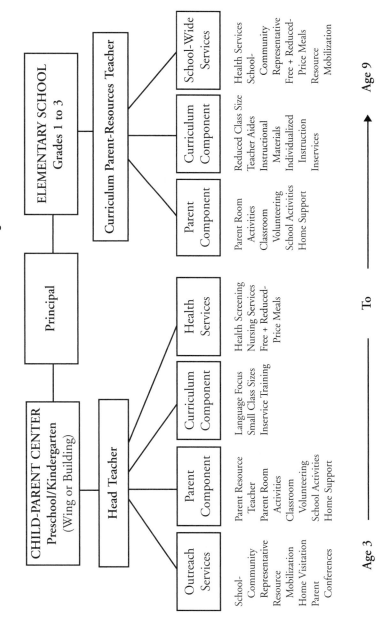

school events, and enrolling in educational courses for personal development under the supervision of the parent-resource teacher.

- Outreach activities coordinated by the school-community representative including resource mobilization, home visitation, and enrollment of children.

- A comprehensive primary-grade program from first to third grade that supports children's transition to elementary school through (a) reduced class sizes (to 25 children), (b) the addition of teacher aides in each class, (c) extra instructional supplies, and (d) coordination of instructional activities, staff development, and parent-program activities by the curriculum-parent resource teacher.

Compared with Head Start/Follow Through, the CPC preschool program has a greater focus on the acquisition of basic skills in language and math and provides more intensive parent involvement, but substantially fewer health services. Most of the centers offer both half-day preschool and half/full-day kindergarten; about half of the participants enter at age 3, and half at age 4. Since 1977, the funding for the preschool/kindergarten and primary grade components was split between federal Title I and State of Illinois Chapter I, respectively. Reduced class sizes (from 35+ to 25) are a major element of the school-age program.

**Research findings.** Evaluations of the CPC program have consistently found that participation is significantly associated with higher levels of school achievement, motivational development, and parent involvement in children's education (see Reynolds, 2000). Many studies have concluded that the instructional focus on basic skills, a strong emphasis on parental involvement, and the provision of follow-on services are critical to the total success of the program. In one of the first controlled studies of the program, Conrad and Eash (1983) found that participation in the extended program from preschool to third grade in the six original sites was associated with higher academic achievement even after participation in preschool and kindergarten was taken into account. Following the progress of another cohort from the six original sites, Fuerst and Fuerst (1993) found that children with four or more years of participation had higher reading and math achievement in eighth grade and had higher rates of high school graduation than a comparison group of children from feeder schools with no participation. As with most of the FT studies, however, these evaluations did not directly compare the effects of participation in extended intervention beyond the effects of participation in preschool and kindergarten. They also did not investigate the impact across all of the centers.

In 1985, the Chicago Longitudinal Study was begun to investigate these issues, including the impact of participation in the CPCs for different lengths of time for all 20 sites with preschool and kindergartens. In the study, 1,150 CPC kindergarten graduates in 1986 (most of whom enrolled in preschool) were compared to a matched comparison group of 389 children who participated in an alternative all-day kindergarten program (i.e., "treatment as usual," or standard treatment) from five randomly selected schools serving low-income families. As the largest and most extensive study ever of the effects of a federally funded early childhood program, several methodological attributes strengthen the validity of the findings: (a) a large sample size for investigating the effects of timing and duration of participation, (b) substantial variation in the number of years of participation including the crucial contrast between children who participated from preschool to third grade (4 to 6 years) and children whose participation ceased in kindergarten (2 or 3 years), and (c) measurement of a variety of family, child, school, and program characteristics that address questions related to who benefits most from participation, and which postprogram events and experiences lead to long-term effects (for more information, see Reynolds, 2000).

Table 6.2 summarizes some of the key findings about the value added by participation in extended intervention in the CPC program. Reynolds (1994) found that at the end of the program in third grade, extended program participation was associated with one half of a standard deviation improvement in both reading and math achievement over participation in preschool and kindergarten alone. This translates into a seven-month advantage in achievement (a typical gain for the academic year). Participation that continued through third grade led to performance advantages over participation through second grade. Children who participated in extended intervention also had significantly lower rates of grade retention and placement in special education services. Reynolds and Temple (1998) found that these effects were stable up to age 13. At the age 15 follow-up (Reynolds, 2000), extended program participants continued to demonstrate significant performance advantages over less extensive participation even after controlling for kindergarten achievement. As shown in Figure 6.3, extended program participation to third grade (4 to 6 years of CPC) was associated with significantly lower rates of school remedial services (grade retention and special education placement), and with lower rates of delinquency infractions as reported by schools. Relative to no participation, six years of enrollment (maximum participation) was associated with over a 50% reduction in school remedial services.

More recently, Temple, Reynolds, and Miedel (2000) found that extended intervention for five or six years was associated with a significantly lower rate of school dropout by age 18 relative to less extensive intervention. These findings are consistent with those of Fuerst and Fuerst (1993), which were based on the six original sites of the program in 1967. These studies provide the only evidence supporting the link between extended childhood intervention and educational attainment. For more recent findings, see Reynolds, Temple, Robertson, & Mann (2001).

In summary, the Chicago Longitudinal Study of the Child-Parent Centers has demonstrated over the past decade that participation in extended early childhood interventions for low-income children in high-poverty neighborhoods substantially improves school success and socialization in the short- and long-term on a variety of outcomes.

## *The Carolina Abecedarian Project*

Like the Chicago study of the CPCs, the Carolina Abecedarian Project (ABC) was specifically designed to investigate the effects of early intervention and the added effect of continuing intervention into the

## FIGURE 6.3 Age 15 Comparisons in the CPC Program

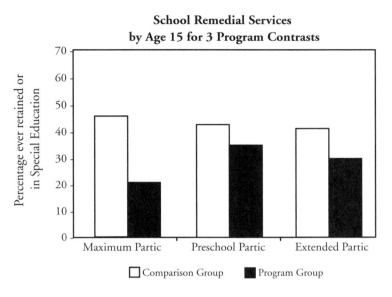

**School Remedial Services
by Age 15 for 3 Program Contrasts**

Percentage ever retained or in Special Education

Maximum Partic     Preschool Partic     Extended Partic

☐ Comparison Group     ■ Program Group

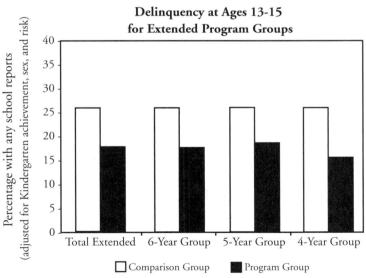

**Delinquency at Ages 13-15
for Extended Program Groups**

Percentage with any school reports
(adjusted for Kindergarten achievement, sex, and risk)

Total Extended     6-Year Group     5-Year Group     4-Year Group

☐ Comparison Group     ■ Program Group

primary grades. Begun in 1972 in rural North Carolina, ABC was a model intervention program consisting of five years of enriched educational day care from age 4 months to 5 years (prior to kindergarten). The innovative program occurred at a single site for yearly cohorts through 1977, followed by a school-age intervention for three years starting in kindergarten and continuing to second grade (age 8). The cohorts entered kindergarten from 1977 to 1982. Children were biologically healthy but economically disadvantaged; 98% were African American and most attended schools populated predominantly by middle-income Caucasian children. As noted by Campbell and Ramey (1995), the goal of the project was "to test the degree to which continual, consistent enrichment of the early environment might alter this negative trend toward developmental retardation and also reduce academic failure in such children [in poverty]" (p. 746).

In addition to the capacity to probe the effects of extended intervention, ABC has two major strengths. First, entry into intervention in the first months after birth and continuing for five years provides a full test of the power of early intervention to alter children's life course development. This level of intensity and duration in infancy and preschool is rare in intervention research. Second, the study design was elegant and powerful for determining program impact. One hundred eleven infants (matched on a high-risk index) were randomly assigned at birth to enriched center-based day care (full-day, year round) or to a no-treatment control group (i.e., typical home care). Prior to kindergarten entry, the preschool intervention and control groups were randomly assigned again to a school-age intervention or to a control group of regular school-age programs. Of the total of four groups at age 5, 25 children participated in extended early childhood intervention for eight years and 24 children participated during only preschool for five years.

While the day care program emphasized language and literacy skills with very small child-to-teacher ratios, the school-age intervention followed a family-support model of intervention. As Campbell and Ramey (1995) explain, the continuation program "was designed to support children's academic development by increasing and enhancing parent involvement in the educational process" (p. 751). This was accomplished through the activities of the home/school resource teacher. Functioning as a case manager for the family and child, the home/school resource teacher (a) provided learning activities for parents to use with their children at home, (b) visited the classroom twice per month to assist with any learning problems, (c) made home visits to the parents twice per month to provide and demonstrate various learning activities, (d) served as a home-school liaison to advocate for children's needs, and (e) provided community outreach associated with transportation, medical services, education, and training. The school-age program also included a six-week summer transition program prior to kindergarten entry. The case-management approach of ABC contrasts with the school-organization and instructional approaches of CPC and FT, respectively.

**Research findings.** Although evaluations of ABC have consistently found that the 5-year preschool program produced greater intellectual and academic outcomes than does participation in the 3-year school-age program, an additional dosage-response effect has been found for children who participate in both preschool and school-age programs. These children have the highest levels of intellectual and scholastic performance at the end of the program at age 8; and the extended intervention group surpassed the performance of the preschool-only group by one-third of a standard deviation (see Table 6.2). At the age 15 follow-up, the extended surpassed the nonextended group only for reading achievement. No differences between groups were found for math achievement, intelligence test scores, and cumulative rates of grade retention and special education placement. As shown in Table 6.2, participation in extended intervention was associated with higher rates of special education services. This finding should be interpreted cautiously because it may reflect greater levels of responsiveness by teachers in the schools children attended.

Although extended intervention was found to enhance children's transition to school, the case-management model ABC had limited long-term effects on children's success, especially in comparison to the intensive 5-year day care experience. Campbell and Ramey (1995) concluded that ABC supports the "primacy of early experience." They go on to observe that "based on the present results, the value of providing only a supplemental program in the primary grades appears doubtful, being by itself, not associated with greatly enhanced academic outcomes" (p. 769). While their own findings support this conclusion, those of FT and CPC discussed above do not. Reynolds and Temple (1998) offered the following explanations for the different longer term findings of the ABC and CPC programs:

> The CPC program also provided reduced class sizes and teacher aides for participating students as well as a staffed parent resource room in the elementary school. Thus, the CPC school-age program provided more comprehensive services. Second, the two programs were implemented at different ages. The Abecedarian Program provides school-age services from kindergarten to second grade; the Child-Parent Center Program provides services from first grade to third grade. Timing of program services could make some difference, especially since in the present study, the three-year follow-on program group had better school performance than the two-year group. Third, the effect of school-age intervention may interact with the extent and quality of earlier intervention experiences. In the Abecedarian Project, all children participated for five years in a preschool program prior to the school-age program. In the CPC program, children had less extensive center-based experiences prior to the school-age program (two or three years, including kindergarten). Finally, the socioeconomic context of the programs were different. The Abecedarian Program was implemented in schools serving mostly middle-income White children while the CPCs are located in inner-city communities serving mostly poor Black children. Extended early childhood programs in high-poverty schools may have a greater impact than programs implemented in more socioeconomically advantaged contexts. (p. 244)

In addition, school-organization models of primary-grade intervention may be more effective than case-management approaches. Evaluation research on the Comprehensive Child Development Program (St. Pierre, 1999) and the Fort Bragg Experiment in children's mental health (Bickman, 1996), for example, indicates that case management models in community-based programs do not result in better child development outcomes for many children.

## National Head Start/Public School Early Childhood Transition Demonstration Project

Implemented in school districts across the country beginning in 1991 and sponsored by the U.S. Department of Health and Human Services, the National Head Start/Public School Early Childhood Transition Demonstration Project (HST) revamped the concept behind Head Start/Follow Through. With a $20 million authorization by Congress in 1990 through P. L. 101-501 (Kennedy, 1993), HST was designed to "implement a coordinated and continuous program of comprehensive services for low-income children and their families" (Federal Register, 1991, p. 31818). Program components included coordination between Head Start and elementary school programs, comprehensive support services in the early school years, and parental involvement (Kennedy, 1993). As discussed above, the decision to use FT to test the effects of different instructional methods reduced the capacity to determine the added value of continuation programs. HST corrected two major shortcomings of the FT experience. First, consistent with the vision of Head Start planners, HST focused on the total transition experiences of Head Start graduates into public schools. A wider range of family and community services were provided and more emphasis was placed on family services, and less emphasis on implementing instructional models. Second, the research design of HST was, in theory, methodologically stronger than in FT. Participation in HST was determined through random assignment of schools within school districts such that the number of Head Start graduates in intervention schools and in comparison schools was equally balanced. Thus, Head Start graduates who attended schools implementing HST were directly compared to those of Head

Start graduates who attended elementary schools without the transition program. Nevertheless, one feature that remained the same in FT and HST was that the gulf between the cultures of the Head Start preschool programs and elementary schools was wide, and the level of integration between these systems was highly variable. Thus, the provision of a coordinated continuum of early childhood intervention was not ideal.

Providing comprehensive services to children and families, HST may best be characterized as a family-service model of intervention rather than a classroom or school environment model. Although differences occurred across sites, a family service coordinator organized a variety of activities for parents at home and in school by overseeing home visits by family service workers, and encouraging parental school involvement (e.g., volunteering in the classroom, attending parent meetings, and helping to coordinate school activities). Staffed parent rooms also were available in many sites. Social services included family referrals for a variety of community-based services (e.g., education, health, and mental health). Drug education programs in the classrooms also were provided. Educational support for children included efforts to encourage the use of developmentally appropriate practices in the classroom. In-service training of teachers occurred on a regular basis and teachers met regularly to plan activities. Finally, health and nutrition activities were organized by nurses placed in each transition site. They helped coordinate breakfast and lunch programs and dental care, documented immunization, conducted health screenings, and visited classrooms to teach nutrition education.

**Research findings.** Because the evaluations of HST are recent, the evidence base is incomplete.[2] I note a few preliminary studies below that have reported findings through third grade, the end of the transition program. The North Carolina HST, for example, compared the performance of 100 intervention children (with and without Head Start experience) and 123 non-HST children in schools randomly assigned to the control condition (Bryant et al., 1998). After analyzing data in a number of ways to account for the different intervention experiences, HST had no effect on children's reading abilities over time (as measured by the Woodcock-Johnson Battery). As explained by the investigators, compensatory equalization occurred in the control sites, and this may account for the no-effect findings: The local schools try to help all children with special needs "so children in the control schools received a number of school-provided interventions and services over their first four years of school" (Bryant et al., 1998, p. 158). This equalization occurred in other sites as well.

Although no overall results were described in the Montgomery County HST (Seefeldt et al., 1998), the investigators found that children of parents who participated in school and social activities as organized by the Family Service Coordinator had higher achievement test scores on the letter-word subtest of the Woodcock-Johnson Test. Qualitative data from parents revealed the importance of family-school connections in HST for supporting children's education.

Preliminary studies of other local sites have revealed a mixed pattern of outcomes through second or third grade, and some evidence indicated that HST participants benefited (Hegland & Colbert, 1998). In the Indiana HST, Mantzicopoulos & Neuharth-Pritchett (1996) found no consistent differences in achievement test scores between intervention and comparison groups. They did note positive effects on social skills in the first two primary grades, and higher teacher ratings of parental involvement in HST schools. Investigators in the West Virginia site (Bickel & Spatig, 1999) also reported no differences in achievement test scores between HST and the comparison group.

While it is too soon to know the overall effects of this program, so far the pattern of findings is mixed with some evidence HST enhances the transition to school (see Ramey, Ramey et al. (2000) for recent findings). Yet in the studies discussed above, performance advantages of children who participated in Head Start and HST relative to children who participated only in Head Start are not evident. As with Follow Through, the added value of the Head Start Transition Program will be difficult to gauge if sample sizes of children in the Head Start/non-HST group are insufficient or if the comparison sites received alternative program services through the process of compensatory equalization or rivalry.

## Conclusion

Although extended intervention programs have been discussed since the founding of Project Head Start in 1965, only recently has sufficient evidence become available to assess their short- and long-term effects above and beyond preschool intervention. Taken together, the evidence described in this chapter indicates that extended early childhood programs can promote more successful transitions to school than preschool interventions alone. Findings from both ABC and the CPC program directly support this conclusion. Studies of the CPC program demonstrate the long-term positive effects of extended intervention over less extensive intervention for several school competence outcomes. As an integrated intervention model within a single delivery system, the design of the CPC program is very similar to the original concept of providing services for several years within one setting. The Head Start/Follow Through experience reveals the benefits of modifications in school learning environments. Although studies of the Head Start Transition Program are ongoing, early evidence from selected sites presents mixed results. In general, the transition programs that directly alter the organization and learning environments of elementary schools demonstrate more consistent and longer lasting effects on children's school success than programs that emphasize case management approaches for promoting successful transition experiences.

Although the CPC program is not perfect (e.g., it provides few health and mental health services), it did from the beginning what Head Start/Follow Through did not: implement an extended early childhood intervention from preschool to third grade under a single administrative system, a system that provides greater continuity for children during the transition to school. Although more longitudinal data from a variety of settings are needed, several lessons about the future success of extended early childhood programs can be drawn from this review of the evidence:

1. Strengthen the continuity of services to children by using schools as the single delivery system for early and extended childhood interventions.

2. Reflect in the program's service provisions the principle that the duration of program participation can matter as much as timing of participation.

3. Implement intensive parent programs through staffed parent-resource rooms emphasizing both personal growth and school participation.

4. Focus children's enrichment activities on language-based school-readiness skills while keeping activities diverse enough to meet the needs of individual children.

5. Focus programs for school-aged children on school organization and instructional improvements, including reduced class sizes and student-teacher ratios, and better instructional coordination and quality.

Extended early childhood interventions are one element of larger reforms of educational and human services occurring today. The overarching principle is the provision of well-coordinated, comprehensive services that occur over many years. After reviewing the evidence on the impact of social programs in the first two decades of children's lives, Weissberg and Greenberg (1998) concluded, "It is now recognized that family-based models that incorporate outreach to the home, offer center-based enriched preschool experiences, and facilitate optimal transitions to elementary school are part of a warranted developmental package of services" (p. 907). Several innovative service models have expanded this vision further: Schools of the 21st century, full-service schools, and several social-competence enhancement programs. They implement early intervention and continue through major transitions during children's formative years (Zigler, 1994).

Given demographic trends showing increasing concentration of poverty and other risk factors in large metropolitan areas (National Center for Children in Poverty, 1997), early interventions today must be better in quality, intensity, and comprehensiveness than in the past to successfully meet the needs of children and families. While the expansion of programs to include children from birth to age 3 is an important area of intervention, the expansion of early childhood programs to include children in grade school also seems critical for supporting the transition to school and reinforcing preschool learning gains. Indeed, extended childhood programs have two practical advantages over programs from birth to age 3. First, educational systems are already in place to support extended childhood intervention in the primary grades. New early childhood systems would not have to be developed. Second, upward expansion of programs into the primary grades may cost less than many of the alternatives, and they are certainly more cost-effective than continuing the current system of providing little or no extra support for children's transition to school. In Chicago's Child-Parent Center Program, for example, the expenditure for one year of school-age services is about $1,500 per child.

Nevertheless, programs for a new age of services should be tailored to the needs of children across the entire first decade of life. Given that many children are entering preschool and school-age environments today at even higher risk than students entering 10 years ago, the "first decade" strategy provides the optimal level of support for children's learning and development and does not presume that any stage of development (infancy, preschool, school-age) alone can immunize children from future underachievement. Indeed, not only do investments in programs and services for children need to be of sufficient duration and intensity, but the knowledge base about the impact of these investments should be commensurate with the high priority the public has for them.

## Acknowledgment

Preparation of this chapter was supported by grants from the National Institute of Child Health and Human Development (No. R29HD34294) and the National Institute for the Education of At-Risk Students, Office of Educational Research and Improvement (No. R306F960055).

# Endnotes

[1] For additional perspectives, see Kagan and Neuman (1998). Another extended childhood intervention was called Project Developmental Continuity (Zigler & Styfco, 1993; Valentine, 1979). This program began after the goals of Follow Through were changed to reflect a planned variation model of intervention rather than a continuous intervention bridging the preschool and early primary grades. Like the original Follow Through model, Project Developmental Continuity was designed to coordinate services between Head Start and the public schools, and it provided health and social services to former Head Start graduates through the early school years. Because of the limited research on this project, I do not consider it further in this chapter.

[2] See Ramey, Ramey et al. (2000) for results of the recently completed national evaluation.

# References

Abelson, W. B., Zigler, E., & DeBlasi, C. L. (1974). Effects of a four-year Follow Through program on economically disadvantaged children. *Journal of Educational Psychology, 66,* 756–771.

Alexander, K. L., & Entwisle, D. R. (1988). Achievement in the first 2 years of school: Patterns and processes. *Monographs of the Society for Research in Child Development, 53*(2, Serial No. 218).

Barnett, W. S. (1995). Long-term effects of early childhood programs on cognitive and school outcomes. *Future of Children, 5*(3), 25–50.

Becker, W. C., & Gersten, R. (1982). A follow-up of Follow Through: The later effects of the Direct Instruction model on children in fifth and sixth grades. *American Educational Research Journal, 19,* 75–92.

Bickel, R., & Spatig, L. (1999). Early achievement gains and poverty-linked social distress: The case of post-head start transition. *Journal of Social Distress and the Homeless, 8,* 241–254.

Bickman, L. (1996). A continuum of care: More is not always better. *American Psychologist, 51,* 689–701.

Bronfenbrenner, U., & Morris, P. A. (1998). The ecology of developmental processes. In W. Damon (Ed.), *Handbook of Child Psychology: Vol. 1. Theoretical Issues* (pp. 993–1028). New York: Wiley.

Bryant, D. M., Campbell, F. A., Taylor, K. B., & Burchinal, M. R. (1998, July). What is 'participation' in North Carolina's Head Start Transition Demonstration? *Summary of Conference Proceedings of Head Start's Fourth National Research Conference.* Washington, DC: Administration on Children, Youth, and Families, U.S. Department of Health and Human Services.

Campbell, F. A., & Ramey, C. T. (1995). Cognitive and school outcomes for high risk African-American students at middle adolescence: Positive effects of early intervention. *American Educational Research Journal, 32,* 743–772.

Conrad, K. J., & Eash, M. J. (1983). Measuring implementation and multiple outcomes in a Child Parent Center compensatory education program. *American Educational Research Journal, 20,* 221–236.

Doernberger, C., & Zigler, E. (1993). Project Follow Through: Intent and reality. In E. Zigler & S. J. Styfco (Eds.), *Head Start and beyond: A national plan for extended childhood intervention* (pp. 43–72). New Haven: Yale University Press.

Durlak, J. A., & Wells, A. M. (1997). Primary prevention mental health programs for children and adolescents: A meta-analytic review. *American Journal of Community Psychology, 25,* 115–152.

Entwisle, D. R. (1995). The role of schools in sustaining early-childhood program benefits. *Future of Children, 5*(3), 133–144.

Entwisle, D. R., & Alexander, K. L. (1993). Entry into school: The beginning school transition and educational stratification in the United States. *Annual Review of Sociology, 19,* 401-423.

Federal Register. (1991, July 11). Vol. 56, No. 133, pp. 31818-31841.

Fuerst, J. S., & Fuerst, D. (1993). Chicago experience with an early childhood program: The special case of the Child Parent Center program. *Urban Education, 28,* 69–96.

Garmezy, N., & Rutter, M. (Eds.). (1988). *Stress, coping and development in children*. Baltimore: Johns Hopkins Press.

Gray, S. W. (1983). Enduring effects of early intervention: Perspectives and perplexities. *Peabody Journal of Education, 60,* 70–84

Greenwood, G. E., Ware, W. B., Gordon, I. J., & Rhine, W. R. (1981). Parent Education Model. In W. R. Rhine (Ed.), *Making schools more effective: New directions from Follow Through* (pp. 49–93). New York: Academic Press.

Hegland, S. M., & Colbert, K. (1998, July). Head Start transition outcomes: Families and children. *Summary of Conference Proceedings of Head Start's Fourth National Research Conference.* Washington, DC: Administration on Children, Youth, and Families, U.S. Department of Health and Human Services.

House, E. R., Glass, G. V., McLean, L. D., & Walker, D. F. (1978). No simple answer: Critique of the Follow Through evaluation. *Harvard Educational Review, 48,* 128–160.

Kagan, S. L., & Neuman, M. J. (1998). Lessons from three decades of transition research. *Elementary School Journal, 98,* 365–379.

Kennedy, E. M. (1993). The Head Start Transition Project: Head Start goes to elementary school. In E. Zigler & S. J. Styfco (Eds.), *Head Start and beyond: A national plan for extended childhood intervention* (pp. 97–109). New Haven: Yale University Press.

Mantzicopoulos, P. Y., & Neuharth-Pritchett, S. (1996, April). *Head Start to second grade: School competence and parental involvement in a public school transition project.* Paper presented at the annual meeting of the American Educational Research Association, New York.

Masten, A. S., & Garmezy, N. (1985). Risk, vulnerability, and protective factors in developmental psychopathology. In B. B. Lahey & A. E. Kazdin (Eds.), *Advances in clinical child psychology* (Vol. 8, pp. 1–51). New York: Plenum.

Mendelsohn, R. (1970). Is Head Start a success or failure? In J. Hellmuth (Ed.), *Disadvantaged child: Vol. 3. A national debate* (pp. 445–454). New York: Bruner/Mazel.

National Center for Children in Poverty. (1997). *Early childhood poverty: A statistical profile.* New York: Columbia University, School of Public Health.

Ramey, C. T., & Ramey, S. L. (1998). Early intervention and early experience. *American Psychologist, 53,* 109–120.

Ramey, S. L., Ramey, C. T. et al. (2000, November). *Head Start children's entry into public school: A report on the National Head Start/Public School Early Childhood Transition Demonstration Project.* Washington, DC: Administration for Children and Families, U.S. Department of Health and Human Services.

Reynolds, A. J. (1991). Early schooling of children at risk. *American Educational Research Journal, 28,* 392–422.

Reynolds, A. J. (1994). Effects of a preschool plus follow-on intervention for children at risk. *Developmental Psychology, 30,* 787–804.

Reynolds, A. J. (2000). *Success in early intervention: The Chicago Child-Parent Centers.* Lincoln: University of Nebraska Press.

Reynolds, A. J., Mavrogenes, N. A., Bezruczko, N., & Hagemann, M. (1996). Cognitive and family-support mediators of preschool effectiveness: A confirmatory analysis. *Child Development, 67,* 1119–1140.

Reynolds, A. J., & Temple, J. A. (1998). Extended early childhood intervention and school achievement: Age 13 findings from the Chicago Longitudinal Study. *Child Development, 69,* 231–246.

Reynolds, A. J., Temple, J.A., Robertson, D.L., & Mann, E.A. (2001). Long-term effects of an early childhood intervention on educational achievement and juvenile arrest: A 15-year follow-up of low-income children in public schools. *Journal of the American Medical Association, 285*(18), 2339-2346.

Rhine, W. R. (Ed.). (1981). *Making schools more effective: New directions from Follow Through.* New York: Academic Press.

Rhine, W. R., Elardo, R., & Spencer, L. M. (1981). Improving educational environments: The Follow Through Approach. In W. R. Rhine (Ed.), *Making schools more effective: New directions from Follow Through* (pp. 25–46). New York: Academic Press.

Schweinhart, L. J., & Wallgren, C. R. (1993). Effects of a Follow Through program on achievement. *Journal of Research in Childhood Education, 8,* 43–56.

Seefeldt, C., Galper, A. R., & Younoszai, T. M. (1998, July). Transition activities and their effectiveness. Washington, DC: Administration on Children, Youth, and Families, U.S. Department of Health and Human Services.

Seitz, V., Apfel, N., Rosenbaum, L., & Zigler, E. (1983). Long-term effects of Projects Head Start and Follow Through: The New Haven Project. In Consortium for Longitudinal Studies (Eds.), *As the twig is bent: Lasting effects of preschool programs* (pp. 299–332). Hillsdale, NJ: Erlbaum.

Slavin, R. E., Karweit, N. L., & Madden, N. A. (1994). *Effective programs for students at risk.* Boston: Allyn & Bacon.

Stebbins, L. B., St. Pierre, R. G., Proper, E. C., Anderson, R. B., & Cerva, T. R. (1977). *Education as experimentation: A planned variation model. Vol. IV-A: An evaluation of Follow Through.* Cambridge, MA: Abt Associates.

St. Pierre, R. G. (1999). The effectiveness of comprehensive, case-management interventions: Evidence from the national evaluation of the comprehensive child development program. *American Journal of Evaluation, 20*(1), 15–34.

Temple, J. A., Reynolds, A. J., & Miedel, W. T. (2000). Can early intervention prevent high school dropout? Evidence from the Chicago Child-Parent Centers. *Urban Education, 35*(1), 31–56.

Valentine, J. (1979). Program development in Head Start: A multifaceted approach to meeting the needs of families and children. In E. Zigler & J. Valentine (Eds.), *Project Head Start: A legacy of the War on Poverty* (pp. 349–365). New York: Free Press.

Weissberg, R. P., & Greenberg, M. T. (1998). School and community competence-enhancement and prevention programs. In W. Damon (Ed.) *Handbook of child psychology: Vol. 4. Child psychology in practice* (pp. 877–954). New York: Wiley.

Wilson, W. J. (1996). *When work disappears: The world of the new urban poor.* New York: Knopf.

Zigler, E. (1994). Reshaping early childhood intervention to be a more effective weapon against poverty. *American Journal of Community Psychology, 22,* 37–48.

Zigler, E., & Styfco, S. J. (Eds.). (1993). *Head Start and beyond: A national plan for extended childhood intervention.* New Haven: Yale University Press.

Zigler, E., Styfco, S. J., & Gilman, E. (1993). The National Head Start Program for disadvantaged preschoolers. In E. Zigler & S. J. Styfco (Eds.), *Head Start and beyond: A national plan for extended childhood intervention* (pp. 1–41). New Haven: Yale University Press.

# Chapter 7

# Grade Retention, Social Promotion, and "Third Way" Alternatives

*Karl L. Alexander, Doris R. Entwisle, and Nader Kabbani*

What's a body to do when Johnny can't read? Not too long ago, many schools simply would have passed the problem along. That's "social promotion" in a nutshell, and if one believes all the furor, it's akin to educational malpractice. School systems throughout the country are responding vigorously to this most recent diagnosis of the crisis in our nation's schools—with new screening tests, mandatory summer schools, and, as a last recourse, retention in grade.

So, the pendulum swings again, just as it has over almost two centuries of U.S. education history (e.g., Larabee, 1984). But things seem different now. For one thing, the periodicity of the swing appears to have accelerated. Social promotion was in vogue during the 1970s; the practice yielded to rigorous promotion standards during the "back-to-basics" 1980s and then resurfaced barely a decade later when it became apparent that those high standards were having a disproportionate adverse impact on minority and low-income children. That's about a 10-year cycle, and as the decade of the 1990s drew to a close, yet another move to "toughen up" was already under way (e.g., Lawton, 1997; Olson, 1990).

A second difference is the extent of White House involvement. President Clinton made ending social promotion a centerpiece of his school reform agenda, and policymakers took heed. In successive State of the Union addresses (1998, 1999), the President challenged the country to "stop promoting children who don't learn." His use of the Presidential office had a galvanizing effect, much like that of Terrell Bell's Excellence Commission Report almost two decades earlier (National Commission on Excellence in Education, 1983). Back then, the Commission's call to action against "a rising tide of mediocrity" in U.S. education proved a surprisingly powerful catalyst for change (e.g., Educational Testing Service, 1990; U.S. Department of Education, 1994). Likewise, President Clinton's exhortation struck a responsive chord. For example, a five-year Lexis-Nexis search of newspaper articles identified 431 references to "social promotion" (with September 30, 1999, the search date). Eighty percent of the citations appeared within two years since the President's 1998 State of the Union speech and over half (51.5%) since his 1999 address.

And what exactly was the President saying about social promotion to warrant such media attention? To begin with (Clinton, 1998) "When we promote a child from grade to grade who hasn't mastered the work, we don't do that child any favors." We agree—who wouldn't? "Social promotion" as conventionally understood is not good educational practice. But the President also called for its end, and that raises the bar. In principle, students who are unprepared for the work ahead shouldn't be passed, but we know that pragmatic considerations often temper principle, and to end social promotion presumes there is a better alternative. Is there?

## Social Promotion and Grade Retention: Surveying the Landscape

A recent U.S. Department of Education report (1999, p. 5) defines social promotion as "the practice of allowing students who have failed to meet performance standards and academic requirements to pass on to the next grade with their peers instead of completing or satisfying the requirements." According to the American Federation of Teachers (hereafter, AFT), social promotion is

> ...an insidious practice that hides school failure and creates problems for everyone—for kids, who are deluded into thinking they have learned the skills to be successful or get the message that achievement doesn't count; for teachers who must face students who know

> that teachers wield no credible authority to demand
> hard work; for the business community and colleges
> that must spend millions of dollars on remediation,
> and for society that must deal with a growing propor-
> tion of uneducated citizens, unprepared to contribute
> productively to the economic and civic life of the
> nation. (1997, p. 1)

In light of such grave, and one would think obvious, consequences, can it really be commonplace for children to be passed on regardless of the quality of their performance? Strange though it may seem, the extent of social promotion has yet to be authoritatively mapped, and we simply do not know. National data are lacking because educational policy is primarily a local matter in the United States (e.g., Weiss & Gruber, 1987), but requisite data are sparse even at the local level.

To determine how many students are promoted despite falling short of prescribed standards requires, first, prescribing standards, and second, knowing the promotion/retention history of a well-defined population of students in relation to those standards. According to an AFT survey of promotion policies in 85 of the nation's largest school districts (1997, p. 12), these information needs are rarely met, "The first and most obvious problem with the policies is the absence of specific academic standards against which student progress is judged... the language often is vague and not useful for ensuring that teachers and administrators have a commonly agreed upon expectation about satisfactory performance."

Tracking social promotions at the local level typically is no better than the specification of standards, which means the extent of social promotion must be determined indirectly. Instead of specifying numbers of unwarranted promotions, the Department of Education offers only the following collateral data: half of teachers admit to having promoted unprepared students, 10–15% of high school graduates cannot balance a checkbook, 32–40% of public school students fall short of the "basic" standard on various National Assessment of Education Progress assessments of math competence, and roughly half the entering freshmen at the California State University System fail entry level math and English placement tests (1999, p. 6). Surely something has gone wrong when so many of our children fall short of reasonable standards, but such lists have little diagnostic value for determining exactly what that something is.

We can also attempt to better gauge social promotion by examining data about retention. At the national level, retention rates usually are inferred from annual census data that map the distribution of October school enrollments by age and grade for large, nationally representative samples. Panel surveys like the National Educational Longitudinal Study of 1988 (NELS88) are a second source for estimating retention rates across the country (for an overview of the NELS88 project, see U.S. Department of Education, 1998a). Individual school systems often keep records on retention also, but because definitions and the quality of recordkeeping differ from place to place, piecing together a general picture from local sources is impractical.

Robert Hauser (1999a) provides prevalence estimates for grade retention based on census data in his report entitled, "How Much Social Promotion Is There in the United States?" an infelicitous title because his work concerns grade retention, not social promotion. Children who are a year or more older than is typical for their grade in school are considered repeaters in the data. But the data are skewed by other students who deviate from the normal grade progression: students who start school late, for example, or who attend multigrade or ungraded special education classes for a time. For this reason and others, calculations based on age and grade correspondence are but a rough guide on the matter. Still, Hauser's use of these data is adept, and his estimates are conservative. For example, he focuses on changes in over-age enrollments comparing successive grades between years as opposed to the number or proportion of over-age children in a given grade in a given year.

Hauser's report considers changes over roughly three decades, and his many comparisons are hard to summarize. Still, he concludes (1999a) that "grade retention is pervasive in American schools." For example, 21% of children age 6–8 in 1987 were overage for grade according to Hauser's calculations. Because of nonretention factors that skew data, Hauser uses the 21% figure not as an estimate of retention, but as a baseline for comparing the same children's later experience (this is why his estimates are conservative). And what happens to this group later? At age 9–11, the percentage of children overage increased to 28%, and at age 12–14 it increased further to 31%.

Overage enrollments thus increase roughly 10 percentage points over the elementary school years into middle school. An indeterminate but presumably large fraction of the baseline rate would have to be added onto this figure to gauge the group's actual retention rate. It appears that about 9% of children who meet the age eligibility cutoff for kindergarten are held out a year by their parents (Zill et al., 1998, p. 17; see also Meisels, 1992). If we assume that 9% of Hauser's overage 6 to 8 year-olds in 1987 were overage for that reason, then the cohort's cumulative rate of retention through middle school (age 12–14) would be close to 22% (Hauser's 21% baseline figure less 9% plus the 10% increase from baseline).

This estimate applies to the country as a whole, but for certain kinds of children in certain kinds of settings, the estimates are much higher. Hauser's report, for example, documents large differences in over-age enrollments comparing Caucasians, African Americans, and Latinos. Though all three groups had similar rates in the 6–8 age range, by age 9–11 the minority children were 5%–10% more likely to be retained than Caucasians, and the difference increased further at age 15–17. Using similar data some years back, Bianchi (1984) showed that retention rates escalate rapidly as socioeconomic risk factors increase. Children of high school dropouts living in poverty, for example, had a retention rate of about 50% for males of all three racial/ethnic groups, and of about 40% for comparably disadvantaged females.

The NELS88 panel study of eighth graders—another national source—asked retrospectively about grade retention. Retrospective accounts are not completely reliable but neither is inferring retention from over-age enrollments. According to Meisels and Liaw (1993, p. 70), 19.3% of NELS88 parents report that their children had been held back at some point, a figure close to our rough estimate from Hauser's analysis. The NELS data also document large differences across social lines: 17% of Caucasians had been held back versus 30% of African Americans and 25% of Latinos. The differences are larger still when families are classified according to socioeconomic level: 34% of those in the lowest socioeconomic status (SES) quartile were retained compared with 8.6% of those in the highest quartile.

Comparisons of retention rates across state lines (e.g., Shepard & Smith, 1989) and across different kinds of school contexts also reveal large differences. High rates of retention in urban school systems that enroll mainly low-income and minority students are a particular concern. In Chicago, for example, the Chicago Longitudinal Study has been following a group of low-income, minority children (95% Black; 5% Hispanic) since 1986, when they were finishing kindergarten. Twenty percent of the group was held back by the time they had reached the third grade (Reynolds, 1992), 28% by the eighth grade (McCoy & Reynolds, 1999).

Our own research in Baltimore likewise focuses on an "at-risk" student population and likewise finds grade retention all too common— even more so than in Chicago. Our Beginning School Study (BSS) has been tracking the educational progress and personal development of a representative sample of Baltimore school children. This ongoing project began in fall 1982 when the youngsters were starting first grade. At the study's inception, two-thirds of the group qualified for free or reduced price meals at school (indicative of low income relative to family size), 42% were in single-parent households in first grade, and 38% of their mothers lacked high school degrees. When the BSS commenced, Baltimore's public school enrollment was about 77% African American. To provide for African American-Caucasian comparisons, schools with majority Caucasian enrollments were oversampled; nevertheless, the panel is 55% African American.

Considering the adverse socioeconomic conditions in Baltimore during this time and the "at-risk" makeup of the BSS panel, it is not surprising that many BSS children struggled academically. This struggle is evident in the group's high rate of grade retention. Over the first nine years of their schooling, half the panel repeated a grade, with 36% of repeaters registering two or more retentions. Reflecting national statistics (e.g., Shepard & Smith, 1989, p. 8), retention risk proved greatest in first grade. Seventeen percent of the cohort was held back then, accounting for a third of all first retentions. However, retention rates remained high, averaging 7.0% annually across years 2 through 9.[1]

The BSS experience aligns with other sources too in that retention risk in the BSS is socially patterned. For example, 41% of Caucasians repeated a grade versus 56.3% of African Americans. This is a large difference, but it pales against an almost 50-point spread across the SES "extremes": 68% of lower SES youngsters experienced one or more retentions as opposed to 21% of the higher SES segment of the sample.[2]

In summary, the BSS accords with other estimates of cumulative risk of grade retention in big-city school systems often reaching and exceeding 50% and above ("Quality Counts, '98," 1998, p. 13; e.g., Shepard & Smith, 1989). Multiple retentions too are commonplace, comprising just under 40% of all BSS retentions. The study also reveals that minority and lower SES youths are at greatest risk of retention, a finding that means that educational effectiveness and educational equity both are involved when promotion/retention policy is being considered.

What, then, do high levels of grade retention in the BSS and elsewhere imply about the extent of social promotion? Very little, unfortunately, because many children who are performing below par probably still get promoted. By one estimate, for example, two-thirds of Los Angeles' 1.1 million elementary school children are reading below grade level (Sahagun, 1999), while in Chicago, elementary schools are declared "reconstitution eligible" when the percentage of students scoring below grade level on standardized tests reaches 85. For the 1996/97 school year, a fifth of Chicago's elementary schools fell short of this standard and were placed on probation (Terry, 1996).

Perhaps reading ability and test scores aren't the right criteria for making promotion/retention decisions (remember, most school systems do not have clear-cut "pass" criteria), but obviously nowhere near two-thirds of Los Angeles's pupils will be held back in a given year (e.g.,

Sterngold, 1999) and retention rates in even the worst of Chicago's schools will fall far short of the 85% mark. One can only conclude that social promotion and grade repetition both are rampant in U.S. education.

Retention in grade is the traditional remedy for children not keeping up, and it would be good to have a sense of its effectiveness before considering the need for alternatives. Repeating a grade is intended to give children who have fallen behind a chance to catch up, but critics of the practice contend that it does harm, not good. Which view of grade retention is closer to the truth? That question is addressed in the next section.

## Grade Retention and School Performance Revisited

The sentiment most often encountered in the results of research on grade retention echo that of Holmes and Matthews (1984):

> Those who continue to retain pupils at grade level do so despite cumulative research evidence that the potential for negative effects consistently outweighs positive outcomes.... the burden of proof legitimately falls on proponents of retention plans to show there is compelling logic indicating success of their plans where so many other plans have failed. (p. 232)

Analogues to this statement appear again later in the 1980s (House, 1989, p. 210; Smith & Shepherd, 1987, p. 134) and still appear regularly (e.g., Hauser, 1999b; Reynolds et al., 1997). When we undertook the research published in our volume *On the Success of Failure,* our expectation was that we would find, and conclude, much the same.

Some years into the BSS, we noticed that many students had been held back, and we wondered if the retention really helped. As a team, we had a longstanding interest in issues of educational tracking, and it is reasonable to think of grade retention as a form of tracking (e.g., Alexander, Entwisle, & Legters, 1998). Certainly that connection had been made before by others. According to Smith and Shepard (1987, p. 133), for example, practices like retention and homogeneous grouping by ability help "advantaged groups, [create] further barriers for the disadvantaged, and [promote] segregation and stratification." Also, research on grade retention typically did not embrace the kind of children we were following—low income, urban—so our work would help fill a void.

We began gathering information on the group's schooling (test scores and marks) in the fall of first grade. First interviews concerning the children's attitudes toward school and their self-regard all took place before first-quarter report cards were issued.

The longitudinal approach to our data-gathering meant we could compare the repeaters' academic standing, self-regard, and liking for school after retention with their circumstances before they were held back. However, the results of our comparisons did not accord with statements like that of Holmes and Matthews with which we began this section. Rather than seeing harmful consequences, in many of our comparisons repeaters appeared to benefit from the experience. This finding obliged us to ponder our procedures and to revisit the then extant research literature to see what might account for our contrary results.

The existing literature, we concluded, was neither as compelling nor as consistent as we had been led to believe. Many of the research studies were quite dated; others were methodologically suspect. "Weak, inconclusive evidence," we concluded (Alexander et al., 1994, p. 220), "has been presented as robust."

And we discovered that this was not our view alone. For example, A. J. Reynolds, whose own research with a panel of Chicago schoolchildren finds against retention, offers the following commentary on a later literature review by Holmes (1989), the most comprehensive research stocktaking at the time of Reynolds' writing. He observes (1992, p.102) that just 25 of the 63 studies covered in Holmes' metaanalysis use matching or statistical adjustments to evaluate retention's effects, that just 16 of those match on students' prior achievements, and that just 4 match "on attributes that are consistently found to be predictive of the decision to retain, including prior achievement, sex and socioeconomic status." Reynolds does not mention that one of the four studies employing all these controls finds positive effects for retention (i.e.,

Peterson et al., 1987), but he does go on to say that the literature of the time "hardly constitutes conclusive evidence for or against retention." Reynolds' position on the lack of conclusive evidence for retention echoes that of Jackson (1975) and has been repeated more recently by N. Karweit (1992). Additionally, some research that is often characterized as negative is in fact more mixed. Holmes' literature, mentioned above, is quoted frequently as though it unequivocally rejected retention—a reading that is easy to understand in light of some of Holmes' own statements (see Wilson's comment, 1990, in his review of the Shepard–Smith volume). In fact, Holmes divides the studies he reviews into two groups: those studies that report "same-age" comparisons between retained students and their chronological peers who were promoted, and those studies that report "same-grade" comparisons between repeaters and their new classmates.

The same-age studies almost always favor promotion (Peterson et al., 1987, is an exception), but results under a same-grade framing often favor retention. Holmes' review covers 10 studies that use the latter approach. These studies produce an effect size advantage accruing to first-year retention of .25 SDs, but the size advantage becomes negligible after three years. Two of the 10 studies, however, consistently favor retention, and for them the effect size advantage accruing to retention remains a robust .73 SDs at three years and afterward. Holmes also looks in detail at nine studies that report positive effects for retention. In most of these, retention was combined with supplemental services, a pattern also commented upon by Karweit (1992).

## Positive Effects of Retention in Recent Research

Given the conflicting and inconclusive nature of the data in the literature up to the time of Holmes' review, unequivocal condemnation of retention is unwarranted. Moreover, four methodologically sound studies in the contemporary corpus of retention research find positive effects on academic outcomes. In addition to our own published work, there is the study just mentioned, by Peterson et al. (1987), a study by Pierson and Connell (1992), and a recent report by N. L. Karweit (1999) that uses the large, national Prospects data set (the Prospects research design is detailed in Bryant, Chu, & Hansen, 1991). Additionally, some studies report positive effects on attitudes (e.g., Reynolds, 1992).

Pierson and Connell (1992) compare achievement scores and attitudes in Grades 3 through 6 in two upstate New York school districts, one urban, one rural. Their research includes four groups: repeaters ($N$ = 74), a matched-ability comparison group ($N$ = 69), a random sampling of students ($N$ = 60), and—this is the interesting comparison—a group of children who were socially promoted ($N$ = 35), meaning that they were promoted despite being recommended for retention. The socially promoted group is small, but its inclusion affords a rare comparison. Here is what Pierson and Connell (1992) say about their results:

> It appears that whereas retention is not a cure-all for below grade-level academic performance, students whose academic performance suggests they should be retained, and who are retained, perform better two or more years later than students with comparable performance who are promoted.... the findings support the use of retention as a potentially effective remediation for academic difficulty in the early elementary grades.... early academic difficulties tend to persist over the course of elementary school and whereas retention does not eliminate these difficulties, social promotion may exacerbate them. (pp. 305–306)

N. L. Karweit (1999) examines retentions in Grades K–3 for children in the Prospects longitudinal first grade cohort ($N$ = 9,240), comparing reading and math achievement as assessed in the fall of first grade (1991), spring 1992, spring 1993, and spring 1994. She reports both same-age and same-grade comparisons from several perspectives (retained versus all promoted; retained versus all promoted after adjusting statistically for background differences; retained versus a low-performing promoted comparison group).[3] Almost 20% of the panel registered a retention over this period, half of them in first grade (first grade is the modal grade of retention in practically all studies that span multiple years).

Karweit's same-age comparisons show no benefit or harm accruing to retention—the achievement gap separating repeaters and promoted children is about the same after retention as it was prior to the former's being held back. Her same-grade comparisons, on the other hand, consistently favor retention. For example, before they were held back, to-be-repeaters were scoring on average 1.21 $SD$s behind to-be-promoted children in reading comprehension, vocabulary, and math. At the end of retainees' repeated year, the deficit was down to .38 $SD$s, and though it increased gradually thereafter, at three years postretention it stood at .55 $SD$s, still well below repeaters' preretention shortfall. Based on these and other results from her analysis, Karweit (1999) concludes as follows:

> Retention appears to be a catching up year that benefits children two or three years afterward. We pay specific attention to the same-grade comparisons because these are the comparisons that are probably most relevant to teachers and parents. That is, parents and teachers are probably most interested in how the retained child does in comparison to his classmates given the retention, not to his former classmates in another grade.... These results, then, are somewhat at odds with the verdict on retention offered by the educational research community over the last 25 years. Why might this be the case? The primary methodological difference between this study and prior studies is the ability in the present study to make comparisons of retained students' performance to non-retained children *before, during and after retention*.... In most cases, studies have looked at the achievement differentials at the end of the year of retention, concluded that retained students were still behind, and therefore concluded that retention was not effective. Even studies that look longitudinally at the effect of retention stress that retention is not effective because the gap between retained and promoted starts to widen after the retained year. However, even with the widening gap, the gap between

retained and promoted children after retention is not
as large as it was before retention. (pp. 43–44)

Using an approach similar to Karweit's, our Baltimore results show
much the same pattern. We examined first grade, second grade, and
third grade repeaters in relation to never-retained children over an eight-
year period beginning in the fall of first grade. Test scores (reading
comprehension, math concepts and their applications) and report card
marks (reading, math) were evaluated as academic outcomes. Table 7.1
shows same-grade retainee-promoted test score differences at several
benchmarks—the fall of first grade when all members of the panel were
just starting school; the spring of retainees' failed year (their "low point"
in all instances); a year later, at the end of their repeated year; and in
seventh grade (that is, eight years for one-time repeaters), which was as
far as BSS coverage extended at the time.

Repeaters' achievement scores fall below promoted youngsters' in
every instance, but the comparisons that predate retention are telling.
To-be-repeaters already are behind in the fall of first grade, and their
preretention trajectories put them even further back relative to promoted
children when they are designated for retention: in the spring of their
failed year, the three repeater groups were behind never retained
youngsters by between 1.33 and 1.90 $SD$s (this range applies to both
verbal and quantitative achievement domains). After retention, repeaters
still lag far behind, but their shortfall is less than it had been before
retention. This reduced shortfall applies to comparisons one year
postretention, when repeaters' progress is most pronounced, but even in
seventh grade—six years after retention in the case of first grade
repeaters—the differences still have not returned to their failed year
levels.

This pre-/post- comparison is just one of the many approaches we
used to gauge how retention affected these children's academic and
emotional development. The indications were not always clear-cut—
sometimes they seemed to conflict—but we concluded that retention
had mainly positive, not negative, consequences for the children in our
study group. This conclusion was not true for all repeaters under all

**TABLE 7.1**

**Differences Between Retainee and Never Retained CAT-R and CAT-M Averages (in Standard Deviation Units) at the Start of First Grade, the End of Each Retainee Group's Failed Year, the End of Each Retainee Group's Repeated Year, and the End of Seventh Grade, for First, Second, and Third Grade Retainees[a]**

| | CAT-R[b] | | | | CAT-M[c] | | | |
|---|---|---|---|---|---|---|---|---|
| | Fall 1st grade | Spring failed year[d] | Spring repeated year[e] | Spring 7th grade | Fall 1st grade | Spring failed year[d] | Spring repeated year[e] | Spring 7th grade |
| 1st grade retainees | .83 | 1.90 | .49 | 1.21 | 1.28 | 1.77 | .52 | 1.44 |
| 2nd grade retainees | .52 | 1.82 | .87 | .96 | .83 | 1.27 | .37 | 1.13 |
| 3rd grade retainees | .44 | 1.51 | .70 | .78 | .75 | 1.33 | .34 | .78 |

[a]Adapted from Table 4.4, Alexander, Entwisle, and Dauber, 1994, p. 92. [b]Originally measured as scale scores on the Reading Comprehension subtest of the California Achievement Test battery. [c]Originally measured as scale scores on the Math Concepts and Applications subtest of the California Achievement Test battery. [d]Failed year differences are calculated for first grade retainees at the end of year 1, for second grade retainees at the end of year 2, and for third grade retainees at the end of year 3. [e]Repeated year differences are calculated for first grade retainees at the end of year 2, for second grade retainees at the end of year 3, and for third grade retainees at the end of year 4.

circumstances, though. Positive effects were most consistently indicated for children held back only once and for children held back after first grade.

We declared retention a qualified success on that basis. However, the "boost" associated with retention in most instances still left repeaters lagging far behind, and we stressed that outcome also. If its goal is to improve the performance of poor achievers, then, according to our results, retention is a valid procedure. However, if the goal is to have children who are far behind catch up, then retention generally is not the answer. Repeaters' test scores and marks do not rise to the level of promoted children's, and when they make it to middle school—a difficult time of school transition under the best of circumstances (e.g., Eccles, Lord, & Midgley, 1991; Eccles & Midgley, 1989)—there are signs that they begin to slip back.

Retention does not turn struggling students into average students. Rather, it helps them hang on, and that leaves them vulnerable to setbacks later. We believe this is why many repeaters' grades and achievement scores decline in the middle grades, and we suspect a similar dynamic may be behind the retention-dropout connection.

## Grade Retention and Dropout: A Preliminary Look

Early grade retention probably is the most well-documented school-based risk factor for dropout (e.g., Grissom & Shepard, 1989; Rumberger, 1995; Rumberger & Larson, 1998; Temple et al., 2000). Hauser's review (1999a, pp. 21–22), for example, cites studies in which grade retention increases dropout risk by 12 percentage points, 70 percentage points, and 2.5 times. These are large and troubling differences, but is the link causal? That is, is grade retention itself an impetus to dropout or are grade retention and dropout both traceable to other factors, like poor school adjustment and low levels of achievement?

Teasing out cause from consequence is never easy and in this area the problem is exacerbated by critical knowledge gaps. According to the Goal 2 Work Group (1993, p. 18), "Few retention studies follow students throughout their school careers, especially studies beginning in the early elementary grades where retention is most likely to occur." The BSS embodies such a longitudinal design, but high school dropout was not addressed in our earlier work because the project at that point had only tracked school progress through the middle school years. Now at age 23–24, the cohort is six years past its "expected" high school graduation date of spring 1994. We have continued to monitor their life progress, which means we are in a position now to revisit the retention issue.

The mode of high school exit is known for 92.3% of the cohort. Concurring with other estimates for Baltimore (Bomster, 1992), 41.6% of the BSS panel left high school without degrees.[4] The likelihood of their dropping out is not random. Sixty percent of children from lower SES households (half the sample) dropped out at some point, for example, as against 15% of those in the upper SES quarter of the sample (Alexander et al., 2001). Dropout risk is nonrandom by retention status also. Sixty-five percent of all retainees over years 1–9 left without degrees; the figure for nonrepeaters is 18%,[5] and multiple retentions appear to be more of a problem than single retentions: 80% of multiple repeaters dropped out (compared to 56.5% of single repeaters), while the risk of dropping out approaches a certainty for children retained in elementary school *and* middle school (94% drop out in the BSS).

In general, the dropout risk associated with grade retention in a given year is greater at the upper grades, which seems reasonable because these older children have arrived or will shortly arrive at the age when school-leaving is legally permissible (age 16 in Maryland). Year 11 is the modal year of dropout in the BSS panel, but ninth grade is the modal grade of dropout, and in many instances these school-leavers are double repeaters.

The retention-dropout link is examined a bit more formally in Table 7.2, using logistic regression to estimate effects of retention on dropout risk in the BSS. Estimates are reported as odds ratios. These express the conditionality of dropout on retention as the ratio of the odds of dropping out for a particular repeater group to the odds for children never retained (the latter constitute the frame of reference throughout). To illustrate, with a dropout rate of 65% among repeaters in the BSS, the odds of dropping out given retention are about 1.857 to 1 (i.e., .650/.350). The corresponding odds for children not held back are .220 to 1 (i.e., .180/.820). The ratio of these two odds (i.e., 1.857/.220) gives the difference in the relative risk of dropout associated with grade retention: Repeaters are over eight times as likely to drop out as are never-retained youngsters. Logistic regression yields similar estimates, but adjusted for the influence of other factors. With no such adjustments, the logistic regression counterpart of the "effect" just calculated is 8.43.

"Effect" is in parentheses because this eightfold increase in the odds of dropout across the retained-never retained divide simply describes the association between retention and dropout in the BSS. We know that a host of other considerations influence both retention risk (Dauber, et al., 1993) and graduation prospects (Alexander, et al., 1997; Alexander et al., 2001), so to gauge retention's role as an impetus to dropout requires a more refined approach that takes account of possible confounding factors.

The estimates in Table 7.2 evaluate several different specifications of the retention experience under a variety of control conditions. All estimates are adjusted for race (African American, Caucasian), gender, and family socioeconomic level—key aspects of personal and social background. Personal resources and school experiences are controlled too, measured in first grade and again in the group's ninth year of school, which for children promoted each year is the first year of high school.[6] These resources include (a) school performance (the average of fall and spring verbal and quantitative test scores and of report card marks averaged across all four quarters), (b) parents' attitudes in support of their children's schooling (from parent interviews), (c) children's school engagement as reflected in their conduct (e.g., absences, teachers' work habit ratings from report cards), and (d) children's school engagement as reflected in their attitudes (e.g., expressed liking of school, academic self-image).

TABLE 7.2

**Odds Ratios Predicting High School Dropout From Measures of Grade Retention, Adjusting for Background Factors, First Grade Resources and Resources From Year 9**

| Independent variable(s)[a] | Background[b] + year 1 controls[c] | Background[b] + year 9 controls[d] | Background[b] + year 1[c] & year 9 controls[d] |
|---|---|---|---|
| 1. Any retention (versus none) | 4.60** | 3.81** | 3.68** |
| N | (665) | (584) | (548) |
| 2. # retentions | 3.07** | 2.51** | 2.65** |
| N | (665) | (584) | (548) |
| 3. Retained once | 3.81** | 3.21** | 3.32** |
| Multiple retentions | 10.81** | 6.58** | 7.38** |
| N | (665) | (584) | (548) |
| 4. Retained once, elem. school | 2.56** | 3.17** | 3.27** |
| Multiple retentions, elem. school | 3.63** | 3.21** | 3.18* |
| Retained once, middle school | 4.57** | 3.12** | 2.90** |
| Multiple retentions, middle school | 26.69** | 8.42+ | 7.29+ |
| Retained both elem & mid school | 29.64** | 26.89** | 29.06** |
| N | (663) | (582) | (546) |
| 5. Retained 1st gr only | 2.97* | 3.31** | 4.71** |
| Retained 1st gr and later | 12.50** | 9.21** | 16.96** |
| Retained once after 1st gr | 3.87** | 2.98** | 3.28** |
| Multiple retentions after 1st gr | 8.76** | 4.50** | 5.12** |
| N | (665) | (584) | (548) |

[a]The "no retention" group is the reference group for all the independent variable contrasts. [b]Background controls include gender, race (African American versus Caucasian) and family socioeconomic level (the average of mother's and father's education, mother's and father's occupational status, and family income—low/not low—after conversion to Z scores). [c]Year 1 controls include school performance (fall and spring CAT-R and CAT-M scores and math and reading marks from all four quarters, all averaged after conversion to Z scores); a composite measure of parents' attitudes in support of their children's schooling; a composite measure of children's attitudes toward self in the student role and attitudinal engagement with school; a composite measure of children's behavioral engagement with school. [d]Year 9 controls include school performance (fall and spring CAT-R and CAT-M scores and reading, math, English, and science marks from all four quarters, all averaged after

**TABLE 7.2 (CONTINUED)**

conversion to Z scores); a composite measure of parents' attitudes in support of their children's schooling; a composite measure of children's attitudes toward self in the student role and attitudinal engagement with school; a composite measure of children's behavioral engagement with school.

\*\*p ≥ .01. \*p ≥ .05. + p ≥ .10.

The first column of Table 7.2 estimates retention's effect with resource controls measured in first grade, prior to anyone's being held back (background factors also are controlled in the first column and throughout). In the second column, the resource controls all are from the panel's ninth year of school, before dropping out begins in earnest. These year-nine controls do not adjust for spuriousness (i.e., covariation that traces to common causes) in the classic sense; they are measured after retention, not before. Instead, they allow us to ask whether students who reach high school with a history of retention are at elevated risk of dropout compared to their never-retained peers even when academic records, levels of behavioral and attitudinal engagement, and parental support all are comparable. The third column reports odds ratio estimates adjusted for both first-grade and year-9 resource measures. These controls thus bracket the retention experience, and so constitute a stringent test of retention's status as a risk factor for dropout.

The estimates in Table 7.2 indicate a sizeable reduction in the "any retention" versus "no retention" zero-order odds ratio of 8.43 (mentioned above) when the relationship is adjusted for background factors and resources. This reduction occurs whether resources are measured prior to retention, subsequent to retention, or both, and this is to be expected. But the independent effect of grade retention, ranging from 3.68 to 4.60, remains quite large (and highly significant) in all three estimations. Whether retention per se is the operative agent still cannot be said with certainty, but such large adjusted differences surely cast strong suspicion on the practice.

The remaining rows of Table 7.2 explore various permutations of the likelihood of dropping out as a result of retention. Panel 2 indicates the odds of dropping out more than doubled with each additional retention. Panel 3 demonstrates that multiple repeaters are at substantially greater risk of dropout than are single repeaters, but single retentions still elevate dropout risk. Panel 4 signifies children held back in middle school are at much greater risk of dropout than are children held back in elementary school, but with odds ratios approaching 30, children held back at both levels of schooling are in serious jeopardy. Finally, Panel 5 indicates that with background and first-grade controls in place, risk is elevated among all repeater groups, but children held back just once (in first grade or later) are at lower risk of dropout than are double repeaters.

In identifying retention as a risk factor for dropout, these findings accord with much other research. Our earlier work on the effects of grade retention focused on performance outcomes and self-attitudes, not dropout. We concluded then that double repeaters and first-grade repeaters were helped least by the practice, so to see elevated levels of dropout in those instances is not surprising. But Table 7.2 indicates that retention also increases dropout risk among single repeaters who were held back after first grade, whereas earlier we concluded that those children profited from an extra year in grade. If repeating a grade in elementary school boosts children's school performance and shores up their self-regard, as we believe it does, why would it later increase dropout risk?

With rates of dropout elevated among repeaters of all classes, it would be easy simply to count the practice a self-evident failure and move on. But there are good reasons for wanting to understand the "why" of such an association. The pattern here, for example, is reminiscent of the "spurt–fade-out" cycle characteristic of early research on compensatory education (e.g., McDill et al., 1969). The cognitive boost children received from participation in Head Start and other early education enrichment programs typically dissipated after a few years, and on that basis some commentators (e.g., Jensen, 1969) deemed compensatory education a failure. But other interpretations are possible.

Perhaps, for example, the "spurt–fadeout" reflects not so much the failure of compensatory education, as the failure of regular schooling to provide the enriching experiences needed to sustain compensatory education's advances. Likewise, we see some benefits accruing to repeaters in the years after their retention, but they are prone to drop out anyway. Does this tendency reflect on the efficacy of retention, or does it say more about the support systems available to repeaters later? Perhaps a bit of both.

Table 7.3 shows report card mark averages year-by-year for never-retained children and various repeater groups over the first nine years of the BSS panel's schooling. In the elementary grades, the public schools in Baltimore evaluate children's performance in the major academic subjects as either "excellent," "good," "satisfactory," or "unsatisfactory." In middle school and high school, percentile rankings are used, with the failure cutoff set at 60%.[7] To put these ranking systems on a common metric, and to allow for other marking schemes outside the city system, marks in Table 7.3 are scored from 13 (A+, equivalent to a percentile grade of 98–100) to 1 ("unsatisfactory" in the primary grades; below 60% in the middle grades and high school). Baltimore's nominal marking distinctions at the elementary level have been set to the following values: Excellent, 12; Good, 9; Satisfactory, 6; Unsatisfactory, 1.

The averages in Table 7.3 do not bear directly on how retention affects children's school performance; the timing is not sufficiently nuanced for that purpose. Still, seeing the time line of children's marks is informative; it shows their standing at different stages of their schooling and thus the feedback they are getting. With a score of 6 indicating "satisfactory" performance and 9 "good" performance, never-retained children's marks fluctuate in the mid-range between "good" and "satisfactory" over the five elementary school years, then drop slightly to just over 7 during middle school (years 6–8), and slip yet again during the first year of high school, averaging just above "satisfactory" at that point. This decline in school performance, seen too in other research, parallels a decline in affective indicators of school engagement (e.g., liking of school, compliance with school routines—see, for example, Anderman & Maehr, 1994; Stipek & MacIver, 1989).

**TABLE 7.3**
**Mark Averages from First Grade Through Nine Years for Promoted and Retained Youngsters**

| Mark average[a] | Never retained | All repeaters | Retained once in elem. sch. only | Multiple rets in elem. sch. | Retained once in mid. sch. only | Multiple rets in mid. sch. | Retained in elem. & mid. sch. |
|---|---|---|---|---|---|---|---|
| Year 1 | 7.99 | 4.65 | 4.31 | 2.43 | 6.83 | 6.61 | 4.35 |
| Year 2 | 8.06 | 5.61 | 5.28 | 4.73 | 6.97 | 6.90 | 5.10 |
| Year 3 | 7.72 | 5.19 | 5.05 | 4.56 | 6.03 | 6.13 | 4.82 |
| Year 4 | 7.55 | 5.06 | 5.31 | 3.91 | 5.89 | 5.10 | 4.61 |
| Year 5 | 8.07 | 5.54 | 5.71 | 4.74 | 6.17 | 5.98 | 5.17 |
| Year 6 | 7.29 | 5.49 | 6.03 | 5.40 | 5.31 | 3.94 | 5.08 |
| Year 7 | 7.01 | 4.71 | 5.56 | 4.95 | 4.52 | 2.97 | 3.38 |
| Year 8 | 7.28 | 4.71 | 5.55 | 4.70 | 4.65 | 2.92 | 3.45 |
| Year 9 | 6.25 | 4.58 | 5.92 | 4.71 | 3.44 | 2.35 | 3.89 |
| Range of N's | (373–237) | (357–286) | (149–112) | (63–54) | (75–64) | (16–14) | (52–46) |

[a]Marks, taken from school records, range from 1 (failing) to 13 (A+), with the following benchmarks used for children in Baltimore public schools: Elementary level: Excellent = 12; Good = 9; Satisfactory = 6; Unsatisfactory = 1; Middle school and high school: 99–100 = 13; 86–87 = 9; 78–79 = 6; below 70 = 1.

This time line for the most successful of Baltimore's schoolchildren is useful as a frame of reference for viewing repeaters' standing. Retainees' marks lag far behind promoted children's marks for all years. Considering all repeaters together, their mark average falls well short of "satisfactory" every year and dips noticeably during the middle school years (which for most retainees includes year 9). The third column of Table 7.2, however, reveals an important qualification to that overall trend: Children held back in elementary school perform noticeably better in middle school than they had in elementary school. In fact, they are the only group for whom this can be said (although their marks still average below satisfactory even at their high point). In contrast, children held back two or more times in elementary school lag behind one-time repeaters initially and, after a spurt in year 2, evidence no more improvement over time; these youngsters are far behind their entire time in school.

One-time middle school repeaters follow yet a different mark trajectory. They attain reasonably good academic success in the primary grades (at least by the standard of all repeaters), but their marks drop off precipitously in the middle grades and then again in year 9. In fact, at 3.44, their year-nine average (right around "D") is the second lowest of any group at that point, "exceeded" only by middle school double repeaters, whose mark decline over the same period is even more precipitous.

Whereas elementary school repeaters' marks modestly improved over time and middle school repeaters fell off from a reasonably good start, children held back at both levels of schooling struggled mightily all along. Their marks during the elementary years register just a shade above those of elementary school double repeaters, and after year 6 their mark average never reaches even 4.0. Almost all these youngsters eventually drop out, and we can see in these comparisons at least one of the reasons why: They were badly behind right from the start and never recovered.

These figures reveal that even the best positioned children, those held back in elementary school who progressed smoothly thereafter, are precariously situated. This tenuous position doesn't leave much room to absorb additional setbacks, yet their history as repeaters suggests they will have some. Roderick (1993, 1994), for example, finds that middle schoolers who are overage for grade are at elevated risk of dropout regardless of whether they achieved that status through retention or by starting school late. This pattern suggests falling out of educational synchronization with their age group, not their status as repeaters, predisposes children to leave school early. Likewise, in the BSS (Entwisle, Alexander, & Olson, 1999), retention predicts dropout in the upper grades with school performance controlled, suggesting that something other than the academic sequelae of retention is at issue. Repeaters' grade disjunction with their age peers seems a likely candidate.

Consider the situation of double repeaters, most of whom eventually drop out. Many of these youngsters reach the legal age for dropout while still in middle school. Their history suggests that academics is not a source of much gratification. Students who are struggling academically sometimes find refuge in the social side of schooling, the extracurriculum (Mahoney & Cairns, 1997; McNeal, 1995) and strong friendships (Hymel, Comfort et al., 1996), but because repeaters are overage for grade, these sources of attachment to school also may be difficult to achieve.

## Our Perspective on Retention

Because we do not univocally condemn retention, we sometimes are misread as enthusiasts for the practice. This is decidedly not the case. Grade retention, especially grade retention without supplemental services, should be a last recourse, not a first recourse. It is expensive (the cost of an extra year or years of schooling), and it separates children from their age-mates, which under present organizational arrangements apparently creates problems for them later. Nor are we saying that grade retention is a solution to children's academic difficulties in the near-term. Our review of the literature has been highly selective. We deliberately have emphasized the positive as a counterbalance to voices that dwell on the negative, but even the most favorable evidence does not find repeaters catching up with their promoted classmates. That said, simply passing them and their problems along in the form of social promotion is not the answer either.

Not all children struggle at school for the same reason, a fact recognized in the recent Department of Education (1999) report on social promotion:

> Some students have learning disabilities, others have behavioral problems, are not ready for school, or face other challenges in their families and in their lives outside school. Some students barely miss meeting the standards, while others perform at levels considerably behind their peers. The point is that in order to help all students meet standards, educators must understand the nature of children's difficulties, and they must do so early. (p. 32)

This important point bears repeating, as it rarely comes up in the often tendentious debate over grade retention: To determine what is the best course in the individual case requires understanding what is behind a particular child's difficulties. The available research offers little guidance for determining individual placements; it informs the issue "on average." Telling people responsible for policy that grade retention "does harm and does not help" misrepresents the evidence and could do harm if it means that children who might benefit from extra time are deprived of it.

Jim Grant, whose "Retention/Promotion Checklist" (Grant & Richardson, 1998) is the rare instance of a research-informed diagnostic inventory, encourages us to think of retention when it seems advised as "additional learning time for misplaced students" (Kelly, 1999, p. 1). In his reconstruction of the concept of retention, Grant shifts the onus from the child to the school and strips away the negative associations. And what kind of children might be candidates for additional learning time? Grant (Kelly, 1999, p. 2) offers the following profile: "younger students in a class, emotionally immature children of average or high ability, and children who are small for their age" (see also Grant & Richardson, 1999). This kind of guidance is sorely needed, but research on retention's effectiveness rarely informs the issue at that level of detail.

Again, we cannot emphasize too strongly that our purpose here is not to push for wholesale retention. Indeed, one of our fears is that former President Clinton's call to end social promotion will be received as a mandate to "toughen up." But if grade retention should be the exception not the rule, and social promotion fixes nothing, then "What's a body to do?" Common sense suggests there ought to be a better way, and evidence is mounting that indeed there is.

## In Search of a "Third Way"

The easiest course would be to maintain present policies. From an administrator's perspective, the surface appeal of grade retention/repetition and social promotion—the two traditional "remedies"—is easy to understand. For one thing, they pose few, if any, burdens: no new programs, no additional staff training, no new technology. They can also help with external pressures. A school's achievement profile will look better, for example, if poor performing 7-year-olds are given tests designed for 6-year-olds (e.g., Gottfredson, 1988), as happens with first grade repeaters.

These approaches entail costs too, but often they are deferred (in the case of children's diminished life opportunities later) or hidden from view. What is the cost, for example, to teachers and to students performing at or near grade level when the span of reading levels in a class increases to four, or five, or six years owing to social promotion? The retention/promotion research literature never addresses those kinds of costs, but school people confront them daily, and parents sense them too (e.g., Natriello, 1998, pp. 16–17).

Even costs in dollars often are submerged. Funding for regular education typically is done by head count (e.g., a school's registration total on October 1), which means that for a principal to have half her enrollment in elementary school for six years instead of five poses no particular fiscal burden. The same holds true when students spend 13 or 14 years getting a diploma instead of only 12. The cumulative cost to the state or town treasury will be substantial, though, especially in localities with high poverty rates. These hidden costs of retention contrast sharply with the conspicuous costs of special programs for poor-performing children.

In light of the surface appeal of resting content with the status quo, the vigor of the current reform climate can't help but impress. School systems throughout the country are experimenting, ambitiously and energetically, with "third way" alternatives to both grade repetition and social promotion for children who are not keeping up. These programs often incorporate research-based "best practice" principles[8]—summer programs (Cooper et al., 2000), reduced class size (Grissmer, 1999), one-on-one or small group supplemental instruction (Farkas, 1998; Wasik & Slavin, 1993)—and preliminary results in many instances are encouraging (for overview, American Association of School Administrators, 1998; see U.S. Department of Education, 1999).

Chicago's public school system has been at the vanguard of this movement, and the experience there is instructive. Mandatory summer school for children who fail to meet promotion requirements is the cornerstone of Chicago's reform package, but it includes many support elements in addition to summer school (e.g., after-school enrichment programs and small transition schools for over-age ninth graders who fall short of promotion standards; see Toch, 1998). Mandatory summer school was instituted in 1996 for eighth graders and extended the following year to Grades 3 and 6. Promotion is determined by performance on the Iowa Test of Basic Skills (ITBS), reading and math grades, and attendance. The ITBS cutoffs are low, but the plan is to gradually raise them. In the program's first year, for example, eighth graders with an ITBS grade equivalent score below 7.2 at year's end were obliged to attend summer school; the next year, the standard was raised to 7.4, and the year after to 7.7. At present, summer school is required for sixth graders scoring more than 1.5 years below grade level and for third graders more than one year below grade level. Flunking reading or math is another road to summer school, as are 20 or more unexcused absences for children whose test scores fall below the national average for their grade (Catalyst, 1998).

The record for the first two years of Chicago's experiment is that about half the third, sixth, and eighth graders assigned to mandatory summer school come close enough to meeting the "pass" criteria to be moved up to the next grade (e.g., Chicago Public Schools, 1998). The others are retained. Such results demonstrate that an intensive, coordinated package of supplemental services can help a great many "at-risk" children avoid failure, even in the most challenging of circumstances (in 1996/97, 85% of Chicago's public school enrollment was low income; see Chicago Public Schools, 1999).[9]

We should take heart in that realization, as such victories are hard-won. But there is another implication of the numbers coming out of Chicago that is less cheery: Even with vigorous remediation, many children still fall short, a situation posing profound challenges. Children who are far behind academically, both repeaters and socially promoted youngsters, are not good prospects to suddenly spurt ahead, but a spurt is what it takes to catch up. Children are better off if they keep pace all along and do not have to catch up, but in Chicago, Baltimore, and our nation's other poverty-stricken urban centers, too many children lack the tools to keep up on their own.

The real need is not so much to find a formula for effective remediation as it is to find a formula for effective education, so that there will be less need later for the kind of rear-guard heroics exemplified in Chicago's reforms. The first priority is to have children start school with the skills to succeed, but we know that not all children do so. Large differences in "readiness" indicators present themselves as early as kindergarten and they are patterned along social lines. Minority children and those from lower SES households, in particular, often start school already behind (U.S. Department of Education, 2000), and this deficit needs to be addressed. The second line of defense should be, according to the American Federation of Teachers (AFT; 1997, pp. 24–25), "just in time" interventions that catch problems early, and we agree. Waiting until third grade, the first of Chicago's "promotion gates," almost certainly is too late. The AFT report quotes from our 1994 book to buttress the point, and we repeat it here for the same purpose:

> Children who will be retained some time in elementary
> or middle school are far behind academically at the start
> of school. Their marks indicate that they are having
> trouble with the curriculum, and their test scores at the
> beginning of first grade show serious deficiencies in
> terms of readiness skills. (Alexander et al., 1994, p. 58)

Children at risk of academic failure require early and ongoing interventions, and to address their needs effectively calls for a more comprehensive reform agenda than resolving the promotion/retention conundrum. Our concluding comments will focus on the school side of the equation, but it is important to recognize that most "school problems" do not originate there. Schools are the venue where low achievement and other problems come to public attention, but the problems themselves trace mainly to resource shortfall in children's home and community environments (e.g., Alexander, 1997; Entwisle et al., 1997, 2000). Still, we often ask our schools to fix problems not of their making, and the current reform climate is no exception.

There is a large group of children, perhaps 20% nationally and an even larger fraction in high-poverty school districts, for whom regular schooling simply is not effective. The externalities that weigh on these children—the drag of poverty and of dysfunctional families—are ever-present in their lives, and so too must be the "correctives" to them. These externalities make unrealistic the expectation of long-term cognitive benefits accruing from a one-time infusion of "extras," be they compensatory education (Barnett, 1995; Ramey, et al., 1998; Schweinhart & Weikart, 1998), full-day instead of half-day kindergarten (e.g., N. Karweit, 1989), or grade retention.

At present there is no sure blueprint for fixing "regular schooling." Classroom and school reform models that combine best practice lessons from basic research on student learning and classroom process to date have shown impressive effectiveness (e.g., Crane, 1998; Farkas, Fischer, Dosher, & Vicknair, 1998; Pinnell, et al., 1994; Ross et al., 1995), but even the best of these programs still leave many children behind, which suggests more radical steps are necessary. Larry Cuban (1989), for one, believes it will take nothing less than the dismantling of graded schooling, and he may be right—remember Jim Grant's characterization of grade retention as "additional learning time for misplaced children."

We observed above the social consequences of retention on older children displaced from their age peer group; however, the consequences of rigid age-grading are even more profound and far-reaching in the early grades. The calendar-driven model of schooling sets a severe pace. Children who aren't caught up when the teacher is obliged to move on to the next lesson plan fall behind, and if they are far behind when the final bell sounds for the year, what then?

The curriculum in the primary grades is the foundation for all later learning, and children need to master it before moving on. But, obviously, children do not all mature on the same timetable, they do not all learn at the same pace, and they do not all learn in the same way. Here is how the National Education Commission on Time and Learning (1994) puts it:

> Decades of school improvement efforts have foundered on a fundamental design flaw, the assumption that learning can be doled out by the clock and defined by the calendar…. Some students take three to six times longer than others to learn the same thing. Yet students are caught in a time trap—processed on an assembly line to the minute. Our usage of time virtually assures the failure of many students. (p. 7)

The challenge—a daunting one—is to build more flexibility into the system without the stigma and other problems that come with being "off-time" for one's age. In tomorrow's classrooms, that some 7-year-olds are working on "first grade" material and others on "third grade" material should hardly warrant notice. With some restrictions, class-mixing of this sort is routine in high school and college, so long as prerequisites are satisfied. With prerequisites appropriately defined in the primary grades, why couldn't similar organizational arrangements be attempted? One barrier is that "age" and "grade" are so closely aligned in how we think about schooling at the elementary level that separating them is hard to conceive. Standardized organizational forms like the age-graded classroom constitute elements of what Tyack and colleagues refer to as a "grammar of schooling" (Tyack & Cuban, 1995; Tyack & Tobin, 1994). Once institutionalized as the understood way of doing things, such practices are highly resistant to change. That's why "break-the-mold" changes in school organization are needed. Examples of reforms that promise to loosen the stranglehold of the clock include multiage or nongraded classes (e.g., Goodlad & Anderson, 1987; Gutierrez & Slavin, 1992; Lloyd, 1999), in which placement is determined by skill level rather than age, and extended-year and summer program alternatives to the archaic nine-month school calendar (e.g., Cooper et. al., 2000; Gándara & Fish, 1994).

For such new structures to work well, they will have to be administered flexibly and incorporate appropriate best practices into the extra learning time they afford.[10] This may not be quite the right formula even then, as circumstances outside school still will conspire to hold many children back. But allowing the clock and calendar to dictate which children will succeed and which will stumble is not good educational practice. The pace of schooling under present organizational arrangements poses obstacles, often insurmountable ones, for children who have the ability but need more time. An extra year in grade might help some of these youngsters, and reforms like those being tested in Chicago and elsewhere might well reduce the need for retention,[11] but until school reform addresses the pace of learning in a serious way, too many of our children will continue to fall behind, the pendulum will continue to swing, and we will find ourselves again pondering, "What's a body to do?"

## Acknowledgments

We thank Jim Grant for helpful comments on an earlier version. Preparation of this chapter was supported by Spencer Foundation Grant No. B-1517 ("Disengagement and Dropout: A Study of the Long-Term Process that Leads to Early Withdrawal from School"), and Grant No. R117D94005 from the Office of Educational Research and Improvement, U.S. Department of Education to the Johns Hopkins University Center for Research on the Education of Students Placed at Risk.

## Endnotes

[1] We also have monitored accelerations. Altogether, 83 children, or 10.6% of the panel, "skipped" a grade at some point, either within or between years. Eighty-one of the 83 had been previously retained, amounting to just over a fifth of all repeaters. According to our checking, though, the consequences of retention are the same whether or not repeaters later moved ahead.

² About one-half of the sample is classified as lower SES and one fourth as higher SES, based on mothers' and fathers' education, mothers' and fathers' occupation, and family income, as reflected in participation in the school meal program. Mothers' education in the lower SES group averages 10 years and 95% qualified for subsidized school meals; in the higher group, mothers' education averages 14.6 years, and 13% received reduced price meals. These distinctions, we believe, meaningfully capture the range of family standing in the city's public school enrollment, but that range embraces few genuinely upper SES, wealthy households. It should be understood that the "lower" and "higher" descriptors are context bound.

³ The NELS88 data also have been used to assess effects of retention, in this case for a nationally representative sample of eighth graders. However, the NELS88 design is deficient for this purpose in at least two key respects. First, the project relies on parent and student recall to identify repeaters and grade of retention, undoubtedly introducing measurement error. Second, when used to assess consequences of early retention, the project provides no controls for conditions that predate retention (e.g., achievement scores; measures of school adjustment). Because of this, when repeaters are found to lag behind promoted children, as in Meisels and Liaw's (1993) analysis, it cannot be said whether the difference is a consequence of retention or a cause of retention.

⁴ Dropout was determined through self-reports, first elicited in the spring of project year 9 and then annually thereafter through project year 18 (five years beyond the panel's expected graduation date). It refers to the first occasion of school-leaving; whether or not dropouts later returned or obtained alternative high school certification is a separate matter. By age 22–23, 39.6% of BSS dropouts completed high school, 9.2% with regular high school degrees, 30.4% by way of the GED (based on information for 293 of 303 dropouts). This is below the estimate of 50% eventual degree completion nationally (U.S. Department of Education, 1989, 1998b).

⁵ Year 9 is a convenient terminus ad quem for these comparisons. For one thing, relatively few dropouts have left school by then, which means we are able to speak to considerations that apply to the entire cohort. Also, through middle school grade, retention usually is an all-or-nothing proposition. In high school, students often can fail one or more subjects and still be moved ahead.

⁶ Measurement details are available in Alexander et al., 2001. That report also develops the rationale for a life-course perspective on dropout in which these several resource measures are evaluated as precursors to dropout.

⁷ This is the cutoff used in Baltimore through December 1994, or through the middle of the panel's 12th year of school. At that point, the failure threshold was changed

to 70%, bringing it into alignment with neighboring school districts. Because this change occurred so late in the group's experience, we use 60% throughout.

[8] The "best practices" approach to reform involves identifying institutions that have accomplished significant improvements in their performance and efficiency. The innovative practices and activities of these organizations are referred to as "best practices" and can be used to spearhead similar reforms at institutions with comparable missions. Benchmarking is frequently used to gauge progress (U.S. General Accounting Office, 1995).

[9] The Chicago Consortium on School Research recently released an evaluation of the first two years of the Chicago reforms (Roderick et al., 1999). In general terms, it finds pass rates in grades 3, 6, and 8 up overall (compared against preform benchmarks), that the largest gains are registered by the poorest performing children, and that summer school helped many children, especially sixth and eighth graders. However, children held back under the new plan are not faring well despite supplemental services and resources.

[10] They also will require a workable management plan and considerable staff training. For a sense of these and other challenges in the context of multiage classes, see Appalachia Educational Laboratory, 1998.

[11] We thank Jim Grant for this insight (personal communication). We have cast the present discussion in terms of alternatives to grade retention, but "retention reduction" no doubt is a more realistic expectation.

## References

Alexander, K. L. (1997). Public schools and the public good. *Social Forces, 76,* 1–30.

Alexander, K. L., Entwisle, D. R., & Dauber, S. L. (1994). *On the success of failure: A reassessment of the effects of retention in the primary grades.* Cambridge, MA: Cambridge University Press.

Alexander, K. L., Entwisle, D. R., & Horsey, C. (1997). From first grade forward: Early foundations of high school dropout. *Sociology of Education, 70,* 87–107.

Alexander, K. L., Entwisle, D. R., & Kabbani, N. (2001). The dropout process in life course perspective: Risk factors at home and school. *Early Teachers College Record, 103*(5), 760–822.

Alexander, K. L., Entwisle, D. R., & Legters, N. (1998, August). *On the multiple faces of first grade tracking.* Paper presented at the annual meeting of the American Sociological Association, San Francisco.

American Association of School Administrators. (1998). *The School Administrator, 7*(55).

American Federation of Teachers. (1997). *Passing on failure: District promotion policies and practices.* Washington, DC: Author.

Anderman, E. M., & Maehr, M. L. (1994). Motivation and schooling in the middle grades. *Review of Educational Research, 64,* 287–309.

Appalachia Educational Laboratory. (1998, September). Evolution of the primary program in six Kentucky schools. *Notes from the Field: Education Reform in Rural Kentucky, 6,* 1–12.

Barnett, W. S. (1995). Long-term effects of early childhood care and education on disadvantaged children's cognitive development and school success. *The future of children, 5*(3), 25–50.

Bianchi, S. M. (1984). Children's progress through school: A research note. *Sociology of Education, 57,* 184–192.

Bomster, M. (1992, September 18). City's dropout rate ranked 9th-worse in nation in 1990. *The Baltimore Sun,* pp. C1–4.

Bryant, E., Chu, A., & Hansen, M. (1991). *Prospects: The congressionally mandated study of educational growth and opportunity: Sample design.* Washington, DC: U.S. Department of Education.

Catalyst. (1998, September). CPS policies: Elementary school promotion policy. Available: http://www.catalyst-chicago.org (Accessed 08/22/99).

Chicago Public Schools. (1998, August 21). Chicago Public Schools has successful summer school. In CPS press release [Online]. Available: http://www.cps.k12.il.us (Accessed 06/30/99).

Chicago Public Schools. (1999). Student characteristics. Available: http://www.cps.k12.il.us (Accessed 08/22/99).

Clinton, W. J. (1998). *State of the union address.* Washington, DC: Department of State, Bureau of Public Affairs.

Clinton, W. J. (1999). *State of the union address.* Washington, DC: Department of State, Bureau of Public Affairs.

Cooper, H., Charlton, K., Valentine, J. C., & Muhlenbruck, L. (2000). *Making the most of summer school: A meta-analytic and narrative review.* Monograph Series for the Society for Research in Child Development 65(1, Serial No. 260).

Crane, J. (Ed.) (1998). *Social programs that work.* New York: Russell Sage.

Cuban, L. (1989). The "at-risk" label and the problem of urban school reform. *Phi Delta Kappan, 70,* 780–801.

Dauber, S. L., Alexander, K. L., & Entwisle, D. R. (1993). Characteristics of retainees and early precursors of retention in grade: Who is held back? *Merrill-Palmer Quarterly, 39,* 326–343.

Eccles, J. S., Lord, S., & Midgley, C. (1991). What are we doing to early adolescents? The impact of educational contexts on early adolescents. *American Journal of Education, 99,* 521–542.

Eccles, J. S., & Midgley, C. (1989). Stage/environment fit: Developmentally appropriate classrooms for early adolescents. In R. E. Ames & C. Ames (Eds.), *Research on motivation in education* (pp. 139–186). New York: Academic Press.

Educational Testing Service. (1990). *The education reform decade.* Princeton, NJ: ETS Policy Information Center, Educational Testing Service.

Entwisle, D. R., Alexander, K. L., & Olson, L. S. (1997). *Children, schools and inequality.* Boulder, CO: Westview Press.

Entwisle, D. R., Alexander, K. L., & Olson, L. S. (1999, August). *Urban teenagers: Work, stopout, and dropout.* Paper presented at the annual meeting of the American Sociological Association, Chicago.

Entwisle, D. R., Alexander, K. L., & Olson, L. S. (2000). Early work histories of urban youth. *American Sociological Review, 65*(2), 279–297.

Farkas, G. (1998). Reading one-to-one: An intensive program serving a great many students while still achieving large effects. In J. Crane (Ed.), *Social programs that work* (pp. 75–109). New York: Russell Sage.

Farkas, G., Fischer, J., Dosher, R., & Vicknair, K. (1998). Can all children learn to read at grade-level by the end of third grade? In D. Vannoy & P. J. Dubeck (Eds.), *Challenges for work and family in the twenty-first century* (pp. 143–165). New York: Aldine de Gruyter.

Gándara, P., & Fish, J. (1994). Year-round schooling as an avenue to major structural reform. *Educational Evaluation and Policy Analysis, 16,* 67–85.

Goal 2 Work Group. (1993). *Reaching the goals: Goal 2, high school completion.* Washington, DC: Office of Research and Improvement, U.S. Department of Education.

Goodlad, J., & Anderson, R. (1987). *The nongraded elementary school.* New York: Teachers College Press.

Gottfredson, G. D. (1988). *You get what you measure, you get what you don't: Higher standards, higher test scores, more retention in grade* [Report No. 29]. Baltimore: Center for Research on Elementary and Middle Schools, The Johns Hopkins University.

Grant, J., & Richardson, I. (1998). *The retention/promotion checklist.* Peterborough, NH: Crystal Springs Books.

Grant, J., & Richardson, I. (1999). One more year. *High School Magazine, 7*(4), 9–13.

Grissmer, D. (Ed.). (1999). *Educational evaluation and policy analysis. Vol. 21: Class size: Issues and new evidence* [Special issue]. Washington, DC: American Educational Research Association.

Grissom, J., & Shepard, L. A. (1989). Repeating and dropping out of school. In L. A. Shepard & M. L. Smith (Eds.), *Flunking grades: Research and policies on retention* (pp. 34–63). London: Falmer Press.

Gutierrez, R., & Slavin, R. E. (1992). Achievement effects of nongraded elementary schools: A best evidence synthesis. *Review of Educational Research, 62,* 333–376.

Hauser, R. M. (1999a). *How much social promotion is there in the United States?* (CDE Working Paper No. 99–06). Madison, WI: Center for Demography and Ecology, University of Wisconsin, Madison.

Hauser, R. M. (1999b, April 7). What if we ended social promotion? *Education Week on the Web, 18*(30). Available: http://www.edweek.org.

Holmes, C. (1989). Grade level retention effects: A meta-analysis of research studies. In L. A. Shepard & M. L. Smith (Eds.), *Flunking grades: Research and policies on retention* (pp. 16–33). London: Falmer Press.

Holmes, C., & Matthews, K. (1984). The effects of nonpromotion on elementary and junior high school pupils: A meta-analysis. *Review of Educational Research, 54,* 225–236.

House, E. (1989). Policy implications of retention research. In L. A. Shepard & M. L. Smith (Eds.), *Flunking grades: Research and policies on retention* (pp. 202–213). London: Falmer Press.

Hymel, S., Comfort, C., Schonert-Reichl, K., & McDougall, P. (1996). Academic failure and school dropout: The influence of peers. In J. Juvonen & K. R. Wentzel (Eds.), *Social motivation: Understanding children's school adjustment* (pp. 313–345). New York: Cambridge University Press.

Jackson, G. B. (1975). The research evidence on the effects of grade retention. *Review of Educational Research, 45,* 613–635.

Jensen, A. R. (1969). How much can we boost I.Q. and scholastic achievement? *Harvard Educational Review, 39,* 1–123.

Karweit, N. (1989). Effective kindergarten practices for students as risk. In R. E. Slavin, N. L. Karweit, & N. A. Madden (Eds.), *Effective programs for students at risk* (pp. 103–142). Boston: Allyn and Bacon.

Karweit, N. (1992). Retention policy. In M. Alkin (Ed.), *Encyclopedia of educational research* (pp. 1114–1118). New York: Macmillan.

Karweit, N. L. (1999). *Grade retention: Prevalence, timing, and effects* (Report No. 33). Baltimore: CRESPAR.

Kelly, K. (1999). Retention vs. social promotion: Schools search for alternatives. *Harvard Education Letter, 15*(1), 1–3.

Larabee, D. F. (1984). Setting the standard: Alternative policies for student promotion. *Harvard Educational Review, 54,* 67–87.

Lawton, M. (1997, June 11). Promote or retain? Pendulum for students swings back again. *Education Week on the Web* [Online]. Available: http://www.edweek.org.

Lloyd, L. (1999). Multi-age classes and high ability students. *Review of Educational Research, 69,* 187–212.

Mahoney, J. L., & Cairns, R. B. (1997). Do extracurricular activities protect against early school dropout? *Developmental Psychology, 33*(2), 241–253.

McCoy, A. R., & Reynolds, A. J. (1999). Grade retention and school performance: An extended investigation. *Journal of School Psychology, 37*(3), 273–298.

McDill, E. L., McDill, M. S., & Sprehe, J. T. (1969). *Strategies for success in compensatory education: An appraisal of evaluation research.* Baltimore, MD: Hopkins Press.

McNeal, R. B., Jr. (1995). Extracurricular activities and high school dropout. *Sociology of Education, 68,* 62–81.

Meisels, S. J. (1992). Doing harm by doing good: Iatrogenic effects of early childhood enrollment and promotion policies. *Early Childhood Research Quarterly, 7,* 155–174.

Meisels, S. J., & Liaw, F.R. (1993). Failure in grade: Do retained students catch up? *Journal of Educational Research, 87*(2), 69–77.

National Commission on Excellence in Education. (1983). *A nation at risk: The imperative for educational reform.* Washington, DC: U.S. Department of Education.

National Education Commission on Time and Learning. (1994). *Prisoners of time.* Washington, DC: Author.

Natriello, G. (1998, August). Failing grades for retention. *The School Administrator,* pp. 14–17.

Olson, L. (1990, May 16). Education officials reconsider policies on grade retention. *Education Week on the Web.* Available: http://www.edweek.org.

Peterson, S. E., DeGracie, J. S., & Ayabe, C. R. (1987). A longitudinal study of the effects of retention/promotion on academic achievement. *American Educational Research Journal, 27,* 107–118.

Pierson, L. H., & Connell, J. P. (1992). Effect of grade retention on self-system processes, school engagement and academic performance. *Journal of Educational Psychology, 84,* 300–307.

Pinnell, G. S., Lyons, C. A., DeFord, D. E., Bryk, A. S., & Seltzer, M. (1994). Comparing instructional models for the literacy education of high-risk first graders. *Reading Research Quarterly, 29*(1), 9–39.

Quality Counts, '98: An Education Week Pew Charitable Trust report on education in the 50 states. (1998, January). *Education Week, 17*(17).

Ramey, C. T., Campbell, F. A., & Blair, C. (1998). Enhancing the life course for high-risk children: Results from the Abecedarian Project. In J. Crane (Ed.), *Social programs that work* (pp. 163–183). New York: Russell Sage.

Reynolds, A. J. (1992). Grade retention and school adjustment: An explanatory analysis. *Educational Evaluation and Policy Analysis, 14,* 101–121.

Reynolds, A., Temple, J., & McCoy, A. (1997, September 17). Grade retention doesn't work. *Education Week on the Web* [Online] 17(3). Available: http://www.edweek.org.

Roderick, M. (1993). *The path to dropping out: Evidence for intervention.* Westport, CT: Auburn House.

Roderick, M. (1994). Grade retention and school dropout: Investigating the association. *American Educational Research Journal, 31*(4), 729–759.

Roderick, M., Bryk, A. S., Jacob, B. A., Easton, J. Q., & Allensworth, E. (1999). *Ending social promotion: Results from the first two years.* Chicago: Chicago Consortium on School Research.

Ross, S. M., Smith, L. J., Casey, J., & Slavin, R. E. (1995). Increasing the academic success of disadvantaged children: An examination of alternative early intervention programs. *American Educational Research Journal, 32*(4), 773–800.

Rumberger, R. W. (1995). Dropping out of middle school: A multilevel analysis of students and schools. *American Educational Research Journal, 32*(3), 583–625.

Rumberger, R. W., & Larson, K. A. (1998, November). Student mobility and the increased risk of high school dropout. *American Journal of Education, 107,* 1–35.

Sahagun, L. (1999, April 17). L.A. school district curtails plan to end social promotions. *Los Angeles Times,* p. 1.

Schweinhart, L. J., & Weikart, D. P. (1998). High/Scope Perry Preschool Program effects at age twenty-seven. In J. Crane (Ed.), *Social programs that work* (pp. 148–183). New York: Russell Sage.

Shepard, L. A., & Smith, M. L. (1989). Introduction and overview. In L. A. Shepard & M. L. Smith (Eds.), *Flunking grades: Research and policies on retention.* London: Falmer Press.

Smith, M. L., & Shepard, L. A. (1987). What doesn't work: Explaining policies of retention in the early grades. *Phi Delta Kappan, 66,* 129–134.

Sterngold, J. (1999, December 2). L.A. may back off get-tough policy; 50% of the schoolchildren would repeat grades if officials ended 'social promotion.' *The New York Times,* p. A23.

Stipek, D., & MacIver, D. (1989). Developmental changes in children's assessment of intellectual competence. *Child Development, 60,* 521–538.

Temple, J. A., Reynolds, A. J., & Miedel, W. T. (2000). Can early intervention prevent high school dropout? Evidence from the Chicago Longitudinal Study. *Urban Education, 35*(1), 31-56.

Terry, D. (1996, October 1). One fifth of schools put on probation in Chicago. *The New York Times,* p. 14.

Toch, T. (1998, October 5). Schools try a new (old) tack: Holding back flunking students. *U.S. News and World Report,* p. 59.

Tyack, D., & Cuban, L. (1995). *Tinkering toward Utopia: A century of public school reform.* Cambridge, MA: Harvard University Press.

Tyack, D., & Tobin, W. (1994). The grammar of schooling: Why has it been so hard to change? *American Educational Research Journal, 31,* 453–479.

U.S. Department of Education. (1989). *Dropout rates in the United States: 1988* (NCES 89-609 by Mary J. Frase). Washington, DC: U.S. Department of Education, National Center for Education Statistics.

U.S. Department of Education. (1994). *Digest of education statistics, 1994* (NCES 94-115). Washington, DC: U.S. Department of Education, National Center for Education Statistics.

U.S. Department of Education. (1998a). *National Education Longitudinal Study of 1988 (NELS:88) base year through second follow-up: Final methodology report* (Working Paper No. 98-06 by Steven J. Ingels, Leslie A. Scott, John R. Taylor, Jeffrey Owings [Project Officer], Peggy Quinn). Washington, DC: U.S. Department of Education, National Center for Education Statistics.

U.S. Department of Education. (1998b). *Subsequent educational attainment of high school dropouts* (NCES 98-085 by Jennifer Berktold, Sonya Geis, and Phillip Kaufman). Washington, DC: U.S. Department of Education, National Center for Education Statistics.

U.S. Department of Education. (1999). *Taking responsibility for ending social promotion.* Washington, DC: Author.

U.S. Department of Education. (2000). *America's kindergartners: Findings from the Early Childhood Longitudinal Study, kindergarten class of 1998-99, Fall 1998* (NCES 2000-070 by Jerry West [Project Officer], Kristin Denton, and Elvie Germino-Hausekn). Washington, DC: U.S. Department of Education, National Center for Education Statistics.

U.S. General Accounting Office. (1995). *Best practices methodology: A new approach for improving government operations* (GAO/NSIAD-95-154). Washington, DC: Author.

Wasik, B. A., & Slavin, R. E. (1993). Preventing early reading failure with one-to-one tutoring: A review of five programs. *Reading Research Quarterly, 28*(2), 179–200.

Wehlage, G. G., Rutter, R. A., Smith, G., Lesko, N., & Fernandez, R. (1989). *Reducing the risk: Schools as communities of support.* Philadelphia: Falmer Press.

Weiss, J., & Gruber, J. (1987). The managed irrelevance of federal education statistics. In W. Alonso & P. Starr (Eds.), *The politics of numbers* (pp. 363–391). New York: Russell Sage.

Wilson, M. (1990). [Review of the book *Flunking grades: Research and policies on retention*]. *Educational Evaluation and Policy Analysis, 12,* 228–230.

Zill, N., Loomis, L. S., & West, J. (1998). *The elementary school performance and adjustment of children who enter kindergarten late or repeat kindergarten: Findings from national surveys* (NCES 98-097). National Center for Education Statistics Statistical Analysis Report. Washington, DC: U.S. Department of Education, National Center for Education Statistics.

# PART III

## National Investments

# Chapter 8

# The Three Types of Early Childhood Programs in the United States

*Lawrence J. Schweinhart*

Head Start, public school prekindergarten programs, and preschool child care programs define the landscape of early childhood programs in the United States today. If we wish to understand and improve early childhood care and education, the current programs are our starting places. These three types of programs have their own histories, forms of governance, and staffing patterns. This differentiation insulates early childhood program workers from each other and can narrow our perspectives on early childhood programs. Staff of one kind of program—even administrators and evaluators—find themselves critical and distant from staff of the other kinds of programs. This is not to say that their criticisms are unwarranted, but rather that we must strive to transcend these narrow job-related perspectives in order to achieve a panoramic view of all the types of early childhood programs. Such a view will enable us to improve programs through better evaluation and design.

## Histories

Some of the roots of the current early childhood program situation lie in the 1960s and the birth of Head Start. Head Start was a part of President Lyndon Johnson's War on Poverty and, as such, participated in the general effort to empower people living in poverty. This effort operated in tandem with the civil rights movement and the empowerment of people of color. Many people living in poverty and people of color held public schools in low regard. They considered the public schools unresponsive to their needs and insensitive to their plight. The federal government established community action agencies as alternative structures for their empowerment and as bureaucratic homes for Head

Start and other federal programs. As a group, the people running these programs were adamantly opposed to having the public schools run Head Start. This attitude expressed itself forcefully in 1980, keeping Head Start in the U.S. Department of Health and Human Services when the U.S. Department of Education became a separate entity. Throughout these years, some public schools did operate some Head Start programs. The point, though, was that the majority of Head Start programs operated independently of the public schools, and even the ones within the public schools were isolated from public school bureaucracies. Thus, Head Start was created as an independent national institution just a few decades ago.

The rift between Head Start and public schools expressed itself programmatically as well. Public schools required certified teachers with bachelor's degrees. Head Start did not require professional teacher certification and took pride in hiring, and thereby empowering, people from impoverished communities. Public school classrooms focused almost exclusively on education at that time. Head Start found its identity by focusing not only on education, but also on parent involvement, health care access, and social services support. The alienation of poor people from the public schools became institutionalized in Head Start and is still there today.

Unlike public schools and Head Start, which have always had full government support, child care began without government support but rather with private, parental support. Occasional child care beyond the family has always existed, but, during World War II, mothers began to move into the workforce, and their numbers there have continued to increase ever since. Maternal employment (combined with the paternal employment away from home that preceded it beginning with the Industrial Revolution) defined the need for regular, extrafamilial child care. But even today, some families choose maternal employment and others do not. Those who do not regularly use child care pursue their self-interest politically by discouraging government from providing preferential financial treatment to those who do use regular child care and thus keep government support for child care lower than it would otherwise be.

## Governance Patterns

Early childhood programs in the United States are governed by federal, state, or local governments, by private organizations, or by some combination of these. Most public programs are either Head Start or public school; private programs are either for-profit or nonprofit. Child care licensing usually comes from state departments of social services. Partial child care subsidies usually come from the U.S. Department of Health and Human Services through state departments of social services. Early childhood programs have a fuzzy boundary with child care by relatives and friends, which is, in turn, only a step removed from family childrearing. Because of this contested area between public and family responsibility, the amount and reach of public regulation and funding is a matter of some dispute.

It is useful to distinguish between local and distal governance of early childhood programs. Local governance is closely related to program administration and directly affects program operation. Distal governance in the United States is either federal, state, or some combination of both and acts through local governance and program administration. The balance of federal and state responsibilities has been a continuing American debate, with insistence upon states' rights once leading to civil war. Within the limits on federal powers set by the U.S. Constitution, the 20th century has seen considerable growth of federal budgets and responsibility, including funding for early childhood programs. The lion's share of public funding for early childhood programs, both Head Start and child care, originates with the federal government. In contrast, most public school funding, including funding for prekindergarten programs, originates with state and local governments.

The strengths and weaknesses of federal and state governance mirror each other. The federal government is much larger than any state government and frequently brings together greater expertise and greater articulation of various perspectives. As a consequence, it takes longer and requires more effort to move from an idea to a plan to reality. States vary in population and resources from Rhode Island to California, but all of their governments are much smaller than the federal government.

As a consequence, in any state it is easier and quicker for an idea to become a plan and then a reality. But of course, that reality applies to only one state, and state policies differ, while federal policy is uniform across states. Having many states is ideal for policy development, experimentation, and testing. Once the experimentation and testing have reached a conclusion, federal policy is the path to uniform quality as well as uniform bureaucracy.

Head Start governance is federal to local. Most state governors do no more than acknowledge that federal Head Start funding is in their states. Head Start is nationally centralized in the federal Head Start Bureau, as particularly expressed in the federal Head Start Performance Standards, rules that all Head Start programs are expected to follow. Beyond these rules, Head Start is locally governed by the program staff and community-based policy councils. Public school governance in the United States is essentially state and local, with various balances between the two in various school districts. From a national perspective, public schools are decentralized, with any federal influence coming from federal funding that they obtain. It is ironic that despite this decentralization, public schools are widely seen as monolithic in their performance. Critiques of this performance led, on the one hand, to the independence of Head Start from the public schools and, on the other hand, to the movement to establish charter schools that operate independently of public school districts.

As compared to Head Start and public schools, child care governance is an open market in a regulatory context set by government. Each state establishes the regulatory context for child care in its boundaries, including what qualifies as regulated child care and what does not. The federal government is involved in child care funding and research, but regulates only the child care it provides as an employer. Government's role—federal, state, or local—in child care is radically different from its role in Head Start or public schools, programs for which it assumes full responsibility. Government does not assume full responsibility for child care, but rather sees itself as keeping the children in child care free from harm.

## Staffing Patterns

In the United States today, early childhood programs follow one of three staffing patterns—Head Start, public school, or child care. These three patterns strongly depend on the corresponding funding and regulatory source, but some hybrids do exist, such as the Head Start program in a public school that uses Head Start funds to implement a public school staffing pattern.

The Head Start staffing pattern is a multidisciplinary team of teachers, family service workers, and various coordinators. The teachers are low-paid and required to have a competency-based Child Development Associate credential. In recent years, Head Start has been engaging in a continuing effort to improve quality, including requiring teachers to have an associate-level college degree and increasing teacher salaries. Nonetheless, the Head Start staffing pattern places teachers alongside family service workers and a step below various coordinators. It places the classroom as one component alongside parental support, health and mental health services, and social services referrals.

The public school staffing pattern places teachers in charge, supervised by a building principal. There are usually no family service workers or coordinators of other services, except sometimes school nurses. Relative to Head Start or child care, teachers are better paid and better educated, generally with a teaching certificate based on a bachelor's degree. Because of this staffing, the classroom teacher predominates, and there is less emphasis on separate positions that provide parent support, health and mental health services, and social services referrals.

Unlike child care, both Head Start and public school prekindergarten programs typically have part-day classes for children and, thus, can serve twice as many children by having double sessions, serving one classroom group in the morning and the other in the afternoon. By dropping the days of class from five to four, teachers can use the fifth weekday for the nonclassroom aspects of the program, such as home visits, teacher planning, and inservice training. The apparent efficiencies do, however, limit the time available for nonclassroom services. For example, double-session teachers have enough time to make two home visits to each family in a school year, but not enough to make weekly or even monthly home visits. If such frequent home visits are critical to programs' long-term effectiveness, as research suggests they may be (e.g., Schweinhart et al., 1993), double sessions cannot achieve such effectiveness.

Both Head Start and public school staffing patterns are designed to help children develop and prepare for school, but the public school pattern focuses primarily on education, while the Head Start pattern provides multiple services with intermediate goals, such as parents' economic self-sufficiency, that sometimes become ends in themselves. Indeed, some Head Start practitioners consider Head Start to be primarily a parent program.

The child care staffing pattern resembles the director and teaching staff portion of the Head Start pattern. The director has similar high status and authority, while teachers are of low status and poorly paid. Unlike Head Start, there are no family service workers and no coordinators of other services. The staffing is set up for teachers to attend to the physical needs of children and supervise their play. The teachers surely engage in some educational activity and may well aspire to do more, but they are not accorded the status and compensation that public school teachers receive. While Head Start and public school programs are fully supported by public tax dollars, child care programs are paid for primarily by families; government subsidies are either partial or nonexistent. Child care hours are longer, in response to family needs. The relatively low cost of child care staffing is a response to families' desire for greater affordability.

Each of these staffing patterns involves trade-offs relative to the other two. Public schools employ tax dollars to give their teachers greater responsibility and compensation than Head Start or child care teachers. Head Start employs tax dollars to give children and families access to other support services as well as education. Child care programs, with no or partial support from tax dollars, strive to take care of children at a level of quality that families can afford.

Head Start, public schools, and child care programs each have their own blend of federal, state, local, and private-sector politics. National

Head Start politics center on the federal Administration and the Congress. Public school politics center on school districts and state governments, with relatively little federal influence. State governments set child care licensing policies, but the federal government has policies for various types of federal child care funding.

## Children Served

The three types of early childhood programs have different criteria defining which children they serve. Head Start serves primarily children living in poverty (at least 90% of those enrolled are below the federal poverty line), along with a significant fraction of children with disabilities (at least 5% of those enrolled have identified disabilities). Public school prekindergarten programs' enrollment criteria differ from state to state, but similarly to Head Start, serve children deemed to be at special risk of school failure. Other public school preschool programs target children with disabilities. Preschool child care programs usually have no explicit enrollment criteria but have hours of operation that are set to meet the needs of working mothers and families.

## Goals

Head Start, public school prekindergarten programs, and preschool child care programs all have the goal of contributing to children's development, and all value and support parental contributions to children's development. But each offers its own variations on these themes. Head Start also has the goal of encouraging and supporting families' self-sufficiency by referrals to needed social, health, and mental health services, as well as offering support for adult literacy, employment, and freedom from drug abuse. Head Start's goals for families generally support children's development, but can on occasion compete with, or even replace, this goal. Public school prekindergarten programs focus single-mindedly on contributing to children's development, but may narrow this goal to focus only on children's academic readiness for school. Preschool child care programs' primary goal is taking care of preschool-aged children while parents are otherwise occupied. Contributing to children's development is an enhancement of this primary goal, an enhancement which is at the discretion of the caregivers involved, their supervisors, and the parents who support these programs.

## Definitions of Quality

These variations on the goal of contributing to children's development translate into a general definition of early childhood program quality that nonetheless comes in three versions. In general, early childhood program quality may be instrumentally defined as those practices that contribute to children's development. In high-quality programs, teaching practices and child outcomes mutually validate each other. However, for many practices, empirical evidence of their efficacy is lacking, and their contributions to children's development simply assumed.

Quality practices are either established or interactional. Established practices set program characteristics, such as group size, staff-child ratio, and teacher qualifications. Interactional practices are the behaviors that adults and children engage in during the program. Established practices are more easily set by rules and regulations, but interactional practices directly affect children's behavior and development, so they mediate any effects of established practices on children's development. For example, smaller group sizes may (or may not) lead to teachers spending more time with individual children and engaging in richer interaction with them, which would in turn contribute to their development.

High/Scope's Program Quality Assessment (High/Scope Educational Research Foundation, 1998) is our effort to comprehensively define early childhood program quality. This assessment battery includes evaluative items in seven areas of concern: learning environment, daily routine, adult-child interaction, curriculum planning and assessment, parent involvement and family services, staff qualifications and staff development, and program management. Some of its items are completed by observing programs, others by interviewing teachers. The items evaluate both established and interactional practices. Program management, for example, has 10 items evaluating structural practices, such as no more than eight children per adult and accessibility for those with disabilities. Daily routine, in contrast, has a dozen items representing interactional practices, such as time for child planning and choices during transition times. Other instruments that examine classroom quality include the revised Early Childhood Environment Rating Scale (Harms et al., 1998) and the Assessment Profile for Early Childhood Programs (Abbott-Shim & Sibley, 1987).

Now let's consider the major variations in the definition of program quality—that is, practices that contribute to children's development— as represented by the three types of programs. Head Start has family self-sufficiency as a secondary goal, so Head Start program quality is defined as those practices that contribute to children's development and families' self-sufficiency. Public school prekindergarten programs (and Head Start, according to Congress) place special emphasis on children's school readiness as their contribution to early childhood development, so the quality assessment of these programs emphasizes those practices that help prepare children for school. Preschool child care programs place a premium on those practices that take care of children while parents are otherwise occupied. One determiner is their ability to adapt to parents' schedules, whether the schedules are in the typical 9-to-5 workday or some other arrangement. Another determiner of quality is breadth of access, including accommodating a range of ages of children and the differing abilities of families to pay.

To the extent that all types of early childhood programs share the goal of contributing to children's development (with an emphasis on getting ready for school), they share a common definition of program quality. To the extent that they have other goals as well—Head Start's goal of families' self-sufficiency, child care's goal of enabling parents to be otherwise occupied—their definitions of program quality are partly unique to each.

## Implications for Interpreting Evaluative Research

There are two basic traditions of evaluative research on early childhood programs—the part-day tradition and the full-day tradition. Head Start and public school prekindergarten programs both contribute to and profit from the part-day evaluation tradition, while preschool child care programs contribute to and profit from the full-day tradition.

The part-day tradition's research question has always been how much good programs contribute to children's short- and long-term development. This tradition boasts evidence of the extraordinary success of high-quality early childhood programs, including the long-term benefits found by the High/Scope Perry Preschool Study (Schweinhart et al., 1993) and the rest of the Consortium for Longitudinal Studies (1983). These studies have impressive internal validity, with strong experimental designs, but limited generalizability, with relatively small sample sizes, The full-day tradition's research question has been whether existing full-day programs are of adequate quality and effectiveness. Its exemplars are the National Day Care Study (Ruopp et al., 1979), the National Child Care Staffing Study (Whitebook et al., 1989), and the Child Care Cost, Quality, and Outcomes Study (Child Care Cost, Quality, and Child Outcomes Study Team, 1995). These studies have strong generalizability, with larger samples from around the country, but weak internal validity, with no experimental designs. Both traditions have essentially the same research question regarding quality and short- and long-term effectiveness of programs, but their emphases differ— hence the strengths and weaknesses of their research designs. Ramey and Campbell's Abecedarian Project (Campbell & Ramey, 1995) is a crossover study—a full-day study that, like the part-day studies, has internal validity as its strong suit. Just as the three types of early childhood programs complement each other, so do these two research traditions complement each other. But the challenge to all evaluative research on early childhood programs is to combine the scientific strength of internally valid, experimentally designed studies with the generalizability of randomly selected, highly representative populations of children and families.

## Implications for Designing Evaluative Research

Evaluative research compares programs and outcomes to criteria for success. Thus, the three definitions of program quality and goals identified herein have large implications for evaluative research on Head Start, public school prekindergarten, and preschool child care programs. Evaluative research can examine program performance in terms of the common core of criteria for all three types of programs—established and interactional practices that contribute to children's development. In addition, evaluative research can examine Head Start program practices that contribute to families' self-sufficiency, public school prekindergarten program practices that contribute to children's readiness for school, and preschool child care program practices that enable parents to be otherwise occupied when they need to be.

It is also possible to apply these idiosyncratic criteria to the other types of programs. We could examine how well public school prekindergarten programs and preschool child care programs contribute to families' self-sufficiency, a particularly apt criterion for programs serving families living in poverty. We could examine how well any of these programs contribute to children's readiness for school, a criterion that is beginning to break boundaries anyway because of our national interest in it. We could examine how well Head Start and public school prekindergarten programs meet families' child care needs. Such ideas go to the heart of the question of whether the differentiation of types of early childhood programs is a good idea. Should publicly funded programs be expected to meet families' child care needs, or should we continue with our national policy of no or partial subsidy of such programs? Should early childhood programs address families' self-sufficiency needs for families not living in poverty? Until these questions are answered, however, we can stick with the universal definition of early childhood program success—established and interactional practices that contribute to children's development.

Although the criteria appropriate to one type of program can be applied to the other two, it is very difficult, perhaps impossible, to compare the effectiveness of Head Start, public school prekindergarten, and preschool child care programs—that is, their effects on children and families—for the simple reason that they serve different populations of children and families. The main entry criterion for Head Start is that families have poverty-level incomes. Low family income may be a factor in the entry criteria for public school prekindergarten programs, but it is only one factor among others. Low family income plays no role at all in the entry criteria for many preschool child care programs. The defining criterion for enrollment in preschool child care is that the family needs child care to permit parents to be otherwise employed, a criterion that tends to increase family income and also renders impossible the idea of randomly assigning children who need child care to an unserved control group. Families who use preschool child care are, by that very fact, different from families who do not; effects attributed to differences in program type could, in fact, be due to these differences in families.

On the other hand, the quality of the various types of early childhood programs can be compared. The question is not which program type is best, but rather what staffing and governance patterns and funding levels per child lead to programs with the best quality and effectiveness. For example, Zill et al. (1998) reported that Head Start classrooms had higher average scores than child care classrooms on the Early Childhood Environment Rating Scale (Harms & Clifford, 1980). The related methodological issue is whether raters were using the scale in the same way in the various studies. Such comparisons lead to thorny dilemmas that need to be resolved. Funding levels and policies interact in complex ways, making interpretation of findings difficult or impossible. Michigan's state prekindergarten program, for example, provides only two-thirds of the funding per child of a Head Start program, but requires teachers to have bachelor's degrees while Head Start does not. Depending on which program's quality is better, is it because of the difference in spending levels or the difference in teacher qualifications?

These questions seldom arise in current early childhood evaluative research because this research is program-specific, dealing only with Head Start, public school prekindergarten, or preschool child care programs. For example, the recent Advisory Committee on Head Start Research and Evaluation (1999) focused exclusively on evaluating Head Start, for the most part regarding public school prekindergarten programs and preschool child care programs as complications for the control group rather than as early childhood program variants. The evaluations of state prekindergarten programs that are under way in Michigan, Kentucky, and other states (Ripple et al., 1999) are evaluations of the state programs, not Head Start or child care programs. Similarly, child care research focuses exclusively on child care.

Conducting evaluative research on early childhood programs— that is, on Head Start, public school prekindergarten, and preschool child care—is reasonable. Indeed, the U.S. study in the IEA Preprimary Project, of which High/Scope is both international coordinator and U.S. sponsor, has done something along those lines, studying children in Head Start, public school preschools, other organized programs, family day care homes, and their own homes. But this multiple setting approach will not become the rule until those who fund evaluative research take a wider view of the whole field of early childhood programs. Federal and state legislators are well positioned to be asking questions of all these programs, but they need to figure out ways to transcend program positioning in the funding agencies. All of us who care about young children should find ways to place their education and welfare above the status of the programs in which they find themselves. Of course, children are too young to develop the blinding loyalties to program types that adults do. This breadth of vision is one respect in which adults—especially policymakers and researchers—would do well to emulate them.

## References

Abbott-Shim, M., & Sibley, A. (1987). *Assessment Profile for Early Childhood Programs.* Atlanta: Quality Assistance.

Advisory Committee on Head Start Research and Evaluation. (1999). *Evaluating Head Start: A recommended framework for studying the impact of the Head Start program.* Washington, DC: U.S. Department of Health and Human Services.

Campbell, F. A., & Ramey, C. T. (1995). Cognitive and school outcomes for high-risk African-American students at middle adolescence: Positive effects of early intervention. *American Educational Research Journal, 32,* 743–772.

Child Care Cost, Quality, & Child Outcomes Study Team. (1995). *Cost, quality, and child outcomes in child care centers, public report* (2nd ed.). Denver: Economics Department, University of Colorado at Denver.

Consortium for Longitudinal Studies. (1983). *As the twig is bent... Lasting effects of preschool programs.* Hillsdale, NJ: Erlbaum.

Harms, T., & Clifford, R. M. (1980). *Early Childhood Environment Rating Scale.* New York: Teachers College Press.

Harms, T., Clifford, R. M., & Cryer, D. (1998). *Early Childhood Environment Rating Scale* (Rev. ed.). New York: Teachers College Press.

High/Scope Educational Research Foundation. (1998). *High/Scope Program Quality Assessment: Preschool version.* Ypsilanti, MI: High/Scope Press.

Ripple, C. H., Gilliam, W. S., Chanana, N., & Zigler, E. (1999, May). Will fifty cooks spoil the broth? The debate over entrusting Head Start to the states. *American Psychologist, 54,* 1–17.

Ruopp, R., Travers, J., Glantz, F., & Coelen, C. (1979). *Children at the center: Summary findings and their implications* (Final report of the National Day Care Study, Vol. 1). Cambridge, MA: Abt Associates.

Schweinhart, L. J., Barnes, H. V., & Weikart, D. P. (1993). *Significant benefits: The High/Scope Perry Preschool Study through age 27* (Monographs of the High/Scope Educational Research Foundation, 10). Ypsilanti, MI: High/Scope Press.

Whitebook, M., Howes, C., & Phillips, D. (1989). *Who cares? Child care teachers and the quality of care in America.* Oakland, CA: Child Care Employee Project.

Zill, N., Resnick, G., McKey, R. H., Clark, C., Connell, D., Swartz, J., O'Brien, R., & D'Elio, M. A. (1998). *Head Start Program Performance Measures—Second progress report.* Washington, DC: Research, Development and Evaluation Branch and Head Start Bureau, Administration on Children, Youth and Families, U.S. Department of Health and Human Services.

# Chapter 9

# The Science and Policies of Early Childhood Education and Family Services

*Robert B. McCall, Lana Larsen, and Angela Ingram*

Over the last three decades, our awareness of the needs and problems of families in the United States has increased substantially, and, although services have proliferated, this increase has not been in proportion to the need. "Children's issues" are at the top of the public's list of government concerns, and citizens with and without children want better outcomes for children and are willing to pay for such programs with higher taxes (Sosin, 1997). Nevertheless, heated political debate often bounces between wanting to improve outcomes for families and children and, on the other hand, wanting to reduce taxes and public dependency on government.

A middle ground may lie between the current limit to the number of years parents are eligible for public assistance and the need for publicly supported care for their children when these parents become employed, likely at low wages insufficient to pay for child care. The political and financial battle then may focus on the quality of that care: Should it be "no frills care," at minimum cost to the government, without expensive standards, supplied primarily to allow parents to work, or should it be mandated to be of high quality (and high cost) so that children and society reap the benefits that such programs can potentially provide?

But providing child care alone is unlikely to help stressed, low-income families to become more effective parents and to restore the family as America's primary socialization agent. Indeed, being employed for low wages and no benefits could add more stress to single parents and reduce the time they have available for their children, unless family programs, which are also expensive, support low-income parents comprehensively until they become financially and psychologically self-sufficient. Given these conflicting aims and needs, knowing which early childhood and family programs are effective at achieving particular goals and what program characteristics contribute to such effectiveness can form the basis of creating more cost-effective services. Such knowledge will be useful regardless of which philosophy dominates the political decisions.

One might presume that the most effective, efficient services would be those that prevent problems from arising, but prevention is more appealing in theory than in practice. Prevention requires a substantial expenditure, and programs are likely to serve more people who do not need the treatment in the course of helping the fewer individuals who do. Also, prevention programs may take years to be evaluated, and they have a checkered record of effectiveness.

Nevertheless, many prevention programs are cost-effective over the long term, and assessing the benefits of a program over a decade or two is crucial for prevention programs for young children, which may save money only after those children become old enough to attend school, commit crimes, and be employed (Barnett, 1995). Unfortunately, it is a rare politician who is willing to invest today for gains that will be realized years or decades later (Steiner, 1976).

Despite these caveats, prevention is, at least philosophically, a preferred approach. During the last three decades, service professionals and researchers from education, social work, public health, psychology, and other disciplines have been exploring different types of prevention programs aimed primarily at low-income, high-risk families and young children. These programs have had three general emphases:

1. Early childhood educational intervention services are primarily directed at low-income children, from birth to 8 years of age, and are aimed at improving mental and social development and preparation for school.
2. Maternal improvement programs are primarily directed at low-income mothers to (a) improve their educational levels, employability, financial status, and psychological self-sufficiency; and/or to (b) improve their ability to promote the health and development of their infants and young children, their knowledge of child development, their relationships with their chil-

dren, and their abilities to manage as parents (see, for example, Olds & Kitzman, 1993; Powell, 1993; Roberts & Wasik, 1990; Roberts et al., 1991; Wasik et al., 1990). Reduction in child abuse rates is also a direct or implicit goal of some programs.

3. Two-generation programs comprise a number of different approaches, the most prominent of which is family support (see, for example, Allen et al., 1992; Family Resource Coalition, 1994; Halpern & Weiss, 1990; Kagan et al., 1987; Weiss & Jacobs, 1988; Weissbourd, 1993), an umbrella for a wide variety of programs. Many two-generation programs provide a case manager who helps the family identify its strengths and goals, and who facilitates access to health, education, and welfare services typically directed at both child and parent.

The purpose of this paper is to review in very general terms what more than three decades of research has revealed about (a) which families and children are most at risk for undesirable outcomes, and who is likely to benefit most from these interventions; (b) the potential effectiveness of these interventions to produce positive outcomes for parents and children and the actual benefits when such interventions are implemented as routine services by community agencies; and (c) the characteristics of successful interventions. Following this review, we discuss how this scientific information can contribute to deciding major policy issues regarding the nature and extent of government support for such intervention services, especially regarding the size and cost-effectiveness of their benefits for children and families, as well as the characteristics of services that are recommended and appear necessary to produce the outcomes research demonstrates are possible?

## What We Know About Intervention Service Programs

In this section, we provide a guide to the general conclusions of the research on preventive intervention and service programs designed for low-income or otherwise at-risk families and young children (as opposed to those with diagnosed disabilities; see Farran, 1990; Guralnick, 1997;

Shonkoff & Hauser-Cram, 1987). The details of this research have been reviewed numerous times (e.g., Center for the Future of Children, 1995; Guralnick, 1997; plus other reviews cited throughout this paper). Instead, we present conclusions and issues intended as background for practitioners, policymakers, and funders to guide the creation of programs and policies.

# Risk Factors

Risk factors are identifiable characteristics that correlate with, but may or may not actually cause, the problems or circumstances that a service program aims to alleviate. Knowing these risk factors provides the potential to target services—for people in greatest need and likely to benefit most from those services—and thereby to reduce costs.

## *General Risk Factors*

Five risk factors commonly correlate with a wide assortment of problems, including but not limited to educational failure, parenting insufficiency, child abuse and neglect, and adolescent delinquency. These five general risk factors are summarized below.

1. Individual family poverty is the single most pervasive risk factor (e.g., Huston, 1995), and the one most commonly used to define eligibility for services. Poverty in turn is associated with the additional risk factors of low parental education, poor parental employability, teenage motherhood, single parent-hood, and large family size (Eckstrom et al., 1986; Farrington, 1985, 1987; Loeber & Dishion, 1983; Slavin, 1989; Weissbourd, 1993).

2. Community poverty, in addition to individual family poverty, correlates strongly with child and family problems. Such communities are urban, densely populated with low-income house-holds, and characterized by high mobility, high crime, and low social cohesion and control (Developmental Research and Programs, Inc., 1993; Feldman, 1990; Garbarino et al., 1992; Sampson et al., 1997).

3. Family problems encompass separation, divorce, family conflict, and violence, including child and spousal abuse and

neglect (Developmental Research and Programs, Inc. 1993; Yoshikawa, 1995).

4. Dysfunctional parenting describes the failure of parents to monitor their children and provide clear expectations for their behavior. Excessively severe, lax, or inconsistent disciplinary practices are related to many undesirable outcomes (Developmental Research and Programs, Inc. 1993; Loeber & Dishion, 1983; Loeber & Stouthamer-Loeber, 1986; Patterson, 1982; Yoshikawa, 1995). These circumstances may be accompanied by parental drug and alcohol abuse and psychopathology.

5. Perinatal hazards—including prematurity, low birth weight, anoxia, respiratory distress, intraventricular hemorrhage, excessive prenatal exposure to drugs and alcohol, and other early medical stresses—are associated with subsequent educational and behavioral problems in children (Day et al., 1994; Infant Health and Development Program, 1990; McGee et al., 1984; Mednick et al., 1988; Sameroff & Chandler, 1975; Werner, 1987).

## Specific Risk Factors

Two risk factors—family history and gender—are related to particular problems. A family history of a certain problem predisposes their children to that same problem. Such problems can include drug and alcohol abuse, criminal activity, teenage parenthood, and school failure (Developmental Research and Program, Inc., 1993). The transmission process may be environmental and/or genetic, but genetic factors are related to the risk of delinquency, violence, criminality, and alcohol abuse (see, for example, DiLalla & Gottsman, 1991; Plomin, 1989; Plomin et al., 1990; Rowe, 1990; Rowe & Rodgers, 1989) as well as low IQ and poor school performance (e.g., Plomin, 1989).

The gender of the child also increases children's risk of certain difficulties. Males have more educational problems (Eckstrom et al. 1986; McCall et al., 1992; Slavin, 1989) and substantially more behavioral problems, including delinquency and criminality, although rates for the latter are increasing among females (Elliott et al., 1989; Werner & Smith, 1992).

## *Risk Factors Accumulate*

Which risk factors exist matters less than how many a family possesses with respect to the likelihood of antisocial behavior (Yoshikawa, 1995), psychopathology (Rutter, 1979), and poor social and mental performance (Sameroff & Fiese, 1990; Sameroff & Seifer, 1983; Werner & Smith, 1982, 1992). Similarly, families and children at greatest risk are likely to benefit most from intervention programs, as long as the risk factors do not reflect biological disabilities and their correlates (e.g., very low birthweight, severe physical disability, mental retardation) or severe psychopathology.

# Program Effectiveness

McCall (1977) divides the issue of program effectiveness into two questions, the answers to which are essential to informed policy decisions. First, can such programs potentially produce the desired outcomes? Second, do programs, after full-scale implementation, actually deliver such outcomes for their participants? Policymakers need to know which components are crucial to a program's effectiveness (which we rarely study), and whether the version of the program that communities can afford to implement is likely to be effective.

## *Program Potential*

We first consider the issue of program potential of the three main types of intervention programs: early childhood education, home visiting, and parental support programs. Of these three, early childhood education shows the most potential, perhaps because it has been the most widely implemented and studied, and therefore refined, type of intervention.

### Potential of Early Childhood Education Programs

Research over the past two decades has indicated that early childhood educational programs can accomplish many of their short-term and some of their long-term goals. Specifically, early education demonstration programs for children—typically begun at 3 to 4 years of age, but some earlier—have been shown to have several benefits for low-income children relative to comparable children who do not experience the program.

These programs increase IQ, language fluency, and other early mental and academic skills. Such advantages, especially with respect to IQ, diminish and may disappear entirely (but see Campbell & Ramey, 1994; Fowler et al., 1995) over the three years following the termination of program attendance. This loss of advantage, however, results in part from the improvement of nonprogram children, presumably as a result of entering school (Bryant & Ramey, 1987b; Caldwell, 1987; Farran, 1990; Guralnick & Bennett, 1987; Hibbs, 1988; Lazar & Darlington, 1982; Schorr, 1988; Zigler & Freedman, 1987).

High-quality early childhood education programs can minimize severe academic problems in grade and high school, including reducing the frequency of class failure, retention in grade, use of remedial and special education services, and dropout rates (Berrureta-Clement et al., 1984; Lazar & Darlington, 1982; Schorr, 1988; Schweinhart & Weikert, 1980). Early childhood program advocates often cite the prevention of severe educational failure as the most compelling evidence for the long-term benefits of these programs.

Children 3 to 5 years of age who have attended early childhood programs are more socially mature and independent than children who experience primarily a home environment (Belsky, 1988; Clarke-Stewart & Fein, 1983; Gamble & Zigler, 1986). Program children are more socially competent, cooperative in shared activities, aware of social norms and conventions, appropriately independent, friendly, responsive, socially confident, comfortable relating to strangers, and oriented more toward peers than adults. A few studies show they can also be more active, assertive, physically and verbally aggressive, rebellious, and less compliant with maternal and teacher directives. These effects, both positive and negative, also diminish after the child leaves the program (but see below), again because comparison children tend to develop the same behaviors upon entering school at a later age. The aggressive behavior, which is not consistently found, is stronger in children attending programs in which modifying or monitoring such behavior is not a main program theme. When curricula are altered to place more attention on behavior control, discipline, and reduced aggressiveness, improvements in child behavior occur (Farran, 1990; Finklestein, 1982; Honig et al., 1982).

A few long-term follow-up studies show program children engage in less noncompliant and delinquent behavior, have fewer teen pregnancies, graduate at higher rates, and are more likely to be employed and less dependent on welfare after high school (Honig & Lally, 1982; Lazar & Darlington, 1982; Schweinhart & Weikert, 1980; Yoshikawa, 1995; Zigler et al., 1992). Despite the possibility of short-term aggressiveness, the long-term prognosis is for less antisocial behavior.

## Potential of Home Visiting Programs

Home visiting programs aimed at improving maternal and child health and development, promoting parenting, and reducing abuse have had only modest and inconsistent effects (Center for the Future of Children, 1999; Olds & Kitzman, 1993). Programs for pregnant women sometimes improve several health-related behaviors and the women's use of prenatal care and health services, but they have neither reduced the number of low-birthweight and preterm deliveries nor consistently increased immunization rates or well-baby visits for children. Other home visiting programs for parents and their low-birthweight and preterm infants increased the children's physical health and developmental status and the stimulating environment of the home. Programs designated for low-income families improved maternal education levels and employment rates, especially for teenage mothers, but only a minority of these programs improved parental caregiving or the behaviors and mental functioning of the children. Home visiting programs improved maternal attitudes and reduced self-reported use of harsh disciplinary practices, but few programs reduced reported child abuse and neglect rates.

Early childhood educational programs, although predominantly focused on children, have frequently also provided services for mothers. These programs, rather than the home visiting programs, have had more impact on increasing maternal education and employment, reducing subsequent fertility, increasing knowledge of child development, and improving mother-infant interaction (Benasich et al., 1992). No one knows why home visiting programs have had limited effects, especially on children. Such findings raise questions about how much "on task" activity takes place and how much direct tuition of specific parenting behaviors that are likely to influence child development and behavior actually occurs during home visits. Effects are more likely to be observed if the visits are very frequent, the program is intense and directly applicable to children, and visitors are professionals rather than paraprofessionals or minimally trained nonprofessionals.

## Potential of Family Support Programs

Contemporary family support programs, which have been evaluated primarily while participants are in the program and immediately upon termination, have shown (Halpern, 1990a) several benefits. They have improved parental coping, adaptation, and personal development as well as parenting behaviors (e.g., increased involvement in reciprocal interaction with infants, more praise and less restrictiveness, more appropriate control practices). Children's cognitive development and social skills improved in about half of the studies. However, major dimensions of the parent-child relationship (e.g., security of attachment) typically do not change.

## *Implementation and Outcomes*

When these intervention programs become implemented as routine services, outcomes are similar but often weaker and less consistently observed.

## Outcomes of Early Childhood Education Programs

The benefits of Head Start, for example, are similar qualitatively to the benefits of the demonstration early childhood education programs, but the size of the benefits, their persistence, and the consistency with which they are found from study to study is often smaller (e.g., Bee, 1981; Copple et al., 1987; Datta, 1979; Fosburg et al., 1984; Goodstein, 1975; Haskins, 1989;

Kresh, 1993; Lee et al., 1988; Lee et al., 1990; Mann et al., 1976; McKey et al., 1985; Monroe & McDonnell, 1981; Royster & Larsen, 1977; Shipman, 1976). Notice that most evaluations of Head Start were conducted nearly two decades ago, because policymakers subsequently favored allocations that increased the number of children enrolled rather than evaluations of the effectiveness of the program. Congress has now mandated a rigorous outcome evaluation of Head Start.

## Outcomes of Home Visiting Programs

Similarly, many parenting programs within the home visiting literature show only modest, sometimes isolated, and frequently inconsistent effects, especially with respect to improving outcomes for children (Center for the Future of Children, 1999; Larner et al., 1992; Wasik, Ramey et al., 1990; Weiss, 1993), although a few reports suggest that very intensive and early programs can produce substantial mental advantages (Fowler et al., 1995; Oakland & Ghazaleh, 1996; Powell & Grantham-McGregor, 1989). Also, "welfare-to-work" programs designed to improve the education levels, employability, employment, and incomes of adults (not all of whom may be mothers) have modest effects and low frequencies of success (Datta, 1982; Gueron & Pauly, 1991). Even when graduate equivalency degrees (GED) are obtained at increased rates, they do not necessarily lead to better literacy or earnings (Cameron & Heckman, 1993; St. Pierre et al., 1994).

## Outcomes of Family Support Programs

Finally, in a review of "two-generation programs," including some substantial federal programs that were less two-generational than they seemed (e.g., the Comprehensive Child Development Program, the Even Start Family Literacy Program, Head Start Family Service Centers), St. Pierre et al. (1994, 1997) report only modest effects (e.g., improved attitudes of parents toward childrearing and the expectation for child success, improved parent-child interaction, increased adult education but not annual household income, increased use of federal benefits such as AFDC and food stamps, and small short-term effects on children's general mental performance).

# Characteristics of Successful Programs

The crucial question is why these programs, once they are implemented as routine services, fail to produce this potential in the level and consistency of benefits. The answer may be revealed by reviewing the literature to identify the characteristics of successful programs and then comparing the services delivered by the implemented programs with those delivered by the demonstration programs. Determining the characteristics of successful programs is a speculative venture because such potential characteristics are rarely manipulated in a single study (Bryant & Maxwell, 1997). Although programs differ in many ways and cannot be compared directly, reviews of successful programs (Barnett, 1995; Bryant & Ramey, 1987a; Clarke-Stewart, 1987, 1988; Gomby et al., 1993; Halpern, 1990a, 1990b; Halpern & Weiss, 1990; Karweit, 1994; Olds & Kitzman, 1993; Phillips & Howes, 1987; Ramey & Ramey, 1992; Wasik & Karweit, 1994; Weiss, 1993; Weiss & Halpern, 1990) seem to agree that they usually have a few common characteristics, which can be included within the concept of "treatment dosage" (Barnett, 1995). "Dosage," as used here, refers not only to the traditional drug-trial meaning of quantity of program but also its quality, because quality in behavioral services often reflects the amount of effective treatment actually delivered to the children.

## *Treatment Dosage—The Quantity of the Program*

Successful programs reveal that the more parents and children experience the services provided, the greater the benefits. Some literature suggests that a minimum dosage is required before benefits are observed at all, and only after that minimum do the benefits increase with additional time in the program (e.g., Reynolds, 1994). The dose-response relation is embodied in three often-confounded components defining program quantity: duration, intensity, and age of the child upon entry into the program.

### Duration

The literature reviews demonstrate that the longer the participants are engaged in programs, the better the outcomes. This phenomenon is clearest for early childhood education programs, for which a voluminous literature of studies is available, but it also characterizes home visiting programs (e.g., Fowler et al., 1995; Oakland & Ghazaleh, 1996; Powell & Grantham-McGregor, 1989) and two-generational programs (St. Pierre et al., 1997). In what may be the most direct test of this proposition, Reynolds (1994) demonstrated for a school-based, Chapter I-funded, comprehensive, preschool-through-third-grade, parent-child support program (i.e., Chicago Child-Parent Center and Expansion Program; see also Reynolds, this volume) that at least four years in the program were necessary to produce noticeable benefits on most education measures at program termination and at two years following termination, with improvements increasing thereafter with five and six years in the program. Outcome benefits also may be more permanent with more years in program (Bryant & Maxwell, 1997; Campbell & Ramey, 1995).

## Intensity

The greater the program intensity—that is, the greater the extent of participant contact and the greater the program's effort at working with the family and providing services—the more benefits accrue and the more consistently they are observed (and perhaps the longer lasting they are). This effect of extent and effort seems to be true for all types of programs (Bryant & Maxwell, 1997), and, as with duration, a minimum intensity may be required before benefits are seen. Further, within programs, families that participate to a greater extent, thereby increasing the intensity of the program they personally experience, attain proportionally greater benefits (e.g., Reynolds, 1994).

## Age of Entry

It has been a continuing premise that the earlier a child starts in such programs, the greater the benefits, but the evidence for such a statement is limited, especially because timing is often confounded with duration and intensity (Bryant & Maxwell, 1997). On the one hand, Fowler et al. (1995) provided intensive training to parents in language and cognitive stimulation in a social context only for several months and found substantial long-term benefits, especially among college educated parents and those whose program began in the first as opposed to the second year of their children's lives. But other programs have not produced clear earlier-is-better outcomes for mental and educational outcomes. Reynolds (1994) demonstrated that duration in the program was much more strongly related to educational outcomes than was the child's age (3, 4, or 5 years) of entry.

The literature suggests that entry into intervention programs before age 3 is not clearly beneficial. Measures of developmental progress in children ages 0 to 2 are not very sensitive to family socioeconomic status variables, and development during this period could be so highly canalized that differences in children's typical environments, including intervention programs, simply do not produce strong effects on children at those ages (McCall, 1979, 1981). Also, because untreated children generally catch up mentally and socially to program children when they enter school, the intervention could be delayed. Moreover, children raised in the unsupportive Romanian orphanages who were adopted into British or Canadian families—if the children spent less than their first 6 months in the orphanage—did not show any higher rates of mental and social problems during childhood than British or Canadian home/parent-reared children. Children had only slightly more problems if they spent the first 6 to 24 months of life in the orphanage (Ames & Chisolm, 1997; O'Connor et al., 1999). One child tragically locked in a dark room until age 6 and found to have only a few guttural utterances attained IQ within the normal range after 18 months of tutoring (e.g., Davis, 1947). Therefore, it is not obvious that interventions designed to improve childhood mental performance must necessarily begin in the first 3 years of life, although early onset of services often is associated with a longer time in program, and intense and extensive programs begun early (by age 3) may have longer lasting if not greater benefits (e.g., Campbell & Ramey, 1994; Reynolds, 1994). Starting the program earlier may nevertheless be beneficial (Zigler & Styfco, 1993), not because the child needs certain treatment in the first few years of life but because his or her parent does (see following).

## *Treatment Dosage—The Quality of the Program*

The participants' intense experience of a program is one major criterion of program success. The other criterion—or aspect of treatment dosage—is high quality (Barnett, 1995; Bryant & Maxwell, 1997; Frede, 1995). Factors that permit and support a high-quality educational and family service with positive child outcomes include early childhood education programs with small groups, low children-to-staff ratios, developmentally appropriate practices, and well-trained personnel. For all types of programs, the involvement of parents and the appropriateness of services provided are indications of quality and often predict positive outcomes.

### Group Size and Children-to-Staff Ratios

Smaller groups of children and lower children-to-staff ratios are associated with better social and cognitive outcomes (see Boocock, this volume; Vandell & Pierce, this volume). This relation was demonstrated by the National Day Care Study (Ruopp et al., 1979) and subsequently supported by additional research (Bailey 1997; The Cost and Quality Team, 1995; Fowler et al., 1995; Seppanen et al., 1993). Frede (1995) suggests that small groups and low child-to-staff ratios provide an instructional climate that permits more effective and appropriate as well as individually intensive teaching. Despite the ease with which such characteristics could be mandated in policies and regulations, only a fraction of the states have required optimal levels of these factors.

### Developmentally Appropriate Practices

Early childhood education programs that implement developmentally appropriate practices produce better child development outcomes. Developmentally appropriate practices emphasize individualized work with children who move at their own pace, include curriculum activities that are child governed and integrated into the flow of children's activities, capitalize on teachable moments during the natural course of children's activities, are responsive to children's ideas and individual choices, and tend to be positive and expansive of children's ideas rather than critical (e.g., Charlesworth et al., 1993; Frede, 1995; Frede et al., 1993; Frede & Barnett, 1992; Marcon, 1992). Such practices produce improved test performance and creativity, greater task orientation, more positive interactions among children, less stress and anxiety, and better social behavior (Bailey, 1997; Charlesworth et al., 1993; Holloway & Reichart-Erickson, 1988; Hyson et al., 1990; Marcon, 1994).

The particular curriculum strategy (e.g., didactic versus direct instruction, open versus traditional classroom, interactive versus cognitive-developmental) seems to matter little (Bailey, 1997; Bryant & Maxwell, 1997; Caldwell, 1997; Frede, 1995; Goffin, 1994; Lazar & Darlington, 1982; Royce et al., 1983), although the research is fragmentary. While the particular curriculum may not matter, interventions work best if they have clear behavioral goals and provide activities that are directly aimed at achieving those goals, although that attempt may be implemented one-on-one and through teachable moments rather than didactic, teacher-controlled instruction (Casto & Lewis, 1984; Madden et al., 1976; Scarr & McCartney, 1988; Wasik et al., 1990).

Unfortunately, we do not know what qualitative aspects of the early childhood program produce certain desirable outcomes. For example, long-term reductions in antisocial behavior and criminality contribute most to such programs' cost benefit (Barnett, 1995; Yoshikawa, 1995), but it is less certain what aspects of early childhood programs produce such outcomes, although the establishment of close, meaningful, warm, caring, stable parent-child, caretaker-child, and child-child relationships is a plausible working hypothesis (Barnard, 1997; Guralnick & Neville, 1997).

## Personnel Training and Supervision

Successful programs have well-trained personnel who are closely supervised (Vandell & Pierce, this volume). Programs employing personnel with higher levels of general education as well as training specific to their roles in the program who are carefully and competently supervised produce better outcomes (Clarke-Stewart, 1987, 1988; Halpern, 1990a; Olds & Kitzman, 1993; Phillips & Howes, 1987).

Such staff also are more attentive and nurturing in their behavior toward children (Berk, 1985; The Cost and Quality Team, 1995; Howes, 1983; Ruopp et al., 1979; Whitebook et al., 1989).

## Parental Involvement

The greater the involvement of parents in the program, the more effective it is. This has been an article of faith for many years with little direct evidence to support it except the retrospective observation that most successful programs had parent involvement components. While parent involvement has still not been experimentally manipulated, the more extensive pattern of outcomes now available conforms to this conclusion (Blair & Ramey, 1997; Bryant & Maxwell, 1997). In addition, more evidence now exists that individual differences in parent involvement within programs are associated with outcomes (Reynolds, Mavrogenes et al., 1996). This simply may be a result of a larger program dose administered by the parent or a subject selection phenomenon, but it is widely believed that long-term effects are mediated by parents after the program has terminated (Fowler et al., 1995; Lazar & Darlington, 1982).

## Appropriately Directed Services

The beneficial outcomes of programs are specific to the family members served and the nature of the services delivered. For example, programs aimed at parents tend to produce parent benefits, whereas programs aimed at children tend to produce child benefits (Bryant & Maxwell, 1997; Crnic & Stormshak, 1996; Wasik et al., 1990). Relatively few parent training programs have produced substantial effects on the children (Center for the Future of Children, 1999), but many such programs are not designed to do so and are not very intense. When high-intensity programs deliberately attempt to train parents to produce developmental changes in their children, they can do so (e.g., Fowler et al., 1995; Oakland & Ghazaleh, 1996; Powell & Grantham-McGregor, 1984; Seitz & Apfel, 1994; Seitz et al., 1985).

Similarly, early childhood education programs that emphasize mental development tend to produce improvements in this domain, whereas programs especially designed to improve social skills have corresponding benefits in this area (Bryant & Maxwell, 1997; Guralnick & Neville, 1997). The specificity of effects constitutes a rationale for family support programs, which have combined child and adult interventions into one program ("two-generation programs") that aims to deal with the complete range of family issues within a single integrated approach. But the specificity of effects may simply reflect differential dosage of program, so, to be effective, two-generation programs must deliver a high dosage of service to both parents and children, which they have not always accomplished (St. Pierre et al., 1997).

### Dosage Components May Combine

The dose-response relationship, however, does not appear to be perfect (Frede, 1995). Some rather minimal programs (e.g., intensive language stimulation for a few months in the first year, Fowler et al., 1995; 2.5 hours per day of preschool for two years begun at age 4, Schweinhart et al., 1993) have produced substantial and long-term benefits. This apparent violation of the dose-response rule—more is better—likely indicates that the several components of dosage accumulate and are mutually compensatory. Thus, for example, a short program of great intensity and high quality may produce greater benefits than a much longer program of less quality and intensity. And certain types of interventions may be more efficacious if performed at certain ages.

## Demonstration Versus Routine Service Programs

Given the characteristics of successful programs outlined above, why are the results for routine service programs less impressive than for demonstration programs? A reasonable hypothesis is that most service programs provide less "dosage" than demonstration programs in terms of both quantity and quality of program (Chubrick & Kelley, 1994; Haskins, 1989; Woodhead, 1988). Head Start, for example, is typically a half-day program, operates 9 months of the year, and children are eligible for one or at most two years—a minimum dosage of intervention relative to many of the most successful demonstrations. Moreover, demonstration programs tend to have a 1:7 ratio of staff to children, whereas only one-third of the routine service programs have such low ratios (Frede, 1995). Similarly, demonstration programs tend to have more parental involvement than service programs (Frede, 1995), are more comprehensive, and have better trained personnel.

The most general conclusion from this literature, therefore, is not that routine service programs have a checkered history of success and are of dubious value; rather, the conclusion is quite consistent with common sense: These programs can and do work, but children and families need more than a few hours a week or vague social support to reverse the consequences that years of impoverishment and stress often produce.

Instead, one obtains benefits in proportion to program dosage, which translates into how much policymakers are willing to spend. Government, it seems, frequently asks service providers to implement a demonstration program on a mass basis at a fraction of the original cost per family, but it nevertheless expects the same beneficial outcomes (Gomby et al., 1995).

## Policy and Program Issues

Science can indicate what works, for whom, and under what circumstances; but what the nation, states, and municipalities actually do to try to help children and families will be decided by policymakers and funders on the basis of many considerations, only one of which will be science or even program efficacy. Below we consider a few of the major policy issues and summarize relevant research. Some issues can be answered clearly; others represent political choice.

## Cost-Effectiveness

The above summary concludes that early childhood and family programs require a fairly substantial investment to return their potential benefits, and some politicians wonder if the benefits of such programs are worth that investment of public dollars. The most pressing concerns relevant to costs are effect size and benefit fade-out.

## Effect Size

Although most easily assessed with respect to educational benefits, the magnitude of effect sizes (e.g., the difference between the means for treatment and comparison groups divided by the pooled standard deviation) from most successful demonstration programs is approximately .5 (although a few have produced effect sizes as high as .75). In terms of IQ, for example, the typical result represents an 8-point increase. Moreover, rarely does the mean for the entire group of children treated by such a program attain the national averages of academic performance (Karweit, 1994). Consequently, opponents of such programs sometimes argue that if six years of intensive programming in some of the most successful interventions (e.g., Campbell & Ramey, 1994; Reynolds, 1994) cannot bring all children to the national average, why should government pay the cost of such programs?

Proponents respond to this argument by suggesting the major benefits of such programs may not be in terms of raising the school and social performance of everyone but of preventing extreme disasters in a few. For example, while advantages in terms of test scores or grades averaged over all participants tend to fade, long-term benefits are found in terms of preventing serious problems in a smaller number of individuals, namely those who would otherwise fail classes, be retained in grade, need specialized educational and family services, commit crimes, become unemployed, use publicly funded services, and produce unwanted pregnancies (Barnett, 1995). And because of the extreme costs of some of these problems, services need only to prevent these disasters in a small number to be cost-effective.

## Benefit Fade-Out

One of the most commonly known research results is the fade-out in the years following program termination of general mental performance benefits for those children enrolled in early childhood educational programs relative to untreated comparison children who subsequently catch up, presumably as a result of attending school. If benefits are so short-lived and untreated children eventually catch up, opponents might argue, why invest billions of dollars for such a short-term gain?

First, the criticism is only half true. As described above, the average IQ and some other mental and social performance indicators fade after program termination; the prevention of school failure, the reduction in antisocial and criminal behavior, and the improved economic self-sufficiency of some program participants are long-term benefits that have not faded out. Indeed, these items, which can only be assessed years later when the children are in school and beyond, are the primary contributors to the cost-effectiveness of these programs (Barnett, 1995).

Second, this political argument reflects unrealistic expectations. Early childhood programs were initially created at a time when it was widely believed that early experiences had very persistent, even permanent, effects on young children. Today, scholars recognize that such programs do not inoculate children permanently against the deleterious effects of poor environments (Zigler & Berman, 1983). The very logic that suggests that an enriching program can produce benefits for low-income 4-year olds, also suggests that those benefits will fade if such children are put back into poor environments and poor schools when they are 6 years of age (Entwistle, 1995; Ogbu, 1986). The conclusion is not that the early childhood programs do not work or work for only a year or two, but that there are no "quick fixes." Therefore, "follow-on" programming is likely needed during the school years (Abelson et al., 1974; Meyer, 1984; Reynolds, this volume; Seitz, Apfel, Rosenbaum, & Zigler, 1983). Quality educational and family programming is essential, not just during early childhood, but throughout childhood and adolescence.

## Recommendations for the Nature of Services

Given that publicly supported early childhood education and family services will be provided, what should be their characteristics to maximize benefits to children and families? The list of characteristics of successful programs given above represents a guideline of what model services should be, but these guidelines raise several specific policy issues.

## Comprehensive Services Are Required

Given that (a) risk factors accumulate, (b) the number rather than the specific factors is significant for defining family risk, and (c) program effects tend to be specific to the individuals and behaviors treated, then services must be able to address directly and with sufficient dosage all of a family's major needs and goals regardless of their specific nature. These needs and goals will be different from family to family, and they likely will change over the treatment period.

Unfortunately, this prescription runs counter to the tendency of government to target services toward specific problems and groups (i.e., "targeted" or "categorical" funding). Instead, services and their funding and administration must be coordinated, if not integrated, across service type, levels of government, different government and service agencies, and ages of children (Zigler & Styfco, this volume). Also, more funding needs to be aimed broadly at families rather than exclusively at particular groups (e.g., teenage mothers), limited age ranges (e.g., birth to 3), and specific problems (e.g., drug and alcohol problems, school failure, teen crime prevention, job training), although such specialized services are also needed. Further, funds must be allocated for case management and coordination of services, items that are not as politically compelling as problems, crises, and direct services. While the federal government has moved in this direction with block grants, it is not yet clear that states will allow localities the same funding breadth and discretion that the federal government has granted them.

## The Dosage Must Be Sufficient to Achieve Program Goals

From the standpoint of attaining major program outcome goals, "lite" programs do not even achieve "lite" results (Ramey & Ramey, 1992). But a high dosage costs money, whether it is implemented in terms of quantity or quality of services. Perhaps the benefits of the demonstration programs have been oversold to policymakers (Zigler & Styfco, 1999), who subsequently invest much less per child in the subsequent service program yet expect champagne benefits on this beer budget.

## Intervention Should Start Early

Interventions should begin early in the lives of participant children, perhaps before they are born, but not necessarily for the reasons child scholars have long assumed. Starting early may be the most effective strategy, not so much because infants and toddlers need enriched early experiences "before it's too late," but because parents do. Instead of working on all goals simultaneously from the beginning, programs might emphasize a developmentally appropriate sequence of goals for parents and children. For example, in the first three years, a program might attempt to (a) establish a relationship of knowledge, trust, and confidence between case manager and parents; (b) identify and concentrate on attaining basic needs (e.g., food, clothing, shelter, drug and alcohol treatment, mental health services, transportation) and the psychological and economic self-sufficiency of the parent; and (c) promote elementary stimulation of the child (e.g., language development) and parent-child relationships. Beginning after the child is 3 years old, the program might (d) train parents to promote emergent literacy, active reading, and basic school readiness in their children; and (e) place children in full-day (if the parent is employed full-time) preschools and care arrangements that emphasize personal-social and pre-academic skills. At ages 5–6, the program might (f) provide follow-on academic services at school with substantial parent involvement. Sequencing in a developmentally appropriate fashion (for family and children) may produce effective programs at less cost than unsequenced omnibus and massive services administered continuously.

Given such a sequenced program, what does one measure in the early years of such a program to demonstrate to funders and policymakers that is it working? First, policymakers must be prepared to make a long-term investment and have realistic expectations about what constitutes progress and benefits at different stages of a program's development. The politically persuasive outcomes that represent cost savings (e.g., reductions in school failure and crime) simply cannot be observed for many years. Second, comprehensive quality programs often take two to three years to become organized to deliver effective services, so indices of program implementation and quality are the initial outcomes. Third, parent-child relationship and parental progress toward economic self-sufficiency (e.g., education, job training, employability skills, employment, income, reduction in use of public assistance and services) and psychological self-sufficiency (e.g., feelings of efficacy and internal locus of control; coping skills; reduction in stress and depression; replacement of hope for hopelessness; increased expectations for a realistic future) should be evaluated as mediators of successful later outcomes. Fourth, the minimization of risk factors is a reasonable short-term goal. In brief, the evaluation of prevention programs should follow a timeline of process and expected outcomes to keep evaluators, program professionals, funders, and policymakers advised of program benefits and when they realistically can be expected to be attained.

## Improve Persistence of Program Benefits

Deliberate attempts should be made to improve the persistence of program benefits. While we lament that some program benefits fade after participants depart from the program, typically little programmatic attempt is made to deliberately extend early gains. For example, preschool benefits may disappear because low-income children go to poor schools after the preschool program ends (Entwisle, 1995). It makes little sense to enrich preschoolers' programs only to subject the children to inferior educational programming thereafter. Consequently, the elementary schools that are likely to receive program children need to provide serious basic education in which poor performance is not accepted and triggers mandatory additional intensive teaching and pupil effort as well as certain family services. What are sometimes considered special follow-on programs (e.g., Reynolds, 1994, and this volume) should be routine educational practice, effectively increasing time-in-program for all such children.

Instead of arbitrary termination from an isolated program (e.g., when the child reaches a certain age or the family has been served for a specified number of years), incentives should be built into the program to encourage families to attain their goals and to "graduate" from the program when those goals are achieved, not when their time is up. After graduation, other programs as well as maintenance and follow-on services should be available (Zigler & Styfco, 1993). Conversely, some provision for terminating services or changing to other types or more intensive services before graduation might be implemented if parental effort and progress is minimal.

## Improve Staff Training

Successful programs have well-trained staff, and general education and staff training, more than experience, is related to beneficial child outcomes (Phillips & Howes, 1987). But training early childhood staff has not kept pace with the increasing severity of problems of low-income families and children (e.g., Hofferth, 1994; Schnur et al., 1992) and with professional advancements. For example, training programs should be more interdisciplinary to match the diverse on-the-job demands of case managers, home visitors, parent and child development specialists, day care and preschool teachers, and educators, and this should be implemented at the undergraduate as well as graduate levels.

## Recommendations for Balancing Cost and Effectiveness

A high-quality program is expensive, so programs must be designed to be cost-efficient. The political choices outlined below to achieve this goal often represent agonizing philosophical, social, and ethical conundra, pitting effectiveness against cost, access, and fairness. Some of the most troublesome debates concern enrollment eligibility, program quality and intensity, administration and physical settings, program standards, training, and parent involvement.

## Eligibility Requirements

Currently, eligibility for most programs is simply determined by family income level or residence in a low-income neighborhood. The evidence reviewed above on risk factors justifies poverty as the single most pervasive risk factor for later problems, and income is easier to measure and verify and has fewer sociopolitical objections than other risk factors. But the literature also suggests that the likelihood of subsequent problems is much greater if a family has more than one risk factor, especially more than three or four, so at least the potential exists for targeting services to a smaller group of families having several of the risk factors.

It is not clear, however, that such a requirement would reduce substantially the number of eligible families from current levels. First, poverty is correlated with other risk factors, although the correlations are more modest (e.g., $rs$ = .20–.35) than one might expect. Second, those families who participate in Head Start, for example, are more disadvantaged in several respects than their impoverished neighbors (Schnur et al., 1992). So most families now in Head Start might actually have several risk factors.

As noted above, low-dosage programs do not work; consequently, it makes little sense to provide ineffective programs to a massive number of families and children. If benefits are produced primarily by programs of high quantity and quality dosage, perhaps it is better to offer such programs, even though costly, to a smaller group of families than to serve a large number of families ineffectively. However, such a limitation of eligibility poses serious problems. Besides deciding who shall be selected for services, denying any services to large numbers of families in favor of fewer well-served families risks producing greater despair and worse outcomes in those not treated and social friction and divisiveness between the "haves" and "have nots" within low-income communities that are already plagued by distrust, stress, and tension. A possible compromise might target extremely low-income neighborhoods, rather than selecting individual families on the basis of risk factors, but poverty is moving out of concentrated inner-city neighborhoods, making this a less effective strategy.

## Universal Early Childhood Programming in Public Schools

Proponents of universal services argue that this programming would eliminate the need to target certain children or to choose quality instead of quantity. Opponents might rebut that universal early childhood services are too expensive to fund in the manner of public schooling and that the public schools in low-income neighborhoods are not doing a very good job of providing quality education for older children and cannot be expected to do so for younger children. These arguments, and a number of others that could be adduced, ultimately resolve into one very messy political issue, one likely to be raised more and more in the future: whether programs should be universal or targeted.

Universal early childhood programming has several potential benefits. Children from diverse backgrounds and skills could learn from each other; and greater public, parental, political, and financial attention might be paid to the quality of the programming if a wider segment of the voting public used the same services. Public costs could be limited by only funding low-income children through a strategy similar to the free-and-reduced lunch program.

Furthermore, the public schools have several assets. They are geographically well distributed; they have physical facilities, or they could be renovated at less cost than building adequate facilities at new sites; they have a financial and administrative structure already in place to support a universal program, and thus a new bureaucracy would not need to be created; and having early childhood services located in the schools (along with nonschool-hour care) would minimize transportation problems and the need for parents to cobble together a patchwork arrangement of school and care for one or more children. Schools could "outsource" the early childhood (and nonschool-hour) programs to independent agencies to deal with the specialized training needed and different salaries and hours of staff, thus circumventing the argument that the public schools are ill-prepared to operate such programs.

## Mandated Quality Standards

Many advocates have lamented that few states have mandated minimum group sizes, child-to-staff ratios, and other indices of quality in early childhood educational programs. Proponents argue that mandated standards would improve the quality and effectiveness of early childhood programs, and they cite the fact that other nations have demonstrated that such regulations can be accomplished and produce benefits for children (e.g., Boocock, 1995, and this volume).

Standards do work (see Boocock, this volume; Vandell & Pierce, this volume), but nations that implement mandatory standards also tend to provide resources to help providers meet and maintain personnel and facility standards, monitor compliance, and ensure that low-income parents can afford and access high-quality services. Not only is this approach costly, it conflicts with some political philosophies of minimizing governmental interference, violations of free enterprise, and the loss of flexibility and creativity that might be produced by excessive regulation. Further, mandatory regulations without additional resources are likely to drive small and low-income providers out of business or underground, forcing low-income families to use substandard or "illegal" services. Government must recognize that quality staff and facilities for early childhood services are not economically sustainable for low-income families without financial supplements. The difficult political and financial choices are what level of quality for how many children are we willing to publicly support, and who will make such decisions and on what basis will they be made?

## Parental Training and Responsibility for Child Development

In a political climate emphasizing personal responsibility, one option is to train parents to promote their own children's development. While parent education programs produce changes in parents' behaviors and create a better home environment, their ability to produce educational and social gains in children are more limited, unless such programs are very high dosage and teach parents of very young children specific behaviors designed to improve their children's development (few programs have attempted to train low-income parents to improve the development of late preschool and school-aged children). While parent training, especially for the parents of very young children, and parent involvement in programming are beneficial, very intense—and thus costly—efforts are required to help parents alone improve the development of their preschool children. Parent training, it appears, is most effective when performed in combination with programming aimed directly at children conducted by well-trained professional staff (Barnes et al., 1995; Weiss, 1993).

## Welfare-to-Work Adults as Caretakers

One current political philosophy suggests employing low-income adults as caretakers for young children, an approach that would provide employment for the adults and child care for the children of other low-income mothers who would then be free to become employed. Such a strategy has economic advantages, but it is less clear that the benefits for children outlined in this review will be attained. Specifically, the amount of general education and of specific training in child development and care of children has been shown to be related to child outcomes, and it is unlikely that low-income adults would be given the necessary levels of such education and training. Although we do not know what aspects of early childhood programming lead to reduced antisocial behavior (e.g., a stable relationship with a caring adult?), and such caretakers may be able to provide that ingredient, we do know that mental and academic benefits are produced in proportion to the educational advantage of the early childhood program relative to the children's home environment (Barnett, 1995). Consequently, caretakers must be well educated and trained to produce educational benefits in the children.

## Summary and Conclusion

The statistics are more dismal than they have been in decades; yet many in government have announced that they will not continue to fund programs for massive numbers of families and children. On the other hand, children and families as a category are politically popular, and a majority of citizens want better programs and are willing to pay for them. This apparent paradox should stimulate inventive academics to seize this situation as an opportunity. If the country needs more effective and efficient programs, academics have some ideas on how to do it, and we should vigorously study those ideas. And there are grounds for hope in improving the cost-efficiency of these programs. Some programs (Reynolds, 1994; Schweinhart et al., 1993; Seitz & Apfel, 1994; Seitz et al., 1985) have produced substantial short- and long-term benefits at modest cost. What made them cost-effective? If the government wishes to fund fewer programs at less cost, then it needs to invest in program evaluation to identify the necessary components of that effectiveness.

Although it does not often sound like it, the government as well as our nation's children and families are calling for help and for revisions. Academics are society's paid revisionists, and we should accept this challenge to improve these services.

## Acknowledgments

Preparation of this paper was supported in part by Urban University Community Services Program Grant P252A50226, awarded by the federal Department of Education to the University of Pittsburgh Office of Child Development and The Frank and Theresa Caplan Fund for Early Childhood Development and Parenting Education.

## References

Abelson, W. L., Zigler, E. F., & DeBlasi, C. L. (1974). Effects of a four-year Follow Through program on economically disadvantaged children. *Journal of Educational Psychology, 66,* 756–771.

Allen, M., Brown, P., & Finley, B. (1992). *Helping children by strengthening families: A look at family support programs.* Washington DC: Children's Defense Fund.

Ames, E. W., & Chisolm, K. (1997). *The development of Romanian orphanage children adopted to Canada. Final report to the National Welfare Grants Program, Canada National Welfare Grants Division*. Human Resources Development. Burnaby, BC: Simon Fraser University.

Bailey, D. B. J., Jr. (1997). Evaluating the effectiveness of curriculum alternatives for infants and preschoolers at high risk. In M. J. Guralnick (Ed.), *The effectiveness of early intervention* (pp. 227–247). Baltimore: Paul H. Brookes.

Barnard, K. E. (1997). Influencing parent-child interactions for children at risk. In M. J. Guralnick (Ed.), *The effectiveness of early intervention* (pp. 249–268). Baltimore: Paul H. Brookes.

Barnes, H. W., Goodson, B. D., & Layzer, J. I. (1995). *Review of research on supportive interventions for children and families: Vol. 1*. Cambridge, MA: Abt Associates.

Barnett, W. S. (1995). Long-term effects of early childhood programs on cognitive and school outcomes. *The Future of Children, 5*(3), 25–50.

Bee, C. K. (1981). *A longitudinal study to determine if Head Start has lasting effects on school achievement. DAI, 42*(5) Section A.

Belsky, J. (1988). The "effects" of day care reconsidered. *Early Childhood Research Quarterly, 3,* 235–272.

Benasich, A. A., Brooks-Gunn, J., & Clewell, B. C. (1992). How do mothers benefit from early intervention programs? *Journal of Applied Developmental Psychology, 13,* 311–362.

Berk, L. (1985). Relationship of educational attainment, child oriented attitudes, job satisfaction, and career commitment to caregiver behavior toward children. *Child Care Quarterly, 14,* 103–129.

Berrureta-Clement, J. R., Schweinhart, L. J., Barnett, W. S., Epstein, A. S., & Weikert, D. P. (1984). *Changed lives: The effects of the Perry Preschool Program on youths through age 19*. Ypsilanti, MI: High/Scope Press.

Blair, C., & Ramey, C. T. (1997). Early intervention for low-birth-weight infants and the path of second-generation research. In M. J. Guralnick (Ed.), *The effectiveness of early intervention* (pp. 77–97). Baltimore: Paul H. Brookes.

Boocock, S. S. (1995). Early childhood programs in other nations: Goals and outcomes. *The Future of Children, 5*(3), 94–114.

Bryant, D., & Maxwell, K. (1997). The effectiveness of early intervention for disadvantaged children. In M. J. Guralnick (Ed.), *The effectiveness of early intervention* (pp. 23–46). Baltimore: Paul H. Brookes.

Bryant, D. M., & Ramey, C. T. (1987a). An analysis of the effectiveness of early intervention programs for environmentally at-risk children. In M. J. Guralnick & F. C. Bennett (Eds.), *Effectiveness of early intervention* (pp. 33–78). Orlando, FL: Academic Press.

Bryant, D. M., & Ramey, C. T. (1987b). Prevention-oriented infant education programs. *Journal of Children in Contemporary Society, 7,* 17–35.

Caldwell, B. M. (1987). Sustaining intervention effects: Putting malleability to the test. In J. J. Gallagher & C. T. Ramey (Eds.), *The malleability of children* (pp. 115–126). Baltimore: Paul H. Brookes.

Cameron, S., & Heckman, J. (1993). Nonequivalence of high school equivalents. *The Journal of Labor Economics, 1,* 1–47.

Campbell, F. A., & Ramey, C. T. (1994). Effects of early intervention on intellectual and academic achievement: A follow-up study of children from low-income families. *Child Development, 65,* 684–698.

Campbell, F. A., & Ramey, C. T. (1995). Cognitive and school outcomes for high-risk African American students at middle adolescence: Positive effects of early intervention. *American Education Research Journal, 32,* 743–772.

Casto, G., & Lewis, A. (1984). Parent involvement in infant and preschool programs. *Journal of the Division of Early Childhood, 9,* 49–56.

Center for the Future of Children. (1995) Long-term outcomes of early childhood programs. *The Future of Children, 5*(3). Los Altos, CA: The David and Lucile Packard Foundation.

Center for the Future of Children. (1999) *Home visiting: Recent evaluations. The Future of Children, 9*(1). Los Altos, CA: The David and Lucile Packard Foundation.

Charlesworth, R., Hart, C., Burts, D., & DeWolf, M. (1993). The LSU studies: Building a research base for developmentally appropriate practice. *Advances in Early Education and Day Care, 5,* 3–28.

Chubrick, R. E., & Kelley, M. F. (1994). Head Start expansion in the 1990's: A critique. *Focus on Early Childhood, 6,* 1–3.

Clarke-Stewart, K. A. (1987). In search of consistencies in child care research. In D. A. Phillips (Ed.), *Quality in child care: What does research tell us?* (pp. 105–120). Washington, DC: NAEYC.

Clarke-Stewart, K. A. (1988). "The effects of infant day care reconsidered" reconsidered: Risks for parents, children, and research. *Early Childhood Research Quarterly, 3,* 293–308.

Clarke-Stewart, K. A., & Fein, G. (1983). Early childhood programs. In P.H. Mussen (Series Ed.) & M. M. Haith & J. J. Campos (Vol. Eds.), *Handbook of child psychology: Vol. 2. Infancy and developmental psychobiology* (4th ed., pp. 917–1000). New York: Wiley.

Copple, C. E., Cline, M. G., & Smith, A. N. (1987). *Path to the future: Long-term effects of Head Start in the Philadelphia School District.* Washington, DC: U.S. Department of Health and Human Services.

The Cost and Quality Team. (1995). *Cost, quality, and child outcomes in child care centers: Executive summary.* Denver: University of Colorado at Denver.

Crnic, K., & Stormshak, E. (1997). The effectiveness of providing social support for families of children at risk. In M. J. Guralnick (Ed.), *The effectiveness of early intervention* (pp. 209–225). Baltimore: Paul H. Brookes.

Datta, L. (1979). Another spring and other hopes: Some findings from national evaluations of Project Head Start. In E. Zigler & J. Valentine (Eds.), *Project Head Start: A legacy of the War on Poverty* (pp. 405–432). New York: Free Press.

Datta, L. (1982). Strange bedfellows. *American Behavioral Scientist, 26*(1), 133–144.

Davis, K. (1947). A final note on a case of extreme isolation. *American Journal of Sociology, 45,* 554–565.

Day, N. L., Richardson, G. A., & McGauhey, P. J. (1994). The effect of prenatal exposure to illicit drugs: Marijuana, cocaine, heroin and methadone. In H. L. Needleman & D. Bellinger (Eds.), *Prenatal exposure to pollutants and development of infants* (pp. 184–212). Baltimore: Johns Hopkins Press.

Developmental Research and Programs, Inc. (1993). *Risk-focused prevention using the social development strategy: An approach to reducing adolescent problem behaviors.* Seattle, WA: Developmental Research and Programs.

DiLalla, L. F., & Gottsman, I. I. (1991). Biological and genetic contributors to violence—Wisdom's untold tale. *Psychological Bulletin, 109,* 125–129.

Eckstrom, R. B., Boertz, M. E., Pollack, J. M., & Rock, D. A. (1986). Who drops out of high school and why? Findings from a national study. *Teachers College Record, 87,* 356–373.

Elliott, D. S., Huizinga, D., & Menard, S. (1989). *Multiple problem youth: Delinquency, substance use and mental health problems.* New York: Springer-Verlag.

Entwisle, D. R. (1995). The role of schools in sustaining early childhood program benefits. *The Future of Children, 5*(3), 133–144.

Family Resource Coalition. (1994). *Family support programs and comprehensive collaborative services: Overview of family support programs.* Chicago: National Resource Center for Family Support Programs.

Farran, D. C. (1990). Effects of interventions with disadvantaged and disabled children: A decade review. In S. J. Meisels & J. P. Shonkoff (Eds.), *Handbook of early childhood intervention* (pp. 501–539). Cambridge, UK: Cambridge University Press.

Farrington, D. P. (1985). Predicting self-reported and official delinquency. In D. P. Farrington & R. Tarling (Eds.), *Prediction in criminology* (pp. 150–173). Albany, NY: SUNY Press.

Farrington, D. P. (1987). Early precursors of frequent offending. In J. Q. Wilson & G. C. Loury (Eds.), *From children to citizens: Families, schools and delinquency prevention* (pp. 27–50). New York: Springer-Verlag.

Feldman, L. (1990). Target population definition. In Y. T. Yuan & M. Rivest (Eds.), *Preserving families: Evaluation resources for practitioners and policymakers* (pp. 16–38). Newbury Park, CA: Sage Publications.

Finklestein, N. (1982). Aggression: Is it stimulated by day care? *Young Children, 37,* 3–9.

Fosburg, L. B., Goodrich, N. N., Fox, M. K.,Granahan, P., Smith, J. H., & Weitzen, M. (1984). *The effects of Head Start health services: Executive summary.* Cambridge, MA: Abt Associates.

Fowler, W., Ogston, K., Roberts-Fiati, G., & Swenson, A. (1995). Patterns of giftedness and high competence in high school students educationally enriched during infancy: Variations across educational and racial/ethnic backgrounds. *Gifted and Talented International, 10,* 31–36.

Frede, E. C. (1995). The role of program quality in producing early childhood program benefits. *The Future of Children, 5*(3), 115–132.

Frede, E. C., Austin, A. B., & Lindauer, S. K. (1993). The relationship of specific developmentally appropriate teaching practices to children's skills in first grade. *Advances in Early Education and Child Care, 5,* 95–111.

Frede, E. C., & Barnett, W. S. (1992). Developmentally appropriate public school preschool: A study of implementation of the High/Scope curriculum and its effects on disadvantaged children's skills at first grade. *Early Childhood Research Quarterly, 7,* 483–499.

Gamble, T., & Zigler, E. (1986). Effects of infant day care: Another look at the evidence. *American Journal of Orthopsychiatry, 56,* 25–41.

Garbarino, J., Dubrow, N., Kostelny, K., & Pardo, C. (1992). *Children in danger: Coping with the consequences of community violence.* San Francisco: Jossey-Bass.

Goffin, S. G. (1994). *Curriculum models and early childhood education: Appraising the relationship*. New York: Merrill, 1994.

Gomby, D. S., Larner, M. B., Stevenson, C. S., Lewit, E. M., & Behrman, R. E. (1995). Long-term outcomes of early childhood programs: Analysis and recommendations. *The Future of Children, 5*(3), 6–24.

Gomby, D. S., Larson, C. S., Lewit, E. M., & Behrman, R. E. (1993). Home visiting: Analysis and recommendations. *The Future of Children 3*(3), 6–22.

Goodstein, H. A. (1975). *The prediction of elementary school failure among high-risk children*. Storrs, CT: Connecticut University.

Gueron, J., & Pauly, E. (1991). *From welfare to work*. New York: Russell Sage.

Guralnick, M. J. (Ed.) (1997). *The effectiveness of early intervention*. Baltimore: Paul H. Brookes.

Guralnick, M., & Bennett, C. (1987). *Effectiveness of early intervention*. New York: Academic Press.

Guralnick, M. J., & Neville, B. (1997). Designing early intervention programs to promote children's social competence. In M. J. Guralnick (Ed.), *The effectiveness of early intervention* (pp. 579–610). Baltimore: Paul H. Brookes.

Halpern, R. (1990a). Parent support and education programs. *Children and Youth Services Review, 12,* 285–308.

Halpern, R. (1990b). Poverty and early childhood parenting: Toward a framework for intervention. *American Journal of Orthopsychiatry, 60,* 6–18.

Halpern, R., & Weiss, H. (1990). Family support and education programs: Evidence from evaluated program experience. In *Helping families grow strong: New directions in public policy: Papers from the Colloquium on Public Policy and Family Support* (pp. 111–129). Chicago: Family Resource Coalition.

Haskins, R. (1989). Beyond metaphor: The efficacy of early childhood education. *American Psychologist, 44*(2), 127–132.

Hibbs, E. D. (1988). *Children and families: Studies in prevention and intervention*. Madison, CT: International Universities Press.

Hofferth, S. L. (1994). Who enrolls in Head Start? A demographic analysis of Head Start eligible children. *Early Childhood Research Quarterly, 9,* 243–268.

Holloway, S. D., & Reichart-Erickson, M. (1988). The relationship of day care quality to children's free play behavior and social problem-solving skills. *Early Childhood Research Quarterly, 3,* 39–54.

Honig, A. S., & Lally, J. R. (1982). The Family Development Research Program: Retrospective review. *Early Child Development and Care, 10,* 41–62.

Honig, A., Lally, R., & Mathieson, D. (1982). Personal-social adjustment of school children after 5 years in a family enrichment program. *Child Care Quarterly, 11,* 138–146.

Howes, C. (1983). Caregiver behavior in center and family day care. *Journal of Applied Developmental Psychology, 4,* 99–107.

Huston, A. (1995, August). *Children in poverty and public policy.* Presidential address to Division 7, Developmental Psychology, at the Annual Meeting of the American Psychological Association, New York, NY.

Hyson, M. D., Hirsh-Pasek, K., & Rescorla, L. (1990). The Classroom Practices Inventory: An observation instrument based on NAEYC's guidelines for developmentally appropriate practices for 4- and 5-year old children. *Early Childhood Research Quarterly, 5,* 475–594.

Infant Health and Development Program. (1990). Enhancing the outcomes of low-birthweight, premature infants. *Journal of the American Medical Association, 263*(22), 3035–3042.

Kagan, S. L., Powell, D. R., Weissbourd, B., & Zigler, E. (1987). Past accomplishments: Future challenges. In S. L. Kagan, D. R. Powell, B. Weissbourd, & E. F. Zigler (Eds.), *America's family support programs: The state of the art* (pp. 365–380). New Haven: Yale University Press.

Karweit, N. L. (1994). Can preschool alone prevent early learning failure? In R. E. Slavin, N. L. Karweit, and B. A. Wasik (Eds.), *Preventing early school failure: Research, policy, and practice.* Boston, MA: Allyn and Bacon.

Kresh, E. (1993). *The effects of Head Start: What do we know?* Unpublished manuscript, Administration for Children and Families, Washington, DC.

Larner, M., Halpern, R., & Harkavy, O. (1992). *Fair start for children: Lessons learned from seven demonstration projects.* New Haven: Yale University Press.

Lazar, I., & Darlington, R. (1982). Lasting effects of early education: A report from the consortium for longitudinal studies. *Monographs of the Society for Research in Child Development, 47* (Serial No. 195).

Lee, V. E., Brooks-Gunn, J., & Schnur, E. (1988). Does Head Start work? A 1-year follow-up comparison of disadvantaged children attending Head Start, no preschool, and other preschool programs. *Developmental Psychology, 24,* 210–222.

Lee, V. E., Brooks-Gunn, J., Schnur, E., & Liaw, F. (1990). Are Head Start effects sustained? A longitudinal follow-up comparison of disadvantaged children attending Head Start, no preschool, and other preschool programs. *Child Development, 61,* 495–507.

Loeber, R., & Dishion, T. (1983). Early predictors of male delinquency: A review. *Psychological Bulletin, 94,* 68–99.

Loeber, R., & Stouthamer-Loeber, M. (1986). Family factors as correlates and predictors of juvenile conduct problems and delinquency. In M. Tonry & N. Morris (Eds.), *Crime and justice: An annual review of research, 7,* 29–150.

Madden, J., Levenstein, P., & Levenstein, S. (1976). Longitudinal IQ outcomes of the Mother-Child Home Program. *Child Development, 46,* 1015–1025.

Mann, A. J., Harrel, A., & Hurt, M. (1976). *A review of Head Start research since 1969.* Washington, DC: Social Research Group, George Washington University.

Marcon, R. A. (1992). Differential effects of three preschool models on inner-city 4-year-olds. *Early Childhood Research Quarterly, 7,* 517–530.

Marcon, R. A. (1994). *Early learning and early identification follow-up study: Transition from the early to the later grades.* A report prepared for the District of Columbia Public Schools. Washington, DC: District of Columbia Public Schools.

McCall, R. B. (1977). Challenges to a science of developmental psychology. *Child Development, 48,* 333–344.

McCall, R. B. (1979). The development of intellectual functioning in infancy and the prediction of later IQ. In J. D. Osofsky (Ed.), *Handbook of infant development* (pp. 707–741). New York: Wiley.

McCall, R. B. (1981). Nature-nurture and the two realms of development: A proposed integration with respect to mental development. *Child Development, 52,* 1–12.

McCall, R. B., Evahn, C., & Kratzer, L. (1992). *High school underachievers: What do they achieve as adults?* Newbury Park, CA: Sage Publications.

McGee, R., Silva, P. A., & Williams, S. (1984). Perinatal, neurological, environmental and developmental characteristics of seven-year-old children with stable behavior problems. *Journal of Child Psychology and Psychiatry, 25,* 573–586.

McKey, R., Condelli, L., Ganson, H. et al. (1985). *The impact of Head Start on children, families, and communities: Final report of the Head Start Evaluation, Synthesis, and Utilization Project.* Washington, DC: U.S. Department of Health and Human Services.

Mednick, S. A., Brennan, P., & Kandel, E. (1988). Predisposition to violence. *Aggressive Behavior, 14,* 25–33.

Meyer, L. L. (1984). Long-term academic effects of the direct instructional project Follow Through. *Elementary School Journal, 84,* 380–392.

Monroe, E., & McDonnell, M. S. (1981). A follow-up of the 1966 Head Start Program. Unpublished manuscript, Rome (GA) City Schools.

Oakland, T., & Ghazaleh, H. A. (1996). *Primary prevention of handicapping conditions among Palestinian children in Gaza.* Unpublished manuscript.

O'Connor, T. G., Bredenkamp, D., Rutter, M., & the English and Romanian Adoptees (ERA) Study Team. (1999). Attachment disturbances and disorders in children exposed to early severe deprivation. *Infant Mental Health Journal, 20,* 10–29.

Ogbu, J. (1986). The consequences of the American caste system. In V. Neisser (Ed.), *The school achievement of minority children* (pp. 19–56). Hillsdale, NJ: Erlbaum.

Olds, D. L., & Kitzman, H. (1993). Review of research on home visiting for pregnant women and parents of young children. *The Future of Children 3*(3), 53–92.

Patterson, G. R. (1982). *A social learning approach: Vol. 3. Coercive family process.* Eugene, OR: Castalia.

Phillips, D. A., & Howes, C. (1987). Indicators of quality in child care: Review of research. In D. A. Phillips (Ed.), *Quality in child care: What does research tell us?* (pp. 1–20). Washington, DC: NAEYC.

Plomin, R. (1989). Environment and genes: Determinants of behavior. *American Psychologist, 44,* 105–111.

Plomin, R., Nitz, K., & Rowe, D. C. (1990). Behavioral genetics and aggressive behavior in childhood. In M. Lewis & S. M. Miller (Eds.), *Handbook of developmental psychopathology* (pp. 119–133). New York: Plenum Press.

Powell, C., & Grantham-McGregor, S. (1989). Home visiting of varying frequency and child development. *Pediatrics, 84,* 157–169.

Powell, D. R. (1993). Inside home visiting programs. *The Future of Children, 3*(3), 23–38.

Ramey, S. L., & Ramey, C. T. (1992). Early educational intervention with disadvantaged children—To what effect? *Applied & Preventive Psychology, 1,* 131–140.

Reynolds, A. J. (1994). Effects of a preschool plus follow-up intervention for children at risk. *Developmental Psychology, 30,* 787–804.

Reynolds, A. J., Mavrogenes, N. A., Bezruczko, N., & Hagemann, M. (1996). Cognitive and family-support mediators of preschool effectiveness: A confirmatory analysis. *Child Development, 67,* 1119–1190.

Roberts, R. N., & Wasik, B. H. (1990). Home visiting programs for families with children birth to three: Results of a national survey. *Journal of Early Intervention, 14*(3), 272–284.

Roberts, R. N.,Wasik, B. H., Casto, G., & Ramey, C. T. (1991). Family support in the home: Programs, policy, and social change. *American Psychologist, 46*(2), 131–137.

Rowe, D. C. (1990). As the twig is bent? The myth of child-rearing influences on personality development. *Journal of Counseling and Development, 68,* 606–611.

Rowe, D. C., & Rodgers, J. L. (1989). Behavioral genetics, adolescent deviance, and "d": Contributions and issues. In G. R. Adams, R. Montemayor, & T. P. Gullota (Eds.), *Biology of adolescent behavior and development* (pp. 38–67). Newbury Park, CA: Sage Publications.

Royce, J. M., Darlington, R. B., & Murray, H. W. (1983). Findings across studies. In Consortium for Longitudinal Studies (Ed.), *As the twig is bent... lasting effects of preschool programs.* Hillsdale, NJ: Erlbaum.

Royster, J., & Larsen, J. C. (1977). *National survey of Head Start graduates and their peers.* Cambridge, MA: Abt Associates.

Ruopp, R., Travers, J., Glantz, F. M., & Coelen, C. (1979). *Children at the center: Summary findings and their implications. Final report of the National Day Care Study: Vol. 1.* Cambridge, MA: Abt Associates.

Rutter, M. (1979). Protective factors in children's responses to stress and disadvantage. In M. W. Kent & J. E. Rolf (Eds.), *Primary prevention of psychopathology: Vol. 3. Social competence in children* (pp. 49–74). Hanover, NH: University Press of New England.

Sameroff, A. J., & Chandler, M. J. (1975). Reproductive risk and the continuum of caretaking causality. In E. M. Hetherington, S. Scarr-Salapabek, & G. M. Siegel (Eds.), *Review of child development research: Vol. 4* (pp. 187–244). Chicago: University of Chicago Press.

Sameroff, A. J., & Fiese, B. H. (1990). Transactional regulation and early intervention. In S. J. Meisels & J. P. Shonkoff (Eds.), *Handbook of early childhood intervention* (pp. 119–149). New York: Cambridge University Press.

Sameroff, A. J., & Seifer, R. (1983). Familial risk and child competence. *Child Development, 54,* 1254–1268.

Sampson, R. J., Raudenbush, S. W., & Earls, F. (1997). Neighborhoods and violent crime: A multilevel study of collective efficacy. *Science, 277,* 918–924.

Scarr, S., & McCartney, K. (1988). Far from home: An experimental evaluation of the mother-child home program in Bermuda. *Child Development, 59,* 531–543.

Schnur, E., Brooks-Gunn, J., & Shipman, V. (1992). Who attends programs serving poor children? The case of Head Start attendees and nonattendees. *Journal of Applied Psychology, 13,* 405–421.

Schorr, L. (1988). *Within our reach: Breaking the cycle of disadvantage.* New York: Doubleday.

Schweinhart, L. J., Barnes, H. V., Weikert, D. P., with Barnett, W. S., & Epstein, A. S. (1993). Significant benefits: The High/Scope Perry Preschool study through age 27. *Monographs of the High/Scope Educational Research Foundation, 10.* Ypsilanti, MI: High/Scope Press.

Schweinhart, L. J., & Weikert, D. P. (1980). *Young children grow up: The effects of the Perry Preschool Program on youths through age 15.* Ypsilanti, MI: High/Scope Press.

Seitz, V., & Apfel, N. (1994). Parent-focused intervention: Diffusion effects on siblings. *Child Development, 65,* 677–683.

Seitz, V., Apfel, N., Rosenbaum, L., & Zigler, E. F. (1983). Long-term effects of projects Head Start and Follow Through: The New Haven Project. In Consortium for Longitudinal Studies (Ed.), *As the twig is bent… lasting effects of preschool programs* (pp. 299–332). Hillsdale, NJ: Erlbaum.

Seitz, V., Rosenbaum, L. K., & Apfel, N. H. (1985). Effects of family support intervention: A ten-year follow-up. *Child Development, 56,* 376–391.

Seppanen, P. S., Godin, K. W., & Metzger, J. L. (1993). *Observational study of Chapter 1-funded early childhood programs. Final report: Volume 2.* Washington, DC: U.S. Department of Education.

Shipman, V. C. (1976). *Stability and change in family status, situational, and process variables and their relationship to children's cognitive performance.* Princeton, NJ: Educational Testing Service.

Shonkoff, J. P., & Hauser-Cram, P. (1987). Early intervention for disabled infants and their families: A quantitative analysis. *Pediatrics, 80,* 650–658.

Slavin, R. E. (1989). Students at risk of school failure: The problem and its dimensions. In R. E. Slavin, N. L. Karweit, & N. A. Madden (Eds.), *Effective programs for students at risk* (pp. 3–19). Boston: Allyn and Bacon.

Sosin, J. (1997, April 21). *The political mandate for children.* Paper presented at the conference Nurturing Neurons, Pittsburgh, PA.

St. Pierre, R. G., Layzer, J. I., & Barnes, H. V. (1994). Two-generation programs: Design, cost, and short-term effectiveness. *The Future of Children* 5(3), 76–93.

St. Pierre, R. G., Layzer, J. I., Goodson, B. D., & Bernstein, L. S. (1997, June). *National impact evaluation of the Comprehensive Child Development Program: Final report.* Cambridge, MA: Abt Associates.

Steiner, G. Y. (1976). *The children's cause.* Washington, DC: The Brookings Institution.

Wasik, B. H., Bryant, D. M., & Lyons, C. M. (1990). *Home visiting: Procedures for helping families.* Newbury Park, CA: Sage Publications.

Wasik, B. A., & Karweit, N. L. (1994). Off to a good start: Effects of birth to three interventions on early school success. In R. E. Slavin, N. L. Karweit, & B. A. Wasik (Eds.), *Preventing early school failure: Research, policy, and practice* (pp. 13–57). Boston: Allyn and Bacon.

Wasik, B. H., Ramey, C. T., Bryant, D. M., & Sparling, J. J. (1990). A longitudinal study of two early intervention strategies: Project CARE. *Child Development, 61*(6), 1682–1696.

Weiss, H. B. (1993). Home visits: Necessary but not sufficient. *The Future of Children, 3*(3), 113–128.

Weiss, H., & Halpern, R. (1990). *Community-based family support and education programs: Something old or something new?* New York: National Center for Children in Poverty.

Weiss H. B., & Jacobs, F. (1988). *Evaluating family programs.* New York: Aldine De Gruyter.

Weissbourd, B. (1993). Family support programs. In C. H. Zeanah, Jr. (Ed.), *Handbook of infant mental health* (pp. 402–413). New York: The Guilford Press.

Werner, E. E. (1987). Vulnerability and resiliency in children at risk for delinquency: A longitudinal study from birth to adulthood. In J. D. Burchard & S. N. Burchard (Eds.), *Primary prevention of psychopathology: Vol. 10. Prevention of delinquent behavior..* Newbury Park, CA: Sage Publications.

Werner, E. E., & Smith, R. S. (1982). *Vulnerable but invincible: A longitudinal study of resilient children and youth.* New York: Adams, Bannister, Cox.

Werner, E. E., & Smith, R. S. (1992). *Overcoming the odds: High risk children from birth to adulthood.* Ithaca, NY: Cornell University Press.

Whitebook, M., Howes, C., & Phillips, D. (1989). *Who cares: Child care teachers and the quality of care in America.* Final report of the National Child Care Staffing Study. Oakland, CA: Child Care Employee Project.

Woodhead, M. (1988). When psychology informs public policy: The cases of early childhood interventions. *American Psychologist, 43,* 443–454.

Yoshikawa, H. (1995). Long-term effects of early childhood programs on social outcomes and delinquency. *The Future of Children, 5*(3), 51–75.

Zigler, E., & Berman, W. (1983). Discerning the future of early childhood intervention. *American Psychologist, 38,* 894–906.

Zigler, E., & Freedman, J. (1987). Early experience, malleability, and Head Start. In J. J. Gallagher & C. T. Ramey (Eds.), *The malleability of children* (pp. 85–95). Baltimore, Paul H. Brookes.

Zigler, E., & Styfco, S. J. (1993). Strength in unity: Consolidating federal education programs for young children. In E. Zigler & S. J. Styfco (Eds.), *Head Start and beyond: A national plan for extended childhood intervention* (pp. 111–145). New Haven: Yale University Press.

Zigler, E., & Styfco, S. J. (1999, July 8). Don't overhaul Head Start—again. *The Wall Street Journal,* p. A18.

Zigler, E., Taussig, C., & Black, K. (1992). Early childhood intervention: A promising preventative for juvenile delinquency. *American Psychologist, 47,* 997–1006.

# Chapter 10

## Lessons from Europe: European Preschools Revisited in a Global Age

*Sarane Spence Boocock*

Rising enrollments in preschool programs and increasing use of nonparental child care are surely among the most significant worldwide trends of the past two decades. The growing demand for early childhood care and education services is, moreover, precipitated by social, political, and economic changes that are themselves global phenomena. The increased participation of mothers in the labor force, declining birthrates, dwindling family size, and disappearing extended-family support that have transformed American family life in the late 20th century have occurred in many other countries as well (Olmsted, 1989; Tietze & Cryer, 1999). Demand for preschool services has also been fueled by the tremendous growth and broader dissemination of knowledge about human development—in particular, about the crucial importance of the early years of life and the untapped learning potential of infants and young children, as well as by concern over the high proportions of children who are doing poorly in school, repeating grades, or dropping out in the first few years (Myers, 1997).

Ironically, growing recognition of the importance of early childhood care and education has coincided with the growing dominance of free market economics that has, among other things, led many countries to reduce social benefits to families and children in order to remain or become more "efficient" and "competitive." This has, in turn, resulted in more children living in poverty, becoming homeless, and entering the labor market, often in violation of national laws prohibiting child labor (Swadener & Bloch, 1997). Particularly disheartening are the curtailments in all forms of support to families with young children in the former communist countries of Eastern and Central Europe, whose programs were once held up as models for emulation by other nations (Ispa, 1994; Zimmerman, et al., 1994). Intense pressures to economize on preschool services by reducing government support or relaxing standards are, moreover, being felt even in nations where programs are well established and have wide public support.

In such a context, continuing support for quality preschool programs may depend upon compelling evidence of their cost-effectiveness. In this chapter, I review research on the long-term effects of early care and education (ECE) programs in European nations, in particular, in the 15 nations comprising the European Union (EU),[1] where, it is generally agreed, some of the world's most highly developed ECE systems can be found. The 1970s and 1980s saw a tremendous expansion of preschool programs for children from age 3 to the age of compulsory schooling (ranging from age 5 to age 7). Enrollment rates doubled, tripled, or in some cases grew even faster during this period. In about half of these countries, publicly funded preschool places are now available for 80% or more of the children in this age group. Most are free of charge or charge small fees taking parental income into account—though the availability and affordability of ECE services for younger children lag considerably behind (Tietze & Cryer, 1999, pp. 180–183).

The opening of national frontiers for trade and travel seems also to have been accompanied by an increased sharing of information, joint planning, and collaborative research. The European Commission Network on Childcare and the European Child Care and Education Study Group have assembled data on the range and nature of services for young children currently provided in each country, have reviewed research on the benefits of participation in preschool programs and identified impediments to their expansion and improvement, and are attempting to standardize the concept of program quality and the instruments used to measure it (Bairrao & Tietze, 1993; Moss, 1990; Tietze & Cryer, 1999; Tietze et al., 1996;). International sharing of information and participation in joint projects have undoubtedly contributed to a growing convergence of thinking, among both professionals and the public in EU countries, that ECE programs should provide "the fundamental requirements for children's personal care, health, safety, socialization, and education in an integrated manner and that those services should be available to support family life, at an affordable cost for all parents who need and want them (Tietze & Cryer, 1999, p. 176).

At the same time, there is still considerable diversity in the availability of preschool programs in EU countries, and each nation's policies and programs retain distinctive characteristics that reflect historical and cultural differences. Table 10.1, based upon figures supplied by the Organization for Economic Cooperation and Development (OECD) for 1995 preschool enrollments, shows, for example, that almost 100% of all French and Belgian children were enrolled in an educational preschool program by age 3, compared to about half of German, Norwegian, and Swedish children, only a few Swiss and Irish children, and no Dutch children. Differences at age 4 are not as sharp but still substantial. Although a consensus is emerging on the importance of providing stimulating environments for young children, there is still considerable debate on whether enrollment in organized and formal provision outside the family is necessarily the best approach, on the appropriate balance of public as opposed to private investment in ECE, and on the appropriate relationships between families and preschools. Rather than present a country-by-country account of research on preschool programs and their outcomes,[2] I have organized the following discussion around four questions, the answers to which, I believe, are being sought by researchers, policymakers, and practitioners throughout the world:

1. What are the most important long-term benefits of preschool programs?
2. What are the most important elements of quality in pre-school programs?
3. How can preschool programs reduce educational inequities?
4. How might the case in support of greater ECE availability and affordability and higher quality of preschool programs be strengthened?

**TABLE 10.1**
**Preschool Participation Rates of European OECD Member Countries, 1995**

| Country | Net enrollment of: | |
|---|---|---|
| | 3-year-olds | 4-year-olds |
| France | 99.50 | 100.00 |
| Belgium | 98.47 | 99.54 |
| Czech Republic | 62.77 | 74.52 |
| Denmark | 59.95 | 78.77 |
| Spain | 57.38 | 100.00 |
| Norway | 54.49 | 65.16 |
| Sweden | 51.00 | 57.61 |
| Germany | 46.61 | 71.02 |
| United Kingdom | 40.59 | 10.64* |
| Portugal | 40.36 | 55.60 |
| Austria | 30.42 | 70.66 |
| Finland | 26.88 | 29.49 |
| Greece | 12.68 | 54.15 |
| Switzerland | 5.87 | 26.97 |
| Ireland | 0.86 | 52.77 |
| Netherlands | -- | 97.18 |
| United States | 34.18 | 61.95 |

*Note:* Adapted from *Education Policy Analysis 1998* (pp. 20, 75), by the Centre for Educational Research and Innovation, 1998, Paris: Organization for Economic Co-operation and Development (OECD). Copyright 1998 by OECD.

*Over 80% of 4-year-olds in the United Kingdom are enrolled, beyond preschool, in primary education.

In the final section, I shall consider the implications of research on European preschool outcomes for the improvement of American preschool programs.

While I have tried to limit my review to studies of "good" quality that allow assessment of preschool effects for at least five years, the studies reviewed here are of varying quality and thus the data in different studies are not always, strictly speaking, comparable. (I shall, in fact, discuss one preschool system, Reggio Emilia, for which the only published "research" is either theoretical or descriptive.) Of course, formidable difficulties arise in comparing data collected in different countries, even if they are close to each other geographically and at similar levels of economic development. Many problems derive from differences in the way ECE services are defined and organized. Some focus upon preparing children for school entry, others provide child care for children with working parents along with some educational activities, and others offer a broad range of health, developmental, and social services. The outcomes measured range from cognitive development and school success or failure, to emotional development and social skills, to reduction of inequalities based on racial, ethnic, gender, and social-class differences. Lack of international consensus regarding the definition and measurement of various outcomes, as well as difficulties in translating from one language to another, make crosscultural comparisons difficult— though the European Child Care and Education Study Group mentioned above has made impressive progress in this regard.

Other problems arise from variations in modes of data collection and analysis. The studies included in this review fall into three major groups: large-scale surveys, studies comparing children having different child care or preschool experiences, and evaluations testing the impacts of particular programs or program models. Few of the studies employed an experimental design with random assignment of children to program and control groups, making it difficult to assess the validity of the findings, since effects that are due to self-selection or other factors not under the researchers' control may be erroneously attributed to a preschool program. (For a fuller discussion of methodological concerns in cross-national analysis of ECE programs, see Boocock & Larner,

1998; Cochran, 1993, especially the introductory chapter; Olmsted, 1989; Tietze et al., 1996).

## What Are the Most Important Long-term Benefits of Preschool Programs?

Some of the best evidence that attendance at high-quality preschool programs is positively associated with children's cognitive and socioemotional development and their success in school can be found in studies from European nations with highly developed ECE systems.

### *France*

Concern over the large number of elementary school children who had to repeat grades was the impetus for broad expansion of the French preschool system in the 1970s and 1980s. The *école maternelle*, or nursery school, is fully funded by the national government and provides a free, full-day program. The curriculum, developed by the Ministry of Education, is used nationwide, and the training and payment of preschool teachers is comparable to that of elementary school teachers. Though not compulsory, the *école maternelle* is now attended by close to 100% of all 3- to 5-year-olds, and a growing number of 2-year-olds.

To discover whether preschool attendance affected retention rates, the French Ministry of Education surveyed a national sample of 20,000 sixth graders, comparing those who had attended preschool for one, two, three, or no years. The survey revealed that every year of preschool reduced the likelihood of school failure, especially for children from the most disadvantaged homes. While children from higher status homes and children in urban areas, who tended to have the most preschool experience, were more likely to be promoted on schedule, each additional year of preschool narrowed the retention rate "gap" between advantaged and disadvantaged children (McMahan, 1992). It should be noted, though, that the magnitude of the estimated effects is considerably smaller than the effects estimated for some programs in the United States. One possible explanation is the relatively large class sizes in the French preschools (Barnett, 1998 and personal communication).

## United Kingdom

Another large-scale survey, the Child Health and Education Study (CHES), examined the effects of preschool and child care programs in the United Kingdom, a nation with a much more diverse system than France. Public investment in full-day child care is limited; many families rely on individual childminders, who may or may not be registered with the government. As indicated in Table 10.1, fewer than half of British 3- and 4-year-olds attend public or private nursery schools, though many children enter public school classes at age 4. Children who have a parent at home during the day often attend organized playgroups several times a week (Curtis, 1992).

The CHES, whose objective was to evaluate "ordinary nursery schools and playgroups, rather than experimental or innovative schemes," followed the development of all the approximately 9,000 children born during one week in 1970 (Osborn & Milbank, 1987). Researchers collected data on cognitive functioning, educational achievement, and behavior ratings by mothers and teachers when the children were 5 years old and again when they were 10. Comparisons between children who attended playgroups, private or public nursery schools, or no preschool indicated that experience in any preschool program contributed to cognitive development and school achievement at ages 5 and 10. Contrary to the researchers' expectations, however, preschool experience did not appear to enhance children's self-concept, skill in getting along with other children, and other aspects of socioemotional development.

## Germany

A study conducted in the former West Germany, where 65% to 70% of children between ages 3 and 6 attended free half-day preschools, produced findings similar to those reported in the French and British studies. Rather than conducting their own survey, the researchers analyzed statistics routinely collected by the elementary schools in one state. The analysis revealed that preschool experience influenced rates of retention in grade, assignment to special education, and other school outcomes more consistently than any other factor studied. The researchers concluded that a well-established preschool system can improve children's school readiness and ease the transition into elementary school (Tietze, 1987). Similar results have been obtained in other German studies as well as in Portugal and the United States. (Bairrao & Tietze, 1993, pp. 40–41).

## Sweden

Of all national ECE systems, Sweden's is arguably the most comprehensive, coherent, and generous. In Sweden, local governments provide carefully supervised, subsidized child care through centers and family child care homes to about half of children between birth and school entry at age 7, although many infants are cared for by their parents during paid parental leaves (Gunnarsson, 1993; Gustafsson & Stafford, 1998). Systematic longitudinal studies of Swedish child care and early childhood education have been carried out since the mid-1960s. Characterized by small but carefully designed samples and meticulous measurement of children's environments, development, and well-being, Swedish research provides a rich source of data on the long-term effects of alternative forms of early child care and education. For example, a study directed by Andersson followed 128 children born in 1975 to age 13, gathering information and assessments from mothers and teachers, as well as administering a series of verbal and nonverbal tests at ages 7 and 13. Whether they attended centers or family child care, children with extensive preschool experience performed significantly better on cognitive tests and received more positive ratings from their teachers on school achievement, social, and personal attributes than children with less or no ECE experience— in fact, children placed in outside-the-home care before age 1 received the most positive ratings on verbal facility, persistence, independence, and confidence, the lowest ratings on anxiety. The positive effects of day care persisted throughout the elementary school period, leading the researchers to conclude that "early entrance into day-care tends to predict a creative, socially confident, popular, open, and independent adolescent" (Andersson, 1992, pp. 32–33). Two other Swedish longitudinal studies (Broberg, Hwang, Lamb, & Ketterlinus, 1989; Cochran & Gunnarsson, 1985) yielded similar findings.

These studies do not fit neatly within the boundaries of this paper, since they cover the entire period from birth to school entry (and sometimes beyond), and it is difficult to separate out the specific effects of preschool programs for children between the ages of 3 and 6 from the effects of other outside-the-home environments and experiences, but two general findings from the Swedish research seem pertinent to our discussion here. One is that the Swedish ECE system is based on a model of childhood and childrearing, sometimes referred to as "dual socialization," which assumes that in contemporary societies, most children from early childhood on are, in effect, living in two different social worlds (in the family and in institutional ECE facilities) on a regular, daily basis, and that if ECE programs are of adequate quality and all families (including those living in unconventional or "alternative" family patterns) receive as entitlements adequate supports from the social welfare system, dual socialization need not have adverse effects on children's development and well-being, and may in fact enhance children's mental flexibility, social sensibility, communication skills, self-reliance, and self-discipline (Dencik, 1995). Andersson's study is often cited as offering empirical support for this model.

Swedish research also indicates that it is possible to make emotional development and socialization to group life an important objective of preschool programs without sacrificing later academic success, a finding that is not reported in the other European studies we have discussed; the French and German studies did not assess socioemotional development, and the CHES found that British preschool experiences that had positive effects on cognitive development did not appear to enhance socioemotional development.[3] On the other hand, findings from studies carried out in several highly industrialized East Asian nations are quite consistent with the dual socialization model. In Japan, Hong Kong, Taiwan, South Korea, and Singapore, as in the European Union countries, the birthrate has dropped in recent years to the extent that most children now grow up in one- or two-child families, and preschools are viewed as providing socialization experiences that few children receive in their homes and neighborhoods. For example, a longitudinal study conducted by the Singapore Institute of Education, in which a stratified random sample of 2,413 3- to 6-year-olds were observed and tested over a two-and-a-half-year period on a broad array of cognitive and behavioral measures, showed that children who attended preschool not only had more highly developed language skills but also showed improved social skills, including sharing and cooperative behavior. In Singapore, as in France, research documenting the benefits of preschool experience has provided empirical support for government efforts to expand the preschool system (Sim & Kam, 1992).

Although most of the research on long-term effects of preschool programs assesses effects on children's development and well-being, research on the Swedish system also provides examples of benefits to parents and to society of good quality ECE services. A comparison of policies and programs in the United States, Sweden, and the Netherlands (Gustafsson & Stafford, 1998) notes that the Swedish teenage birthrate is comparatively low, and the probability of having a child is much higher for more educated than for less educated Swedish women, even controlling for social background and marital status—just the reverse of the American situation. The authors conclude that comprehensive preschool services combined with generous parental leave policies not only alleviate the financial and other problems of single motherhood that haunt the United States, but also provide incentives to postpone childbearing until a career has been established.[4]

## What Are the Most Important Elements of Preschool Quality?

Though positive outcomes for children are associated with program quality throughout the world, consensus on what constitutes a high-quality program has yet to be achieved. On the one hand, few ECE professionals would agree with the conclusion of the British Child Health and Education Study: "Provided the child receives proper care, has interesting activities and other children to play with (which are common elements in the majority of preschool institutions) the actual type of preschool experience matters very little" (Osborn & Milbank, 1987, p. 239).[5] On the other hand, few would deny that

> The quality of early childhood care and education
> can be compared from many differing perspectives
> and with many different issues in mind…. Selecting

which aspects of ECE system quality to compare is a
major task, with possibilities for comparisons
ranging from factors that are far removed from the
child's actual experiences, such as the economic or
political environment that provides the underpinnings for ECE systems, to factors that are more
closely but not directly experienced by children,
such as the structural and philosophical characteristics of ECE programs, and finally to the process
quality of programs that children actually experience, either as a group or as individuals. In addition,
the varying priorities and visions of the different
stakeholders including parents, ECE providers,
employers, the children themselves, and the society
as a whole, might well be considered when comparing ECE system quality (Tietze et al., 1996, p. 448).

The study from which the above quotation derives, an evaluation of
preschools in Austria, Germany, Portugal, Spain, and the United States,
using the Early Childhood Environment Rating Scale (ECERS) and the
Caregiver Interaction Scale (CIS) as the measures of quality, found,
however, (a) few significant national differences despite differences in
the infrastructures that support ECE programs in each country; (b) the
ECE system in all five countries rated "mediocre"—in most cases, mean
scores exceeded minimal standards of quality but did not meet the
ECERS standard of high quality; and (c) the data did not enable the
researchers to identify which specific regulations or societal conditions
were the strongest determinants of program quality, or how variations in
quality were linked to the development of the children served (Tietze et
al., 1996, pp. 468–469, 472).

Although specification of the crucial components of program
quality continues to elude ECE researchers, most would agree that a
high-quality preschool program should be based upon a rich variety of
developmentally appropriate activities that engage children as active
learners. For example, the curriculum of the French *école maternelle*
includes emergent literacy and other activities designed to acculturate
children to the rules and rhythms of a formal school setting, but gives
equal attention to the cultivation of children's curiosity, creativity,

psychomotor development, and social skills. The Ministry of Education guidelines for the professional training required of all preprimary teachers emphasizes active participation of teachers in children's play and other activities, "supportively accompanying, supplying the needs of, and assisting children as they undertake particular projects or endeavors" (Atkinson, 1989, p. 80).

Attentiveness to the child's ideas and interests is carried even further in the highly regarded community preschools in the Northern Italian town of Reggio Emilia. Following the dictum of Loris Malaguzzi, founder of the Reggio Emilia preschool system (RE), that "things about children and for children are only learned from children" (quoted in Edwards, Gandini, & Forman, 1998, p. 51), teachers are encouraged to follow children's leads in pursuing avenues of inquiry and to take cues from children for curriculum development. Children's intellectual, aesthetic, emotional, social, and moral potentials are to be cultivated through "long-term engrossing projects... carried out in a beautiful, healthy, love-filled setting" (Gardner, 1998, p. xi). Since a given group of children and their teacher stay together for three years, they get to know each other so well that a day's activities can be scheduled not by the clock but by the children's "own sense of time and their personal rhythms" (Gandini, 1993, p. 65). Extensive documentation of the children's activities—via transcriptions of their remarks and conversations, photos and videotapes of classroom activities, teachers' written observations, and collections of children's art work—is an important element of the Reggio Emilia model (Palius, 1999, p. 5). Visitors' accounts are glowing, and the system has been rated by some as the best in the world. It is important to keep in mind, however, that to date, assessments of the RE program based upon longitudinal, experimental, or any other systematic analysis of outcomes are lacking.

Some indicators of quality considered essential by American evaluators are accorded less importance elsewhere. For example, the Reggio Emilia preschools and the *écoles maternelles* routinely have class sizes and child-to-staff ratios far in excess of National Association for the Education of Young Children (NAEYC) standards—though they also have training requirements that ensure most classroom personnel have professional credentials. Teachers in the *écoles maternelles* are required to have graduate level training. The staff of a Reggio Emilia preschool have access to a number of specialists, including *atelierista*, teachers with special training in the teaching of visual arts, and *pedagogista*, teams of experts who work intensively with teachers and facilitate interaction among teachers, families, and municipal administrators (Palius, 1999, p. 4). Not surprisingly, in nations with high proportions of well-trained teachers and caretakers, salaries tend to be relatively high and staff turnover relatively low—as, for example, in France, where preschool teachers have civil service status and salaries comparable to those of primary school teachers.

Rigorous training and certification requirements for ECE staff tend to develop in nations with comprehensive national policies regarding children and families, and the means to implement them. A national law passed in 1968 established funding of public preschools for all 3- to 6-year-old Italian children, and the Reggio Emilia preschools are part of a well-subsidized system of social services (New, 1990). The *école maternelle* is part of a national system comprised of child care and education for children from infancy to school entry, income support programs including child allowances and paid parental leave, and universal health care for children and their parents (Bergmann, 1990). Swedish ECE facilities differ considerably in group composition, atmosphere, and staff experience and working methods, but government funding and oversight ensure that variations stay within specified limits, and do not fall below an agreed-upon threshold of quality (Lamb et al., 1991, p. 117). In contrast, in nations where caring for young children is widely viewed as temporary work requiring no special expertise ("any woman can do it"), many caretakers are unpaid volunteers (as in the Netherlands) or untrained babysitters with very low pay (as in the United States), and turnover is high.[6]

In Europe as in the United States, the involvement of parents in their children's preschools is often postulated as an important element of program quality, on the grounds that it improves both parenting skills and child outcomes.[7] Among European countries, the extent and ways in which preschool programs involve parents varies substantially from country to country. In Denmark, national laws mandate that parents be involved in decisions concerning curriculum, budget, and personnel, though few other nations routinely involve parents to this extent. (For a summary of parent involvement policies and practices in the countries participating in the European Commission Network on Child Care, see Bairrão & Tietze, 1993, p. 34.)

However, virtually no solid empirical evidence supports the claims regarding the benefits of parental involvement. A few cross-cultural studies in which parents' and teachers' views have been elicited indicate that parents and professionals agree on a need for improved communication between home and preschool but differ on the ways in which parents should be involved (Carlson & Stenmalm, 1989; Sharpe, 1991). A key feature of the U.K. playgroups included in the CHES was the greater extent of parent involvement—not just attending visiting days and helping with outings or fundraising events, but helping directly with the children and assuming various management responsibilities. However, parental involvement made no significant difference to a child's development unless that child's own mother was involved (Osborn & Milbank, 1987, p. 217).

## How Can Preschool Programs Reduce Educational Inequities?

In Europe, as in the United States, preschool experience appears to be a stronger force in the lives of poor children than more advantaged children. In the French and British studies discussed earlier, preschool experience was found more advantageous for the most disadvantaged— though the British researchers are quick to point out that preschool alone, at least in a diverse system like that of the UK, is unlikely to close the gap caused by social background.

Efforts to use the preschool system as a means of reducing the rates of early school failures and the vast inequalities among children from different social backgrounds are usually based upon one of two general strategies. One is to provide preschool programs as universal entitlements, ensuring that the programs are of high enough quality so that they are supported and used by high- and low-income families alike. As we have seen, this strategy has been used in France and Sweden, where it has had some success in reducing the achievement gap between disadvantaged children and their more affluent peers, and greater success in reducing the number of children who are held back in elementary school. In fact, what may be most impressive about these systems is that free or affordable preschool programs are just one component of a comprehensive social insurance system, resulting in dramatic reductions in child poverty (Smeeding & Torrey, 1988). The European accomplishment is especially striking when compared to the United States, where over 20% of young children live in poverty, and many experience the "worst of both worlds"—that is, children from families with the fewest resources are also likely to attend low quality ECE programs (Goelman & Pence, 1987). Whether the most comprehensive and generous European systems will survive the economic strains resulting from globalization and the large influx of poor immigrant families remains to be seen.

A second strategy to reduce school failures and inequalities is to develop compensatory preschool programs targeted specifically at children in poverty. An experimental program developed for children living in an impoverished area of Dublin exemplifies this approach. As indicated in Table 10.1, very few 3-year-old children attend preschools in Ireland, and most programs for 4-year-olds are conducted in primary schools. Early childhood services outside the primary school are scarce and poorly coordinated, though some children defined as "at risk" can be placed in publicly funded social service nurseries run by the Department of Health (Bairrao & Tietze, 1993, p. 18).

Based upon developmental theory and influenced by U.S. compensatory education programs like Head Start, the Dublin project offered a two-year, half-day preschool program to 90 children beginning at age 3. Measures of cognitive development, school achievement, and parental involvement were collected, at ages 5, 8, and 16, from the 90 participants and from a control group of 60 children from the same neighborhood. Although the participating children showed significant improvements on standardized tests at age 5, these initial gains faded by age 8. The preschool participants were less likely than nonparticipants to drop out of high school and more likely to take the examinations required for further education, but no differences were found between the two groups in employment or in the percentage who had been in trouble with the police. These mixed results led the researchers to conclude that the extent and seriousness of the problems experienced by disadvantaged children limit the power of a single intervention to bring about major change (Kellaghan & Greaney, 1993).[8]

Another mode of delivering ECE services to children from poor or immigrant families is through home-based "enrichment" programs. These are generally cheaper than center-based programs and, by definition, involve parents more directly in their children's preschool experience (and thus offer opportunities for adding to the skimpy research literature on the effects of parental involvement). One of the most widely disseminated home-based programs is Home Instruction Program for Preschool Youngsters (HIPPY), in which mothers are trained by paraprofessionals to work with their children on a series of activities designed to promote cognitive, social, and emotional development and school readiness. Originally designed for disadvantaged Israeli children, especially children of immigrant families, HIPPY has been adopted in over a dozen nations throughout the world including Germany, the Netherlands, and the United States.

Evaluations of program effects generally show some positive results, though most of the study designs leave much to be desired.[9] For example, in 1991, HIPPY was introduced in two German cities, where the targeted populations were Turkish immigrants and repatriated Germans from Romania, Russia, and Poland. Information from questionnaires distributed to participants at the end of the first year indicated general satisfaction with the program, but no systematic evaluation of outcomes has been attempted and future funding is doubtful given recent budget cuts for "enrichment" programs. In the Netherlands, HIPPY was adopted as a national program in 1990 to meet the special needs of immigrant and migrant families. A quasi-experimental study comparing 141 mother-child pairs (56 Native Dutch, 33 Turkish, 29 Surinamese, and 23 Moroccan) who participated in the program for two years with a control group matched for neighborhood, school, ethnicity, age, sex, and mother's education level, found statistically significant differences in eye-hand coordination (which is emphasized in a number of HIPPY activities), but no meaningful differences in general intelligence, language skills, or other measures of children's cognitive performance. Unfortunately, implementation of the Dutch project was flawed in so many respects (40% of the participants dropped out, most in the early months of the program; no families completed all of the activities scheduled over the two years of the project; and in many cases materials seem to have been distributed without the guidance by trained paraprofessionals that is a critical requirement of the program) that it is impossible to determine to what extent the disappointing results were due to inappropriateness of the HIPPY program in the Dutch context, failure to implement the program properly, and/or weaknesses in the design of the project evaluation (Lombard, 1994, pp. 72–78, 84).

An alternative form of home-based program is the parent-run center or playgroup, sometimes viewed also as a strategy for "empowering" impoverished families and communities. As we saw above, the British parent-run playgroups appeared to be as effective as center-based ECE programs, but it was also noted that a disproportionate number of playgroups were organized by middle-class mothers who were not employed outside the home. A smaller scale but well-controlled study of the elementary school performance of a sample of British working-class children, half of whom had attended a playgroup and half of whom had attended a well-funded comprehensive preschool program provided by the local education authority, showed that the latter scored significantly higher than the former on measures of adjustment to school and cognitive gains and received higher ratings from their elementary school teachers. The authors attributed the difference in outcomes in part to the greater availability of educational toys and equipment, and more frequent opportunities for verbal interaction with trained staff in the preschools, concluding, "It may be unwise to expect the scant resources of playgroups, especially those in working-class areas, to provide the same opportunities for children as the better-resourced nursery classes" (Jowett & Sylva, 1986, p. 30).

## How Might the Case in Support of Greater ECE Availability and Affordability, and Higher Quality of Preschool Programs Be Strengthened?

The international research reviewed here provides considerable if not conclusive evidence that high-quality early childhood programs can substantially improve children's cognitive, social and emotional development, that such programs are especially beneficial for children in poverty, that some of the benefits are impressively long lasting, and that the long-term benefits of effective programs can far outweigh their costs. Many European Union countries are far ahead of the United States in making free or very inexpensive preschool programs available to 3- to 6-year-olds. At the same time, some European researchers maintain that most of their national ECE systems are underfunded and that program quality, commonly viewed as the hallmark of these systems, leaves much to be desired. (As we saw above, none of the European systems scored on the Early Childhood Environment Rating Scale (ECERS) received an overall rating higher than "mediocre.")

We have also seen that much remains to be done in conceptualizing and assessing program quality. Even in the studies carried out by the European Child Care and Education Study Group—the most extensive and well-designed international research on European preschool programs—"information about structural features of ECE programs has been used as a proxy for an actual measurement of process quality," and these studies have yet to link specific aspects of program quality to specific outcomes for children (Tietze et al., 1996, pp. 450, 472. See also Centre for Educational Research and Innovation, 1998, p. 23).

Examination of the political and economic trends threatening social welfare systems throughout Europe reminds us, moreover, that even positive research results do not guarantee continuing public support. It is instructive to recall that as recently as the early 1970s, researchers and practitioners in many Western European nations were castigating their countrymen for failing to provide the high-quality preschool programs that were available in most Soviet bloc countries at that time (for example, Blackstone, 1971). Now those Central and Eastern European programs that were held up as models have been decimated or forced to operate with drastically reduced resources, while the Western European countries that were viewed as the ECE trendsetters in the 1980s and early 1990s are having difficulty protecting their extensive social welfare systems and cushioning children and their families from the shocks of globalization and the free market. Indeed, some argue that the high taxes, high unemployment rates, and increasing emigration of highly educated young people that currently bedevil Europe's social democracies are partly the result of their comprehensive but costly social services (Cherlin, 1998).

Yet there are also some heartening countertrends. One is evidence of economic upturn (industrial growth and higher productivity, especially in the areas of information technology and service companies, combined with declines in unemployment, inflation, and national deficits) in some of the Western European countries with the most comprehensive and generous social welfare systems (Andrews, 1999). A second countertrend is resistance to further cutbacks in popular ECE programs, not only in the affluent European Union nations that are currently the world's leaders in system coherence and comprehensiveness, but also in some areas of Central and Eastern Europe where there has been

> activism in support of social support for families,
> children, teachers, and programs through union
> activities, through pressure from parents, the media,
> and advocacy groups, and through the emergence of
> democratic processes in local elections of municipal
> officials. These processes are still new in countries
> where control has been highly centralized in the
> past, but they represent some of the transitions we
> see as international trends in the 1990s (Swadener &
> Bloch, 1997, p. 215).

In Sweden, while overall public spending cuts and a shift toward financing ECE programs at the local level resulted in a scaling down of all aspects of preschool education, from reduction of staff and staff-to-child ratios to cutting back special programs for immigrant and refugee children (Nasman, 1995), the current government has been able to prevent further cutbacks in social welfare programs, including ECE, by raising personal taxes as well as industrial productivity and governmental efficiency, a strategy that challenges some of the central tenets of the free market model embraced by Britain and the United States. Successful efforts to strengthen economic competitiveness while maintaining popular social services for children and their families have also been reported for France, Finland, Italy, and the Netherlands, though the strategies used differ from one country to another (Andrews, 1999; Swedish Ministry for Foreign Affairs, 1997; Simons, 1997; Bohlen, 1996).

Finally, it is noteworthy that the Western European research groups that have been most active in promoting rigorous international research on preschool policies and practices are also turning their attention to political strategies for sustaining high-quality publicly supported programs and making them available to more children. Among the results of this kind of collaborative activity is a 10-year action plan developed by the European Commission Network on Childcare (1995), which proposes construction of an overall infrastructure for planning and monitoring programs and services of member countries, but which will at the same time, accommodate their national traditions and cultures. Western European ECE researchers and practitioners are also reaching out to their counterparts in Central and Eastern Europe who are attempting to create new models of preschool education in a radically altered political and economic environment (Organization Mondiale pour l'Education Prescolaire, 1991).

## Lessons for Americans?

The United States has invested more than any other nation in rigorous research on the effects of preschool programs, and has, I would argue, produced a body of evidence of the long-term benefits of good quality programs, especially for children in poverty, that is even stronger than the European studies reviewed here. Yet we continue to have one of the world's most fragmented, incoherent, and incomplete—some would say downright stingy—ECE systems. In the United States, as Gustafsson and Stafford (1998, p. 237) put it, "You get the child care you pay for, and the types and costs of child care as well as its quality differ between families according to their incomes."

Improving the overall quality of the American ECE system would require massive increases in public funding and oversight, which would in turn require overcoming the ambivalence of many Americans about large public investments in "other people's children." This dilemma is exemplified in the efforts of reformers in New Jersey to revise the state's system of financing of public education and improve the quality of education for the state's poorest children. In May 1998 and again in March 2000, the New Jersey State Supreme Court mandated that preschool programs be provided for all 3- and 4-year-olds in the state's 30 poorest districts. So far, the results of this statewide educational experiment have been mixed. On the one hand, the first preschools actually opened in fall 1999. On the other hand, the proposed model for these preschools—full-day programs with small classes, certified teachers, well-planned curriculum, and an array of social services—has been honored mainly in the breach. Places are available for fewer than half of the 49,000 eligible children, and many of the programs lack properly trained teachers. A spokesperson for the organization that has spearheaded the effort to provide quality preschool programs for New Jersey's most disadvantaged children has characterized the situation at present: The entitlement is there, but the implementation is lacking (J. Ponessa, Education Law Center, personal communication, 1999).

It is also noteworthy that the plan envisioned for New Jersey's poorest districts does not even address a crucial issue raised by Edward Zigler's comments (National Invitational Conference, Early Childhood Learning: Programs for a New Age, November, 29–December, 1, 1999) and by Zigler and Styfco's chapter in this volume regarding the preferability of publicly funded universal preschool programs over segregated programs designed specifically for poor children, like Head Start. Probably the greatest advantage of the ECE systems in many European Union countries over the American system is the greater availability of affordable preschool programs for all children. Moreover, while wholehearted acceptance of new roles for women and new forms of family life is rare in most nations, the European countries with the most comprehensive and generous ECE systems tend to be the countries that are also farthest ahead of the United States in facilitating flexible work schedules, encouraging egalitarian parental roles, and enabling parents to be away from home without negative consequences for children.

Improving the quality of preschool programs in the United States is also impeded by the reluctance of many Americans to learn from other nations. The authors of a recent review of drug policy in several European nations argued that American "exceptionalism" makes us too quick to draw broad conclusions about the "failure" of European social programs from any apparent shortcomings, while "we are all too ready to attribute their successes to some characteristic of their population or traditions that we could not achieve or would not want—a homogeneous population, more conformity, more intrusive government" (MacCoun & Reuter, 1999, p. 30).

Such a perspective with respect to programs for young children seems especially myopic, for it fails to see that the long-term costs of failure to provide high-quality early childhood programs—higher costs for education, social services, police, and prisons, and lost productivity and tax payments—are likely to be far higher than the costs of these programs. A just-released study of recent welfare reform, by Bruce Fuller and Sharon Lynn Kagan, indicates that the effects on the development of young children have been devastating: While about a million preschool children have been added to the ECE system, many, perhaps most, are in low-quality care and are already lagging in language and social development (Lewin, 2000). The "dual socialization" experienced by many European children seems distinctly preferable to a system that condemns so many American children to spending their early years being passed back and forth between harried parents trying to juggle home and work responsibilities and untrained, underpaid caretakers.

Although the long-term benefits of current European preschool policies and programs are by no means decisively demonstrated, the results thus far show the plausibility of an array of policies and services that merit more serious consideration in this country. The European

Commission Network on Childcare's plan, mentioned in the previous section, outlines a model—of an ECE system that is coherent but flexible, that provides unity of purpose while accommodating national and within-nation diversity, that offers programs and services to all families but allows choices among them—a model that seems equally applicable to the American situation. In a rapidly changing world in which economic interdependence and electronic exchanges of information at ever greater speeds are blurring national boundaries in important respects, a greater willingness to view our own preschool policies and programs in a larger context could facilitate our efforts to improve them.

## Acknowledgments
Support for this research, from the David and Lucile Packard Foundation and the Graduate School of Education, Rutgers University, is gratefully acknowledged.

## Endnotes

[1] Austria, Belgium, Denmark, Finland, France, Germany, Greece, Ireland, Italy, Luxembourg, Netherlands, Portugal, Spain, Sweden, and United Kingdom.

[2] For profiles of the early childhood services provided in each European Union country, see Bairrao and Tietze, 1993, pp. 13–24, and Appendices D, E, F, and G.

[3] Barnett (1998) has found that government policy and ECE research in the United States have also focused more upon children's cognitive development and school achievement than upon their development of social skills.

[4] Reviews of research by Australian and New Zealand scholars note positive associations between ECE availability and the upgrading of parents' education or training credentials, improved employment status, alleviation of stress, and enhanced parent-child relationships (Podmore, 1993; Wylie, 1994).

[5] The CHES claim is supported to some degree by a South Korean longitudinal study that explored the effects of four different ECE models (Montessori, open education, child-centered traditional, and academic drill) on children's cognitive and

socioemotional development and school success in elementary and middle school. No single model appeared to maximize all developmental outcomes, and most between-program differences faded by fourth grade and disappeared by seventh grade. However, significant differences between children who attended any of the preschool programs and children in a control group who had no preschool experiences persisted throughout the period studied on all measures except IQ (Rhee & Lee, 1990).

[6] An evaluation of ECE facilities in Victoria, Canada, found that even a little governmental oversight can help. Those regulated by government authorities tended to be of better quality than unlicensed facilities, even when the regulations were "minimal" and "minimally enforced" (Goelman & Pence, 1987).

[7] At the National Invitational Conference on Early Childhood Learning, sponsored by Temple University Laboratory for Student Success (Alexandria, Virginia, November 29–December 1, 1999), comments by parents as well as by scholars associated with innovative ECE programs in San Diego and Baltimore exemplified this point of view.

[8] Research on the outcomes of compensatory programs in several developing nations have been more encouraging, indicating that interventions targeted at disadvantaged groups can ameliorate some of the adverse effects of poverty and discrimination if they (a) combine nutritional and health services with good quality educational components, (b) ensure adequate training of staff, and (c) begin early in a child's life and continue over sustained periods of time (Granthem-McGregor et al., 1994; McKay et al., 1978; Myers, 1992;). Barnett's (1998) review of research on comparable American programs indicates that effects on employment and arrests are unlikely to be evident by age 16—suggesting that the Irish researchers may have been unduly pessimistic—and underscores the importance of long-term longitudinal evaluations.

[9] The most-often-cited study (Kagitcibasi, 1991), which tested the simultaneous effects of HIPPY and three alternative forms of child care on a sample of 251 children from low-income Turkish families, indicated that children whose mothers received the HIPPY training had more positive attitudes toward school, had higher achievement throughout primary school, and were more likely to be still in school at age 13 to 15 than children whose mothers were not trained. Further, it found that HIPPY appeared to benefit mothers as well, leading them to take a more active role in family decisionmaking, to have more say in disciplining the children, and to enjoy more communication and role sharing with their husbands than mothers in the control group. However, because assignment of children to the three child care settings was not random, these findings must be interpreted with caution.

# References

Andersson, B. E. (1992). Effects of day care on cognitive and socio-emotional competence in thirteen-year-old Swedish school children. *Child Development, 63,* 20–36.

Andrews, E. L. (1999, October 8). Sweden, the welfare state, basks in a new prosperity. *The New York Times,* pp. C1, C4.

Atkinson, A. H. (1989). French preprimary education: A tradition of responding to children. *Early Child Development and Care, 46,* 77–86.

Bairrao, J., & Tietze, W. (1993). *Early childhood services in the European Community.* A report submitted to the Commission of the European Community, Task Force Human Resources, Education, Training, and Youth.

Barnett, W. S. (1998). Long-term effects on cognitive development and school success. In W. S. Barnett & S. S. Boocock (Eds.), *Early care and education for children in poverty* (pp. 11–44). Albany, NY: State University of New York Press.

Bergmann, B. R. (1990, August). *The French child welfare system: An excellent system we could adapt and afford.* Paper presented at 85th annual meeting of the American Sociological Association, Washington, DC, August 14.

Blackstone, T. (1971). Some aspects of the structure and extent of nursery education in five European countries. *Comparative Education 7*(3), 91–105.

Bohlen, C. (1996, May 12). Where every day is Mother's Day: The state of welfare in Italy. *The New York Times,* Section 4, pp. 1, 5.

Boocock, S. S., & Larner, M. B. (1998). Long-term outcomes in other nations. In W. S. Barnett & S. S. Boocock (Eds.), *Early care and education for children in poverty* (pp. 45–76). Albany, NY: State University of New York Press.

Broberg, A., Hwang, C.-P., Lamb, M. E., & Ketterlinus, R. D. (1989). Child care effects on socioemotional and intellectual competence in Swedish preschoolers. In J. S. Lande, S. Scarr, & N. Gunzenhauser (Eds.), *Caring for children: Challenge to America* (pp. 49–76). Hillsdale, NJ: Erlbaum.

Carlson, H. L., & Stenmalm, L. (1989). Professional and parent views of early childhood programs: A cross-cultural study. *Early Childhood Development and Care 50,* 51–64.

Centre for Educational Research and Innovation. (1998). *Education Policy Analysis 1998.* Paris: Organization for Economic Co-operation and Development.

Cherlin, A. J. (1998, April 5). By the numbers. *The New York Times Magazine,* 39–41.

Cochran, M. M. (1993). *International handbook of child care policies and programs.* Westport, CT: Greenwood.

Cochran, M. M., & Gunnarsson, L. (1985). A follow-up study of group day care and family-based childrearing patterns. *Journal of Marriage and the Family, 47,* 297–309.

Curtis, A. (1992). Early childhood education in Great Britian. In G. A. Woodill, J. Bernhard, & L. Prochner (Eds.), *International handbook of early childhood education* (pp. 231–249). New York: Garland.

Dencik, L. (1995). Modern childhood in the Nordic countries: "Dual socialization" and its implications. In L. Chisholm, P. Buchnerm, H.-H. Kruger, & P. Brown (Eds.), *Growing up in Europe: Contemporary horizons in childhood and youth* (pp. 105–119). Berlin & New York: deGruyter.

Edwards, C., Gandini, L., & Forman, G. (Eds.). (1998). *The hundred languages of children: The Reggio Emilia—Advanced reflections* (2nd ed.). Greenwich, CT: Ablex.

European Commission Network on Childcare. (1995). *Quality targets in services for young children: Proposals for a ten year action programme.* Brussels: European Commission.

Gandini, L. (1993). Fundamentals of the Reggio Emilia approach to early childhood education. *Young Children, 48,* 63–67.

Gardner, Howard. (1998). Forward: Complementary Perspectives on Reggio Emilia. In C. Edwards, L. Gandini, & G. Forman. (Eds.), *The hundred languages of children: The Reggio Emilia—Advanced reflections* (2nd ed., pp. ix–xiii). Greenwich, CT: Ablex.

Goelman, H., & Pence, A. (1987). Effects of child care, family, and individual characteristics of children's language development: The Victoria Day Care Research Project. In D. A. Phillips (Ed.), *Quality in child care: What does research tell us?* (pp. 89–104). Washington: National Association for the Education of Young Children.

Grantham-McGregor, S., Powell, C., Walker, S., Chang, S., & Fletcher, P. (1994). The long-term follow-up of severely malnourished children who participated in an intervention program. *Child Development, 65,* 428–439.

Gunnarsson, L. (1993). Sweden. In M. M. Cochran (Ed.), *International handbook of child care policies and programs* (pp. 491–514). Westport, CT: Greenwood.

Gustafsson, S. S., & Stafford, F. P. (1998). Equity-efficiency tradeoffs and government policy in the United States, the Netherlands, and Sweden. In W. S. Barnett & S. S. Boocock (Eds.), *Early care and education for children in poverty* (pp. 211–244). Albany, NY: State University of New York Press.

Ispa, J. (1994). *Child care in Russia in transition.* London: Bergin & Garvey.

Jowett, S., & Sylva, K. (1986). Does kind of pre-school matter? *Educational Research, 28*(1), 21–31.

Kagitcibasi, C. (1991). *The early enrichment project in Turkey.* Paris: UNESCO-UNICEF-WFP.

Kellaghan, T., & Greaney, B. J. (1993). The educational development of students following participation in a preschool programme in a disadvantaged area. Dublin: St. Patrick's College, Educational Research Centre.

Lamb, M. E., Hwang, C. P., & Broberg, A. (1991). Swedish child-care research. In E. Melhuish and P. Moss (Eds.), *Day care for young children: International perspectives* (pp. 102–120). London: Tavistock/Routledge.

Lewin, T. (2000, February 4). Study finds welfare changes lead a million into child care. *The New York Times,* p. A17.

Lombard, A. D. (1994). *Success begins at home* (2nd ed.). Guilford, CT: Dushkin.

MacCoun, R. J., & Reuter, P. (1999). Does Europe do it better? Lessons from Holland, Britain and Switzerland. *The Nation, 269*(8), 28–30.

McKay, H., Sinisterra, L., McKay A., Gomez, H., & Lloreda, P. (1978). Improving cognitive ability in chronically deprived children. *Science, 200,* 270–278.

McMahan, I. D. (1992). Public preschool from the age of two: The *école maternelle* in France. *Young Children, 47*(5), 22–28.

Moss, P. (1990). Childcare in the European Community. *Women of Europe*, Supplement No. 31. Brussels: European Commission Childcare Network.

Myers, R. G. (1992). *The twelve who survive: Strengthening programs of early childhood.* New York: Routledge, in cooperation with UNESCO.

Myers, R. G. (1997). Removing roadblocks to success: Transitions and linkages between home, preschool, and primary school. *Coordinators' Notebook, 21,* 1–21.

Nasman, E. (1995). Childhood, family and new ways of life: The case of Sweden. In L. Chisholm, P. Buchnerm, H.-H. Kruger, & P. Brown. (Eds.), *Growing up in Europe: Contemporary horizons in childhood and youth* (pp.121–131). Berlin & New York: deGruyter.

New, R. (1990, September). Excellent early education: A city in Italy has it. *Young Children,* 4–10.

Olmsted, P. P. (1989). *A look at early childhood education in the United States from a global perspective.* Paper commissioned by the National Center for Educational Statistics. (ERIC Document Reproduction Service No. ED 346-950).

Organization Mondiale pour l'Education Prescolaire (OMEP). (1991). The universal and the national in preschool education. Papers from the OMEP International Seminar (Moscow, Russia, December 4–7). YCF Series 3. (ERIC Document Reproduction Service No. 368-447).

Osborn, A. F., & Milbank, J. E. (1987). *The effects of early education. A report from the Child Health and Education Study.* Oxford, UK: Clarendon Press.

Palius, M. (1999, May). *The Reggio Emilia approach to early childhood education as developed in Italy and adopted in the United States.* Paper presented at Rutgers Graduate School of Education, Rutgers University, New Brunswick, NJ.

Podmore, V. N. (1993). *Education and care: A review of international studies of the outcomes of early childhood experiences.* Wellington: New Zealand Council for Educational Research.

Rhee, U., & Lee, K. (1990). The effectiveness of four early childhood program models: Follow-up at middle school. *Journal of Educational Research, 28*(3), 147–162.

Sharpe, P. (1991). Parental involvement in preschools, parents' and teachers' perceptions of their roles. *Early Child Development and Care, 71,* 53–62.

Sim, K. P., & Kam, H. W. (Eds.). (1992). *Growing up in Singapore: The preschool years.* Singapore: Longman Singapore.

Simons, M. (1997, December 12). Child care sacred as France cuts back the welfare state. *The New York Times,* pp. A1, A8.

Smeeding, T. M., & Torrey, B. B. (1988, November 11). Poor children in rich countries. *Science, 242,* 873–877.

Swadener, E. B., & Bloch, M. N. (1997). Children, families and change: International perspectives. *Early Education & Development, 8,* 207–218.

Swedish Ministry for Foreign Affairs. (1997). *Statement of government policy presented by the Prime Minister to Parliament on Tuesday 16 September 1997* (unofficial translation). New York: Swedish Information Service, Consulate General of Sweden.

Tietze, W. (1987). A structural model for the evaluation of preschool effects. *Early Childhood Research Quarterly, 2*(2), 133–153.

Tietze, W., & Cryer, D. (1999). Current trends in European early child care and education. *Annals, AAPSS, 563,* 175–193.

Tietze, W., Cryer, D., Bairrao, J., Palacios, J., & Wetzel, G. (1996). Comparison of observed process quality in early child care and education programs in five countries. *Early Childhood Research Quarterly, 11,* 447–475.

Wylie, C. (1994). *What research on early childhood education/care outcomes can, and can't tell policymakers.* Wellington: New Zealand Council for Educational Research.

Zimmerman, S. L., Antonov, A. I., Johnson, M., & Borisov, V. A. (1994). Social policy and families. In J. W. Maddock, M. J. Hogan, A. I. Antonov, & M. S. Matskovsky (Eds.), *Families before and after perestroika: Russian and U.S. perspectives* (pp. 186–219). New York: Guilford Press.

# Chapter 11

## Understanding the Promise of Universal Preschool

*Darcy A. Olsen*

During the 1990s, issues concerning the expansion of preschool became matters of public debate as three states opened state-run preschools. Georgia, New York, and Oklahoma implemented preschool for all 4-year-olds regardless of family income in 1993, 1997, and 1998, respectively. Connecticut, Kentucky, Massachusetts, New Jersey, and Ohio have taken significant steps in that direction, although they typically exclude from enrollment children from upper-income families (Mitchell, Ripple et al., 1998; Schulman et al., 1999). In these states and elsewhere, differing ideas about the expansion of public schools to include preschool for 3- and 4-year-old children, the voluntary or compulsory nature of such preschooling, and the extent of benefits to all children have been central to the debate.

Few legislators have openly proposed mandatory attendance, although some have alluded to the possibility (Geggis, 1998; Morse, 1998). If the history of public education is any indicator, such mandates will likely appear in time. For example, in 1898 only 10 states had compulsory school attendance laws, and they generally applied to children between the ages of 8 and 14 and required attendance for a few months per year. Today all 50 states have compulsory attendance laws, and many apply to children between the ages of 5 and 18 and require attendance for at least eight months per year (Education Commission of the States Information Clearinghouse, 1997, March, April; Novello, 1998). The trend has been to expand the duration of required attendance to include younger students, those age 5 and below, and older students up to age 18. The U.S. Department of Education's Office of Educational Research and Improvement currently reports that "The notion of transforming schools into all-day, year-round learning centers appears to be a popular one" (1998). Given historic and current trends, it seems likely that the mandatory participation of 3- and 4-year-old children in preschool could be required by many states soon after they open state-run preschools. What might this mean for American children?

Supporters of universal preschool contend that most parents fail to provide their children with the experiences and environment necessary to promote their healthy development. The result is that many children are not "ready to learn" when they enter kindergarten. Consequently, such children perform at a substandard academic level, which leads to long-term problems, including low educational attainment and juvenile delinquency. Proponents of universal preschool say they can prevent those problems by intervening before children enter kindergarten. According to California Department of Education's Superintendent's Universal Preschool Task Force (1998), "Extensive research in recent years has demonstrated the undeniable influence of preschool education on children's later success in school. When children experience success in school, numerous other problems, such as dropping out of school, delinquency, crime, and teenage pregnancy, are prevented" (see also, California Department of Education, Superintendent's Universal Preschool Task Force, 1997; Carnegie Corporation, 1996; Kagan & Cohen, 1997; New York State Board of Regents, 1993).

Yet beneath this enthusiastic endorsement of early intervention programs lurks a body of evidence that universal preschool is unlikely to benefit most children in any lasting manner. The data presented by supporters of universal preschool are often mitigated or contradicted by other more persuasive evidence. While many programs have had meaningful short-term effects on cognitive ability, grade retention, and special education placement, few programs have led to measurable long-term benefits, one of the keystones of the proponents' arguments; their claims for long-term benefits are simply not borne out by the evidence. In fact, the two major studies of long-term effects are critically flawed and misrepresentative. The results from the Georgia Preschool Project have been disappointing, and Head Start, the only large-scale, long-term project, likewise shows limited benefits. Furthermore, the positive gains attributed to early intervention programs are unlikely to be generalizable to the whole population. This paper will examine this body of evidence and discuss implications for public policy (see also Olsen, 1999).

## Day Care and School Preparedness: Dubious Reasons for Expansion

Interest in universal preschool has been increasing for several reasons. Many advocates for universal preschool believe it is a good means by which to provide day care in a safe, school-based setting. Notably, Edward F. Zigler, director of the Bush Center in Child Development and Social Policy at Yale University and a cofounder of Head Start, has supported universal preschool for 3- and 4-year-olds as a school-based approach to child care (Zigler, 1987; Zigler & Styfco, 1999). Yet there is significant evidence from nationally representative surveys conducted under the auspices of the U.S. Department of Education and the U.S. Department of Health and Human Services that families across socioeconomic levels are satisfied with the quality and costs of their child care services (Olsen, 1997, 1998; Rector, 1998).

A second reason for increased interest in universal preschool is a belief among advocates that many children are not "ready to learn" when they enter kindergarten because they have not been provided with the correct educational and social experiences. Researchers argue that inadequate preparation for kindergarten is largely the result of an underregulated system of early child care and education, and that affects all children, not only those from low-income families (Carnegie Corporation of New York, 1996; Clinton, 1996; Kagan & Cohen, 1997).

Yet there is little evidence that parents fail to provide their children with appropriate educational experiences before kindergarten. In the Goals 2000 literature, for example, researchers use preschool participation rates and how often parents read to their children as the two main proxies for school readiness. Those measures show that a higher percentage of American preschoolers than ever before are entering kindergarten ready to learn. Census data also show that at least half of 3- and 4-year-olds attend preschool at least part time. Proportionately that is five times as many children as attended preschool in 1964, just one generation ago. In addition, Goals 2000 has reported that since 1990, the gap in preschool participation rates between preschoolers from high- and low-income families narrowed from 28 percentage points to just 13 points. At the same time, parents are reading to their children with increasing frequency: 83% of preschoolers are read to three or more times a week, up from 70% in 1991, and 65% are taught letters, words, or numbers. While there may be room for improvement, these proxy measures for readiness suggest that most children entering kindergarten today are ready to learn.

At the same time, the standards for what young children are expected to know at kindergarten entrance have been rising steadily for the past 30 years, so that kindergarten is sometimes described as "what first grade used to be." Reflecting those curriculum changes, the first-grade-level content of the 1964 Stanford Achievement Test had become kindergarten content on the 1973 edition, and that same content dropped even below kindergarten level on the 1982 edition; and the incidence of high-stakes testing has been rising (Bryant & Clifford, 1992; Elkind, 1996; Freeman, 1990; May et al., 1994; Shepard, 1997; Shepard & Smith, 1988; Walsh, 1989). The available evidence suggests that greater percentages of American preschoolers are learning more at earlier ages than did preschoolers of previous generations.

The most recent evidence that American children are ready to learn when they enter kindergarten comes from *America's Kindergartners*, a nationally representative longitudinal study by the U.S. Department of Education's National Center for Education Statistics (2000). This study is the first attempt to provide nationally representative descriptive data on children's status at kindergarten entry, and the researchers reported positive findings regarding the majority of first-time kindergartners. On factors that kindergarten teachers say are among the most important for school readiness—physical health, enthusiasm, and curiosity—children fared remarkably well. As children enter kindergarten, parents report that 92% seem eager to learn, about 85% demonstrate creativity in their work and play, and no more than 3% have fair or poor general health. In terms of specific skills in reading and math, nearly all, 94%, are proficient at recognizing numbers, shapes, and counting to 10, and two in three know their ABCs. This study demonstrates that the vast majority of children entering kindergarten do indeed have a strong start (see also U.S. Department of Education, National Center for Education Statistics, 1996).

## The False Promise of Long-Term Benefits

Policymakers have shown an increasing interest in preschool largely because researchers and advocates have advanced the theory that it can ensure a child's healthy development and buffer children from problems that are often associated with poor and one-parent families, including below-average school performance, drug use, teenage pregnancy, juvenile delinquency, unemployment, and welfare use (California Department of Education, Superintendent's Universal Preschool Task Force, 1997, 1998; Kagan & Cohen, 1997; New York State Board of Regents, 1993). Sharon L. Kagan, senior research scientist at the Bush Center in Child Development and Social Policy at Yale University, and Nancy E. Cohen, a graduate student in the Department of Psychology at the University of California at Berkeley, offer an opinion typical of those found in the advocacy literature:

> Many of these positive effects [of early care and education programs] may linger and contribute to children's increased cognitive abilities, positive classroom learning behaviors, long-term school success, and even improved likelihood of long-term social and economic self-sufficiency.... Indeed, investments in quality early care and education save society future costly and lengthy expenditures for incarceration or welfare. (1997, p. 5)

A review of the literature finds that such claims continue to be recycled, yet they are based on evidence from only a handful of studies.

### An Overview of Research

Most research indicates that the cognitive effects of early intervention, namely increases in IQ and standardized achievement scores, fade after children leave the programs. "Fade-out" is important to any discussion of universal preschool because it means that early intervention may be virtually irrelevant to how a child "turns out" in adolescence or early adulthood. However, a number of experimental projects have had meaningful effects on grade retention and special education placement. These findings have been widely documented (Bryant & Maxwell, 1997; General Accounting Office, 1997; Karoly et al., 1998; Karweit, 1989; McKey et al., 1985; Reynolds et al., 1997).

A second problem with basing proposals for universal preschool on findings from early intervention studies is that most interventions have concentrated on severely disadvantaged children and children from low-income families, so there is no evidence of universal replicability with the general population of young children. Scholars have noted that many findings have been uncritically appropriated to children in average-income families (Elkind, 1987/1997; Zigler, 1987).

Not only have early intervention findings been inappropriately generalized to the general population, but evidence also indicates that early schooling is inappropriate for many preschool-aged children and may even be harmful to their development. Research has shown that conversations children have at home may be the richest source of linguistic and cognitive enrichment for children from all but the most deprived backgrounds and that premature schooling can potentially slow or reduce a child's overall development by replacing valuable play time (Elkind, 1981, 1996, 1997/1987; Shepard & Smith, 1988; Zigler, 1987). David Elkind, Professor of Child Study at Tufts University and author of several books on the impact of early education, states, "There is no evidence that such early instruction has lasting benefits, and considerable evidence that it can do lasting harm" (1997/1987, p. 4).

Because most early intervention studies have concentrated on disadvantaged children and because some evidence suggests that preschool programs may not suitable for all children, significantly more research on children from the general population would need to be conducted in order to show that all children would benefit from preschool. The results from Georgia's universal preschool program are instructive in this regard because they move beyond theoretical and experimental constructs into a real-life situation. Those findings will be discussed in the last section of this paper.

Finally, few studies have examined or demonstrated long-term (that is, four or more years after program participation) effects of intervention on children's development. Most long-term studies have significant methodological problems, and they are impaired by small sample size, attrition, and selection bias. Furthermore, most programs studied are model programs, not large-scale programs, which means they are severely limited in statistical power and generalizability (Bryant & Maxwell, 1997; Karweit, 1989; Reynolds et al., 1997). A few long-term studies provide reasonably valid estimates of the long-term effects of early intervention on disadvantaged children. The best known are the Perry Preschool Project and North Carolina Abecedarian study. However, as the following two sections demonstrate, neither study makes a convincing case for universal preschool.

## Perry Preschool

The Perry Preschool Project was a longitudinal experiment designed to study the effects of early intervention on disadvantaged children. It was the early childhood intervention program most frequently cited in research reviews between 1983 and 1997 (Reynolds et al., 1997) and is repeatedly cited in the literature and legislation in support of universal preschool. The Perry Preschool Project was an intervention program for 3- and 4-year-olds deemed at risk for retarded intellectual functioning and eventual school failure and was conducted by investigators at the High/Scope Educational Research Foundation in Ypsilanti, Michigan, from 1962 to 1965. The investigators reported their most recent findings in *Significant Benefits: The High/Scope Perry Preschool Study Through Age 27* (Schweinhart et al., 1993). The preschool involved either one or two years of half-day sessions for seven months each year and periodic home visits. One hundred twenty-three children participated, 58 children in the experimental group and 65 in the control group. All of the children were of low socioeconomic status and had IQs in the range of 70 to 85.

The High/Scope study is frequently cited because it is the most comprehensive longitudinal study of any comparable intervention program. Participants were studied through age 27. Analyses show that students who participated in the preschool program fared better over the long term on a variety of educational and social measures than did children in the control group. Among other findings, an examination of the Perry children at age 27 found the following: participants had 11.9 years of schooling versus 11 years for the control group, 7% of participants had been arrested for drug dealing versus 25% of the control group, and 59% of participants received welfare assistance as adults versus 80% of the control group. On the basis of those and other findings, Schweinhart concluded that the program provided taxpayers a return on investment of $7.16 on the dollar (Schweinhart, 1994; Schweinhart et al., 1993). That is the sole cost-benefit analysis upon which advocates rely to make the case that preschool is an investment that pays for itself in the long term.

The High/Scope researchers' interpretation of the long-term findings is that the preschool program prepared children for kindergarten, a preparation which resulted in a more positive reaction by kindergarten teachers that, in turn, caused the children to have a stronger commitment to school. Others posit that the home visitation component was largely responsible for the results. They hypothesize that people became more effective parents as a result of their involvement in the program. Experiences such as building relationships with teachers may help parents establish a more supportive home environment and effective "home-school linkages" (Zigler et al., 1992). In short, there is no consensus on what components of the program were responsible for the children's gains, and two critical questions remain: How could a one- or two-year half-day preschool program produce such outstanding results? Why have the results never been replicated?

The High/Scope researchers have been sharply criticized for using nonstandard significance levels. Among other critics, Charles Locurto, Professor of Psychology at the College of the Holy Cross, Massachusetts, has argued that if standard significance levels are substituted for those used in the High/Scope study, many of the most "significant" differences between the experimental and control groups disappear (1991). Locurto further argues that the Perry results are less remarkable when all findings, not just those that favor the Perry Preschool Project, are considered:

> We might marry the large number of nonsignificant and unfavorable findings into a different picture of the Perry Project's outcomes. We might argue that preschool training resulted in no differences in school motivation or school potential at the time of school entry, no lasting changes in IQ.... There were no differences in their average grades as compared to former control-group children, in their personal satisfaction with their school performance or in their self-esteem. Their parents were no more likely to talk with teachers about schoolwork or to attend school activities and functions than control-group parents. (1991, pp. 303–304)

Even enthusiastic supporters of preschool have raised questions about the Perry Project, particularly concerning sampling and methodology. According to Edward Zigler,

> [The Perry sample] was not only nonrepresentative of children in general; there is some doubt that it was representative of even the bulk of economically disadvantaged children.... The Perry Project poses a number of methodological difficulties... Children had to have a parent at home during the day, resulting in a significant difference between control and intervention groups on the variable of maternal employment... [and] assignment to experimental and control groups was not wholly random. (1987, pp. 30–31)

Whether or not one believes the Perry findings are reliable, several differences between the Perry program and universal preschool should prevent legislators from basing policy recommendations for universal preschool on it. First, no other program or study has produced results as dramatic as those found for Perry. That suggests that some unique but unidentified conditions at the Perry Preschool simply cannot be duplicated. Certainly, as a general principle, science requires an experiment to be replicable before it can be considered valid, and advocates of universal preschool should be scientifically cautious before applying the findings of High/Scope—or any other program—to millions of children.

Second, the benefits at Perry were obtained only for severely disadvantaged children at risk of "retarded intellectual functioning"; to generalize the effects of Perry to all children is inappropriate. This last point is particularly important because most American children are not severely disadvantaged nor at risk, and, as noted above, research suggests preschool may be harmful to some mainstream children.

Third, Perry children may have outperformed children in the control group, but they still fared poorly compared with mainstream children. For example, nearly one-third of participating children dropped out of high school, nearly one-third of the children were arrested, and three of five participating children received welfare assistance as adults (Schweinhart et al., 1993). Such statistics have led many researchers to caution advocates against overstating the potential benefits of early childhood and preschool programs even for the population studied (Gomby, Larner, Stevenson, Lewit, & Behrman, 1995; Zigler, 1987; Zigler & Styfco, 1999).

Finally, as an intense, experimental program, Perry differed significantly from regular preschool programs or what one could expect from universal prekindergarten. Large-scale programs tend to have smaller effects than model programs, in part because model programs have smaller classes, more educated and enthusiastic staff, more staff members, and more attention and supervision per child (Barnett, 1995; Haskins, 1989; Zigler, 1987).

## The Carolina Abecedarian Project

The Abecedarian Project was launched in 1972 by researchers at the Frank Porter Graham Child Development Center in Chapel Hill, North Carolina. The project involved 111 children deemed at risk on the basis of their parents' income, education, and other factors. The mean age at entry was 4.4 months, and the infants were placed in an eight-hour-a-day, five-day-per-week, year-round educational day care center. They received free medical care, dietary supplements, and social service support for their families. From ages 5 through 8, half of the children from both the experimental and the control groups were given extra help in school and at home by specially trained teachers (Campbell & Ramey, 1995).

At every age from 1 1/2 to 4 1/2 years, children treated in preschool significantly outscored the control group on measures of intellectual development. At age 8, test data showed significant positive effects of preschool treatment on intellectual test scores. A follow-up test at age 12 showed that the effects of preschool treatment on children's performance on intellectual tests and on reading and mathematics tests had been maintained into early adolescence. As the Abecedarian Project researchers note, "This represented a longer maintenance of preschool intervention gains than has typically been reported from previous projects concerned with similar children and families" (Campbell & Ramey, 1995, p. 752).

Recently researchers examined the children's intellectual and academic performance at age 15 and found that students who had received preschool treatment scored higher on reading and mathematics tests and had fewer instances of grade retention and assignments to special education than did the control group. The average IQ score advantage for children treated in preschool was 4.6 points. The researchers hope that benefits from the preschool program will be retained through adulthood: "Extrapolating from long-term outcomes of the Perry Preschool Project, it is the hope of the Abecedarian investigators that the benefits found through mid-adolescence in our sample will eventually be reflected in better life circumstances in adulthood" (Campbell & Ramey, 1995, pp. 768–769).

As with the Perry project, there is no consensus on what components of the program were responsible for the children's gains, although it has been suggested that the early cognitive gains were associated with greater mastery of academics, which led, in turn, to better performance thereafter (Campbell & Ramey, 1995). The findings also provide support for an intensity or duration hypothesis, which predicts that longer, more intense programs result in the most advantages for children. The project investigators concluded

> The long-term results from the Abecedarian Project underscore the need for high quality learning environments for impoverished infants, toddlers, and preschoolers… these results should not, however, be construed as proof that out-of-home care was the key element…. It is quite likely that this type of early intellectual enhancement can occur in a variety of settings…. The key factor is likely to be that the environment was appropriately responsive to the needs of the developing child and provided continuing experiences from which enhanced intellectual development and literacy and mathematics skills emerged. (Campbell & Ramey, 1995, p. 768)

The Abecedarian Project is not without critics, the most notable of whom is Herman H. Spitz, former director of the Research Department at the E. R. Johnstone Training and Research Center in Bordentown, New Jersey. Spitz expressed concern that the project results were presented in ways that bias the findings in favor of Abecedarian. For example, by combining the IQ findings of the four cohorts studied, the researchers concluded that the intervention raised IQ. According to Spitz, however, they neglected to report that scores improved only for two of the four groups. In fact, for the third and fourth cohorts, the experimental group actually lost 3.68 IQ points more than did the control group, providing no support for the efficacy of the intervention (Spitz, 1992).

Spitz also notes that differences favoring the intervention group first emerged at 6 months of age, when those children's advantage was six points. He writes, "This is a rather surprising finding when one considers that the mean age of entry into the day care center was 4.4 months" (Spitz, 1997, p. 72). In terms of IQ, the intervention groups' IQ advantage at 5 years of age was essentially the same as it had been at

6 months of age. Spitz asks, "What happened during the initial 1.6 months to produce essentially the same advantage for the intervention group that later was found at 5 and 12 years of age?" (Spitz, 1997, p. 72). "We need to understand why an additional 4.5 years of intensive intervention had so little effect that, at 6 years of age (and older), the difference between the intervention and control groups was not appreciably different than it had been at 6 months of age" (Spitz, 1993, p. 35). Spitz also notes that some of the reported test results may be biased in favor of the Abecedarian Project because of the ways the tests were conducted. For example, mothers of the experimental group were present at the testing and assisted in the administration of some tests, which means that the mothers may have provided their children with practice on some of the test items (Spitz, 1992).

Whether or not one believes the Abecedarian findings are wholly valid, as is the case with Perry Preschool, several facts should prevent legislators from basing policy recommendations for universal preschool on the study. First, benefits were obtained only for a small group of "economically disadvantaged African-American children." Again, Abecedarian faces the problem of applicability: one cannot assume that the findings would apply evenly, if at all, to mainstream children. Second, the Abecedarian Project has not been replicated. Because the Abecedarian Project is the first of its kind to demonstrate such lasting, positive results, it is critically important that it be replicated before being used as a model for further intervention. Finally and most importantly, even if the Abecedarian Project is widely replicated in the future, the intervention is far more intense than that offered or intended through universal preschool. The positive outcomes of the Abecedarian Project occurred at least partly because the children entered the unprecedented intensive program at such an early age. One could not expect to see—indeed, one has never seen—Abecedarian-type results from a one- or two-year preschool program. Universal preschool is simply not comparable to what in the Abecedarian Project was essentially an adoptive or second-home environment.

## Head Start

Even if there were reliable evidence of lasting, long-term effects of early intervention on disadvantaged children, showing that those effects could be generalized to a program of state or national scope would still be necessary. Research on Head Start, consequently, is relevant to this discussion because it has many characteristics of a large-scale, public preschool program. Unlike model programs, which typically have been small in scale and conducted under ideal circumstances, Head Start is a large-scale program operating under real-world conditions and constraints. Unlike research on model programs, which usually offers synchronic rather than diachronic studies and local rather than national evidence, research on Head Start has been conducted across the country over a 35-year period. Furthermore, fundamental to the program's philosophy is the notion that communities should have considerable latitude to develop their own programs. That variability is likely to be comparable to the variability one would find among public preschools within school districts and across states. Ron Haskins, administrative director of the Abecedarian Project from 1977 to 1980, explains:

> [Many] intervention programs were conducted under ideal circumstances: skilled researchers, capable staffs with lots of training, ample budgets, and perhaps in the glow of Hawthorne effects. It seems unwise to claim that the benefits produced by such exemplary programs would necessarily be produced by ordinary preschool programs conducted in communities across the United States. Research about Head Start, then, is valuable because Head Start has all the characteristics of a large-scale preschool program: It has more than 1,300 preschool projects serving about 457,000 children [by 2000, this figure is over 800,000]; it focuses on poor children; and its quality varies widely across sites. Thus, information about the effects of Head Start can be offered as a close approximation of what could be expected from universal preschool education for poor children. (Haskins, 1989, p. 277)

Head Start was the child-centered component of the War on Poverty. It was designed to improve the poor child's opportunities and achievements in order to end the "pattern of poverty." Its seven major objectives were to improve the child's physical health, help the child's emotional and social development, improve the child's mental processes, establish patterns and expectations of success, increase the child's ability to relate positively to family members, develop in the child and his family a responsible attitude toward society, and increase the sense of dignity and self-worth of the child and his family (*Recommendations for a Head Start Program by a Panel of Experts*, 1965). President Lyndon Johnson enthusiastically announced Head Start's opening in 1965:

> We set out to make certain that poverty's children would not be forevermore poverty's captives. We called our program Project Head Start... [this program] reflects a realistic and a wholesome awakening in America. It shows that we are recognizing that poverty perpetuates itself. Five- and six-year-old children are inheritors of poverty's curse and not its creators. Unless we act these children will pass it on to the next generation, like a family birthmark.... This program this year means that 30 million man-years—the combined lifespan of these youngsters—will be spent productively and rewardingly, rather than wasted in tax-supported institutions or in welfare-supported lethargy. (Johnson, 1965, p. 556)

Like today's advocates for universal preschool, President Johnson sold his program to the public by promising that early intervention could prevent delinquency, poverty, and welfare use. The reality of Head Start has been much different.

As have model intervention programs, Head Start programs have had mixed short-term results (General Accounting Office, 1997). However, there is no evidence of Head Start's having a positive, lasting impact on children. The General Accounting Office (GAO) conducted the most recent and thorough analysis of Head Start's impact in 1997.

After speaking with early childhood researchers and practitioners and searching through electronic databases to locate published and unpublished manuscripts, GAO found nearly 600 citations and documents. Of those, only 22 studies fit their criteria for review and all of those "had some methodological problems." Selection criteria included whether Head Start participation had occurred in 1976 or later, whether studies compared outcomes for participants with those for children not attending any preschool or another preschool, whether studies compared Head Start outcomes with test norms, and whether studies used tests of statistical significance. Not one study used a nationally representative sample so that findings could be generalized to the national program. The GAO concluded that "the body of research on current Head Start is insufficient to draw conclusions about the impact of the national program" (GAO, 1997, p. 8).

Although the 1990 act that reauthorized Head Start funding directed the Department of Health and Human Services to conduct "a longitudinal study of the effects that the participation in Head Start programs has on the development of participants and their families and the manner in which such effects are achieved," the Department of Health and Human Services says that funds were never appropriated for the study; consequently, it is being conducted only now.

The Department of Health and Human Services (HHS) maintains that early research has proven Head Start's effectiveness. In a letter to the GAO, June Gibbs Brown, Inspector General of HHS, wrote, "There is clear evidence of the positive impact of Head Start services" (GAO, 1997, p. 48). For supporting evidence, HHS cited findings from a comprehensive synthesis of Head Start impact studies conducted under its auspices in 1985 (McKey et al., 1985). The study showed that Head Start can have an immediate positive impact on cognitive measures, social behavior, and child health, among other things. HHS failed, however, to mention the rest of the synthesis's findings, namely that the short-term impact of Head Start quickly diminishes once the children enter school. Regarding cognitive development measures—IQ scores, school readiness, and achievement test scores—the report concluded:

> Once the children enter school there is little
> difference between the scores of Head Start and
> control children.... Findings for the individual
> cognitive measures—intelligence, readiness and
> achievement—reflect the same trends as the
> global measure.... By the end of the second year
> there are no educationally meaningful differences
> on any of the measures. (McKey et al., 1985, p. 8
> and p. III-11)

Findings on the impact on children's socioemotional development—social behavior, achievement motivation, and self-esteem—are similar. The evidence showed,

> On social behavior, former Head Start enrollees...
> drop to the level of comparison children by the end
> of the third year. On achievement motivation and
> self-esteem, Head Start children drop below non-
> Head Starters a year after Head Start, then score
> about the same as comparison children for the next
> two years. (McKey et al., 1985, pp. 12–13)

Head Start's inability to produce lasting cognitive, social, or emotional gains after more than three decades confirms the research findings from early intervention experiments—short-term gains are sometimes possible, but those gains do not last. The Head Start study concluded, "In the long run, cognitive and socioemotional test scores of former Head Start students do not remain superior to those of disadvantaged children who did not attend Head Start" (McKey et al., 1985, p. 1).

The GAO is correct in maintaining that the body of research literature on Head Start is imperfect. Like the literature on early intervention, many of the studies are methodologically flawed, and the Head Start program has undergone significant changes since many of the studies were conducted. Given these problems, one might suggest that more and better research is needed before concluding that the program has failed. Yet the literature on Head Start, however imperfect, is remarkably consistent with the past 40 years of research findings on early intervention in general. Both bodies of research consistently show that early intervention programs may have short-term gains, but those gains fade within a few years of exiting the programs.

## Results from Georgia

The nation's first test of statewide universal preschool comes from Georgia, which began funding preschool for every 4-year-old in the state in 1995. Preschool providers primarily include public schools, Head Start agencies, nonprofit child care agencies, for-profit child care agencies, churches, and private schools. Programs operate a minimum of five days a week and for a minimum of six and one-half hours per day.

Researchers at Georgia State University, funded by Georgia's Office of School Readiness, recently completed the second year of a longitudinal study of children in the universal preschool program. Using the Georgia Kindergarten Assessment Program (GKAP), the progress of participating children was assessed during their kindergarten year (1997–1998) in five domains: communicative capability, logical-mathematical capability, physical capability, personal capability, and social capability. Findings revealed that 94% of the students were reported as capable in the first and second areas followed by 97% in the third, 93% in the fourth, and 94% in the fifth. Student scores for this sample were then compared to all students across the state, and researchers concluded, "The study sample does not differ from the entire kindergarten population in GKAP capability scores." (Henderson, Basile, & Henry, 1999). In other words, children in the universal prekindergarten program performed no better than students from the general population.

Furthermore, reports show that GKAP scores are essentially the same as they were before the adoption of universal prekindergarten. Georgia State School Superintendent Linda Schrenko says there has been an improvement of less than 1% on the test scores from 1992 to 1996 and expressed the state's disappointment with the findings, "If you look at the whole test, from 1992 to 1996, we have gained nothing…. The only message you can get from it is that our kindergarten non-ready rate is the same, regardless of what we do" (Salzer, 1999). Despite the implementation of universal preschool, children's performance and readiness levels have not improved. Judged against the goal of benefiting children in a measurable manner, then, Georgia's universal preschool program has not proven itself successful.

## Conclusion

Empirical findings from early intervention experiments and evidence from real-world applications of preschool suggest that those who seek to improve children's outcomes through universal preschool are likely to meet with disappointment. Expectations for these programs far exceed their empirical record.

Although research shows that some preschool and early intervention projects have had meaningful short-term effects on disadvantaged children's cognitive ability, grade retention, and special education placement, other effects, including IQ, social, emotional, and academic gains have not proven sustainable over the long-term. The Perry Preschool and Abecedarian projects offer some evidence that intensive early intervention with highly disadvantaged children can provide lasting benefits, yet neither program is comparable to universal preschool: Both studied severely disadvantaged children only, both were far more intense than regular preschool programs, and neither has been replicated.

When one moves beyond an examination of experimental programs into the real-world application of intervention, the results have been even more disappointing. In more than 35 years, Head Start has failed to benefit participating children academically, socially, or emotionally in a lasting manner. And in the five years since Georgia adopted the nation's first universal preschool program, Georgian preschoolers are no better off academically than they were prior to the program's adoption.

The answer to why preschool does not confer more lasting benefits on children continues to elude researchers. Is it because a few years of preschool are an insufficient weight against the heavier influences of genetics, family, neighborhood, and culture? Is it because preschoolers enter troubled schools that are ill equipped to maintain short-term gains? Is it some combination of the two or other factors entirely?

Researchers seeking answers to these questions should work to conduct high-quality, replicable studies that trace a child's development from the earliest years through the high school years and beyond. Such studies will help researchers tease out the answers to these confounding questions.

Given the evidence that preschool does not lead to long-term gains in IQ scores, nor to many academic, social, or emotional gains, policymakers should leave decisions about preschool in the hands of parents. Research clearly shows that those who advocate universal preschool as a solution to academic underachievement are making a false promise to American children and families.

## References

Barnett, W. S. (1995). Long-term effects of early childhood programs on cognitive and school outcomes. *The Future of Children 5*(3), 25–50.

Bryant, B., & Maxwell, K. (1997). The effectiveness of early intervention for disadvantaged children. In Michael J. Guralnick (Ed.), *The effectiveness of early intervention* (pp. 42–43). Baltimore: Paul H. Brookes.

Bryant, D., & Clifford R. (1992). 150 years of kindergarten: How far have we come? *Early Childhood Research Quarterly, 7*(2), 147–154.

California Department of Education, Superintendent's Universal Preschool Task Force (1997). *Ready to learn: Quality preschool programs for California's young children—draft.* Sacramento, CA: California Department of Education. http://www.facilitate.com/clients/CDE/RPT1224B.html.

California Department of Education, Superintendent's Universal Preschool Task Force (1998). *Universal preschool: Urgent education priority.* Sacramento, CA: California Department of Education. http://www.cde.ca.gov/preschool/priority.htm

Campbell, F. A., & Ramey, C. T. (1995). Cognitive and school outcomes for high-risk African-American students at middle adolescence: Positive effects of early intervention. *American Educational Research Journal, 32*, 743–772.

Carnegie Corporation of New York (1996). *Years of promise: A comprehensive learning strategy for America's children.* Report of the Carnegie Task Force on Learning in the Primary Grades. New York: Author.

Clinton, H. R. (1996). *It takes a village and other lessons children teach us.* New York: Simon & Schuster.

Education Commission of the States Information Clearinghouse (1997, March). Compulsory school age requirements. *Clearinghouse Notes.*

Education Commission of the States Information Clearinghouse (1997, April). *Kindergarten: State characteristics.* Online at www.ecs.org.

Elkind, D. (1981). *The hurried child: Growing up too fast too soon.* Reading, MA: Addison-Wesley Publishing Co.

Elkind, D. (1996). Early childhood education: What should we expect? *Principal, 75*(5), 11–13.

Elkind, D. (1997). *Miseducation: Preschoolers at risk.* New York: Knopf. (Original work published 1987).

Freeman, E. B. (1990). Research review: Issues in kindergarten policy and practice. *Young Children, 45*(4), 29-34.

Geggis, A. (1998, February 16). Mandatory preschool? *Burlington Free Press,* 1A, 7A

General Accounting Office (1997). *Head Start: research provides little information on impact of current program. U.S. Government Accounting Office report to the Chairman, Committee on the Budget, House of Representatives* (GAO/HEHS-97-59). Washington, DC: Author.

Gomby, D. S., Larner, M. B., Stevenson, C. S., Lewit, E. M., & Behrman, R. E. (1995). Long-term outcomes of early childhood programs: Analysis and recommendations. *The Future of Children, 5*(3), 6–24.

Haskins, R. (1989). Beyond metaphor: The efficacy of early childhood education. *American Psychologist, 44,* 274–282.

Henderson, L. W., Basile, K. C., & Henry, G. T. (1999). *Prekindergarten longitudinal study 1997–1998 school year annual report.* Atlanta: Georgia State University Applied Research Center, School of Policy Studies.

Johnson, L. B. (1965). *Public papers of the presidents of the United States: Lyndon B. Johnson* (Vol. 1). Washington, DC: U.S. Government Printing Office, 1966), p. 556.

Kagan, S. L., & Cohen, N. E. (1997). *Not by chance: Creating an early care and education system for America's children.* Hew Haven: Bush Center in Child Development and Social Policy, Yale University.

Karoly, L. A., Greenwood, P. W., Everingham, S. S., Hoube, J., Kilburn, M. R., Rydell, C. P., Sanders, M., & Chiesa, J. (1998). *Investing in our children. What we don't know about the costs and benefits of early childhood intervention.* Santa Monica, CA: The Rand Corporation.

Karweit, N. L. (1989). Effective preschool programs for students at risk. In R. E. Slavin, N. L. Karweit, & N. A. Madden (Eds.), *Effective programs for students at risk* (pp. 75–102). Needham, MA: Allyn & Bacon.

Locurto, C. (1991). Beyond IQ in preschool programs? *Intelligence, 15,* 298–305.

May, D., Kundert, D., Nikoloff, O., Welch, E., Garrett, M., & Brent, D. (1994). School readiness: An obstacle to intervention and inclusion. *Journal of Early Intervention, 18,* 290–301.

McKey, R., Smith, A. N., & Aitken, S. S. (1985, June). *The impact of head start on children, families, and communities* (DHHS Publication No. (OHDS) 85-31193). Washington, DC: U.S. Government Printing Office.

Mitchell, A., Ripple, C., & Chanana, N. (1998). *Prekindergarten programs funded by the states: Essential elements for policymakers.* New York: Families and Work Institute.

Morse, J. (1998, November 9). Preschool for everyone. *Time, 152,* p. 98.

New York State Board of Regents (1993). *Background paper in support of the Policy Statement on Early Childhood.* Albany, NY: Commission for Child, Family, and Community Development, State of New York Department of Education.

Novello, M. K. (1998, March). *A Case against compulsion.* Washington Institute Foundation Policy Brief. Seattle: Washington Institute Foundation.

Olsen, D. A. (1997, October 23). *The advancing nanny state: Why the government should stay out of child care* (Cato Institute Policy Analysis No. 285). Washington, DC: Cato Institute.

Olsen, D. A. (1998, January 30). *State of the union, issue: Child care* (Cato Institute Fact Sheet). Washington, DC: Cato Institute.

Olsen, D. A. (1999, February 9). *Universal preschool is no golden ticket: Why government should not enter the preschool business* (Cato Institute Policy Analysis No. 333). Washington, DC: Cato Institute.

*Recommendations for a Head Start Program by a panel of experts* (1965, February). Washington, DC: U.S. Department of Health, Education, and Welfare, Office of Child Development.

Rector, R. (1998, January 23). Facts about American families and day care (Heritage Foundation FYI No. 170). Washington, DC: Heritage Foundation.

Reynolds, A. J., Mann, E., Miedel, W., & Smokowski, P. (1997). The state of early childhood intervention: Effectiveness, myths and realities, new directions. *Focus: Newsletter of the Institute for Research on Poverty of the University of Wisconsin-Madison, 19,* 5–11.

Salzer, J. (1999, November 1). School readiness the same for tots; results unchanged despite pre-k. *The Florida Times-Union,* p. A1.

Schulman, K., Blank, H., & Ewen, D. (1999). *Seeds of success: State prekindergarten initiatives 1998–1999.* Washington, DC: Children's Defense Fund.

Schweinhart, L. J. (1994). *Lasting benefits of preschool programs.* ERIC Digest EDO-PS-94-2.

Schweinhart, L. J., Barnes, H. V., Weikert, D. P., with Barnett, W.S., & Epstein, A. S. (1993). Significant benefits: The High/Scope Perry Preschool study through age 27. *Monographs of the High/Scope Educational Research Foundation, 10.* Ypsilanti, MI: High/Scope Press.

Shepard, L. A. (1997). Children not ready to learn? The invalidity of school readiness testing. *Psychology in the Schools 34*(2), 85–97.

Shepard, L. A., & Smith, M. L. (1988). Escalating academic demand in kindergarten: Counterproductive policies. *The Elementary School Journal, 89*(2), 135–145.

Spitz, H. H. (1992). Does the Carolina Abecedarian Early Intervention Project prevent sociocultural mental retardation? *Intelligence, 16,* 225–237.

Spitz, H. H. (1993). Spitz's reply to Ramey's response to Spitz's first reply to Ramey's first response to Spitz's critique of the Abecedarian Project. *Intelligence, 17,* 31–35.

Spitz, H. H. (1997). Some questions about the results of the Abecedarian Early Intervention Project cited by the APA Task Force on Intelligence. *American Psychologist, 52*(1), 72.

U.S. Department of Education, National Center for Education Statistics (1996) Kindergarten teacher survey on student readiness. *The Digest of Education Statistics.* Table 48.

U.S. Department of Education, National Center for Education Statistics (2000). *America's kindergartners* (NCES 2000-070). Washington, DC: U.S. Department of Education, Office of Educational Research and Improvement.

U. S. Department of Education, Office of Educational Research and Improvement (1998, fall). Dramatic expansion proposed for after-school programs. *OERI Bulletin,* 1-12.

Walsh, D. J. (1989). Changes in kindergarten: Why here? Why now? *Early Childhood Research Quarterly, 4,* 377–391.

Zigler, E. (1987). Formal schooling for four-year-olds? No. In Sharon L. Kagan & Edward F. Zigler (Eds.), *Early schooling: the national debate* (pp. 27–211). New Haven: Yale University Press.

Zigler, E., & Styfco, S. J. (1999, July 8). Don't overhaul Head Start—again. *Wall Street Journal,* p. A18.

Zigler, E., Taussig, C., & Black, K. (1992). Early childhood intervention: A promising preventative for juvenile delinquency. *American Psychologist, 47*(8), 1000–1002.

# Epilogue

## Themes and Recommendations for a New Century

*Arthur J. Reynolds, Margaret C. Wang, and Herbert J. Walberg*

This book is unique in that it provides a "first decade" approach to early childhood education rather than the traditional "preschool" perspective that often downplays the transition to formal schooling. The foregoing chapters describe progress in knowledge about the effects of new and established early education programs and identify emerging directions for the field. The high priority given to investments in early childhood programs reflects the social need for quality early education and the accumulated evidence that these programs can have substantial benefits for children and families.

In this Epilogue, we briefly discuss integrative themes from the chapters that highlight directions for the future. We then describe some program and policy recommendations derived from the Laboratory for Student Success conference, in which most of the chapter authors participated together with practitioners and parents.

### Integrative Themes

The chapters highlight three major themes for the early childhood field. The first is the importance of promoting successful transitions from home to community and school settings. Programs and policies that take account of and support children's transitions are more likely than others to positively impact learning and development. As described in the chapters, high-quality child care can provide a strong foundation for cognitive and socioemotional development, comprehensive preschool education enhances children's readiness for school, and early school-age programs and services help strengthen learning gains and pave the way for healthy development.

A second theme is the emergence of greater consensus on key principles of effective programs. Eight principles for enhancing early childhood programs follow from the chapters: (a) target services to children with relatively greater educational needs, (b) begin program enrollment as early in the life course as possible, (c) implement programs for a length of time that is sufficient to impact children's learning and support a smooth transition to school, (d) provide comprehensive services in meeting children's needs, (e) encourage parent involvement in children's learning, (f) encourage age-appropriate practices, (g) support ongoing professional development for all staff, and (h) provide adequate levels of support for research and evaluation. These principles can help policymakers and program administrators better prioritize investments in early education.

The third theme of the volume is the need for an integrated and unified system of early childhood programs. As noted in many chapters, the current system lacks coherence in several respects. Funding, administration, goals, populations served, and availability and quality vary substantially across programs. The next century of programs can have greater benefits than the programs of the preceding one if they implement the principles described above and if they are better designed to support children's transitions throughout the first decade of life. Improving early childhood programs by enhancing levels of consistency and coordination was a common theme in the volume.

Given that over 90% of the nation's children attend public schools in kindergarten and the early grades, public school districts would need to take a leadership role in such an effort in collaboration with community providers. In addition, standards of quality would be an important component of expansion. The State of Georgia lottery-funded universal access program demonstrates that public institutions can organize and coordinate large-scale programs. Many other states also have initiated preschool programs. Indeed, collaborative ventures between schools, community agencies, and child-care providers are continuing to be developed.

As discussed in several chapter, two cautions should be considered in designing and implementing an integrated early childhood program serving greater proportions of children. First, programs that are not of sufficient quality and length are unlikely to promote children's school readiness or later success. Thus, expansion should not come at the cost of sacrifices in quality. Second, participation in early childhood programs is one of many influences in children's adjustment. It would not be expected to greatly alter the course of children's lives. As Zigler and Styfco explained in Chapter 1:

> Many intervention attempts tried over the years have proven the difficulty of remediating the effects of poverty. No amount of early brain stimulation, no year of preschool, or no class periods of compensatory studies will ensure a bright future for a child raised in economic deprivation. Intervention must begin early and last long enough to have a meaningful impact on children's development.

McCall and colleagues sounded a similar theme in Chapter 9:

> The most general conclusion from this literature is not that routine service programs have a checkered history of success and are of dubious value; rather the conclusion is quite consistent with common sense: These programs can and do work, but children and families need more than a few hours a week or vague social support to reverse the consequences that years of impoverishment and stress often produce.

## National Invitational Conference

In the rest of the Epilogue, we provide a summary of key recommendations drawn from the work groups at the national invitational conference "Early Childhood Learning: Programs for a New Age." In addition to examining the research base and the next-step recommendations generated by the authors of commissioned papers, conference participants devoted much of their discussion to strategies for addressing the pressing national concern of providing quality universal child care and preschool programs and sought to bring this urgent call to the forefront of the national dialogue.

Conference participants formed small work groups that included a cross section of practitioners, policymakers, and researchers from multiple disciplines, including sociology, psychology, early childhood development, and social work. A consensus was reached on the need to provide universal access to day care, improve the quality of teacher and staff professional development, and increase parental involvement in early childhood programs.

The key recommendations listed below should not be viewed as representing the conference consensus. They do, however, reflect the overall tone of the discussion and represent several prospects for the future of early childhood education in this country.

## Key Recommendations

### *Universal Day Care and Preschool Education*

- Access to publicly supported day care and preschool programs should be universal, regardless of family income, social status, or ethnic and racial backgrounds. These programs should be full-day, full-year programs that do not distinguish between child care and education.

  The conference participants are fully cognizant of the requirement for major increases in public funding and oversight. They are equally aware of the need to articulate clearly the long-term benefits to children and to the nation's future.

  The participants noted that universal access to day care and preschool education would attract greater numbers of middle and lower socioeconomic status families to early childhood programs, which would lead to increased diversity and ultimately to better quality programs. The current "you get what you pay for" mentality that exists would be eliminated, and all children would begin their education on a level playing field.

- Universal access to day care and preschool programs should be seamless, creating a continuity of learning for children.

Curriculum and assessment standards must be aligned and services should be comprehensive and aimed at intellectual, physical, and social development of children and their readiness to achieve learning success in elementary schools.

## Quality and Standards

- Early childhood programs must incorporate developmentally appropriate practices. They should also individualize work and include a variety of learning activities for promoting language and math skills, socioemotional development, and physical health.

- Smaller groups of children and lower child to teacher ratios should be mandated in early childhood programs. Child to teacher ratios of 5 to 1 in infant programs and 8 to 1 in preschool programs are often recommended. Early school-age programs also should have reduced class sizes.

- Develop standards for curricula content and program quality. Collaboration between funders, policymakers, and local service providers will be important to the success of this effort.

## Professional Development

- High-quality, well-trained, well-compensated educators and staff are key to student achievement at all levels of education. Professional development for early childhood educators and staff must be improved and focused on early childhood development, curriculum design, best practices, pedagogy, and parental involvement.

- A balance of focus in preservice and inservice professional development programs must be maintained. The issue of maintaining a substantive balance of pedagogy as opposed to subject matter mastery in teacher preparation and inservice professional development programs has been a persistent debate among educators. It was a key concern raised at the conference.

Teacher education programs often emphasize subject matter knowledge and offer little training in developing a thorough understanding of the learning processes of young children. It was generally agreed by the participants that teaching, teacher development, and curriculum delivery need to focus on what has the greatest impact on healthy development and lifelong learning of each child. Professional development should not only strengthen staff and teachers' knowledge of subject matter and curricular issues but also should emphasize methods for recognizing and addressing children's developmental and learning needs.

### *Parental Involvement*

- Parental involvement is crucial to the success of early childhood programs. Involving parents at all levels of decision making, including curriculum design and professional development, increases parents' sense of ownership of these programs and encourages collaboration between schools and the communities they serve.

  Most parents want to be involved in every aspect of their children's education. By including parents in the early childhood equation, learning that begins in the classroom is reinforced at home. A critical element of this reinforcement is the development of a common vocabulary that teachers and parents can use to discuss a child's progress and methods for improvement.

- Parents should receive information on relevant research on effective practices in readable and useful forms. Parents should not only be informed but also should be involved in providing input and making programming decisions about the education of their children.

## Next-Step Recommendations

In addition to the broad-based issues of universal day care, professional development, and parental involvement, the conferees made the following specific recommendations for moving forward with an advocacy action agenda for universal quality child care and preschool education.

- Convince policymakers that (a) early childhood programs can be cost effective, (b) the extent and quality of programs are crucial to achieving success, and (c) programs can be successful at a relatively small cost if integrated into existing structures.

- Initiate discussions between early childhood education advocates and members of the National Parent-Teacher Association. Form coalitions with other child advocacy groups to create better political climates for children and their families.

- Identify champions of the child care and early childhood education movement who are influential. Promote leadership advocacy for early childhood educators.

- Focus on what sells. Advocates need to get the media on the side of quality child care and early childhood education. Inform the public about relevant research on what works in providing quality child care and preschool education.

- Use new technologies and mass communication avenues to forge a national dialogue on the need for quality child care and preschool education for all, and to foster increased parent-school connections.

- Work to eradicate the risk factors that continue to challenge and mitigate human capital investment and confront racial and social stratification. Examine the assumptions behind the term "at risk" and devise a new term that reduces stereotyping.

- Use the research on preventing reading difficulties in young children to minimize severe academic problems in the primary grades.

- Increase research and development spending in early childhood care and education to mirror R & D spending in other domestic programs such as biomedicine and transportation.

- Investigate through evaluation research how well programs are implemented as much as how effective they are for promoting children's success.

- Improve articulation alignment of what is taught in colleges and of the professional expertise required for quality child care providers and preschool educators. There is a critical need to increase collaboration and coordination between higher education institutions that provide preservice education of child care and preschool education professionals and child care and preschool education-providing agencies.

- Place attention on preservice and inservice programs that focus on bringing research-based knowledge to bear on improving practice.

- Require child care and early childhood education programs to involve parents as much as possible.

- Work intensively to educate colleagues and the public on viewing the 21st century as the "Century of the Child" and on creating for the United States a strategy for investing in its human potential.

## Conclusion

This volume illustrates that effective parenting and early childhood programs in the first decade of life are investments that can contribute positively to children's learning and development. Enhancing their quality, intensity, and effectiveness to serve the changing needs of families is a major challenge in the new century. As derived from the literature, the themes and recommendations discussed in this chapter may be useful in planning and carefully evaluating new initiatives. Hopefully, they can contribute in some small way to a more coherent system of early education that links high-quality services to the needs of families.

# About the Editors

**Arthur J. Reynolds** is professor of social work, educational psychology, and human development and family studies at the University of Wisconsin-Madison. His major areas of interest are child development and social policy, prevention research, and program evaluation. As director of the Chicago Longitudinal Study, a federally funded investigation of the effects of a large-scale early childhood intervention, he has published widely on the short- and long-term effects of participation for both child and family outcomes. The age 15 follow-up study, *Success in Early Intervention: The Chicago Child-Parent Centers,* was published in 2000 by the University of Nebraska Press. Early adulthood findings have been recently reported. He also has published in the fields of program evaluation and educational psychology, most recently as coeditor (with Herbert Walberg) of *Evaluation Research for Educational Productivity* with JAI Press and guest editor of a special issue on the Chicago Longitudinal Study in the *Journal of School Psychology.* Professor Reynolds is affiliated with the Institute for Research on Poverty and the Waisman Center on Mental Retardation and Human Development.

**Herbert J. Walberg,** Emeritus Research Professor of Education and Psychology at the University of Illinois at Chicago (UIC), was awarded a Ph.D. in Educational Psychology by the University of Chicago and was formerly Assistant Professor at Harvard. He completed a term as Founding Member of the National Assessment Governing Board, sometimes referred to as "the national school board," because it has been given the mission to set subject matter standards for U.S. students. He has written and edited more than 50 books and contributed more than 380 articles to educational and psychological research journals on such topics as educational effectiveness and productivity, school reform, and exceptional human accomplishments. He frequently writes for widely circulated practitioner journals and national newspapers, serves as an advisor on educational research and improvement to public and private agencies in the United States and other countries, and testifies before state and federal courts and U.S. Congressional committees.

A fellow of four academic organizations, he has won several awards and prizes for his scholarship and is one of three U.S. members of the International Academy of Education. He holds appointments in the UIC Center for Urban Educational Research and Development and the Mid-Atlantic Laboratory for Student Success. He currently serves on not-for-profit boards and is Chairman of the Board of the Heartland Institute, which provides policy analyses for federal and state legislators and news people and publishes the magazine Intellectual Ammunition and two newspapers, including School Reform News.

The late **Margaret C. Wang** was Professor of Educational Psychology at Temple University and the founding director of the Temple University Center for Research in Human Development and Education (CRHDE). Dr. Wang also served as Director of the Laboratory for Student Success, the Mid-Atlantic Regional Educational Laboratory, and the National Center on Education in the Inner Cities, both funded by the Office of Educational Research and Improvement of the U.S. Department of Education.

Dr. Wang published 15 books and more than 100 articles. She was the senior editor of the four-volume *Handbook for Special Education: Research and Practice.* Other publications include *Adaptive Education Strategies: Building on Diversity; Rethinking Policy for At-Risk Students, and Social and Emotional Adjustment and Family Relations in Ethnic Minority Families.* In addition to her research, Dr. Wang has developed an extensive network of collaborating schools across the country, including schools in such urban centers as Houston, Los Angeles, Washington, DC, and Philadelphia. Professor Wang died at her home in Gladwyne, PA, on November 22, 2000. She will be missed greatly.

# About the Contributors

**Karl L. Alexander** is a professor of sociology at Johns Hopkins University. His research explores why some children, and some kinds of children, are more successful in school than others. He is particularly interested in the role schools play in perpetuating historic patterns of advantage and disadvantage and in identifying features of the home, of the school, and of the individual that seem to promote or impede positive school adjustment. Alexander has published over a hundred journal articles and book chapters and has written four books: *Achievement in the First Two Years of School: Patterns and Processes* (with Doris R. Entwisle), *On the Success of Failure: A Reassessment of the Effects of Retention in the Primary Grades* (with Doris R. Entwisle and S. L. Dauber), *Children, Schools, and Inequality* (with Doris R. Entwisle and L. S. Olson); and, currently in preparation, *Development in Tandem: Self-Image and School Performance from First Grade into High School.*

**Sarane Spence Boocock** is a professor of sociology at the Rutgers University Graduate School of Education. Formerly a staff sociologist at the Russell Sage Foundation, she has also taught at Yale University, the University of Southern California, Johns Hopkins University, and Hebrew University of Jerusalem, Israel. She is the author of *An Introduction to the Sociology of Learning, Simulation Games in Learning, Turning Points: Historical and Sociological: Essays on the Family, International Comparisons of Childrearing: Children, Parents, and Society,* and most recently (with W. Steven Barnett), *Early Care and Education for Children in Poverty: Promises, Programs, and Long-Term Results.* Her current research includes a study comparing childrearing values and practices in Japan, China, France, and the United States, and a study comparing the educational problems of minority children in Japan and the United States.

**Doris R. Entwisle**, Professor Emerita of sociolgy at Johns Hopkins University, has focused her research on human development over ages 5 to 20+, and the social and psychological factors that impinge on that development. With Karl L. Alexander, she has been engaged since 1982 in the Beginning School Study (BSS), which has followed a cohort of about 800 Baltimore youngsters who began first grade in 1982. At present she is involved in two major subprojects. One is a study of BSS drop-outs, supported by the Spencer Foundation, that strives to determine the causes and consequences of drop out. The other is a descriptive study of the work histories of BSS youngsters beginning in middle school and continuing through high school, supported by the W.T. Grant Foundation. Both studies are primarily quantitative. Entwisle has authored or co-authored ten books and numerous articles and book chapters, has been a Guggenheim Fellow, and was presented with the Award for Distinguished Scientific Contribution to Child Development by the Society for Research in Child Development in 1997.

**Elizabeth M. Graue** is a Professor of Early Childhood Education in the Department of Curriculum and Instruction at the University of Wisconsin, Madison. A former kindergarten teacher, she teaches courses in early childhood policy and practice and on kindergarten practices, readiness, and home school relations. She is the author of *Read for What? Constructing Meanings of Readiness for Kindergarten and Studying Children in Context: Theories, Methods, and Ethics* (with Daniel Walsh). She is former Associate Editor of the *Review of Educational Research.*

**Angela Ingram** is at XTRIA (formerly Ellsworth Associates, Inc.) in McLean, Virginia. She previously worked in the Office of Child Development at the University of Pittsburgh.

**Nader Kabbani** is on the staff of the Economic Research Service at the U. S. Department of Agriculture. He earned a Ph.D. in Economics in 2000 at Johns Hopkins University, where he worked on the Beginning School Study.

**Lana Larsen** is employed at Andrews Air Force Base, Maryland. She previously worked in the Office of Child Development at the University of Pittsburgh.

**Robert B. McCall**, Ph.D., is Professor of Psychology and Co-Director of the University of Pittsburgh Office of Child Development. Dr. McCall is a specialist in early mental development, the effects of early experience including early childhood interventions, longitudinal research methodology, developmental changes in mental performance, infant assessment, underachievers, applied statistics, and program evaluation. He has published two dozen editions of textbooks, including a statistics text; more than 150 books, monographs, chapters, and empirical articles, and 140 articles and columns in newspaper and magazines. A particular component in McCall's scholarship and administrative experience is the relations between academics on the one hand and human service professionals, policymakers, and the general public on the other. This has been manifested in the human service, policy, and evaluation initiatives of the Office of Child Development and in McCall's extensive science communication activities in local and national media, accomplishments that won him the American Psychological Association's national award for Contribution to Public Service, six media and special commendations from national professional organizations, and the University of Pittsburgh Chancellor Awards in Research and in Public Service.

**Darcy A. Olsen** is the executive director of the Goldwater Institute in Phoenix, AZ. She is the former director of education and child policy at the Cato Institute, Washington, DC, where she explored education reform policies and private initiatives to strengthen the independent education system. She has worked extensively on children's issues, including childcare, preschool, school-age childcare, and social services. She worked for three years as a transitional house manager for the Washington DC Coalition for the Homeless. She has testified before Congress and appeared on numerous programs, including *Inside Politics, the O'Reilly Factor, the Today Show, CNN, C-SPAN, and the NBC Nightly News.* Olsen holds a bachelor's degree from the School of Foreign Service at Georgetown University and a master's degree in international education from New York University.

**Kim M. Pierce** is a researcher at the Wisconsin Center for Education Research, University of Wisconsin, Madison. She received her B.S. in psychology from the University of Wisconsin–LaCrosse and her M.S. and Ph.D. in educational psychology/human development from the University of Wisconsin–Madison. Dr. Pierce is site coordinator for the

Wisconsin site of the NICHD Study of Early Child Care and Youth Development. Her research has examined the quality of and children's experiences in after-school programs, and the effects of program quality variations on children's development, both concurrently and longitudinally.

**Anthony Raden** is the associate director of the Columbia University Institute for Child and Family Policy. A 1998 graduate from Yale University with a Ph.D. in developmental psychology, Dr. Raden's research focuses on the evaluation and analysis of programs and policies for children and youth at risk due to poverty, violence, and maltreatment. In addition, Dr. Raden consults with community-based programs on issues related to children's mental health and violence, as well as local, state and national agencies and organizations, such as the Foundation for Child Development, the State of Connecticut Commission on Children, and the National Health Policy Forum.

**Craig T. Ramey** is Distinguished Professor of Health Studies in the School of Nursing and Health Studies at Georgetown University. He specializes in the study of factors affecting the development of intelligence, social competence, and academic achievement in young children. During the past 30 years, Dr. Ramey has led research and development teams involving over 500 professionals and 14,000 children and families in over 40 states. This research and development has been supported by numerous grants from federal and state agencies and from private foundations. He is an author of over 200 publications, including five books. Dr. Ramey has won professional and civic awards for his work on the prevention of intellectual disabilities and for exemplary early childhood education programs. He is currently focusing on the creation of a new generation of early childhood education, health, and family support programs. His latest books, written with his wife Dr. Sharon Ramey, are *Right From Birth: Building Your Child,s Foundation for Life* and *Going to School: A Complete Handbook for Parents of Children Ages 3-8.* Prior to arriving at Georgetown, Dr. Ramey was codirector of the Civitan International Research Center at the University of Alabama at Birmingham.

**Sharon Landesman Ramey** is the Susan H. Mayer Professor of Child and Family Studies in the School of Nursing and Health Studies at Georgetown University. Dr. Ramey's professional interests include the study of the development of intelligence and children's competency, early experience and early intervention, the changing American family, and the transition to school. She is the recipient of many citations and awards for her scientific and policy contribtions, and the Distinguished Research Contributions Award of the American Association on Mental Retardation. She serves on many national review and advisory panels, including the National Academy of Sciences and NIH review panels. Dr. Ramey is the author/editor of four books and has written more than 160 articles, and has made more than 275 presentations at local, state, regional, national, and international conferences. She frequently conducts workshops for parents, educators, health care professionals, and policymakers about how to enhance young children's development. Until this year, Dr. Ramey was codirector of the Civitan International Research Center at the University of Alabama at Birmingham.

**Lawrence J. Schweinhart** is an early childhood program researcher and speaker. He has conducted research at the High/Scope Educational Research Foundation in Ypsilanti, Michigan, since 1975 and has chaired its research division since 1989. He currently directs High/Scope's Head Start Quality Research Center, the state evaluation of the Michigan School Readiness Program, and the development and validation of the High/Scope Child Observation Record. He is the lead researcher on the High/Scope Perry Preschool Study and the High/Scope Preschool Curriculum Comparison Study. He has served on the Governing Board of the National Association for the Education of Young Children. He received his Ph.D. in education from Indiana University in 1975.

**Sally J. Styfco** is a writer and policy analyst specializing in matters pertaining to children and families, particularly early childhood and later educational intervention. She is a noted synthesizer of the literature for policymakers, scholars, and students. Her writings span the topics of Head Start, child care, children with disabilities, federal education initiatives, child maltreatment, the effects of poverty on child development, and the historical progression of government policies in these areas. She is the asssociate director of the Head Start Research Unit at the Yale University Bush Center in Child Development and Social Policy and a research associate at the Yale Psychology Department.

**Deborah Lowe Vandell** is a professor of educational psychology at the University of Wisconsin, Madison. Professor Vandell is a core investigator at the Wisconsin Center for Education Research, the Institute for Research on Poverty, that Waisman Center on Mental Retardation and Human Development, and the Wisconsin Center for Affective Sciences. She is a member of the Maternal and Child Health Research Subcommittee at the National Institute of Child Health and Human Development (NICHD) and a member of the Steering Committee for the NICHD Study of Early Child Care and Youth Development. Dr. Vandell has served as an associate editor for the journal *Child Development* and on the editorial boards of *Developmental Psychology, Contemporary Psychology,* and the *Journal of Family Issues.* Much of her research has examined effects of early child care and after-school care on children's development. Children's relationships with their parents, siblings, peers, and teachers provide another unifying theme to her work.

**Edward Zigler** is the Sterling Professor of Psychology, head of the psychology section of the Child Study Center, and director of the Bush Center in Child Development and Social Policy at Yale University. He is the author, coauthor, and editor of numerous scholarly publications and has conducted extensive research on topics related to normal child development and to psychopathology and mental retardation. Dr. Zigler regularly testifies as an expert witness before congressional committees and has served as a consultant to a number of cabinet-rank officers. He was one of the planners of Project Head Start and was the first director of the U.S. Office of Child Development (now the Administration on Children, Youth, and Families) and chief of the U.S. Children's Bureau.

# Author Index

## A

Abbott-Shim, M., 120, 121, 249
A.B.C. Task Force, 87
Abelson, W. B., 171, 172, 175, 274
Abelson, W. D., 11
Abt Associates, 20
Achenbach, T. M., 122
Adams, G., 76
Administration on Children, Youth and Families, 6, 7, 14
Advisory Committee on Head Start Quality and Expansion, 24
Advisory Committee on Head Start Research and Evaluation, 16, 252
Advisory Committee on Services for Families with Infants and Toddlers, 19
Advisory Panel for the Head Start Evaluation Design Project, 15
Alamprese, J., 22
Alberts, D. M., 153
Alexander, K. L., xxviii, 116, 166, 167, 197–227, 363
Allen, M., 257
American Association of School Administrators, 223
Ames, E. W., 267
Anderman, E. M., 217
Anderson, K., 5
Anderson, R., 172, 226

Andersson, B. E., 306
Andrews, E. L., 317, 318
Apfel, N., 172, 270, 274, 283
Arroyo, C. G., 20, 21
Atkinson, A. H., 310
Auinger, P., 153, 154
Austin, A. B., 269
Ayabe, C. R., 206

## B

Bailey, D. B. J., Jr., 268, 269
Bairrao, J., 300, 304, 306, 309, 312, 313, 316
Baker, L. S., 116
Barnard, K. E., 269
Barnes, H. V., 15, 40, 58, 246, 250, 264, 271, 283, 335, 336, 338
Barnes, H. W., 282
Barnes, R., 98
Barnett, W. S., xvii, xxi, 10, 11, 15, 20, 40, 53, 58, 71, 100, 165, 225, 246, 250, 256, 261, 265, 268, 269, 271, 273, 274, 282, 283, 304, 335, 336, 338
Barrett, B., 12, 264, 334, 344–345
Basile, K., 96, 97, 104, 105, 106, 346
Bauer, C., 54, 122
Beatty, B., 4
Becker, W. C., 172
Bee, C. K., 263

Bee, H. L., 38
Behrman, R. E., 265, 272, 338
Beinart, P., 75, 101
Bellisimo, Y., 152, 153
Belsky, J., 261
Benasich, A. A., 263
Bennett, C., 261
Bennett, F. C., 54
Bergmann, B. R., 311
Berk, L., 270
Berman, W., 274
Bernbaum, J. C., 54
Bernstein, L. S., 18, 264, 266, 271
Berrueta-Clement, J. R., 53
Berrureta-Clement, J. R., 261
Besharov, D., 105
Bezruczko, N., 167, 270
Bianchi, S. M., 201
Bickel, R., 187
Bickman, L., 185
Black, K., 262, 336
Blackstone, T., 316
Blair, C., 225, 270
Blank, H., 71, 329
Blau, D. M., 127–129, 133–134
Bloch, M. N., 299, 317
Boertz, M. E., 258, 259
Bohlen, C., 318
Bomster, M., 212
Bond, J. T., 40
Boocock, S. S., xvii, xxi, xxix–xxx, 268, 281, 299–321, 363
Bowman, B., xx, xxii
Bracken, B. A., 122

Bradley, R. H., 122
Bredekamp, S., 116, 152
Bredenkamp, D., 267
Brennan, P., 259
Brent, D., 152, 153, 332
Broberg, A., 306, 311
Bronfenbrenner, U., xxi, 6, 37, 164
Brooks-Gunn, J., 54, 61, 263, 264, 278, 279
Brown, J. G., 344
Brown, P., 257
Brush, L. R., 24
Bryant, B., 332
Bryant, D., 40, 59, 60, 124, 125, 186, 187, 257, 261, 264, 265, 266, 268, 269, 270, 271, 334, 335
Bryant, E., 207
Bryk, A. S., 225
Burchinal, M. R., 40, 60, 115, 124, 125, 132, 186, 187
Burns, M. S., xx, xxii
Burts, D., 269
Butterfield, E. C., 11, 37
Byler, P., 115, 125
Byrd, R. S., 153, 154

## C

Cabrera, N. J., 15
Cairns, R. B., 220
Caldwell, B. M., 122, 261, 269
California Department of Education's Superintendent's Universal Preschool Task Force, 330, 333

Cameron, M. B., 153
Cameron, S., 264
Campbell, F. A., 40, 53, 60,
    182, 183, 186, 187, 225,
    250, 261, 266, 267, 273,
    339, 340
Carlson, H. L., 312
Carnegie Corporation, 330, 331
Carnegie Task Force on
    Learning in the Primary
    Grades, xvii
Carpenter, J., 145, 149
Carville, J., 75
Casey, J., 225
Casey, P. H., 54
Casto, G., 63, 257, 269
Catalyst, 223
Catto, S. F., 153
Ceci, S. J., 53
Center for the Future of
    Children, 258, 262, 264,
    270
Cerva, T. R., 172
Chafel, J. A., 24
Chanana, N., 24, 25, 105, 329
Chandler, M. J., 259
Charlesworth, R., 269
Charlton, K., 223, 227
Cherlin, A. J., 317
Chicago Public Schools, 223,
    224
Chiesa, J., xx, xxi, xxii, 334
Chin-Quee, D. S., 119–120
Chisolm, K., 267
Chu, A., 207
Chubrick, R. E., 271
Cicirelli, V. G., 9

Clarke, A. D. B., 38
Clarke-Stewart, K. A., 261,
    265, 269
Clewell, B. C., 263
Clifford, R. M., 115, 118, 125,
    249, 252, 332
Cline, M. G., 263
Clinton, H. R., 331
Clinton, W. J., 197–198, 221
Cochran, M. M., 304, 306
Coelen, C., 126, 132, 250,
    268, 270
Cohen, N., 71, 101, 105, 330,
    331, 333
Colbert, K., 187
Collins, M., 143
Collins, R. C., 10
Comfort, C., 220
Condelli, L., 12, 264, 334,
    344–345
Connell, J. P., 206, 207
Conners, C. K., 9
Conrad, K. J., 178
Cook, M., 116
Cooke, R., 5
Cooper, H., 223, 227
Copple, C. E., 263
Cosden, M., 152
Cost, Quality, and Outcomes
    of Child Care Study
    (CQO), 125, 250
The Cost and Quality Team,
    268, 270
Council for School
    Performance, 84, 98, 100
Council of Economic Advisors,
    xvii

Cowan, C. P., 38
Cowan, P. A., 38
Cowen, E., 23
Crampton, F., 101
Crane, J., 225
Crnic, K., 270
Cryer, D., 249, 299, 300, 301,
    304, 309, 316
Cuban, L., 225, 226
Culkin, M. L., 115, 125
Cunningham, A., 145
Cupp, R., 153, 154
Currie, J., 12
Curtis, A., 305

**D**
Daniels, D., 97
Darlington, R., 39, 261, 262,
    269, 270
Datta, L., 9, 263, 264
Dauber, S. L., 205, 213
Davis, K., 267
Day, N. L., 259
Deater-Deckard, K., 120
DeBlasi, C. L., 171, 172, 175,
    274
DeFord, D. E., 225
DeGracie, J. S., 206
Dencik, L., 307
Department of Education, 198,
    200, 221, 223, 224, 329,
    332, 333
Department of Health and
    Human Services, 7, 13, 24
Derman-Sparks, L., 87
Deutsch, M., 38

Developmental Research and
    Programs, Inc., 258, 259
Dewey, John, 36
DeWolf, M., 269
Dichter, H., 101
DiLalla, L. F., 259
DiPerna, J. C., 152, 153, 155
Dishion, T., 258, 259
Doernberger, C., 19, 169
Dolan, L. J., 21
Donovan, M. S., xx, xxii
Dosher, R., 225
Dubrow, N., 258
Durlak, J. A., 166

**E**
Earls, F., 258
Early Childhood Environment
    Rating Scale (ECERS), 118
Eash, M. J., 178
Eccles, J. S., 211
Eckstrom, R. B., 258, 259
Educational Testing Service,
    198
Education Commission of the
    States Information
    Clearinghouse, 329
Edwards, C., 310
Eisenberg, L., 9
Eisenberg, M., 120, 121
Elardo, R., 169
Elkind, D., 332, 334
Elliott, D. S., 259
English and Romanian
    Adoptees Study Team, 267

Entwisle, D. R., xxviii, 116, 165, 166, 167, 197–227, 274, 277, 363–364
Epstein, A. S., 15, 40, 53, 58, 246, 250, 261, 271, 283, 335, 336, 338
Escobar, C. M., 53
Evahn, C., 259
Everingham, S. S., xx, xxi, xxii, 334
Ewen, D., 71, 329

**F**

Family Resource Coalition, 257
Farkas, G., 223, 225
Farran, D. C., 257, 261, 262
Farrington, D. P., 258
Farris, E., 145, 149
Federal Register, 185
Feiler, R., 97
Fein, G., 261
Feldman, L., 258
Fendt, K. H., 40
Fiese, B. H., 260
Finklestein, N., 262
Finley, B., 257
Finn-Stevenson, M., 21
Fischer, J., 225
Fish, J., 227
Forman, G., 310
Forum on Child and Family Statistics, xx
Fosburg, L. B., 263
Fowler, W., 261, 264, 266, 268, 270, 271
Fox, M. K., 263

Frede, E. C., 268, 269, 271, 272
Freedman, J., 261
Freeman, E. B., 152, 332
Froebel, F., 36
Fuerst, D., 179, 180
Fuerst, J. S., 179, 180
Fuller, B., 320

**G**

Gaidurgis, A., 24
Gallagher, R. J., 116
Galper, A. R., 187
Gamble, T., 12, 261
Gamse, B., 22
Gándara, P., 227
Gandini, L., 310
Ganson, H., 12, 264, 334, 344–345
Garbarino, J., 258
Garber, H. L., 38, 40, 45, 54, 60, 61
Garcia, C., 38
Gardner, H., 310
Garmezy, N., 166
Garrett, M., 332
Geggis, A., 329
General Accounting Office (GAO), xvii, xviii, xxii, xxiii, 12–13, 334, 343–344
Georgia Department of Education, 80, 82
Gersten, R., 172
Ghazaleh, H. A., 264, 266, 270
Ghodse, H., 101
Gilliam, W. S., 18, 24, 25, 105
Gilman, E., 163

Gilmore, J. E., 156

Glantz, F., 126, 132, 250, 268, 270

Glass, G. V., 172

Glasser, W., 163

Godin, K. W., 268

Goelman, H., 313

Goffin, S. G., 269

Golightly, S., 94

Gomby, D. S., 265, 272, 338

Gooding, K., 99

Goodlad, J., 226

Goodrich, N. N., 263

Goodson, B. D., 18, 24, 264, 266, 271, 282

Goodstein, H. A., 263

Gordon, I. J., 172

Gottfredson, G. D., 222

Gottsman, I. I., 259

Granahan, P., 263

Grant, J., 221, 225

Grantham-McGregor, S., 264, 266, 270

Graue, E. M., xxvii, 143–158, 364

Gray, S. W., 38, 163

Greaney, B. J., 314

Greenberg, M. T., 165, 166

Greenwood, G. E., 172

Greenwood, P. W., xx, xxi, xxii, 334

Griffith, E. M., 153

Griffiths, M., 101

Grissmer, D., 223

Grissom, J., 211

Gross, R. T., 61

Gruber, J., 199

Gueron, J., 264

Gunnarsson, L., 306

Guralnick, M. J., xxiii, 257, 258, 261, 269, 271

Gustafsson, S. S., 306, 308, 318–319

Gutierrez, R., 226

**H**

Hagemann, M., 167, 270

Halpern, R., 257, 263, 264, 265, 269

Handy, J., 106

Hansen, M., 207

Harkavy, O., 264

Harms, T., 118, 249, 252

Harrel, A., 264

Harris, K., 116

Hart, C., 269

Haskins, R., 10–11, 263, 271, 338, 342

Hatch, J. A., 152

Hauser, R., 200–201, 204, 211

Hauser-Cram, P., 258

Hausken, E. G., 143

Head Start Bureau, 14, 17

Heaviside, S., 145, 149

Heckman, J., 264

Hegland, S. M., 187

Heming, G., 38

Henderson, L., 96, 97, 104, 105, 106, 346

Henderson, V. K., 130

Henke, R. R., 115

Henry, G., 76, 85, 96, 97, 99, 104, 105, 106, 346

Hess, R. D., 38
Hibbs, E. D., 261
High/Scope Educational
    Research Foundation, 248
Hirsh-Pasek, K., 269
Hofferth, S. L., 115, 278
Hogan, A., 122
Holloway, S. D., 269
Holmes, C., 204, 205, 206
Honig, A. S., 24, 262
Horsey, C., 213
Hoube, J., xx, xxi, xxii, 334
House, E., 172, 204
Howes, C., 105, 115, 125, 127,
    131, 133, 250, 265, 269,
    270, 278
Huber, R., 156
Huizinga, D., 259
Hunt, J. McV., 38
Hurt, M., 264
Huston, A., 38, 258
Hwang, C. P., 306, 311
Hymel, S., 220
Hyson, M. D., 269

**I**

Infant Health and
    Development Program,
    259
Ingram, A., xxix, 255–283,
    355, 364
Institute for Research on
    Poverty, xxi
Ispa, J., 300
Itard, J., 35

**J**

Jackson, G. B., 206
Jacobs, F., 257
Jensen, A. R., 216
Johnson, L. B., 4–5, 8, 169,
    241, 343
Johnson, L. J., 116
Jones, T., 101
Jowett, S., 315

**K**

Kabbani, N., xxviii, 197–227,
    364
Kagan, S. L., 71, 101, 105,
    115, 116, 125, 152, 257,
    320, 330, 331, 333
Kam, H. W., 308
Kandel, E., 259
Karoly, L. A., xx, xxi, xxii, 334
Karweit, N. L., 165, 206, 207–
    209, 225, 265, 273, 334,
    335
Kaufman-McMurrain, M., 94,
    95
Keefe, N., 120, 121
Kellaghan, T., 314
Kelley, M. F., 271
Kelly, K., 221
Kennedy, E. M., 19, 185
Ketterlinus, R. D., 306
Kilburn, M. R., xx, xxi, xxii, 334
Kitzman, H., 257, 262, 265, 269
Klaus, R. A., 38
Knudsen-Lindauer, S. L., 116
Kostelny, K., 258
Kraemer, H. C., 61

Kratzer, L., 259
Kresh, E., 264
Kroeker, R., 36
Kronchite, R., 83, 84
Kundert, D., 152, 153, 332

## L

Lally, J. R., 262
Lally, R. J., 24
Lamb, M. E., 118, 121, 126,
    132, 306, 311
Landesman, S., 37, 61
Landesman-Dwyer, S., 37
Larabee, D. F., 197
Lareau, A., 148, 149, 153, 155
Larner, M., 264, 272, 303, 338
Larsen, J. C., 264
Larsen, L., xxix, 255–283, 355,
    364
Larson, C. S., 265
Larson, K. A., 211
LaVange, L. M., 40
Lawrence, R., 81, 93, 99
Lawton, M., 197
Layzer, J. I., 18, 24, 264, 266,
    271, 282
Lazar, I., 39, 261, 262, 269, 270
Leckie, M. S., 38
Lee, V. E., 11, 264
Legters, N., 204
Leiter, V., 18
Leonard, C. O., 61
LeTendre, M. J., 25
Levenstein, P., 269
Levenstein, S., 269
Levine, E., 11

Lewin, T., 320
Lewis, A., 269
Lewit, E. M., 116, 265, 272, 338
Liaw, F., 201, 264
Lindauer, S. K., 269
Lloyd, L., 226
Locurto, C., 336–337
Loeb, S., 11
Loeber, R., 258, 259
Logue, M. E., 145
Lombard, A. D., 315
London, M., 101
Loomis, L. S., 153, 154, 201,
    252
Lord, S., 211
Lorion, R. P., 23
Love, J. M., 145
Lyons, C. A., 225

## M

Maccoby, E., 38
MacCoun, R. J., 320
MacIver, D., 217
Madden, J., 269
Madden, N. A., 21, 165
Maehr, M. L., 217
Magenheim, E., 101, 104
Mahoney, J. L., 220
Malaguzzi, L., 310
Mangione, P. L., 24
Mann, A. J., 264
Mann, E., 10, 20, 180, 204,
    334, 335
Mantzicopoulos, P. Y., 187
Marcon, R. A., 97, 269
Martin, J., 38

Martin, S. L., 61
Marx, F., 76
Masten, A. S., 166
Mathieson, D., 262
Matthews, K., 204, 205
Mavrogenes, N. A., 167, 270
Maxwell, K., 59, 60, 265, 266,
    268, 269, 270, 271, 334,
    335
Maxwell, S., 83
May, A., 75
May, D., 152, 153, 332
McAllister, D., 75
McCaig, R., 153
McCall, R. B., xxix, 10, 23,
    255–283, 355, 364–365
McCartney, K., 119, 120, 121,
    124, 269
McCarton, C. M., 54
McConkey, C., 12, 264, 334,
    344–345
McCormick, M. C., 54
McCoy, A. R., 202
McDill, E. L., 216
McDill, M. S., 216
McDonnell, M. S., 264
McDougall, P., 220
McGauhey, P. J., 259
McGee, R., 259
McKey, R. H., 12, 264, 334,
    344–345
McLean, L. D., 172
McLoyd, V., 38
McMahan, I. D., 304
McNeal, R. B., Jr., 220
McNeil, J. T., 40
Mednick, S. A., 259

Meinert, C. L., 54
Meisels, S., xvii, xx, 145, 147,
    150–152, 201
Menard, S., 259
Mendelsohn, R., 163
Mergendoller, J. R., 152, 153
Metzger, J. L., 268
Meyer, L. L., 274
Michel, S., 4
Midgley, C., 211
Miedel, W., 10, 20, 180, 204,
    211, 334, 335
Milbank, J. E., 305, 308, 312
Milburn, S., 97
Miller, Z., xxv, 74–78, 81, 82,
    83, 84, 85, 86, 87, 88, 92,
    93, 98, 99, 102, 103
Mitchell, A., 76, 101, 102, 329
Monroe, E., 264
Montessori, M., 36
Moore, E., 116
Morris, P., xxi, 164
Morrison, F. J., 153
Morse, J., 329
Moser, H. W., 61
Moss, M., 24
Moss, P., 300
Muenchow, S., 5, 62
Muhlenbruck, L., 223, 227
Murray, H., 39, 269
Myers, R. G., 299

N
Nasman, E., 317
National Center for Education
    Statistics, 144, 145, 148,
    332, 333

National Educational Goals
    Panel, xviii, 14
National Head Start
    Association, 24
National Institutes of Child
    Health and Human
    Development (NICHD),
    116–117, 122, 131
National Science and
    Technology Council, xvii
Natriello, G., 222
Neebe, E., 124, 125, 265
Neuharth-Pritchett, S., 187
Neville, B., 269, 271
New, R., 311
Newman, J., 155
New York State Board of
    Regents, 330, 333
Nikoloff, O., 332
Nitz, K., 259
Noel, A. M., 155
Novak, M. F. S. X., 36
Novello, M. K., 329
Nyman, B. A., 38

O
Oakland, T., 264, 266, 270
Observational Record of the
    Caregiving Environment
    (ORCE), 118
O'Connor, T. G., 267
Office of Educational Research
    and Improvement, 329
Office of School Readiness, 92
Office of the Inspector General,
    24
Ogbu, J., 274

Ogston, K., 261, 264, 266,
    268, 270, 271
Olds, D. L., 257, 262, 265, 269
Olmsted, P. P., 299, 304
Olsen, D. A., xxx, 329–348, 365
Olson, L., 197, 220
Organization Mondiale pour
    l'Education Prescolaire, 318
Osborn, A. F., 305, 308, 312
Osborn, C., 81, 82
Osofsky, J. D., 38

P
Palacios, J., 300, 304, 309, 316
Palius, M., 310, 311
Pardo, C., 258
Parke, R. D., 153, 154
Patterson, G. R., 259
Pauly, E., 264
Peisner-Feinberg, E. S., 115, 125
Pence, A., 313
Perlman, E., 101
Pestalozzi, J. H., 35–36
Peterson, S. E., 206
Phillips, D., 15, 105, 119, 120,
    121, 133, 250, 265, 269,
    270, 278
Piaget, J., 36
Pierce, K. M., xxvi, 115–136,
    268, 269, 281, 365–366
Pierson, L. H., 206, 207
Pilcher, L. C., 94, 95
Pinkerton, R., 120
Pinnell, G. S., 225
Plantz, M., 12, 264, 334, 344–
    345
Plomin, R., 259

Poersch, N. O., 71
Pollack, J. M., 258, 259
Powell, C., 24, 264, 266, 270
Powell, D. R., 152, 257
Powers, C. P., 130
Price, R. H., 23
Proper, E. C., 172

**Q**

Quinn-Leering, K., 145

**R**

Raden, A., xxv–xxvi, 71–106, 366
Ralph, J., 23
Ramey, C. T., xxv, 35–64, 165, 182, 183, 187, 225, 250, 257, 261, 264, 265, 266, 267, 269, 270, 273, 275, 339, 340, 366
Ramey, S. L., xxv, 35–64, 165, 187, 265, 275, 367
Ramos-McKay, J., 23
Raudenbush, S. W., 258
Raver, C. C., 13
Rector, R., 331
Reichart-Erickson, M., 269
Rescorla, L., 269
Reuter, P., 320
Reyes, O., xvii
Reynell, J., 122
Reynolds, A. J., xvii–xxxii, 10, 20, 163–190, 202, 204, 205–206, 207, 211, 265, 266, 267, 270, 273, 274, 277, 283, 334, 335, 353–360, 361

Rhine, W. R., 169, 172
Richardson, E., 10
Richardson, G. A., 259
Richardson, I., 221
Richmond, J. B., xxxi
Riggins, R., Jr., 124, 125, 265
Rimdzius, T., 22
Ripple, C., 18, 24, 25, 105, 253, 329
Roberts, J. E., 124, 125, 265
Roberts, R., 63, 257
Roberts-Fiati, G., 261, 264, 266, 268, 270, 271
Robertson, D. L., 180
Rocheleau, A., 120, 121
Rock, D. A., 258, 259
Roderick, M., 220
Rodgers, J. L., 259
Rogers, W., 86
Rosenbaum, L., 172, 270, 274, 283
Rosenthal, R., 124
Rosenthal, S., 120, 121
Ross, S. M., 225
Rowe, D. C., 259
Royce, J., 39, 269
Royster, J., 264
Ruh, J., 120, 121
Rumberger, R. W., 211
Ruopp, R., 126, 132, 250, 268, 270
Rustici, J., 115, 125
Rutter, M., 166, 260, 267
Rydell, C. P., xx, xxi, xxii, 334

# S

Sack, K., 101
Sackett, G. P., 36, 53
Sacks, C. H., 152, 153
Sahagun, L., 203
Salzer, J., 346
Samari, N., 105
Sameroff, A. J., 259, 260
Sampson, R. J., 258
Sanders, M., xx, xxi, xxii, 334
Sandfort, J., 76
Scarr, S., 118, 119, 120, 121, 269
Schnur, E., 264, 278, 279
Schonert-Reichl, K., 220
Schorr, L., 23, 261
Schrenko, L., 86, 87, 346
Schulman, K., 71, 329
Schulz, M. S., 38
Schweinhart, L. J., xxviii–xxix, 15, 40, 53, 58, 172, 225, 241–253, 261, 262, 271, 283, 335, 336, 338, 367
Scott, D. T., 54
Scott, K. G., 122
Seefeldt, C., 187
Seifer, R., 260
Seitz, V., 11, 18, 24, 172, 270, 274, 283
Seligson, M., 76
Seltzer, M., 225
Seppanen, P. S., 268
Shapiro, P., 90
Shapiro, S., 61
Sharpe, P., 312
Shauman, K. A., 115

Shepard, L. A., 144, 145, 148, 150, 152, 153, 155, 202, 203, 204, 211, 332, 334
Shepherd, R., 101
Shipman, V., 38, 264, 278, 279
Shonkoff, J. P., xvii, xx, 258
Shore, R., 64, 147
Shriver, S., 4–5, 6
Sibley, A., 249
Silva, P. A., 259
Sim, K. P., 308
Simons, M., 318
Slavin, R. E., 21, 165, 223, 225, 226, 258, 259
Smeeding, T. M., 313
Smith, A. N., 263
Smith, J. H., 263
Smith, L. J., 225
Smith, M. L., 145, 148, 150, 152, 153, 202, 203, 204, 332, 334
Smith, R. S., 259, 260
Smith, S., 62
Smokowski, P., 10, 20, 204, 334, 335
Snipper, A., 39
Sosin, J., 255
Sparling, J. J., 40, 257, 264, 269, 270
Spatig, L., 187
Spencer, L. M., 169
Spiker, D., 61
Spitz, Herman H., 340–341
Spitzer, S., 153, 154
Sprehe, J. T., 216
St. Pierre, R., 18, 22, 172, 185, 264, 266, 271

Stafford, F. P., 306, 308, 318–319
Stark, E., 6
Stebbins, L. B., 172
Steele, D. M., 145
Steiner, G. Y., 256
Stenmalm, L., 312
Sterngold, J., 204
Stevenson, C. S., 272, 338
Stipek, D., 97, 217
Stoney, L., 101
Stormshak, E., 270
Stouthamer-Loeber, M., 259
Streissguth, A. P., 38
Styfco, S. J., xxiv–xxv, 3–26, 62, 100, 163, 267, 275, 276, 278, 319, 331, 338, 355, 367–368
Sullivan, L. M., 176
Superintendent's Universal Preschool Task Force, 91, 106
Swadener, E. B., 299, 317
Swanson, M., 54
Swedish Ministry for Foreign Affairs, 318
Swenson, A., 261, 264, 266, 268, 270, 271
Sylva, K., 315

**T**

Takanishi, R., 4
Tao, F., 22
Taussig, C., 262, 336
Taylor, K. B., 186, 187
Temple, J. A., 180, 184, 211

Terry, D., 203
Thayer, K., 145
Thomas, D., 12
Tietze, W., 299, 300, 301, 304, 306, 309, 312, 313, 316
Tobin, W., 226
Toch, T., 223
Tonascia, J., 54
Torrey, B. B., 313
Travers, J., 126, 132, 250, 268, 270
Trickett, P., 11, 13
Trudeau, J. V., 145
Tuss, P., 152
Tyack, D., 226
Tyson, J., 54

**U**

U. S. Department of Education, 198, 200, 221, 223, 329, 332, 333
U. S. Department of Health and Human Services, 7, 13, 24
Uphoff, J., 156

**V**

Valentine, J., 5, 6, 223, 227
Vandell, D. L., xxvi, 115–136, 268, 269, 281, 368
Van Egeren, L. F., 38
Vicknair, K., 225
Volmer, Mike, 85, 88, 89, 90, 92, 98–99
Vygotsky, L. S., 38

# W

Walberg, H. J., xvii–xxxii, 353–360, 361–362
Walker, D. F., 172
Wallace, I. F., 54
Wallgren, C. R., 172
Walsh, D. J., 332
Wang, M. C., xvii–xxxii, 353–360, 362
Ware, W. B., 172
Wasik, B. A., 21, 223, 265
Wasik, B. H., 40, 60, 63, 257, 264, 269, 270
Watson, C., 75, 102
Weikert, D. P., 15, 40, 53, 58, 225, 246, 250, 261, 262, 271, 283, 335, 336, 338
Weiss, H., 257, 264, 265, 282
Weiss, J., 199
Weissberg, R. P., xvii, xxi, 165, 166
Weissbourd, B., 257, 258
Weitzen, M., 263
Weitzman, M., 153, 154
Welch, E., 332
Wells, A. M., 166
Werner, E. E., 259, 260
West, J., 115, 143, 153, 154, 201, 252
Wetzel, G., 300, 304, 309, 316
White, B., 87
Whitebook, M., 105, 133, 250, 270
Whitney, T., 101
Wilgoren, J., 71
Williams, S., 259

Wilson, B. J., 153
Wilson, K. S., 130
Wilson, M., 206
Wilson, W. J., 166
Wong, P., 116
Wood, R., 101
Woodhead, M., 10, 271
Wooten, Jim, 75

# Y

Yazejian, N., 115, 125
Yoshikawa, H., 100, 259, 260, 262, 269
Younoszai, T. M., 187

# Z

Zeisel, S. A., 124, 125, 265
Zelazo, J., 115, 125
Zero to Three: National Center for Clinical Infant Programs, 19
Zigler, E., xxiv–xxv, 3–26, 38, 62, 100, 105, 163, 169, 171, 172, 175, 257, 261, 262, 267, 274, 275, 276, 278, 319, 331, 334, 336, 337, 338, 355, 368
Zill, N., 143, 153, 154, 201, 252
Zimmer, J., 152

# Subject Index

Page numbers followed by italicized *f* and *t* refer to figures and tables, respectively.

## A

Abecedarian Project (ABC), 40, 180–185, 338–341
  amount and nature of intervention in, 41, 42, 339
  control group for, 43
  critics of, 340–341
  findings of, 43, 44*f*, 174*t*, 183–185, 339
  general ecological context of, 42
  key attributes of, 170*t*
  long-term benefits of, 53– 54, 55*f*–56*f*, 57*f*, 60, 183– 184, 340
  participants in, 41, 338–339
  strengths of, 182
Achievement tests, 9
ACYF. *See* Administration on Children, Youth and Families
Adaptive Social Behavior Inventory, 122
Administration on Children, Youth and Families (ACYF), research on Head Start by, 14
Adult education services, 22

Advisory Committee on Head Start Research and Evaluation, 16, 252
Advisory Panel for the Head Start Evaluation Design Project, 15
African American children
  grade retention of, 201, 202–203
  intervention programs for, 54, 182
AFT. *See* American Federation of Teachers
Age of entry
  to early childhood programs, 266–267, 276–277
  to kindergarten, 144–145, 146*t*
Aggressive behavior, 261–262
American Federation of Teachers (AFT)
  on "just in time" interventions, 224
  on social promotion, 198– 199
*America's Kindergartners* (study), 332
Appropriately directed programs, 270–271

Assessment Profile for Early
    Childhood Programs, 249
*Atlanta Journal and
    Constitution,* 74–75, 76,
    87, 101–102
Attendance laws, 329

# B
Bank Street Model of
    Developmental-Interaction,
    171, 172
Beginning School Study (BSS)
    on dropping out of school,
        xxviii, 212–213, 220
    on grade retention, 202–
        203, 209–211, 210*t*
    on mark averages, 217, 218*t,*
        219
    participants in, 202
Behavioral Analysis Model,
    171, 172
Behavior assessment, 122
Behavior problems, 261–262
Benefit fade-out. *See* Fade-out
    effect
Benefits from early childhood
    programs, 261–262, 263–
    264
    age of entry and, 266–267,
        276–277
    child-adult ratio and, 127,
        268
    duration of program and,
        265–266
    fade-out effect and. *See*
        Fade-out effect
    group size and, 127, 268

improving persistence of,
    277–278
intensity of program and, 266
long-term, 46–58, 119–120,
    262, 304–308, 333–347
magnitude of, 273
maternal education and IQ
    and, 61–62
teacher training and, 269–270
"Best practice principles," 223
Birthweight, and IQ scores, 45–
    46, 47*f*–52*f,* 54–58
Boys, "redshirting," 152, 153
Bracken School Readiness
    Scale, 122
Brain development, 64
BSS. *See* Beginning School Study

# C
California Department of
    Education,
    Superintendent's Universal
    Preschool Task Force, 330
CAPs. *See* Community Action
    Programs
Caregiver Interaction Scale
    (CIS), 309
Caregivers. *See also* Teachers
    welfare-to-work adults as, 282
Carolina Abecedarian Project.
    *See* Abecedarian Project
CCDP. *See* Comprehensive
    Child Development
    Program
CDA programs, 17–18
CHES. *See* Child Health and
    Education Study

Chicago Child-Parent Center
    and Expansion Program
    (CPC), 20, 170*t*, 173*t*–
    174*t*, 175–180, 177*f*, 181*f*
Chicago Longitudinal Study,
    179, 202
Child-adult ratio
    and child care quality, 126–
    132, 268
    in Europe, 310
Child and Family Resource
    Program, 18
Child Behavior Checklist, 122
Child Care and Development
    Funds, xviii
Child care quality, xxvi, 24,
    115–136
    and child development, xxvi,
    118–126, 123*t*
    conceptual model of, 116–
    117, 117*f*
    definitions of, 248–249
    elements of, 308–312
    in Europe, 308–312
    and math skills, 126
    and receptive language skills,
    126
    recommendations for, 357
    research on, 117–132
    structural-regulable factors
    of, 126–132, 268
    of successful programs, 268–
    271
Child Care Staffing Study,
    132–133
"Child-centered" teaching
    approach, 97

Child Development Associate
    (CDA) programs, 17–18,
    245
Child Health and Education
    Study (CHES), 305
Children
    age of entry
        to early childhood
        programs, 266–267,
        276–277
        to kindergarten, 144–
        145, 146*t*
    aggressive, 261–262
    attentiveness to ideas and
        interests of, 310
    development of
        child care quality and,
        xxvi, 118–126, 123*t*
        early childhood education
        and, xxi, 59–61, 94–96
        middle-ear infections
        and, 124–125
        parental training and,
        281–282
        structural-regulable
        factors and, 126–132
    educational success of
        child care quality and,
        115–136
        extended intervention
        programs and, 165–166
        grade retention and, 219
        preschool and, 330
        school readiness and,
        147–152
    gender of, as risk factor, 259
    parents reading to, 332

in poverty, programs for. *See*
    Head Start
struggling at school, 221. *See*
    *also* Grade retention;
    Social promotion
CIS. *See* Caregiver Interaction
    Scale
Class size, and child care
    quality, 126–132, 268
Coats Human Services
    Reauthorization Act
    (1998), 14
Cognition, research on, 8–10, 40
Cognitive advantage
    hypothesis, 167
Community Action Programs
    (CAPs), 4
Community poverty, 258
Comprehensive Child
    Development Program
    (CCDP), 18
Compulsory attendance laws,
    329
Consortium for Longitudinal
    Studies, 10, 39–59, 250
Continuation programs. *See*
    Extended intervention
    programs
Control group
    for Abecedarian Project, 43
    for Infant Health and
        Development Program,
        42–43
    for Milwaukee Project, 43
Cost, Quality, and Outcomes
    of Child Care Study
    (CQO), 125–126, 133, 250

Cost-effectiveness, 272–274,
    278, 300
CPC. *See* Chicago Child-Parent
    Center and Expansion
    Program
CQO. *See* Cost, Quality, and
    Outcomes of Child Care
    Study

**D**
Delayed kindergarten entry. *See*
    "Redshirting"
Demonstration programs, 271–
    272
Denmark, parental involvement
    in preschool in, 312
Department of Education
    intervention programs by,
        20–21, 25
    National Center for
        Educational Statistics of,
        xix, 332
    Office of Educational
        Research and Improvement
        of, 329
    on social promotion, 198
Department of Health and
    Human Services (DHHS)
    child care subsidies from, 243
    Head Start operated by, 242
    research on Head Start by,
        13, 344
Deprivation
    experiments on, 36–37
    reversing or minimizing, 37
Developmentally appropriate
    programs, 268–269

DHHS. *See* Department of Health and Human Services
Direct Instruction Model, 171, 172
Distal governance, 243
Dropping out of school
extended intervention programs and, 180
grade retention and, xxviii, 211–220
predicting, 213, 214*t*, 215–216
Dual socialization, 307, 320
Dysfunctional parenting, 259

**E**

Early Childhood Division of Georgia Department of Education, 79, 81, 84
Early Childhood Environment Rating Scale (ECERS), 118, 120, 133, 249, 252, 309
Early Childhood Learning: Programs for a New Age (conference), xxiii, 355–356
Early childhood programs, 241–253. *See also specific programs*
appropriately directed, 270–271
availability and affordability of, 316–318
benefits from. *See* Benefits from early childhood programs

challenges of, xxii–xxiii
characteristics of successful, 265–271
and child development, xxi, 59–61, 94–96
children served by, 247
cost-effective, 272–274, 278, 300
demand for, 299
developmentally appropriate, 268–269
ecology of, 103
effectiveness of. *See* Effectiveness of early childhood programs
eligibility for, 279
emerging trends in, xviii–xxx
and emotional development, 307–308
entrance age to, 266–267, 276–277
in Europe, xxix–xxx, 299–321
extended. *See* Extended intervention programs
federal commitment to, 3–26. *See also* Head Start
full-day, 249–250
goals of, 247–248
governance patterns of, 243–244
history of, 241–242
and infrastructure, 106
integrated and unified system of, 354–355
investments in, xviii, xix*f*
mandated standards for, 281

model *vs.* large-scale, xxix, 62
parental involvement in, 270
part-day, 249–250
participation in
    in Europe, 301, 302*t*
    family income and, xx
    increase in, xviii–xx, xx*f*
    parent education and, xx
policies of, 272–282
potential of, 260–262
preventive, 62–64
    cost of, 63
    effectiveness of, 256
    types of, 256–257
quality of. *See* Child care
    quality
reducing educational
    inequities, 312–315
risk factors and, 258–260
science of, 258–272
staffing, 245–247
transition from, 165–166
universal access to. *See*
    Universal access to early
    childhood programs
Early Head Start, 18–19
ECERS. *See* Early Childhood
    Environment Rating Scale
*École maternelle,* 304, 309–310,
    311
Ecological transition, 165–166
Economic Opportunity Act
    (EOA) (1964), 4
Education for Parenthood, 18
Effectiveness of early childhood
    programs, xxix, 260–264

and cost, 272–274, 278, 300
elements of, 23–25
in Georgia, 94–96
principles of, 353–354
research on, xxi–xxiii, xxv,
    8–17, 35–64, 333–347
    benefits and limits of,
        39–59
    child care quality and,
        117–132
    designing, 250–253
    implications of, 62–64
    interpreting, 249–250
    origins of, 35–38
    for prevention of mental
        retardation, 40–43
Effectiveness of extended
    intervention programs,
    172–175, 178–180, 183–
    187
Elementary and Secondary
    Education Act (ESEA)
    (1965), 20–21, 25, 175
Emotional development, early
    childhood programs and,
    307–308, 345
Empiricist (environmental)
    approach to school
    readiness, 150, 151*t*
Enrichment programs, home-
    based, 314–315
Entrance age
    to early childhood programs,
        266–267, 276–277
    to kindergarten, 144–145,
        146*t*

Environmental (empiricist)
approach to school
readiness, 150, 151*t*
Environmental enrichment,
reversing or minimizing
deprivation, 37
EOA. *See* Economic
Opportunity Act
ESEA. *See* Elementary and
Secondary Education Act
Europe
early childhood programs in,
xxix–xxx, 299–321
demand for, 299
long-term benefits of,
304–308
parental involvement
and, 311–312
participation in, 301, 302*t*
quality of, 308–312
reducing educational
inequities, 312–315
research on, 303
universal access to, 312–
313
social welfare system in,
316–318
European Child Care and
Education Study Group,
303
European Commission
Network on Childcare, 318
Even Start Family Literacy
Program, 22
Experiments, on deprivation,
36–37

Expressive language skills,
assessment of, 122, 124–125
Extended intervention
programs, xxvii–xxviii,
163–190. *See also specific
programs*
effectiveness of, 172–175,
178–180, 183–187
evaluation of, 172–175,
178–180, 183–185, 186–
187
focus of, 167
and grade retention, 180,
181*f*
participation in, 166, 178–
180
rationale for, 165–167

**F**

FACES. *See* Family and Child
Experiences Survey
Fade-out effect, 273–274
in Abecedarian Project, 340–
341
Consortium for
Longitudinal Studies on,
40
grade retention and, 216–
217
in Head Start programs, 9–
10, 11
in Perry Preschool Project,
53, 58
prevention of, 277
reasons for, 11–12
and universal preschool, 334

Family and Child Experiences
    Survey (FACES), 16
Family characteristics, as
    predictors of child
    outcomes, 116–117
Family Connections, 79
Family history, 259
Family income, and preschool
    attendance, xx
Family poverty, 258
Family problems, 258–259
Family support hypothesis, 167
Family support programs. *See
    also* Maternal improvement
    programs
    in Even Start, 22
    in Georgia, 92–93
    in Head Start, 18–19, 247
    importance of, 23–24, 255–
        256
    outcomes of, 264
    potential of, 263
Federal commitment to early
    childhood programs, 3–26.
    *See also* Head Start
Federal governance, 243
Federal investment in early
    childhood programs, xviii,
    xix*f*
    Chicago Child-Parent
        Center and Expansion
        Program, 175
    Head Start, xviii, 7, 241
    Head Start/Follow Through,
        169

Head Start/Public School
    Early Childhood
    Transition Demonstration
    Project, 185
public school
    prekindergarten, 242
Fixed-effects model, 134
Follow Through (FT), 169–
    175, 170*t,* 173*t*
For-profit providers, 82–83,
    103–104, 242
France, preschool in, 304, 309–
    310, 311, 313
FT. *See* Head Start/Follow
    Through
Full-day early childhood
    programs, 249–250
Full-day kindergarten
    programs, 145

## G

Gender of child, as risk factor,
    259
General Accounting Office
    (GAO), research on Head
    Start by, 12–13, 343–345
Georgia, universal access to
    prekindergarten in, xxv–
    xxvi, 71–106
    challenges to, 80–84
    controversy about, 84–87
    corrections for, 89–94
    designing and
        implementing, 78–80
    effectiveness of, 94–96

evaluation of, 96–97, 346–347
for-profit providers in, 82–83
funding, xxv, xxvi, 74–78, 84, 98
future of, 98–99
guidelines for, 79–80
and Head Start, 81–82, 93–94, 104–105
Office of School Readiness and, 88–89, 89–94, 98–99, 346
popular support for, 98–99
public perception of, 89
Georgia Child Care Council, 83
Georgia Department of Education, 78–79, 83–84, 89, 90
Georgia Kindergarten Assessment Program (GKAP), 346
Georgia Lottery for Education, 74–78
Germany
home-based enrichment programs in, 314
preschool in, 305–306
GKAP. *See* Georgia Kindergarten Assessment Program
Goals 2000, 79, 331, 332
Government Performance and Results Act (1993), 14
Grade retention
cost of, 220
and dropping out of school, xxviii, 211–220
estimating rates of, 200–203
extended intervention programs and, 180, 181*f*
in France, 304
guidelines for, 221
hidden costs of, 222
intervention programs and, 53, 57*f*
and mark averages, 217, 218*t*, 219
multiple, 203, 212, 220
positive effects of, 206–211
research on, 200, 201–203, 204–209
and school performance, 204–206, 207, 208, 209
"Grammar of schooling," 226
Great Society, 4
Group size, and child care quality, 126–132, 268

**H**

Half-day kindergarten programs, 145
Head Start, xxiv–xxv, xxviii–xxix, 3–17, 241. *See also* Early Head Start
benefits from, 263–264
children served by, 247
development of, 4–8, 241–242
and Georgia prekindergarten program, 81–82, 93–94, 104–105

goals of, 5, 14, 247, 343
governance of, 244
investment in, xviii, 7
quality of, 24, 249
research on, 251–253, 342–
    346
    early, 8–12
    goals and measures of,
        13–15
    planning, 15–16
    recent, 12–17
and school readiness, 14, 16
and social competence, 14
structure of, 6–7, 62
teachers of, 242, 245–247
Head Start Bureau, 14, 16
Head Start/Follow Through
    (FT), 169–175, 170*t*, 173*t*
Head Start/Public School Early
    Childhood Transition
    Demonstration Project
    (HST), 19–20, 170*t*, 174*t*,
    185–187
High/Scope Cognitively
    Oriented Curriculum
    Model, 171, 172
High/Scope Educational
    Research Foundation, 335–
    336
High/Scope Perry Preschool
    Study, 250
High/Scope's Program Quality
    Assessment, 248–249
HIPPY. *See* Home Instruction
    Program for Preschool
    Youngsters

Hispanic children, grade
    retention of, 201, 202
"Holding out." *See*
    "Redshirting"
Home-based enrichment
    programs, 314–315
Home Instruction Program for
    Preschool Youngsters
    (HIPPY), 314–315
Home/school resource teacher,
    183
Home visiting programs
    duration of, 266
    outcomes of, 264
    potential of, 262–263
Home visits
    in Head Start/Follow
        Through, 171, 172
    in Perry Preschool Project,
        336
    time available for, 245–246
HST. *See* Head Start/Public
    School Early Childhood
    Transition Demonstration
    Project
Human Services
    Reauthorization Act
    (1994), 18, 19

**I**

IDEA. *See* Individuals with
    Disabilities Education Act
Ideal (nativist) approach to
    school readiness, 150, 151*t*
Immigrants, home-based
    enrichment programs for,
    314

Improving America's School
Act (1994), 21
Inclusive (interactionist)
approach to school
readiness, 150, 151*t*
Individuals with Disabilities
Education Act (IDEA),
xviii
Infant Health and
Development Program, 40
amount and nature of
intervention in, 42
control group for, 42–43
findings of, 45–46, 47*f*–52*f*
general ecological context of,
42
long-term benefits of, 54–58
participants in, 41
Infants, research on, 38
Infrastructure, 106
Inoculation hypothesis, 46
Institute of Medicine, 15
Institutions, research on, 37–38
Interactionist (inclusive)
approach to school
readiness, 150, 151*t*
Intervention programs, 17–22.
*See also* Early childhood
programs; *specific programs*
for African American
children, 54, 182
appropriately directed, 270–
271
characteristics of successful,
265–271
and child development, 59–
61

for children at risk of
academic failure, 223–225
cost-effective, 272–274, 278
developmentally
appropriate, 268–269
effective, 23–25, 260–264
eligibility for, 279
extended. *See* Extended
intervention programs
and grade retention, 53, 57*f*
mandated standards for, 281
parental involvement in, 270
for parents, 18, 22, 23–24
policies of, 272–282
preventive, 62–64
cost of, 63
effectiveness of, 256
types of, 256–257
quality of, 24
research on
benefits and limits of,
39–59
implications of, 62–64
origins of, 35–38
for prevention of mental
retardation, 40–43
risk factors and, 258–260
science of, 258–272
Iowa Test of Basic Skills
(ITBS), 223
IQ scores
birthweight and, 45–46,
47*f*–52*f,* 54–58
fade-out effect on, 9–10, 11,
40, 53, 58, 274, 340–341
intervention programs and,
43, 45, 46, 54, 273

maternal, and benefits from
    intervention programs,
    61–62
IQ tests, in Head Start research,
    9–10, 11
Ireland, preschool in, 313–314
Italy, preschool in, 310–311
ITBS. *See* Iowa Test of Basic
    Skills
ITERS, 120, 121, 133

**J**

"Just in time" interventions, 224

**K**

Kindergarten, 143–158
    children not "ready to learn"
        when entering, 330, 331
    curriculum of, 332
    delayed entry to. *See*
        "Redshirting"
    entrance age to, 144–145,
        146*t*
    origins of, 35–36
    participation in, xxvii
    program configuration in,
        145–146
    and school readiness, xxvii,
        147–152
    state policies related to, 143–
        145, 146*t*

**L**

Language skills, assessment of,
    122, 124–125
Large-scale early childhood
    programs, xxix, 62

Leadership, and universal access
    to early childhood
    programs, 102–103
Local governance, 243
Lottery, as funding mechanism,
    xxv, xxvi, 74–78, 84, 98,
    101–102

**M**

Mandatory attendance laws, 329
Mark averages, 217, 218*t*, 219
Maternal education
    and benefits from
        intervention programs,
        61–62
    improved, 262
Maternal improvement
    programs, 256–257, 262–
    263
Maternal IQ scores, and
    benefits from intervention
    programs, 61–62
Math skills
    child care quality and, 126
    intervention programs and,
        53, 54, 56*f*
Mental retardation
    poverty and, 37–38
    prevention of, 40–43, 62–64
Middle-ear infections, 124–125
Milwaukee Project, 40
    amount and nature of
        intervention in, 41, 42
    control group for, 43
    findings of, 43–45
    general ecological context of,
        42

long-term benefits of, 54
  participants in, 41
Model early childhood
  programs, xxix, 62
Motivational advantage
  hypothesis, 167
Multiple grade retention, 203,
  212, 220

# N

National Association for the
  Education of Young
  Children (NAEYC), 87
National Center for
  Educational Statistics, xix,
  332
National Child Care Staffing
  Study, 250
National Day Care Study, 126–
  127, 132, 250
National Educational
  Longitudinal Study of
  1988 (NELS88), 200, 201–
  202
National Education
  Commission on Time and
  Learning, 226
National Head Start/Public
  School Early Childhood
  Transition Demonstration
  Project, 19–20, 170t, 174t,
  185–187
National Institute of Child
  Health and Development
  (NICHD), study on child
  care quality by, xxvi, 115,
  116–117, 121–124, 123t,
  129, 131, 133

National Laboratory, 17–20
National Longitudinal Survey
  of Youth (NLSY), 128
National Research Council, 15
Nativist (ideal) approach to
  school readiness, 150, 151t
NELS88. See National
  Educational Longitudinal
  Study of 1988
Netherlands, The
  home-based enrichment
    programs in, 314–315
  preschool in, 311
Newborns, research on, 38
New Jersey, preschool in, 319
NICHD. See National Institute
  of Child Health and
  Development
NLSY. See National
  Longitudinal Survey of
  Youth
Nonprofit providers, 82–83,
  103–104

# O

Observational Record of the
  Caregiving Environment
  (ORCE), 118
Office of Educational Research
  and Improvement, 329
Office of School Readiness
  (OSR), 88–89, 89–94, 98–
  99, 346
ORCE. See Observational
  Record of the Caregiving
  Environment

Organization for Economic Cooperation and Development (OECD) countries, preschool participation rates of, 301, 302*t*

Orphanages, research on, 37–38

OSR. *See* Office of School Readiness

Otitis Media Study, 124–125

# P

Parental involvement, 270
    in Abecedarian Project, 183
    benefits of, 312
    in Europe, 311–312
    in Head Start, 5
    in Head Start/Follow Through, 171
    in home-based enrichment programs, 314–315
    importance of, 358

Parent and Child Centers (PCCs), 18

Parent Education Model, 171, 172

Parenting
    dysfunctional, 259
    home visiting programs and, 262, 264

Parent-run playgroups, 315

Parents
    education of, and preschool attendance, xx
    intervention programs for, 18, 22, 23–24

reading to children, 332

and "redshirting," 153, 155

satisfied with Georgia prekindergarten program, 96–97

on school readiness, 148–149

Parent training, 281–282

Part-day early childhood programs, 249–250

Participation
    in early childhood programs in Europe, 301, 302*t*
    family income and, xx
    increase in, xviii–xx, xx*f*
    parent education and, xx
    in extended intervention programs, 166, 178–180
    in kindergarten, xxvii

PCCs. *See* Parent and Child Centers

Peabody Individual Achievement Test (PIAT), 128

Peabody Picture Vocabulary Test (PPVT), 128

Peer skills, assessment of, 122

Perinatal hazards, 259

Perry Preschool Project, 40, 335–338
    amount and nature of intervention in, 41, 335
    fade-out effect in, 53, 58
    general ecological context of, 42
    long-term benefits of, 52–53, 336–337
    participants in, 41, 335

Person X Environment
  interaction, 37
PIAT. *See* Peabody Individual
  Achievement Test
Poverty
  children in, programs for.
    *See* Head Start
  as eligibility requirement,
    279
  and mental retardation, 37–
    38
  as risk factor, 258
PPVT. *See* Peabody Picture
  Vocabulary Test
Prekindergarten. *See* Public
  school prekindergarten
Preschool child care programs,
  xxviii–xxix, 241. *See also*
  Early childhood programs
  children served by, 247
  goals of, 247–248
  governance of, 244
  history of, 242
  quality of, 249
  research on, 251–253
  teachers of, 246
Prevention programs, 62–64
  cost of, 63
  effectiveness of, 256
  types of, 256–257
Private providers, 82–83, 103–
  104, 242
Process quality
  and educational success,
    117–126
  and structural-regulable
    factors, 132–134

Program Performance
  Standards, 7
Project CARE, 40
  amount and nature of
    intervention in, 41–42
  findings of, 43
  general ecological context of,
    42
  long-term benefits of, 53–
    54, 60
  participants in, 41
Project Head Start, 3, 4. *See
  also* Head Start
Public school prekindergarten,
  xxviii–xxix, 241. *See also*
  Early childhood programs
  children served by, 247
  goals of, 247
  governance of, 244
  history of, 242
  quality of, 249
  research on, 251–253
  teachers of, 242, 245–247
  universal, 280

**Q**

Quality of child care. *See* Child
  care quality

**R**

RCs. *See* Resource
  Coordinators
Readiness. *See* School readiness
Reading skills, intervention
  programs and, 53, 54, 55*f*
Reauthorization Act (1994), 18,
  19

Receptive language skills
  assessment of, 122, 124–125
  child care quality and, 126
"Redshirting," xxvii, 152–157,
  154t
  evaluation of, 156–157,
    157t
  and individual outcomes,
    153–154
  social influences and, 155
Reggio Emilia preschool
  program, 310–311
Resource Coordinators (RCs),
  92
Retention. See Grade retention
Reynell Developmental
  Language Scales, 122
Roundtable on Head Start
  Research, 15
Routine service programs, 271–
  272

S

"Savage of Aveyron," 35
"Schomes," 176
School performance, grade
  retention and, 204–206,
  207, 208, 209
School readiness
  conceptions of, 150, 151t
  day care and, 331–333
  definition of, 147, 150–152
  differences in, 224
  factors of, 332–333
  Head Start and, 14, 16
  kindergarten and, xxvii,
    147–152

measuring, 122
parents on, 148–149
social meanings of, 155
teachers on, 149–152
School remedial services. See
  also Grade retention
  extended intervention
    programs and, 180, 181f
School support hypothesis, 167
SECC. See Study of Early Child
  Care
SES. See Socioeconomic status
Singapore, preschool in, 307–
  308
Small-scale early childhood
  programs. See Model early
  childhood programs
Small-school homes
  ("schomes"), 176
Social adjustment hypothesis,
  167
Social competence
  alternative paths leading to,
    167–169, 168f
  child care quality and, 119
  Head Start and, 14
Social constructivist approach
  to school readiness, 151t
Social ecology, 37
Socialization
  dual, 307, 320
  early childhood programs
    and, 307–308, 345
Social promotion
  Clinton on, 197–198
  cost of, 222
  definition of, 198–199

extent of, 199–200
and mark averages, 217, 218*t*, 219
Social welfare system, in Europe, 316–318
Socioeconomic status (SES)
and grade retention, 201, 202
and school readiness, 224
Socioemotional development, early childhood programs and, 307–308, 345
Special education, cost of, 63
Spurt—fade-out effect. *See* Fade-out effect
Staff. *See* Teachers
Stanford Achievement Test, 332
State governance, 243–244
State investment in early childhood programs, xviii, xix*f*
State kindergarten policies, 143–145, 146*t*
Structural-regulable factors, 268
and child development, 126–132
and process quality, 132–134
Study of Early Child Care (SECC), 121–124, 123*t*, 129, 131, 133
Summer school, 223–224
Sweden, preschool in, 306–308, 311, 313, 317
Synthesis Project, 12

**T**
TANF. *See* Temporary Assistance for Needy Families
Teachers
assessment of, 118, 122
attentive to ideas and interests of children, 310
certification of, 91, 245
in Europe, 311
evaluation of, 96
of Georgia prekindergarten program, 80
of Head Start, 242, 245–247
preparation of, 105–106
of preschool child care, 246
of public school prekindergarten, 242, 245–247
recommendations for, 357–358
on "redshirting," 155
on school readiness, 149–152
training of
and child care quality, 126–132, 269–270
improving, 278
Temporary Assistance for Needy Families (TANF), xviii
"Third way" alternatives, 222–227
Title I education funding, xviii, 20–21, 25, 175
Transition, ecological, 165–166

Transition from home to
    school, 353
Transition from preschool to
    school, 165–166, 169, 172
Transition Project, 19–20,
    170*t*, 174*t*, 185–187
Two-generation programs, 257,
    271
    duration of, 266
    outcomes of, 264

## U

United Kingdom
    parent-run playgroups in,
        315
    preschool in, 305
        parental involvement in,
            312
Universal access to early
    childhood programs, xxx,
        329–348, 356–357
    in Europe, 312–313
    funding, 101–102
    in Georgia, xxv–xxvi, 71–
        106
        challenges to, 80–84
        controversy about, 84–87
        corrections for, 89–94
        designing and
            implementing, 78–80
        effectiveness of, 94–96
        evaluation of, 96–97
        for-profit providers in,
            82–83
        funding, xxv, xxvi, 74–
            78, 84, 98

future of, 98–99
guidelines for, 79–80
and Head Start, 81–82,
    93–94, 104–105
Office of School
    Readiness and, 88–89,
    89–94, 98–99, 346
popular support for, 98–
    99
public perception of, 89
and infrastructure, 106
leadership and, 102–103
popular support and, 99–
    101
preparation of teachers for,
    105–106
in public schools, 280

## W

War on Poverty, 4, 241, 343
Welfare-to-work programs,
    264, 282
Westinghouse Learning
    Corporation, study on
    Head Start by, 9
"Whole child" approach, 171